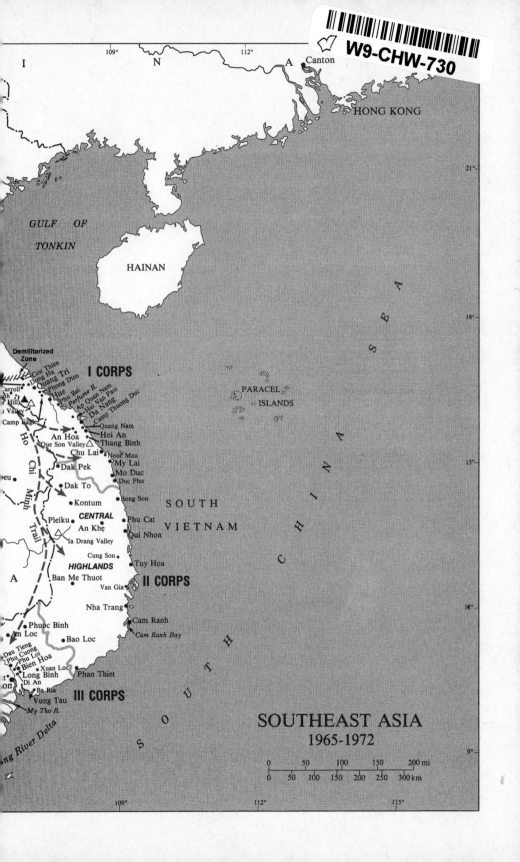

109°   112°

Canton

HONG KONG

21°

I   N   A

GULF OF

TONKIN

HAINAN

18°

Demilitarized
Zone

Con Thien
Dong Ha
Quang Tri
Phong Dien
Hue
Phu Bai
Ap Quan Nam
Hai Van Pass
Da Nang
Camp Thuong Duc
Quang Nam

I CORPS

Carroll
Hill
Valley
Camp Eagle

Perfume R.

PARACEL
ISLANDS

An Hoa
Que Son Valley
Chu Lai

Hoi An
Thang Binh

Nout Mau
My Lai
Mo Duc
Duc Pho

S   O   U   T   H   C   H   I   N   A   S   E   A

Dak Pek

eu

Dak To

15°

Kontum

Bong Son

SOUTH

Pleiku

CENTRAL

An Khe

Phu Cat

VIETNAM

Qui Nhon

Ia Drang Valley

Cung Son

HIGHLANDS

Tuy Hoa

II CORPS

Ban Me Thuot

Van Gia

Ho Chi Minh Trail

A

Nha Trang

12°

Cam Ranh
Cam Ranh Bay

Phuoc Binh
n Loc

Bao Loc

Dau Tieng
Phu Cuong
Phu Loi
Bien Hoa
Long Binh
Di An
Ba Ria
Vung Tau
My Tho R.

Xuan Loc

Phan Thiet

on

III CORPS

SOUTHEAST ASIA
1965-1972

ng River Delta

9°

0   50   100   150   200 mi
0   50 100 150 200 250 300 km

109°   112°   115°

UNKNOWN WARRIORS
Canadians in Vietnam

Fred Gaffen

Dundurn Press
Toronto & Oxford
1990

Editor: Judith Turnbull
Design and Production: JAQ
Printing and Binding: Gagné Printing Ltd., Louiseville, Quebec, Canada

The writing of this manuscript and the publication of this book were made possible by support from several sources. The publisher wishes to acknowledge the generous assistance and ongoing support of **The Canada Council, The Book Publishing Industry Development Programme** of the **Department of Communications**, and **The Ontario Arts Council.**

Care has been taken to trace the ownership of copyright material used in the text (including the illustrations). The author and publisher welcome any information enabling them to rectify any reference or credit in subsequent editions.

J. Kirk Howard, Publisher

Dundurn Press Limited
2181 Queen Street East, Suite 301
Toronto, Canada
M4E 1E5

Dundurn Distribution Limited
73 Lime Walk
Headington
Oxford OX3 7AD
England

Canadian Cataloguing in Publication Data

Gaffen, Fred
    Unknown warriors : Canadians in Vietnam

ISBN 1-55002-073-0

1. Vietnamese Conflict, 1961-1975 - Personal
narratives, Canadian. 2. Vietnamese Conflict,
1961-1975 - Participation, Canadian.
3. Canadians - Vietnam. I. Title.

DS558.6.C3G34 1990   959.704'3371   C90-095151-6

To Canada's Vietnam Veterans

CONTENTS

PREFACE, 8
ACKNOWLEDGEMENTS, 12
PROLOGUE, 13
RETROSPECT, 14

PART I: **HISTORICAL INTRODUCTION,** 19
    The War in Vietnam, 20
    Canadian Participation in the War, 29
    Enlistment of Canadians, 33

PART II: **WAR EXPERIENCES OF CANADIANS,** 41

PART III: **COMING HOME,** 259
    Introduction, 260
    The Struggle for Equal Benefits, 262
    Post-Traumatic Stress Disorder, 264
    Prisoners and Atrocities, 277
    Agent Orange, 282
    Vietnam Veterans' Groups, 284
    Imposters, 291
    Problems with the Royal Canadian Legion, 294
    The Wall and the Dead, 299
    Conclusion, 332

APPENDIX A: Canadian Casualties of the Vietnam War, 334
APPENDIX B: Ranks, 341
APPENDIX C: Chronology, 342

NOTES, 345
BIBLIOGRAPHY, 350
INDEX, 362
CONTRIBUTORS, 367

PREFACE

Picture a Memorial Day parade in an American town not far from the Canadian border. There are flags waving, marching bands playing, and columns of veterans of past wars on parade. The American Vietnam veterans, many in camouflage clothing, draw loud applause. Behind them comes a much smaller group of soldiers wearing various types of uniforms and led by an individual bearing a Canadian flag. The crowd's reaction is muted at first, but then there are cheers and loud clapping, for these are members of the Canadian Vietnam Veterans — Canadian volunteers who fought with the American forces in Vietnam. In U.S. cities and towns further south there would not be this recognition. Most Americans are unaware of the Canadian veterans' existence. Canada is better known as a haven for draft dodgers and deserters than as a source of volunteers for Vietnam.

Unlike Canadian veterans of the Second World War and Korea, who wear their association blazers and campaign medals on appropriate occasions, most of Canada's Vietnam veterans remain an invisible minority. Many do not let it be known to neighbours, employers or new friends that they served in Vietnam. A large number of those who have attained a certain status within their communities do not wish to go public. Some regard their military service with the American forces as a youthful adventure better not dwelt upon. Still, even though they have put that part of their lives aside, they cannot erase it from their memories.

For almost 20 years, I have met and talked with Canadian veterans of the First World War, the Second World War, Korea and peacekeeping assignments. Canadian Vietnam veterans as a group are different. They are more difficult to find. They are more reluctant to talk about their experiences than any other veterans I have encountered. Knowing that I was seeking personal stories, a considerable number of Canadian Vietnam veterans telephoned saying they did not want to reveal who they were because they were married with families and had good jobs. Most did not want to discuss the unpleasant aspects of fighting in Vietnam. Some still carry feelings of guilt, shame, anger and suppressed rage over their experiences in the war. Like soldiers anywhere, Canada's Vietnam veterans are victims of war. Although many do not carry outward wounds, some carry some form of psychological scarring from their experiences.

Like the climate in Canada, their welcome back home after the war was cold. Readjustment to "normal" life proved difficult. This was especially true in the larger urban centres. Taking up their lives in small towns or rural areas was often less traumatic.

Fifteen years ago, the long and painful conflict in Vietnam officially came to a close. Although Canada was not directly involved, Canadians did take part as members of the American forces. The time has come to find out why.

There are persistent myths in this country about Canada's Vietnam veterans. Many Canadians label Vietnam vets as mercenaries; yet no Canadian Vietnam vet could rationally say that he risked his life only for the basic pay offered in the American military. In the course of my research I have not come across a single Canadian who fought in Vietnam just for the money. Some Canadians think of all Vietnam veterans as "baby killers." Yes, there were a few who killed children, but only a few, and acts such as these were carried on in the horrific and confusing conditions of guerrilla warfare — often in self-defence or in defence of comrades. The label "baby killer" is clearly a generalization.

While some Canadians accuse their countrymen who fought in Vietnam of being solely mercenaries, they often fail to realize that Canadian companies supplied American firms with billions of dollars worth of materiel for the war. It was not only those businesses that gained financially; the entire Canadian economy benefited from the Vietnam War. Although there were official pronouncements urging restraint and the cessation of American bombing, this country's financial involvement was greater than some Canadians now seem willing to admit.

To many Americans, Canadians who served with the American forces in Vietnam are heroes because they came to America's side in order to fight against Communist aggression. In Canada, however, those volunteers are generally looked upon in an unfavourable light because of the unpopularity of the war and the negative image of the Vietnam veteran conveyed by the media.

This book provides an opportunity for Canadian Vietnam veterans and others to find out for the first time facts of which they are unaware. Who else went? What did they experience? How have others readjusted?

A member of the American Legion in Toronto, Patrick Luongo, a New Jersey native and Marine Corps veteran who served in Vietnam, 1967-68, wrote to express his concerns about the book:

> I served in a military organization that neither called for or asked for the services of Canadians. Nevertheless, these men fought gallantly and served Corps and my country in

the highest tradition of the United States Naval Service, replacing American draft dodgers and deserters on the battlefield. Initially, I questioned the sanity of these men who, for ideological or frivolous reasons, volunteered to fight a war under a foreign flag that was unpopular and not formally declared. A war that did not directly concern them. I later came to understand that the Canadians shared the same ideals as myself; simply put "that freedom isn't free" and they literally placed their lives on the line for that belief. As for myself, I have nothing but respect and admiration for these men and the camaraderie shared between us is as strong now as it was then. Do these men justice with your book because to men such as myself, the Canadian veterans are truly the unsung and forgotten soldiers, sailors, airmen and marines of the Vietnam War.

This work is by no means the complete account of Canadian military involvement in the Vietnam War. Many government documents will not be released for years to come. Nevertheless, it seems to me that it is time Canadians looked back on those years, in the words of Abraham Lincoln, "with malice toward none; with charity for all."

For the Canadian veterans — who served as individuals, not as a national contingent — the Vietnam War consists essentially of their own experiences. Reflecting these diverse experiences, this book is mainly comprised of veterans' individual stories. Since the Canadian soldiers were interspersed among the American forces throughout the war, there is no uniquely Canadian veterans' perspective on issues such as Agent Orange or prisoners of war. These subjects, however, are part of the Canadian Vietnam veterans' experiences and so are included.

While Canadian Vietnam veterans may learn something by reading this account, writing it has provided me with the invaluable opportunity to meet and get to know a very special group of men. I have also derived an immense amount of satisfaction from helping some veterans with information or advice. The information presented here should help many of them to view their experience and their participation in better perspective. With additional knowledge perhaps will come more understanding.

I hope this book will make Canadians more aware that some of their fellow countrymen served in the American forces in Vietnam. To a considerable number of Canadians, the term Vietnam vet has a negative connotation. This is unfortunate, as the majority are honest, industrious, sane individuals, married with families. They have overcome the many negative aspects of military service in Vietnam. I am proud to be associated with them.

Although they may occasionally rib one another, Canadian veterans of the two world wars and Korea have always been on good terms with one another. Canadian Vietnam veterans, however, have not been accepted into this circle. There is not only an age gap, but also a psychological barrier between them. Both groups have yet to make an effort to understand each other's military experiences and points of view. It is my wish that this book may assist in that reconciliation process.

A hope, perhaps forlorn, is that this study will help to expose the nature and especially the consequences of war. On Remembrance Day, my children wear poppies and attend school ceremonies. The realities that this book lays bare will perhaps help them and others towards an understanding of the meaning of war, and thus increase the chance that collective and individual mistakes will be avoided in the future.

The Wall in Washington, D.C., is most appropriate as a memorial for the Vietnam War. For me it will always symbolize the wall of silence I often met in researching this book. Had I known initially of the difficulties to be encountered, I likely would not have embarked on this project. But now that the book is a reality, I hope that the reader will find my efforts to have been worthwhile.

ACKNOWLEDGEMENTS

I am grateful to the following individuals and institutions: Carol-Ann Kennedy and Philip Robert of the Canadian War Museum; Lee Hitchins of the Canadian Vietnam Veterans Ottawa; Linda Hanson of the Lyndon Baines Johnson Library; Byron A. Parham of the National Archives, Washington, D.C.; and the noted historian, the Honourable George F.G. Stanley, who read the manuscript and offered his comments. I also owe a very special debt to the Ontario Arts Council for its support.

To all those who responded to my ads in various publications, sincere thanks. My appreciation also goes to William Constable, who prepared the map, and to Frank McGuire for editorial assistance. My wife, Susan Audrey, allowed me the use of weekends to work on this book. Thanks also to Judith Turnbull, my editor, for her superb work.

Above all, I would like to express my gratitude to those Canadian Vietnam veterans who contributed their stories. For most, it was a very painful and difficult task. A special word of thanks also to those who tried to help but could not bring themselves to relive their Vietnam experiences, and to mothers of those killed who endured the pain of going back to their late sons' belongings to search for items of possible use.

PROLOGUE

While the Vietnam War was going on, it was known that Canadians were enlisting or serving in the American forces, but there was very little information about them. Following their service, these veterans compounded the situation by keeping out of public view. They became Canada's unknown warriors. It is only recently that spokesmen and individuals have begun to identify themselves. The time has come to find out more about Canada's Vietnam veterans.

American movies about the Vietnam War such as *The Deer Hunter, Apocalypse Now, Platoon, Full Metal Jacket, Casualties of War* and *Born on the Fourth of July* have played to large audiences in this country. On television there is "China Beach." Few Canadians, however, realize that their fellow citizens served in the American forces in Vietnam.

Particularly among the young, the Vietnam War today conjures up various heroic images — Rambo, Chuck Norris and others. The object of this book is to help show that the Vietnam War was definitely not glorious and to introduce a degree of realism into the revisionist trend to romanticize that war.

Although the U.S. government kept accurate records during the Vietnam War, a problem in identifying and learning about the Canadian volunteers arises from the addresses they gave on enlisting. If a Canadian citizen, by reason of employment or sojourn, had a U.S. address upon entering the service, that address was treated as his home town in the event of his being listed as a casualty.

The situation of Canadians going off to fight in a foreign war was not something new. Canadians have fought in other people's wars for generations. Some Vietnam veterans have used arguments based on past history to try to justify full recognition, even pensions, from the Canadian government. But historically there has been a difference in the recognition accorded Canadian veterans of wars involving Canada and that accorded Canadian veterans of other conflicts.

A good deal of the difference between Canadian Vietnam veterans and veterans of the Second World War and Korea has to do with the way the former are perceived by themselves and by the veterans of the earlier wars. Canadian Vietnam veterans see themselves in the same light as they see Americans who enlisted in Canada during either of the world wars when their own country was still neutral. In contrast, Canadian veterans of the Second World War tend to regard Canadian Vietnam veterans in the same light as they view Canadians who fought in the Spanish Civil War. Differing impressions of what happened in the past account for some of these differences.

RETROSPECT

Prior to Confederation

In recent years there has been a dispute between Royal Canadian Legion members and Canadian Vietnam veterans over the issue of the latter's full membership in the Legion and their participation in Remembrance Day ceremonies. A reminder of Canadian involvement in other wars is necessary for an understanding of the historical roots of the disagreement.

The involvement of Canadians in the military service of other countries is not a recent phenomenon. There were several examples prior to the Vietnam War, and a brief glance at the historical background of this cross-border movement will help set the Vietnam episode in context.

In May 1861 Queen Victoria proclaimed that Britain would not intervene in the American Civil War. Many Canadians, however, in disregard of British neutrality, enlisted in the armies of the North and South. During the American Civil War, an unknown number of Canadians crossed the border to fight.

The Papal Zouaves, 1868-1870

A notable 19th-century instance of Canadians enlisting for military service outside the British Empire was the case of the Papal Zouaves. By the mid-19th century the pursuit of the political unification of Italy had reduced much of the papal territory. Volunteers came to Rome to defend the patrimony of Saint Peter (that is, the papal territory) in response to the universal appeal of Pope Pius IX. These forces were known as the Papal Zouaves. Among them were some 400 Canadians, mostly francophones from Quebec. One contingent departed from Montreal in February 1868 but saw little fighting.

At the outbreak of the Franco-Prussian War in the summer of 1870, French troops defending the Papal States were withdrawn to fight the Germans on French soil. Rome fell on 20 September and the Papal States were then incorporated into Italy. On the dissolution of the temporal powers of the Papacy, the Canadian Zouaves, apart from nine who had died (mainly from disease), were repatriated.

The Nile Voyageurs, 1884-1885

The first instance of a distinct Canadian contingent sent to help Britain in an overseas conflict was the Nile Expedition of 1884-85. The purpose of the expedition was to rescue a popular British general, Charles Gordon, who was besieged in Khartoum. About 400 voyageurs were recruited by the governor general, Lord Lansdowne. Some 60 of the total were Iroquois from Caughnawaga, now known as Kahnawake, Québec. The efforts of the Canadian boatmen, however, were in vain. An advance party discovered that the city had been captured, and General Gordon killed, two days before the expedition came within striking distance of the city.

The South African War, 1899-1902

Volunteers were raised, equipped and transported to South Africa by the Canadian government to support Britain against the Boers, the descendants of Dutch settlers. Once in South Africa, the Canadian force was maintained by Britain. Almost all of the volunteers were regular soldiers or militiamen. When they enlisted, they agreed to serve a minimum of 6 and a maximum of 12 months. A second contingent was also sent. Several additional units, for which the government accepted no financial responsibility, were raised in Canada. In all, Canada provided Britain with over 7,000 officers and men to serve in South Africa.

The First World War, 1914-1918

With Britain's declaration of war on Germany on 4 August 1914, Canada was automatically at war as well. It was not until three years later, 6 April 1917, that the U.S. entered the war. Before that, volunteers from the United States crossed the border into Canada and enlisted.

The statutory basis of official American policy in effect at the time was the Foreign Enlistment Act of 1818, which made the recruitment of American citizens on United States soil for service against a friendly state a criminal offence. However, this did not prevent an individual from crossing the border and presenting himself for enlistment on British territory. American enlistment in the Canadian Expeditionary Force (CEF) was not discouraged. As a result, many thousands of Americans joined the CEF. Americans also crossed the border to join the British flying services. The Canadian training scheme for the Royal Flying Corps led to direct recruiting of Americans following their country's entry into the war.

While over 35,000 Americans enlisted in the CEF in the First World War, according to figures supplied by National Personnel Records Centre in Ottawa, some 29,000 joined the Canadian armed services during the Second World War. The flow of Canadians to join the U.S. forces was much less.

Canadians who served on the Nile, in South Africa, and even during the First World War fought as British subjects. Canadian nationality did not appear on passports until after the Statute of Westminster in 1931. Thus, there is no parallel here with Canadian citizens who enlisted in the American forces to fight in Vietnam.

The Spanish Civil War, 1936-1939

Between 1937 and 1939 some 1,200 Canadians of various ethnic origins fought in the Spanish Civil War on the Loyalist side. A few others fought for Franco on the Nationalists' behalf. Like the French Canadians who served as Papal Zouaves in Italy, Canadians who fought in Spain were not recognized by the Canadian government. In fact, the Foreign Enlistment Act of 1937[1] expressly forbade Canadians from joining or recruiting others to enlist. More than a third of them were killed in the two years of bitter fighting that followed. The Soviet Union gave assistance until Stalin realized there was little in the Republican cause for the U.S.S.R. It was the Soviet withdrawal that really decided the issue in favour of the Fascists.

The characteristics of the Canadian troops who formed the Mackenzie-Papineau Battalion during the Spanish Civil War reflected the economic and political climate of the 1930s. Just as Spain became a battleground for a segment of one Canadian generation in 1937-39, so Vietnam attracted another segment of a generation between, for the most part, 1965 and 1970. Although their political philosophies were opposite, they shared a common thirst for adventure and a desire to test themselves. Like those who went to fight in Spain, the Canadian volunteers who enlisted or were drafted into the American forces and fought in the Vietnam War constitute a part of Canada's history.

Surviving veterans of the Mackenzie-Papineau Battalion were given a large reception by their supporters at Massey Hall in Toronto in February 1939.[2] One of the complaints of some Canadian Vietnam veterans is the fact that, unlike past Canadian war veterans, they never received a "Welcome Home" parade or ceremony in this country.

The Second World War, 1939-1945

Two days after Hitler's troops invaded Poland, Britain declared war on Germany, and one week later, on 10 September 1939, the Canadian Parliament made its first independent declaration of war. As in the First World War, the United States was for a time neutral. In April and May 1940, Norway, Denmark, The Netherlands, Belgium, Luxembourg and France fell to the German forces. When France finally signed an armistice on Germany's terms on 22 June, Britain and the Commonwealth stood alone. Germany invaded the Soviet Union on 22 June 1941. It was not until the Japanese attack on Pearl Harbor on 7 December 1941 that the United States was brought into the war. Four days later Germany declared war on the United States, which then declared war on it.

At the outbreak of the Second World War, only British subjects could be enrolled in the Canadian armed services. By an order-in-council of 14 September 1939, Canada created the Royal Canadian Air Force (RCAF) Special Reserve, which could accept aliens. A few months later the Canadian Active Service Force made similar provisions to permit the enlistment of Americans and other aliens.

Since the end of the Second World War, again only Canadian and British subjects could be accepted into the Canadian Forces. An American or any other foreign citizen cannot be accepted into the Canadian Forces unless there is a specific need for which no Canadian is sufficiently qualified.[3]

Based on information from the U.S. National Archives — and their data is incomplete — Canadians were the largest single group from a foreign country within the U.S. forces during the Second World War. Canadians were also the foreign nationals with the highest total number of casualties, killed and wounded.[4]

During the Vietnam conflict, the American government followed the letter of the law and did not recruit Canadians on Canadian soil for American military service. Yet the pervasiveness of the American media, particularly television, saturated Canadians with American news and opinion about the Vietnam War and encouraged many young Canadians to enlist for service there. Statements by American officials also contributed to the enlistment of Canadians. In March 1965, Henry Cabot Lodge, U.S. ambassador to South Vietnam, then between tours, stated that "if any Canadians wish to go out and help, if it appeals to their sense of adventure, I can assure them they will be very welcome."[5]

PART I

HISTORICAL INTRODUCTION

General Westmoreland at a briefing, Phu Bai, May 1967. (Courtesy G. Webster.)

THE WAR IN VIETNAM

The Geography of South Vietnam

The southern half of Vietnam, where most of the fighting took place, consists of a strip of land stretching along the eastern seaward rim of Southeast Asia. From the 17th parallel, which separated South from North Vietnam, a chain of mountains stretches southward along a spine whose branches run in an easterly direction until they fade away into the vast alluvial plain of the Mekong River. The ragged peaks of the Annamese (or Truong Son) Mountains — a steep wilderness of dense rain forest, plunging rivers and tortuous ridges — are characteristic of the northern highlands of northwestern Vietnam. The central highlands is a plateau area located at the southern edge of the mountains. The most southerly area of the country is generally flat lowland, covered with rice paddies.

As of 1966, the population of North Vietnam was about 18 million. The majority of the 16 million inhabitants of South Vietnam lived in the rice-bearing southern region of the Mekong Delta. South Vietnam's coast was fronted by long white sand beaches with many coves and bays washed by the South China Sea. About 40 per cent of the total land was uninhabited and covered with jungle, scrub bush, elephant grass and swamp. Saigon, the capital, was the South's largest city with 1.5 million inhabitants. In the fertile delta, the climate alternates generally between hot, rainy, monsoon weather from

May to October and very hot, drier weather for the rest of the year. The northern central coastal regions receive much of their rainfall between the months of September and January. To the north and in the mountains, the temperatures are cooler.

The Vietnamese Struggle for National Independence

From the Vietnamese perspective, recent colonial history began in the latter half of the 19th century. It was during this period that the country was taken over by the French. Vietnam remained under French colonial domination until 1940, when the Japanese gained control of the country. Following the Japanese withdrawal, Ho Chi Minh, a Communist, proclaimed the country's independence and through warfare resisted French attempts to reassert their authority. The fight for national independence came to be identified with the struggle led by Ho Chi Minh. Anti-Communist nationalists were often eliminated.

The period 1946-54, frequently referred to as the first Indochina war, culminated in the French defeat at Dien Bien Phu on 7 May 1954. That year, an agreement was signed at Geneva dividing the country in two at the 17th parallel. The Communists were given full control of the North (Democratic Republic of Vietnam), and in the South (Republic of Vietnam) an American-supported regime took over.

Following the Geneva Conference, the Communists very brutally consolidated their power in North Vietnam. Many of the more able intellectuals and businessmen were killed. Agriculture was collectivized and a program of industrialization embarked upon.

In the South, Ngo Dinh Diem, a Roman Catholic, formed an anti-Communist regime with himself as president. Using police and army terror tactics, Diem tried to suppress any opposition, Communist or otherwise. A modest land reform program was attempted, but it was much too limited in scope and was effectively sabotaged by the landlord class. Administratively, the country was divided into 44 provinces, headed by provincial chiefs, which were further subdivided into districts, each with its own government. Life in the countryside centred on the local village. Much of the aid supplied by the United States was used to build up the army, the regime's secret service and security forces. Few social benefits reached the general populace.

As part of the Geneva agreement, an international commission consisting of Canadian, Polish and Indian members under an Indian chairman was created to supervise the withdrawal of the French, the movement to the North of Ho Chi Minh's Communist supporters and the movement south of the 17th parallel of those not wishing to remain under a Communist government. Further, the International Commission for Supervision and Control for Vietnam was to supervise the terms of the agreement, which provided for elections in North and South Vietnam in July 1956 to unify the country. Ho Chi Minh and the other Communist leaders in North Vietnam were confident they would win these elections. The refusal by Diem to hold such elections brought about attempts by the Viet Cong, the Communist organization in South Vietnam, to overthrow the Saigon government. Further terrorist and military activities of the Viet Cong, designed to destabilize the southern regime, led to increasing intervention by both the United States and North Vietnam.

Internal opposition to Diem began to mount in South Vietnam. This opposition finally resulted in his overthrow by a military coup on 1 November 1963. Both Diem and his brother were killed. With the fall of the Diem regime, a series of coups and counter-coups followed. There were many changes of government before the military, led by Air Vice Marshal Nguyen Cao Ky, took over completely in June 1965. Presidential elections on 3 September 1967 resulted in the election of General Nguyen Van Thieu with Ky as his running mate.

Until 1960 the United States supported the Saigon regime with some 700 advisors for the training of the South Vietnamese army as permitted by the Geneva agreement. By the end of 1963 that figure had grown to about 17,000 plus a growing number of U.S. helicopter pilots. By the fall of 1964, there were 23,000 Americans in South Vietnam. Their assistance proved insufficient. In early 1965 the U.S. bombing of North Vietnam began. Soon afterwards Washington officially sent its first regular combat troops, 3,500 marines, who arrived 7 March 1965. By early 1968 some 500,000 Americans were serving along with over 600,000 South Vietnamese troops. There were also some 50,000 South Koreans and lesser numbers of troops from Australia, New Zealand and Thailand at that time. The Philippines sent two civic action groups totalling 3,300 personnel. The North Vietnamese regular soldiers at first supplemented and then took over from the Viet Cong guerrillas. Communist forces now numbered about 235,000.

In spite of three years of intensive bombing of the North and fierce warfare in the South, the North Vietnamese and Viet Cong continued to fight fiercely. On 31 January 1968, the Viet Cong initiated the Tet holiday offensive, attacking about 100 cities and military bases in South Vietnam. The very attempt, though militarily unsuccessful, shattered the belief of many that an American military victory was possible. The week of 10-17 February saw U.S. casualties rise to over 500 killed and 2,500 wounded in action. A request by the U.S. commander, General William Westmoreland, for an additional 200,000 troops was not granted. Continuing a war of attrition at such a high casualty level was no longer politically acceptable; clearly domestic support for the war had collapsed. Although the aerial bombing continued and spilled into Laos and Cambodia, the United States was in the process of gradually withdrawing its troops; by April 1970, only 115,000 American troops remained in South Vietnam. The eventual American pull-out in 1973 left the South Vietnamese to fight the North Vietnamese alone.

The United States' Involvement in Vietnam

Following the Second World War, the United States assumed the mantle of defender of the free world against communism. It supported the resumption of French rule over Indochina and gave financial and material assistance to France in its efforts to reimpose its control of the area. Fear of the spread of communism was the American government's primary consideration in reaching that decision.

John F. Kennedy, who succeeded Dwight D. Eisenhower as president in 1961, augmented U.S. involvement in Vietnam with military "advisors." Following Kennedy's assassination on 22 November 1963, Lyndon B. Johnson stepped up the military intervention. When U.S. warships in the Gulf of Tonkin were mistakenly reported attacked by North Vietnamese torpedo boats in August 1964, retaliatory air strikes were ordered and Johnson secured congressional support to take "all necessary measures to repel any armed attack against the forces of the United States and to prevent further aggression."

To meet the growing manpower requirement created by the Vietnam War, the draft was invoked. In July 1965, President Johnson requested authorization to increase the strength of the armed services by 440,000 men. In January 1966, the administration asked for another 112,800. By August, draft calls averaged about 30,000 a month. In August 1966, Secretary of Defense Robert McNamara announced a plan to salvage a number of men who would ordinarily be rejected by the armed services as mentally below standard. The September call-up rose to 37,500, and in October 46,200 men were drafted. Existing military training facilities became cramped; these were expanded and new ones built to meet the influx.

The draft at the height of the Vietnam War became a major

source of dissension. Those who benefited most from American society — the wealthy and well educated — were the least likely to serve. College deferment did not end until December 1971. Ordinarily, in order to be accepted into the American forces, a recruit had to be 18 years of age or over. Boys of 17 were eligible only with the consent of their parents. The maximum age on enrolment was 28 for officers and 34 for other ranks.

As American casualties mounted without any end in sight, public opinion turned against the war. Opposition intensified in the winter of 1967-68, and President Johnson announced he would not accept nomination for a second term. In May 1968 peace discussions began in Paris, and in November the bombing of North Vietnam was curtailed.

Richard M. Nixon won the 1968 election. He cut back U.S. ground forces to fewer than 70,000 by early 1972, leaving the South Vietnamese to defend themselves, the so-called Vietnamization of the war. The American policy of escalating the bombing of North Vietnam while reducing U.S. troop involvement only served to stiffen the resolve of the North Vietnamese. Bombing by B-52 aircraft did succeed in breaking up North Vietnamese troop concentrations but did not give the Americans control of the territory they were bombing.

In January 1973, a cease-fire agreement was reached by means of the Paris peace accords. The agreement provided for the exchange of prisoners and an American withdrawal from South Vietnam within 60 days. Almost 600 American prisoners were released by the North Vietnamese.

The Vietnamization of the War

On 30 March 1972, North Vietnamese regular troops began a massive invasion of South Vietnam using vast quantities of artillery and armour. North Vietnamese troops under cover of the seasonal monsoon moved to establish control of the northernmost provinces of South Vietnam. The South Vietnamese forces and American advisors were overwhelmed initially, but the more experienced South Vietnamese troops were thrown into the battle and held their own. Their spirit was exemplified by their holding of An Loc, 65 air miles north of Saigon, for 95 days until the Communists withdrew. Quang Tri City fell to the North Vietnamese on 1 May and was retaken on 17 September. Although Saigon won the battle, it was at great cost. Stalemate set in.

With the new year of 1973 came the Paris peace accords and the withdrawal of U.S. forces (except for 50 military advisors and some

7,000 civilians, many ex-military) by the end of March. When it became obvious that the cease-fire was not being observed, Canada withdrew as a member of the international commission supervising the accords.

The Final Offensive

In December 1974, the North Vietnamese again took the offensive. Phuoc Binh, the capital of Phuoc Long province, was seized. The United States failed to react. In March 1975, Ban Me Thuot fell and on the same day the U.S. House of Representatives refused to fund a supplemental military aid package proposed by President Gerald Ford. Both actions severely damaged the morale of the South Vietnamese and gave a psychological boost to the North Vietnamese.

The South Vietnamese forces were stretched out thinly in the north and central highlands. They faced some 20 North Vietnamese divisions. Outnumbered and outgunned, President Thieu decided on a military evacuation southwards. It turned into a rout, and only a small number of military units ever reached the Saigon area.

The North Vietnamese launched heavy attacks on Saigon's perimeter before government troops could establish firm defensive positions. Although one division put up a determined resistance at Xuan Loc, the South Vietnamese defenders were eventually overwhelmed and Saigon came under siege. Tan Son Nhut Air Base was bombed and shelled. The North Vietnamese under the command of General Van Tien Dung entered Saigon unopposed at the end of April 1975. The South Vietnamese government collapsed, and as many as could fled the country.

The Americans did not again intervene militarily as many South Vietnamese expected. With the attack on Saigon they began to evacuate both their own people and South Vietnamese. Mobs surged at the American embassy gates in their panic to leave the country via helicopters landing on the roof. Some South Vietnamese soldiers and civilians escaped by South Vietnamese aircraft to Thailand, some were evacuated by the Americans, but most escaped in boats. In 1976 Vietnam was united under a Communist government as the Socialist Republic of Vietnam, and Saigon was renamed Ho Chi Minh City.

Summation

Some 2.7 million Americans served in some capacity in the Vietnam War zone between August 1964 and May 1975. Of these about 60,000 were killed, 300,000 wounded and 75,000 permanently disabled.

Another 2,500 were listed as missing in action. (In comparison, there were 55,000 Americans killed and 100,000 wounded in the Korean conflict in 1950-53.) This protracted war also cost the United States many billions of dollars.

With the help of the United States, the South Vietnamese armed forces increased to over a million men by January 1969. Modelled, perhaps too closely, after conventional American forces, the army consisted of 4 corps organized into 12 divisions. The air force — the fourth largest in the world — had 2,000 aircraft, while the navy had 1,500 vessels.

South Vietnam reported 220,000 of its military personnel killed in the war and 500,000 wounded. North Vietnam and the Viet Cong suffered over 600,000 military casualties. In North and South Vietnam combined, it is estimated that 400,000 civilians were killed in the war and 1,000,000 wounded. Most were South Vietnamese. South Korea lost 4,400 troops killed fighting in Vietnam; Australia and New Zealand together had some 500 killed and over 2,000 wounded of the almost 50,000 who served there; 350 Thais and 7 from the Philippines were killed in action.

The ratio of Communist troops in the field to Communist support personnel was much higher than was the case among the U.S. forces, which were top-heavy in rear echelon manpower. The cost of equipping, feeding and supporting one American in the field vastly exceeded that for a Viet Cong or North Vietnamese. If one does not include the South Vietnamese army, U.S. effective ground troops actually looking for and fighting the North Vietnamese and Viet Cong troops were, in fact, outnumbered by total Communist troops in the field.

The U.S. Army consisted of a mixture of career soldiers and conscripts whose objective was not to win but to survive their tours. Having mastered the skills necessary to survive, they would be replaced after a year by new recruits. The average age of Americans fighting in Vietnam was 19, compared with 26 for those who fought in the Second World War, but 79 per cent of those who served in Vietnam had a high school education by contrast with only 45 per cent in the Second World War. There was bound to be some racial friction between black and white soldiers, since there was serious racial tension in the United States at the time.

The reasons for the Americans' defeat in Vietnam were many. In the Korean War, a generally static front during two years meant that infiltration could be more easily detected than was the case in South Vietnam, which could be infiltrated overland by North Vietnamese through its neighbours Laos and Cambodia. Furthermore, the

Americans did not invade North Vietnam with troops for fear of possible Chinese or Soviet retaliation. It was American domestic opposition to the war, however, that brought about the eventual U.S. withdrawal.

There were other, more subtle, reasons as well. It could be said the Americans were defeated in Vietnam because their overall strategy was flawed. The U.S. government and media generally misunderstood Vietnam and its people. Many Americans viewed North Vietnam as an appendage of Communist China. They ignored Vietnam's history, particularly its long struggle against foreign domination. China and North Vietnam were only temporary allies as a result of America's intervention. After the U.S. withdrawal, old animosities were renewed.

This was a war requiring the active support of the people in the rural areas of South Vietnam, since control of the countryside was the key to holding the country. The American forces, by dint of numbers and firepower, could gain possession of a certain area but that would not give them overall mastery. They achieved many military victories yet lost the war. There was a great need for patience and good human relations with the Vietnamese villagers — neither of which the American war machine had in abundance.

In contrast, the Vietnamese Communists, in seeking and holding support, made extensive use of political indoctrination and propaganda. This was given in substantial doses to their troops as well as to the civilian populace. An effective government of reform in South Vietnam would have gone a long way to counteract Communist propaganda, but this was largely lacking.

While some Americans made a positive contribution to help the South Vietnamese through civic action programs, others turned the people against them. Incidents such as military vehicles running cyclists and pedestrians off the road, empty beer cans being thrown at Vietnamese from a moving vehicle, or water buffalo and cattle being killed for sport served to alienate those whom the Americans were supposedly there to help.

The Vietnam War differed considerably from both world wars in which the United States fought. In the Vietnam struggle, American soldiers never received general public acclaim at home. There was no formal declaration of war. There was no public raising of large military units, no large troop send-offs. Instead, men volunteered or were drafted individually, assembled for training and then were sent, usually by aircraft, to South Vietnam. Their return was often equally quiet and unnoticed. It was the large-scale television coverage that brought the war to the home front. In *The Ten Thousand Day War*,

Michael Maclear quotes Dean Rusk as saying: "This was the first struggle fought on television in everybody's living room every day."

Another way in which Vietnam was different from other wars was in the nature of the wounds suffered by the combatants. Permanently disabling wounds were sustained at a far greater rate in Vietnam than in previous wars. As a result of improvements in field medicine, as well as the use of helicopters and other aircraft to move the wounded quickly to hospital, a good many who would have died in the earlier conflicts survived. The percentage of Vietnam GIs who suffered amputation or crippling wounds to the lower extremities was much higher than in the Second World War and Korea. This was largely the result of the more extensive use of anti-personnel land mines in Vietnam.[1]

The war in Vietnam was also utterly unlike campaigns most American or Canadian soldiers had previously faced in that it was a war waged for the most part in dense jungles and underbrush. To counter overwhelming American firepower, the enemy usually resorted to hit-and-run battles. They controlled the pace of the war. The Americans could never really be sure who was friend and who was foe. One area of the country that might seem safe at one time could be extremely dangerous another time.

Like a chain, an army is only as strong as its weakest link. A "couldn't care less" attitude gradually caused a weakening of the chain. A few Canadian Korean veterans of both the Canadian and American armies noted this attitude in Vietnam as the war dragged on. In their estimation, there evolved a lapse in tight mental discipline among some U.S. Army troops, although there were extenuating circumstances. American political and military leaders tended to underestimate the enemy.

In contrast to the American troops, the Viet Cong and North Vietnamese soldiers were fighting for their country. The Communist forces were generally well trained, well armed, experienced in jungle warfare and highly motivated. Most Communist Vietnamese troops believed in their cause and were willing to die for it.

The United States was unable to achieve a military victory even with overwhelming firepower and resources. The Soviet Union's withdrawal from Afghanistan in 1989 points out again that a foreign superpower cannot impose its hegemony upon a people that has the will and the means to resist.

CANADIAN PARTICIPATION IN THE WAR

Canada's Position

During and following the Vietnam War, some Canadians looked down on the Americans with a good deal of self-righteousness and smugness. Many Canadians considered their country immune to the happenings south of the border. A good number were unaware that fellow Canadians were taking an active part in the war as members of the U.S. forces. While stories appeared in Canadian newspapers partial to the draft dodger, there was almost complete silence about Canadians crossing the border to enlist.

According to a Canadian Institute of Public Opinion survey of 28 September 1966, 31 per cent of Canadians felt the United States should get out of Vietnam, 18 per cent wanted the Americans to maintain the same level of fighting and 27 per cent called for stepped-up attacks on the North. These percentages indicate substantial Canadian support for American policy at the time.

In 1966, in Canada, a Liberal minority government under Prime Minister Lester B. Pearson was in office, while John Diefenbaker headed the Conservative opposition. In 1967, Robert Stanfield succeeded Diefenbaker as leader of the Conservatives and Pierre Trudeau took over as prime minister in April. Trudeau was given an overwhelming mandate in the election of June 1968. One of the federal government's foreign policy objectives under Pearson and

Trudeau was to explore ways in which Canada could help in settling the war in Vietnam. At home, Prime Minister Trudeau continued a policy of integrating the armed forces and began to cut their size substantially.

During the war, the Canadian Forces helped the American military, particularly in the area of training. For example, to ease the problem of a shortage of pilots in Southeast Asia, the U.S. Air Force took some pilots out of Training Command and replaced them under an existing exchange agreement with some Canadian Forces pilots. The latter served as instructors for a couple of years in the United States. The U.S. Air Force, however, did not send any instructors in exchange to Canada.

The Canadian economy helped supply the American military-industrial complex. As well, Canadian economic support was channelled to South Vietnam as part of the Free World Assistance Program. As the Vietnam War intensified, Canada's diplomatic role shifted from one of favouring the United States to one of trying to constrain the Johnson administration and to persuade it to negotiate an end to the war.

Canadians Who Fought in Vietnam

Who were the Canadians who found themselves fighting in South Vietnam? They were not only the many who voluntarily crossed the border to enlist. Some were drafted while living in the United States, and a good number were already serving in the American forces. They came from all social classes and from all parts of Canada. Most joined the army, others the marines, the air force and, lastly, the navy.

While a major proportion of the Canadians in the U.S. forces were about 19 or 20, there was also a significant number of older men. The latter were largely army sergeants — career soldiers already in the regular U.S. Army who retained their Canadian citizenship. After the war, most of these men remained in the United States. Some of the younger Canadians who had enlisted for three years returned to Canada, while others in the younger group decided to make the United States their home.

Canada's involvement in two world wars and in the United Nations "police action" in Korea had a largely positive effect on those who served. The personal impact of war can be attested to by many of the veterans. For some of Canada's Vietnam veterans, however, the war has had severe negative, long-term effects that will never leave them.

The word "Vietnam" has many connotations among Canadians today. Some think of the recent arrivals from that country who have made their homes here. A few think of the two peacekeeping commissions for Vietnam on which Canada served. (As noted earlier, the first was formed after the Geneva conference in 1954, the second following the Paris peace accords.) But most Canadians asked about Vietnam associate it with the war in the latter half of the 1960s.

Vietnam was not a popular war, even in the United States. In Canada, there was considerable sympathy for the anti-war movement. The medium of television brought the horrors of the war into everyone's homes. Atrocities, such as the My Lai massacre of 16 March 1968, served to reinforce an abhorrence of the war and the American soldiers fighting there.

While the two world wars and Korea involved troops fighting other troops in uniform for certain territory, the Vietnam War was largely a guerrilla war fought in all areas of South Vietnam amidst the civilian population. The enemy was often indistinguishable from the general populace. Body counts, not territorial gains, were the criteria of American success.

Previous books written on the war in Vietnam usually mention the contribution of America's allies, including Australia, New Zealand, South Korea, the Philippines and Thailand. Canadians are not mentioned at all — perhaps because the other countries provided separate contingents. Canadian volunteers were intermingled within the U.S. forces.

What is the feeling of Canadians towards the Canadian Vietnam veteran? The common reaction generally remains one of distaste. (On the positive side, a bumper sticker with "Vietnam Veteran" on it does help prevent tailgating.) A younger generation of Canadians, however, wishes to know more about Canadian Vietnam veterans.

The majority of Canadians who enlisted were in their late teens or early 20s. Most were from blue-collar and lower middle-class backgrounds. Ontario, with the largest population, was the home province of many of the recruits. During the years 1958-68, there was considerable Canadian support for the American cause in Vietnam and this encouraged young Canadians to enlist for military service in the American forces. Many joined specifically to get to Vietnam for adventure. Ideologically, those from Canada in the American forces were generally against communism, although most were not too familiar with the subject or with the true political situation in Vietnam.

A phrase from the Vietnam War new to Canadian veterans of other conflicts was "rules of engagement." This phrase applied to the conditions under which allied troops in Vietnam were permitted to fire on suspected enemy, reflecting the difficulties in waging guerrilla warfare in South Vietnam. For example, according to initial orders, persons were not to be shot at by troops on the ground "unless they open fire first." Canadians who fought in the Second World War or Korea never operated under such restraints.

As for postwar readjustment, it often proved more difficult for Canadian Vietnam veterans than for Canadian veterans of other wars. For example, they cannot attribute their physical or emotional problems to their having fought for their country against Naziism, and thereby gain the sympathy of their communities. While Canadian veterans of the First and Second World War were given preference in job hiring in the federal civil service, Canadian Vietnam veterans cannot look to the public sector for preferential employment. Employers in the private sector are much less sympathetic to Canadian Vietnam veterans than they were to veterans of the Second World War. As well, soldiers who fought in Vietnam must struggle with the consequences of a different type of stress, since they fought a very different kind of war — a guerrilla war is not the same as a conventional war for territory.

While American Vietnam veterans were not given sufficient recognition for their sacrifices, Canadian Vietnam veterans were forgotten. The establishment of the Vietnam Veterans Memorial in Washington, D.C., consisting of a black granite wall (1982) and a statue of three combat-weary servicemen (1984), has helped to ease some of the bitterness.

ENLISTMENT OF CANADIANS

The Foreign Enlistment Act

During the Vietnam War, the Canadian government did not discourage the enlistment of Canadians in the American forces. No Canadians were prosecuted for violating the Foreign Enlistment Act[2] in joining to fight in Vietnam. While the American government did not openly recruit on Canadian soil, it did facilitate their enlistment. For example, expanded or new recruiting offices were set up in northern Washington and New York states. At these offices, "letters of acceptability" for American military service were issued to potential Canadian recruits. These documents enabled the prospective enlistees to receive residency visas (equivalent to landed-immigrant status) from U.S. immigration. The U.S. military then proceeded with induction. To be eligible for commissioned rank, however, a recruit usually had to be a U.S. citizen.

Canada, as a member of the International Control Commission, was not supposed to compromise its impartiality. However, the government permitted the entry of its nationals into the U.S. military forces throughout the Vietnam War. The departments of External Affairs and Justice, after studying the situation, refused to prosecute anyone, considering it "very questionable that a Canadian could be successfully prosecuted under the Foreign Enlistment Act for serving in the U.S. forces in Vietnam."[3] Canadians who enlisted in the

American forces during the Vietnam War were generally unaware of the Foreign Enlistment Act. They certainly were not informed about it at American recruiting offices.

American Visas and Citizenship

For an alien, the normal period of residency to qualify for U.S. citizenship was, and remains, five years. However, three years' service in the armed forces entitles one to American citizenship. When the United States is involved in hostilities, as in Vietnam, and an alien is going to be sent overseas for military service, he can become an American citizen with less than a year's residency. A few Canadians going to Vietnam did take advantage of the latter provision. A year's service in a war zone also enabled many to become American citizens. But qualifying for American citizenship was generally not the main reason most Canadians wanted to go to Vietnam. They usually had decided to enlist before they had found out details about American citizenship.

Canadian Vietnam veterans who decided to return to this country after their military service did so because they preferred the lifestyle here. Others decided to become American citizens for a variety of reasons. That decision had usually been made during the Vietnam War.

At the time of the Vietnam conflict, there was no requirement for enlisted men (other ranks) to become American citizens. The U.S. Navy and Marine Corps still do not require an alien to take out U.S. citizenship. An alien may serve four years in the U.S. Air Force, but as of 1 November 1982, in order to re-enlist an alien must become an American citizen. As of 1 January 1986, an alien serving in the U.S. Army must take out citizenship within seven years of enlistment.

Canadian/American Political Relations

Early in 1965, President Lyndon Johnson approached Prime Minister Lester Pearson about the possibility of the government of Canada providing military assistance to the government of South Vietnam. In the face of intense pressure from L.B.J., Pearson retorted that although Canada would not send combat forces, the issue of sending military medical and non-combatant battlefield support personnel would be referred to Cabinet. Pearson's proposal involved sending Canadian officers into battlefield areas for such tasks as staffing field hospitals and disease prevention centres for soldiers. On 20 January, the matter was brought up in Cabinet where the idea met stiff resistance and was shelved.[4]

In February 1966, a group in Toronto called "Canadian Volun-teers-Vietnam" (CVVN), headed by Donald T. Echlin and T. David Mitchell, sought permission from the Canadian government to re-cruit a battalion in Canada for combat duty in Vietnam. The aim was to stop the spread of Chinese communism as well as to help the United States. Members would undergo full U.S. armed forces in-duction procedures. Officers and, initially, non-commissioned offic-ers (NCOs) would be provided by the U.S. Army. The battalion would be trained, equipped and paid for by the U.S. government, but would retain its Canadian identity by virtue of special distinctive insignia.

Prime Minister Pearson was against the creation of such a force in view of Canada's responsibility as a member of the International Commission for Supervision and Control. The Toronto group was advised that its proposal appeared incompatible with the laws of Canada, in particular with the Foreign Enlistment Act, which pro-hibits recruitment in Canada for service in foreign armed forces. It was suggested that the organizers discuss their plans with private legal counsel. Nothing further was heard concerning this group.

The right of individual Canadian volunteers to cross the border to enlist was queried. In response to a question raised in early 1966 by W.B. Nesbitt, the member of Parliament from Oxford, Ontario, concerning the status of Canadian volunteers who were already serving with the U.S. armed forces, some of them in Vietnam, the minister of external affairs, Paul Martin, replied, "... this is a free country." John Diefenbaker, leader of the opposition, retorted, "I thought the Foreign Enlistment Act prevented that." Martin simply replied, "No."[5]

Aliens and U.S. Military Service During the War

Those called up for training and service in the U.S. armed forces were usually between the ages of 18 and 26. The period of duty was 24 months. American draft laws applied to all aliens, including Cana-dian citizens, living in the United States. All male Canadian citizens of call-up age who entered the United States were required to regis-ter with a selective service board. Registration was required within six months of entry within the country. However, such individuals were not usually eligible for military service unless they spent a total of more than 365 days (not necessarily continuous) in the United States. While the draft generally applied to Canadians working in the United States, it did not include those who entered on a student visa or an exchange visitor's visa, the foreign press, or officials of government agencies or international organizations. Dual nationals of the United States and Canada, even though residents of Canada, were required to register. Dual Canadian-American citizens in Canada could be relieved of that obligation by divesting themselves of American citizenship before a U.S. consul. They would, however, be barred from applying thereafter from becoming citizens or permanent residents of the United States. Any alien who was not seeking permanent residency, and prior to being called for induction, could make an application to be relieved from U.S. military service. A Canadian citizen charged with violation of the U.S. Military Service Act could not be extradited from Canada to the United States. Canadian police officers were instructed not to concern themselves with such violators.

A major concern of Canadian families in the United States with draft-age sons was the Vietnam War. Some young men returned to Canada but most remained. The draft, which was abolished in 1973, discouraged some Canadian families from immigrating to the United States.

Numbers of Canadians in Vietnam

It is impossible to determine exactly how many Canadians fought in Vietnam. In newspaper articles, a variety of figures have been suggested as to the number of Canadians who entered the United States to enlist. Estimates vary from 20,000 to 30,000. Higher figures have been cited by members of the media and the public, but based on current information, the number of Canadian volunteers from this country who went to Vietnam was closer to 6,000.[6] If one includes Canadians who were already in the United States for one reason or another, the total is over 12,000.[7] Of that number, perhaps one-third enlisted for idealistic reasons, one-third for what might be termed adventure and one-third for other reasons. In fact, Vietnam was the locale of the largest number of Canadian citizens ever serving in a war in which their country was not officially involved.

The only way to establish the exact number of Canadians who served in Vietnam would be to check the nationality cited in the record of military service of each person who served in the American forces in Vietnam. Thus far, the American government has been unwilling to do this.

The failure of the United States to order full mobilization during the Vietnam War resulted in a growing need to find replacements as American casualties increased. Along the border with Quebec, American recruiting stations displayed signs such as "Bienvenue

Canadiens." Canadian volunteers entering the U.S. Army's recruiting office in Plattsburgh remember being greeted by "surly Al, the soldier's pal."[8] Many Canadians from the greater Montreal area enlisted at Plattsburgh and gave that town as their home address. Recruiters accepted some men who would have been rejected under normal peacetime conditions. Thus, men who could not qualify for the Canadian Forces had a ready alternative, available also to those being squeezed out of the Canadian Forces by reduction. A print-out supplied by the Military Archives Division of the General Services Administration, Washington, shows that, of aliens killed while serving in the American forces in South Vietnam, the largest single national group was Canadian.

Motives for Enlistment

With the beginning of the sustained U.S. bombing of North Vietnam in 1965, the war came to occupy an increasing amount of Canadian newspaper space and television time. TV's coverage of the many protests against the war throughout the United States incited similar demonstrations in Canada. Flag-burning and protests at the U.S. embassy and at consulates across Canada, sit-ins, and marches for peace became commonplace. Canadians also crossed the border to join in massive demonstrations against the war. The majority, however, remained silent, but there were some Canadians who strongly disagreed with the demonstrators; among these were some who enlisted to fight in the American forces. A good number of volunteers from Canada had a personal connection with the United States. Some had been born there and had moved to Canada as youngsters; others had one parent who had been born in the United States.

As the American forces expanded to meet the commitments of the Vietnam War, there were increased opportunities for those Canadians who wanted a military career but were unable to pursue one in Canada. Canadians who could not meet the higher physical and educational requirements of their own country's armed forces gravitated to the U.S. forces at this time. Some who had previously served in the Canadian Forces joined the American forces in order to go to Vietnam.

A few Canadians who enlisted in the U.S. forces at the time of the Vietnam War did so with the intention of distinguishing themselves on the battlefield and then returning to Canada as heroes. They believed that combat experience in Vietnam would open the road to rapid promotion in the Canadian Forces. Those who returned with that idea learned that their service in Vietnam counted for little or nothing. The public ignored them and the few who did join the Canadian Forces after their return experienced no preferential treatment.

Most Canadians who enlisted were not highly qualified academically or technically. For some, the war offered the opportunity to pick up a trade or skill they could use in future civilian life. A good many enlisted to escape the boredom of school or a civilian job. Some aimed at acquiring American citizenship, which they believed was the key to a better economic future. The idea of fighting communism was not the central motivating factor initially for many Canadians who joined up. Fighting communism became the main justification for many later, beginning at boot camp.

Some Canadians volunteered in order to satisfy a need for adventure. They did their stint in the U.S. forces, returned to Canada, and then tried to put what happened behind them. The subsequent letdown has some similarities with the depression experienced after the ending of an intense love affair. Still they had wanted a chance at honour and glory.[9] "You're young and you're strong and you want to use that energy," recalled Arthur Diabo, a Mohawk from Kahnawake, Quebec, who served in the Marine Corps. "And Vietnam was a good place to do that — for about two weeks. After that, you just tried to stay alive."[10] Diabo brought back a left forearm shattered by a sniper's bullet. After being released from medical care, he began drinking heavily until a near-fatal car accident. In 1972, he married and turned his life around. Diabo now heads a Canadian Vietnam Veterans organization in Montreal.

Another who enlisted was Richard Dextraze, the son of General Jacques Dextraze, chief of the Canadian defence staff from 1972 to 1977. General Dextraze gives his son's reasons.

"I asked him why he wouldn't join the Canadian Forces and he said we weren't at war anywhere. He kept saying the Americans were our friends and we had to do our bit to help them. He honestly believed that.

"It might sound corny coming from a 20-year-old fellow, but he told us, 'I want to do my share. You fought in the last war for freedom and I'd like to go for a couple of years. When I come back I'll feel a better man. I'll feel I've contributed.'"[11]

Richard had finished high school and was working at Molson's Breweries when he left his Montreal home to join the U.S. Marines in 1967. He arrived in Vietnam in the winter of 1968. On 23 April 1969, when he was on a patrol close to the Demilitarized Zone, his company encountered the enemy and Richard was fatally wounded. His body was brought back to Montréal for burial. Richard was awarded the Silver Star Medal. Says General Dextraze of those Canadians who fought in Vietnam: "People say they were cranks, that they were stupid to go over there because it wasn't our war. But this war was to fight a common enemy."[12]

A significant number of Canadian Indians, especially those living close to the border, enlisted to fight in Vietnam. Their motives for joining the American forces were many; for some, a thirst for adventure, and for others, a need to assert their manhood. Some were living or working in the United States and felt obliged to enlist in the American forces. For many, the American military forces offered a means of escape from an otherwise bleak economic future.

While a good number of Canadians who enlisted lived near the border, geographical location was not generally the determining factor. Through the media, young Canadians in all parts of the country knew about the Vietnam War. If they had the desire to enlist in the American forces, the obstacle of distance would be surmounted.

Joe Collard, president of Chapter No. 180 of the Vietnam Veterans of America at Sault Ste. Marie, Michigan, summed up his view of the main reason for cross-border enlistment: "I don't think that those who enlisted sat around discussing whether it was a just or an unjust war; I think it was neighbours helping neighbours."[13]

Is he correct? The following accounts from a cross-section of Canadians Vietnam veterans do not entirely bear out Collard's opinion. It is hoped that the stories will shed some light on the individuals who were there.

PART II

WAR EXPERIENCES OF CANADIANS

Bob Hope show. (Courtesy K. McVeigh/CVVO.)

REID FELTMATE

Vietnam: June 1969 to December 1970   Service: Army

Warrant Officer Reid Feltmate (left) leaning on the door of his helicopter, Bao Loc, Vietnam, January 1970. (Courtesy R. Feltmate.)

The following account by Reid Feltmate of Timmins, Ontario, is not typical — there is no one typical Canadian experience — yet it is representative. Each Canadian who went to Vietnam has his own personal story of why he went, of his experiences there and of postwar readjustment. Taken together, the individual stories of Canadians in this section offer a glimpse of their collective experiences.

When I write this, it has been 20 years to the month since I arrived in Vietnam as a 20-year-old helicopter pilot. The time I spent there amounted to 1,600 hours of flight time and as many recollections. War stories are easy, especially as time dulls the need for veracity, but one incident still seems particularly clear and poignant to me these 20 years later.

I was assigned to the 92nd Assault Helicopter Company, a unit comprised of 20 UH-1H troop carriers and 10 UH-1C gunships. Split into three platoons, these aircraft provided daily lift and support to the units assigned to the II Corps military region situated in the central highlands. We flew every variety of mission, from Special

Forces insertion missions, to tedious day-long resupply and, combining with our sister companies, brigade-size air assaults.

Everything not associated with "movie-style" combat assault missions we conveniently referred to as ass and trash, alluding to the variety and value of cargo carried when supporting a modern army in the jungle with helicopters. This was the mission, and I was on my fifth or sixth outing as a co-pilot when the following incident occurred.

The aircraft commander was my platoon leader, whom I remember simply as Captain Ferguson. He was huge, in the athletic sense, and he filled his side of the cockpit with no effort whatsoever. He seemed even larger as he scrunched behind his chicken plate (chest protector) and snuggled into the armoured seat. As a result, large portions of him just protruded around and over this protection.

We talked as we flew, and the discovery that I was a Canadian only fuelled his reminiscences about a year or so he had spent as a football player in Canada. He had played for the Toronto Rifles for a season or two and his stories of that experience and his exposure to Canadians formed the basis for hours of conversation. We had started around seven in the morning flying some colonel around his sector, showing the flag and delivering the mail, and it was a little after lunch on a short hop from Bao Loc to Ban Me Thuot that we picked up the peculiar wail of an aviation emergency locater beacon.

It seemed strongest in the area of dense jungle we were flying over at the moment, so we noted the location and proceeded to our destination. En route, we contacted "King," a surveillance aircraft, and reported the beacon. High overhead the small country, King assured us that they were not receiving the signal and that no aircraft were missing or reported down at that time. About 30 minutes later we had turned around at Ban Me Thuot and were returning to Bao Loc, when we received the same signal again in that section of the jungle previously overflown.

Again King confirmed that our find was a false signal but Captain Ferguson would have no part of it. He declared a tactical emergency to our colonel passenger, delivered him to Bao Loc, refuelled and set out again for the area of the signal. Whether it was concern, curiosity or plain boredom that affected his decision, I will never know, but it turned out to be the right one. I never again underestimated the value of a hunch.

It was now about two o'clock, and the signal was as strong as ever. From our circuits around the area, we narrowed the source down to about a 10-square-mile section of double-canopy jungle reaching up about a hundred feet. It was solid cover. We crisscrossed the area trying to sense the focus of the signal, and had gotten the strongest tone now down to about a square city block. This had gone on for about two hours, and prior to leaving for refuel, we hovered over a larger outgrowth to tie a large fluorescent distress marker to help us refind the spot should we return and the signal had faded.

We returned, now about four o'clock, to a relatively weak signal, but found our marker and continued the pattern search in what we hoped was the right location. We would hover at treetop height, slowly manoeuvring back and forth with all four crew members peering down through the foliage. More than once the thought crossed our mind that we were falling right into an ambush, but the sense that we were about to rescue someone was so strong that that minor fear seemed inconsequential. Then about 4:30, we spotted it, about 500 yards from our marker. I will never forget the surge of electrical awareness that I experienced when we spotted the tail section of an army Bird Dog observation plane.

It had crashed into the treetops, only clipping minor limbs, almost unnoticeable, and had descended vertically into the trees almost to the ground. There was only a five- or six-foot hole where the fuselage could even be seen. We could see the two bodies in the cockpit, but no movement. Then as we hovered over the scene, I observed the most delirious sight. A single hand reached painfully out the broken left windscreen and waggled, just a few inches. Someone was alive in that airplane.

Now King was more than interested in our find and called for a "dust-off," a Huey evacuation helicopter out of Phan Thiet. That was a 30-minute flight. We dropped a rope on the wreckage to signal the occupant that we had spotted him and returned to Bao Loc for a squad of Rangers to help in the rescue. It was obvious that getting the victim out was going to be difficult, if not dangerous, in view of the possibility of Viet Cong in the area. As it turned out, the Bird Dog had been shot down with small arms from a point about 10 miles away, and we never did find out if the other occupant had been killed in the air or in crashing.

We returned with the Rangers about the same time as the medevac Huey arrived and were prepared to let the troops down by rope when dust-off spotted a bomb crater about 200 yards from the crash. We had seen it earlier but had forgotten about it in the excitement of the discovery. It had been created by a 500-pounder, and with a few clips going in, we were able to land the men. Our sidekick gunships also arrived on station at this time to help cover the extraction and the dust-off bird as it went in for the pickup.

It seems like only minutes later that the two bodies were on the medevac headed for the coast. We extracted the Rangers and flew escorted back to Bao Loc. Drained, both from concentration and excitement, we called our operations to tell them we would have to spend the night at the outpost.

The passenger in the back of the Bird Dog, a colonel, lived. He had a broken neck and legs and had lost a lot of blood. The pilot was dead. That is about all we heard. It is not difficult to put oneself in the colonel's shoes: in a crashed airplane, the enemy a few miles away probably looking for you, extremely mangled and weak, the pilot dead, and the sound of this Huey working overhead, sometimes close, then far, and just praying you would be found; knowing also that if you weren't found, you would probably die during the night.

People want to know about war, especially combat, about heroics and all the incumbent nuances of Vietnam. But I will never forget that moment: the hand waving weakly through the broken glass. To save a life in that maelstrom just seemed so valuable.[1]

A helicopter takes off from Da Nang, 1966-67. (Courtesy of K. McVeigh/CVVO.)

CHARLES JAMES PHELPS

Vietnam: May 1965 to May 1966   Service: Army

Specialist 4 C.J. Phelps, Saigon, January 1966. (Courtesy C.J. Phelps.)

Another Canadian who served in Vietnam was Charles James "Mike" Phelps. Born in Toronto, 4 July 1940, he attended school at Niagara-on-the-Lake. On 17 October 1963 he enlisted in the U.S. Army at Buffalo. When he joined, he had no idea where his service in the U.S. forces would take him. Mike's father had been in the Canadian Expeditionary Force and Royal Flying Corps in the First World War. His three older brothers had served Canada honourably during times of war as well as in peace. His third-oldest brother, now living in Niagara Falls, New York, was with the Canadian Army in Korea and joined the U.S. Army to go to Vietnam from 1966 to 1967. Mike was single and he had never been very far from home. He saw the U.S. Army as an opportunity for him to broaden his experience. After training at Fort Jackson, South Carolina, Mike went on to the U.S. Army Finance School at Fort Benjamin Harrison, Indianapolis. Being a high school graduate, Mike was able to join the Army Finance Corps. Until April 1965 he was posted to the 15th Financial Disbursing Section at Fort Benning, Georgia. Then while he was on leave back in Canada, he received notice that he would be going to Vietnam.

Corporal (later Sergeant) Phelps served in Vietnam from May

1965 to May 1966. He was stationed at Tan Son Nhut Air Base and
Saigon with the 7th Financial Disbursing Section attached to Headquarters U.S. Army Vietnam (USARV). When he first arrived, the
troops were being paid in American currency. About September the
United States began using scrip to pay its troops to discourage black
marketeering. It did not solve the problem. There grew a flourishing
black market in U.S. currency. The legal rate of exchange was 80 Vietnamese piastres to the dollar obtained at the Army Finance Office.
On the black market, the rate was 120 piastres to the dollar. The rate
differential increased as the war progressed.

Mike was discharged from the army on 16 October 1966, and six
days later he married a girl he had met on a blind date just prior to
his departure overseas. Happily married with a family, he is a
member of the Ontario Provincial Police at Sault Ste. Marie, Ontario.[2]

The Vietnam War generally conjures up images of infantry patrolling through dense jungle, helicopters hovering, and fighter jets
bombing and strafing enemy positions. In reality, for every infantryman in the field or pilot in the air, there were more than five
support personnel. Those engaged in combat support, referred to as
"service and support," included cooks, paymasters and even radio
announcers as portrayed, for example, by Robin Williams in the
movie *Good Morning Vietnam*. The stories of those in the rear form an
integral part of the total picture, and Canadians also served among
that group .

Huge concentrations of American military personnel first developed around air bases and ports in South Vietnam. These facilities
grew to be rear echelon base cities, strung out mainly along or not far
from the coastline of South Vietnam. They included Quang Tri, Phu
Bai, Da Nang, Chu Lai, Nha Trang, Cam Ranh and the biggest of all,
the Tan Son Nhut-Bien Hoa complex on the outskirts of Saigon.

The general layouts of many of these base cities were similar. In
the core area was the original Vietnamese city, usually with archi-
tectural reminders of the French colonial background. Around this
core were to be found American service-and-support buildings.
Surrounding the Americans were shantytown settlements, referred to
by the American GIs as "Dogpatch," derived from the "Li'l Abner"
comic strip. They were inhabited by refugees — Vietnamese peasants
driven from their villages. From these people came the "mama-sans"
— Vietnamese women who did the Americans' laundry; youngsters
who dealt in the black market and in drugs; prostitutes; and even
recruits for the Viet Cong.

Among the facilities in the rear were clubs for American military
personnel, the American equivalent of the off-duty social centres

called "messes" in Canada. There were also the PXs (post exchanges), which sold everything from potato chips and aftershave lotion to stereos. Cameras were extremely popular among GIs. Vietnam became the most unofficially photographed war in history.

THOMAS TOMPKINS

Vietnam: May 1965 to June 1966   Service: Army
           August 1968 to January 1969
           January 1972 to January 1973

Sergeant Tom Tompkins (right), at Marble Mountain, Da Nang, September 1968. (Courtesy T. Tompkins.)

Thomas Tompkins, born in Amherst, Nova Scotia, in 1937, served in the militia with the North Nova Scotia Highlanders. Tom went on active duty with the Royal Canadian Electrical and Mechanical Engineers from 1955 to 1961. Seeking action, he joined the U.S. Army in 1963. Private 1st Class Tompkins served in Vietnam with the 173rd Airborne Brigade as a machine gunner from May 1965 to June 1966.

It was during an operation, April 1966. I was a machine gunner with the 2nd Platoon, Company B, 1st Battalion, 503rd Infantry Regiment, 173rd Airborne Brigade. We had been humping for what seemed like days without any real contact with the forces we were looking for. We would be under sniper fire occasionally and hit-and-run tactics of no great significance except that each time we would lose a man or two. We were informed that we were to link up with our 2nd Battalion at an LZ (landing zone) sometime during the afternoon hours and that we would receive our resupply at that time. We continued to move through the jungle for what seemed forever and eventually came to a small clearing in the jungle which we stopped at, and cleared, to receive supplies by helicopter. Everyone was curious as to what had happened to the 2nd Battalion, as it was late when we arrived and there was no sign of them. We bedded down for the night and gave it no further thought. Thinking is not the job of privates in the infantry.

Before dawn the following morning the sounds of gunfire, intense and prolonged, filtered to us from a distance that alerted us and worried us. It was too close and too intense to be a casual contact. Our platoon was hastily assembled, and briefed that the 2nd Battalion had been attacked with an enemy force of regimental size and we were to fight our way through the enemy to aid them. We then were told that the only reason we were not with the 2nd Battalion was that our battalion (1st Battalion) had missed the LZ and had gone too far. We immediately started at the indication of dawn breaking towards the heavy fighting. We were aware that we must first fight our way through the enemy just to get to the 2nd Battalion. We all realized that we were not in for a good day.

We could hear air strikes and artillery pounding the positions around the 2nd Battalion and we needed no compass or any other means of navigation to go in the direction that we were going. We moved out and travelled light. A small security force was left at our original position with any heavy equipment, and all we carried was grenades, ammunition and a poncho. We were ambushed five or six times en route and those small groups were driven off by rushing them and firing as much ammo at them as was needed to overcome their desire to stop us. We were determined that our sister battalion not be overrun and slaughtered. We were U.S. Airborne. No one could stop us if we decided not to let them. We were wild men on a mission and damn the results. When we were fired on we did not even slow down. We just fired and kept moving. It must have scared the hell out of the enemy seeing us so totally fearless. Our wounded and dead were left to those elements behind us. We were the lead platoon and anyone who didn't keep up was also left for the following platoons to take care of. We went into the 2nd Battalion perimeter with great shouts of welcome from the men of the 2nd Battalion and we saw the carnage that they had gone through in such a short period of time. The entire area was chewed up from weapons fire and the men seemed exhausted and mechanical. Two helicopters had crashed inside the perimeter, having been shot down attempting to resupply and take out the casualties.

As our platoon was the first inside the perimeter we were immediately assigned to the hardest hit part of the perimeter. We moved into a position that had been held by a platoon of the 2nd Battalion except that it was no longer defended by a platoon, but a squad, one quarter of a platoon. We took what positions we could and were called upon immediately to get ready to go on a platoon-size fighting patrol. We were to clear the enemy from in front of our positions. We saw many dead North Vietnamese in front of us and we knew there were a lot more out there waiting for us. When we were attacked by the NVA from close range (25-50 feet), it was a slaughter. We hit the ground and sprayed the entire area with fire. None came within 10 feet of us.

That night we were attacked again, mortared and anything else that the enemy could think of. We had blown all our mines. We had only enough ammunition to stand one more heavy attack, but we stayed and were prepared to meet our fate. We walked out of that place three days later, less a lot of men.

I thought at the time I would never forget who all those men were. Today, I have a hard time putting a face to some actions, let alone names. To have gone through so much and today it means so little.

Not long after his return from Vietnam, Tom joined the Special Forces and became an American citizen in order to be eligible for top-security clearance. Sergeant Tompkins's second tour in Vietnam was from August 1968 to November 1969. It ended prematurely because he was wounded. His final tour was from January 1972 to January 1973. Among the awards he earned was the Bronze Star Medal with "V" device and the Silver Star Medal. The citation reads:

> On the night of 30 October 1968, an estimated enemy platoon assaulted his six-man team which had established an observation post on a rocky mountain peak. Sergeant Tompkins, with complete disregard for his personal safety, left his defensive position and quickly

killed two of the aggressors, but in so doing was severely wounded in the chest. A second Communist attack was perpetrated immediately and Sergeant Tompkins, though weak and in severe pain from his wounds, rallied his men and forced the enemy into the jungle with a heavy volume of automatic weapons fire and grenades. Throughout the night, he and his men, with the aid of flare ships, repulsed all enemy attempts to overrun their position. The early morning light of 31 October gave the reinforced enemy element a new chance to attack. Sensing this opportunity, Sergeant Tompkins consolidated and readied his team and when the assault began it was quickly halted with a devastating volume of fire. During the battle, the team's radio man was seriously wounded by a grenade. Sergeant Tompkins, ignoring the intense enemy fire, crawled to his comrade and dragged him to safety. Realizing that most of his men were seriously wounded and required evacuation, he radioed for an ambulance ship and then called and directed air strikes on the Communists' positions. Although extremely weak from loss of blood, Sergeant Tompkins guided the medical helicopter onto the mountain top and supervised the loading of his injured men into the craft. Staff Sergeant Tompkins' gallantry in action was in keeping with the highest traditions of the military service and reflects great credit upon himself, his unit, and the United States Army.

Tom describes in more detail what happened as he recalls it:

The target was distant and required the setting up of a refuelling location before crossing into or over an international boundary. When I went in, there were three 37-mm radar-controlled anti-aircraft guns that we knew about. That alone indicated that there were at least three infantry platoons ready to look for us. The fact that each were about a kilometre and a half from the LZ did in no way put a halt to the operation. My usual 1.1 (one one — second in command of the team or assistant team leader) was away and I requested an experienced 1.1 to take his place and go with me. What I got was a person who had been on a reconnaissance team for six months and had never been on a mission. This I discovered after the operation. I was not scheduled to make this mission as I was on "stand-down" because of just returning from another mission. No one could be ordered to perform cross-border operations without his consent and the primary and secondary teams that were supposed to take this one quit because of the low possibility of returning alive. One other team had made it into this target and they had remained on the ground for a total of 17 minutes. They never left the LZ. I picked my own LZ, not exactly the one I really wanted, but it was close, so at least I got in without fighting on the LZ.

We went in two UH-34 "King Bee" helicopters flown by Vietnamese, two because one with the weight of all of us would not have made the distance. As the terrain was quite mountainous, the altitude also played a role in lift capability. Now that the scene is set, I will try to tell what happened as best as I can remember.

In the first helicopter there was myself, code "one zero" (10), team leader with radio, Ly my interpreter and Thanh my Vietnamese team leader, "zero one" (01). In the second helicopter was my second in command, an American, "one one" (1.1 or assistant team leader) and two other Vietnamese. Our helicopter went into the LZ and I was first out, never looking back, and out came the two others right behind me. The helicopter was gone and we watched for the second to come in. It came in about 200 metres west of us and downhill. This meant a loss of half an hour or so in locating them and climbing back up. This was accomplished without a word being said by anyone. But it was a critical loss of time getting away from our location and gave the enemy time to deploy troops to intercept us. We all knew that the enemy knew we had landed but our advantage was our small size, six men, and our ability to get away into the jungle as soon as possible. I pointed in the direction I wanted to go and we went in that direction. Nothing was spoken. My plan was to climb a mountain 2,434 metres and establish an observation point just below the top of it. We were inserted by helicopter about 10 in the morning and we had time to move slowly and cautiously.

At times the climb was difficult and sometimes just a rock face to climb. When we got to a rock face I would climb up first and have the remainder of the team follow me up by me dragging or pulling them up on a short rope. Every time I began a rock face climb I expected a sniper round to knock me off. I felt totally naked but could not stop. This constant climbing continued until four in the afternoon and was non-stop except for a break about noon where we all ate one small can of C-rations and those who smoked took a smoke. We lay near the top almost totally exhausted from the climb, and the temperature appeared to be about 20 degrees colder than in the valleys. We were drenched in sweat and could see the entire valley floor both to the northeast and west from the top of the mountain. I thought that I had found the perfect observation post, as we would, in my mind, camp below the top and keep two men on the top during daylight hours to see what was going on. We could see ant-sized people moving around far below us on the infiltration route and it appeared that they had no idea of our presence. I was proud of myself for getting in and setting up without them knowing where we were. The thought about them continuously searching the valley for us until we were to come out made me feel great. At about six o'clock I decided to put in our Claymore mines to the north and to start to prepare our RON (rest over night). My interpreter, Ly, and my Vietnamese sergeant "zero nine" (09), nicknamed Batman, went down the north side of the mountain about 30 feet and began to emplace the mines. In one quick move, the bushes approximately 20 feet below them began to rustle with no apparent reason. The air was dead calm. About 10 North Vietnamese, dressed in full combat gear, had started towards those of us putting in the mines. I could not fire as the enemy was on the other side of my people. A second later we noticed the enemy and my men started towards me. The North Vietnamese opened fire and threw grenades at them as they ran past me. My interpreter got shot through the side of his stomach and Batman had a live grenade bounce off his head. Ly hardly bled and Batman, the lesser damaged, bled like a stuck pig. Now I opened fire and four or five went down at about 30 feet from me but I wondered what all the dust and other pieces of trees and branches were doing flying around me. Their fire was all around me and that was what was causing the dust, dirt and leaves falling about me. I was hit three times not realizing it at the time, twice in the shoulder and once in the chest. I went flying backwards and, when I landed, wondered what had happened. I regained my senses and rolled behind a small mound about a foot high. Bullets were kicking up dirt all around me and I still had my CAR-15 (smaller version of the M-16 rifle) and all my equipment with me. I was caught in the crossfire between the enemy and the team and could not move. One team member motioned for me to throw my CAR-15 back to him. He was the M-79 (grenade launcher) man and at 20 feet, with me in the centre, his M-79 was of little use. I threw him my CAR-15. I looked to my left and right and two of the enemy were crawling past me, but just below me, approximately 15 feet. I pulled out a grenade and pulled the pin, smoked the grenade a couple of seconds, and let it roll towards them. They saw it before it went off and they did not get the chance to crawl farther. Finally, my American assistant threw a white phosphorus grenade at the enemy and they broke contact and all went quiet. I crawled to the team and surveyed the situation. I was seriously wounded, my interpreter was seriously wounded and Batman may have had a concussion. I decided to declare an emergency and called "Hillsboro," a friendly high-flying Lockheed C-130 Hercules aircraft that stayed up over Southeast Asia day and night, and asked for extraction. The C-130 had no idea where we were or who we were. Time was wasted getting clarification and authentication. The end result was that it was too late to get aircraft and helicopters to us that night. After about 20 minutes, the pain began to seep through the numbness and I got the other American to give me a shot of morphine to stop the pain. He did not want to but I told him either that or I would be lying there screaming my head off like a fool. (Never inject morphine if wounded above the waist.) The pain subsided and I was breathing six breaths per minute. I crawled around our mountain top. We held the top of the south side. They had control of the north side. I stationed my remaining able-bodied Vietnamese members in defensible positions and placed myself and the Vietnamese team leader in the centre. We were attacked half-heartedly once at dusk, more of a five-to-six man probing attack team, and these were easily killed. We set in for a long night .

A friendly aircraft came over us about two in the morning and asked for our exact location. I told the other American to take out his strobe light and indicate our position to the pilot. He took out his light and turned it on. The whole top of the mountain lit up. He did not have a "barrel" on the strobe and it was non-directional. When his light went on, I grabbed it and smashed it against a rock. The first notion that this guy was not able to perform came into my thoughts. I asked him to make sure that all the Vietnamese were awake and he refused to move. I checked them myself. Dawn brought us the hope for extraction but we could see a cloud front coming towards us from the northeast and I informed Hillsboro of this. We were attacked in force about half an hour after dawn by a force that I estimated to be two platoons. We slaughtered them with rifle fire and grenades. We were again attacked about an hour later and were at this time completely covered by the clouds. This attack cost us dearly, as my Vietnamese leader who was fighting next to me got hit just above the right eye and he lay unconscious next to me. The enemy grenades just bounced off the top of our side of the mountain except for once during this attack. We all knew that this one was staying on top and in the middle of us and we all hollered "grenade" and sought cover behind rocks — all except my fellow American, who never moved. After it went off, he was lying with blood spurting out the left side of his head. I crawled to him and clamped my free hand on his head and with the other hand reached for the radio handset. I had a radio handset with dangling wires because the grenade had got our radio too. I reached into the wounded American's pocket and got out his URC-10 radio and turned it on. It worked but the short battery life was on my mind.

We had enemy bodies stacked around us and at this stage I could not figure a way to count them, but I estimated 50 to 60 were in our immediate area — all within about 30 feet of us. The enemy could no longer attack full speed at us as they had to cross their own dead lying in mixed patterns. I now had two Vietnamese and myself able to fight. I had forgotten about my wounds; in fact, I had picked up a wound from the grenade but was not yet aware of it.

A friendly aircraft came on the radio and asked for our exact location. I tried to fire a flare from the M-79 through the clouds but it was not seen. I next tried firing a magazine of tracers from the CAR-15 through the clouds and these were not seen either. Finally, I asked that they drop a bomb at what they thought was our location. Five minutes later I heard an explosion about two kilometres south of us. I asked if that was their bomb and they said yes. I informed them they were that distance south of us and that the valley below us was clear. Ten minutes later two Cobra helicopter gunships came up the valley. About halfway up they began to engage targets not seen by us and then they peeled off and disappeared. Seconds later the first fixed-wing aircraft came up the valley and climbed up towards us. It was a propeller-driven SPAD (Douglas Skyraider) and he let napalm go at about the same height as where the Cobras had attacked. The next SPAD attacked in a matter of seconds and fired his guns and dropped bombs close to the top. The radar-controlled enemy anti-aircraft 37-mm guns opened up and we could see pieces of the aircraft falling off as the 37s hit it. The pilots were clearing our mountain and disappearing into clouds not 40 to 50 feet above us. At this time the North Vietnamese decided to attack again and the aircraft kept coming in. We continued fighting them both on and off the ground. It kept up that way until the aircraft had run out of ammunition and napalm. The aircraft stated that they still had cluster bomb units on board and asked if I wanted it and where. It was apparent that without some major assistance we were not going to live for another 10 minutes and I requested it on top of us. I screamed for us to duck and in it came. It cleared the mountain of anything standing and filled me with fear they might use another one. I yelled not to drop any more. The attack ceased. Cobra gunships took up the attack after the SPADs and they tore up the north side of the mountain with 40-mm grenades and their guns. Every one of them — the aircraft and the helicopters — had hits from the 37s and one aircraft took a 37 through the wing.

At this stage we had no grenades, few magazines of ammunition and everyone was at least slightly wounded as well as being totally exhausted. Over the radio they said they were going to try to evacuate us and a UH-34 came up to the top and looked at us. Our position would not let a helicopter land and it flew off into the clouds. We thought we were abandoned. A couple of minutes later a Huey flew up and dropped a ladder. It was a J-model Huey and had the capacity to retrieve us all. To my surprise, everyone got up and moved to the ladder (made of rope with solid rungs).

Batman and I started firing in the direction of the enemy and the first four of the team got up the ladder. The door gunner grabbed me as I reached to get inside and I passed out. He hauled me in. The next thing I was aware of was extreme pain as Batman climbed over me and stepped on my shoulder. The helicopter was taking many hits and it peeled off the mountain and down into the valley. Every light on the control panel was red and the front window was a mass of holes and broken plexiglass. On the way, in the helicopter, the pilot indicated that we were not going to make it. I checked to see how much ammunition we had and all that remained was eight magazines. We crash-landed at a place called Dak Pek.

The American with me, as far as I know, never fired his weapon all the time we were in that area. He did throw that one grenade. He wrote himself up for the Medal of Honor and signed my name to the recommendation. It took me about a year to stop all the paperwork to insure he got nothing. Thanh, the Vietnamese leader, lost his eye and a lot of grey matter but lived. Ly never went on another mission. Batman was killed on a mission two months later and the other Vietnamese never went again on missions. I ended up with a chest tube and a long recovery but no long-range ill effects. Reading documents that came from the helicopter pilots who pulled us out, I discovered they estimated between 175 to 200 dead North Vietnamese around us.

Recently Tom read a book describing a Special Forces operation. He found it so inaccurate that he wrote the following:

Having led a few behind the set lines and deep penetration missions, I will construct the sequence of events that led up to a team's departure. When a mission was assigned to our group, the officers and senior NCOs would select the team for the mission. The leader would be called into the launch bunker and be asked if and when the team could be deployed. He would then be given a designated-target code, i.e. V1, C6, etc. From there the team leader would go to the command bunker and sign out the folder for the designated target. He would have no access to any other targets and could not remove the folder from a room set aside to study the target. These folders would vary in size from a couple of pages to a thick manuscript depending on the amount of interest and intelligence that was taken about the area. This folder would normally have air photos (not up-to-date) and a map of that area alone. After careful study of the folder, the leader would decide whom he was to take on the mission and the equipment needed. The leader then told those Americans who were to go to come to the study room and look over the data found in the folder. The "little people" (locals) who were chosen never saw any of this information and never knew where they were headed. The next step was to draw the weapons, meals, ammunition and necessary special equipment. This varied with each mission. The little people who were selected were now told that they were going and all equipment would be centrally placed, packed and secured until departure time. Although I secured all the rucksacks and equipment to prevent any possible loss, not all leaders did this. Needless to say, it cost some of them dearly later on. My own rules were to have every man carry a minimum of 25 magazines for all rifles, six hand grenades each, three canteens of water, one meat ration per day with one vitamin pill, one Claymore mine, four M-14 mines, two white phosphorus grenades, an M-79 with 40 rounds (various), a platoon radio (I carried) with six batteries, one emergency radio per American, one indigenous poncho per man, five morphine syringes per American, "speed" as needed (carried it, never used it), one signal mirror per American, signal panels (one each), plus specialized equipment, such as a camera. All this would be locked in a room, normally my sleeping area, and no one had access to this except myself. The team as a whole would then commence training but this was limited, as normally we would only have 24 to 48 hours from notification until launch time. Our diet would be changed only at the leader's request and baths and shaving would cease. I preferred that we go in clothes that were stinking and dirty. On the day of launch, all persons would assemble at my location. I would issue the rucksacks to each individual, inspect each again, issue a map to the U.S. personnel (normally for an area only 12 km by 12 km in size), pick up the classified codes for the mission, encode and decode materials (classified), and then we would go directly from there to the load/launch. All personnel were also strip-searched to ensure that they had no ID, no pictures or any other identifiable papers.

The launch was normally by helicopter and depending on the depth of penetration, one or two would be used because of lift capability, weight, range, altitude and many other determining factors. Needless to say, at this stage your senses were extremely alert and you knew that the next contact with friendly forces would be the following day when a light aircraft would fly within 10 to 15 miles of you and make radio contact. That was your only contact until extraction. From then on it was you alone against whatever you had out there. Fear was with you at all times. It was just something you had to control. I never took a man with me that wanted to kill and none that I ever led killed for the fun of it. It was all just for survival.

I had the chance on a couple of occasions to find and return U.S. personnel that were captured by the North Vietnamese Army. It was never a pretty sight and would turn you into an animal at what they did to persons they captured. It made you vow never to get captured. Anyone who ever said that they would accept capture usually were in that situation sooner or later. None of them ever returned alive.

The saddest part of the war in my mind was the sending of 18-year-olds not properly trained and most important of all, very poorly led. The regular officer corps in Vietnam were only interested in medals and promotions. All in all, the war was not worth one American or Canadian life. Many of my Canadian relatives accused me of fighting to make the U.S. wealthier but I would destroy their statement simply by saying that the country had no material wealth of any significance. I was the family black sheep during the war, especially on going back for the third time. On many occasions, I accepted the fact that I would not see the sun come up or the sun go down. I just continued to do the job and somehow or other I survived.[3]

Master Sergeant Tompkins retired from the U.S. forces after 20 years' service. He works as a deputy sheriff for Osceola County, Florida.

ARNE SUND

Vietnam: June 1965   Service: Navy
          July 1966 to November 1966
          September 1967 to March 1968

I was born 19 July 1946 and raised in Winnipeg. At the age of 16 I quit high school, worked at several jobs and eventually got in trouble with the law. At my last court appearance I was told that an open warrant was going to be issued because shortly I would be considered an adult and would therefore be looking at penitentiary time.

Petty Officer 3rd Class Arne Sund, 1966. (Courtesy A. Sund.)

At this point I made the decision to start a new life in a new environment. I was issued an American visa on 10 August 1964 on condition that I would enlist in the United States Navy, which I did on 4 September at Fargo, North Dakota. During my time in the U.S. Navy, I went on three western Pacific cruises aboard the USS *Perkins*.

First Western Pacific Cruise
6 March 1965 to August 1965

On the morning of 6 March the *Perkins*, a destroyer, departed San Diego. A short stay in Subic Bay, the Philippines, in early June was made even more brief to avoid a typhoon. The following 18 days off South Vietnam — our first exposure to the conflict — were perhaps the most eventful. Our mission ranged from service with the coastal patrol to brief stops at Qui Nhon and Nha Trang for liaison work and medical assistance. Suspicious small craft had to be inspected regardless of the hour, and when gunfire support became our primary mission, we answered calls at all hours of the day and night.

Second Western Pacific Cruise
28 July 1966 to 3 February 1967

On 28 July 1966 the *Perkins* departed San Diego for another period off Vietnam. She served off I Corps area, mainly patrolling for North Vietnamese logistics craft. On 4 November in company with a destroyer, the USS *Braine*, *Perkins* came under heavy shore battery fire off the North Vietnamese coast. All six guns let loose into the enemy position and effectively suppressed their fire.

While refuelling on the night of 20 November during heavy weather, two men were swept overboard from a destroyer, the *Philip*. In spite of high seas and 45-knot winds, the men were successfully rescued by the *Perkins*. In February 1967 I completed another cruise in the western Pacific.

Third Western Pacific Cruise
22 September 1967 to 12 March 1968

Upon arrival with the Seventh Fleet, the *Perkins* was assigned to naval gunfire support. During this cruise the ship fired in all four corps areas. In February 1968 she joined the aircraft carrier USS *Kitty Hawk* in the Tonkin Gulf and later the aircraft carrier *Coral Sea*.

Accuracy is the key word in naval gunfire support. It enables cruisers and destroyers to fire projectiles up to 15 miles inland at any enemy who may be within a few hundred yards of friendly forces. That accuracy is backed by a mobility unmatched by ground-based artillery and also heavier volume of shelling than of readily available fighter aircraft.

Geographically, the Republic of Vietnam proved ideal for naval gunfire. The country's sprawling coastline, narrow breadth and navigable coastal waters meant that cruisers and destroyers could move in close and hit targets deep inland. The country's dependence on the sea means that many villages and towns, and much of the enemy's activities, were near the coast and within easy range of naval guns.

Gunfire support ships have the ability to loiter in an area indefinitely or to speed along the coast at more that 30 knots. A ship assigned to gunfire support might spend her early morning hours softening up the beach before an amphibious assault, answer a call for an emergency mission against enemy troops in the afternoon, and fire illumination rounds and harassment and interdiction fire through the night.

A gunfire mission begins with a request from a naval liaison officer ashore in South Vietnam. When a ship arrives on station, she contacts spotters by radio for last-minute instructions. At first the ship fires her rounds slowly and deliberately. Under the guidance of the spotter, the projectiles find their mark and the pace of firing quickens.

I found it particularly interesting operating with the battleship *New Jersey*. We would go in close to shore where the Viet Cong had artillery in rock caves in the hillsides. The *New Jersey* would go 20 to 25 miles out to sea and we would act as a spotter. You could hear their huge shells going over our heads to shore. They sounded like a freight train.

My most exciting experience was being fired on by enemy shore batteries north of the Demilitarized Zone. The *Perkins* and another ship were given the job of flushing out the guns' location. We went so far into a harbour inside the three-mile limit that our propellers were kicking up sand from the bottom. We were all so confident that the operation would be easy that the four boilers were not even placed in battle-ready condition for full power.

We were cruising as close as possible to the shore when the enemy began lobbing shells at us. They were coming fairly close to us — in our wake. At that point, there was panic on the bridge. The officer in charge decided the ship's steering was not reacting properly and transferred steering to the stern for local control. From the talk on the battle phones, it appeared no one knew who was doing the steering. We ended up doing one hell of a zig-zag manoeuvre out of the harbour. The other ship sustained some minor damage trying to escape but lost power due to high water in a forward boiler. We were out to open sea when we noticed the other ship in trouble and went back to help her escape.

In the United States no one is drafted into the navy, only the army. People were drafted for two-year hitches in the army or voluntarily signed up for four years in the navy and air force, with the aim of avoiding combat. Of the men aboard 85 per cent were temporary and 15 per cent permanent.

Recreation aboard ship consisted of sleeping, sunbathing, playing cards and movies. Occasionally we would stop at sea and have swim call. On those occasions, the captain's launch would patrol for sharks. You would be so tired because watches consisted of four hours on, eight hours off, plus working eight hours during the daytime, that all a person wanted to do was sleep. In combat zones we would go four hours on, four hours off, around the clock.

There were no open racial problems, but blacks when together had a tendency to ignore whites. On the other hand, whites acted nice to their faces but used derogatory terms behind their backs. I was friends with several blacks and I think I was accepted to a certain degree because I was Canadian.

There was ample space to sleep in — cramped, but ample. The food aboard ship was reasonably good and you could get as much as you liked. Most other people on board were not impressed with the food, and wasted more than they ate.

The other ranks were not enthusiastic about being in the Vietnam War Zone. We felt we were victims of circumstances and simply did what we were told.[4]

After serving from 1964 to 1968 in the U.S. Navy, Arne left active naval service as a petty officer 3rd class, and settled in Orange County, California. He remains a Canadian citizen.

NICHOLAS CARUSO

Vietnam: July 1965 to July 1966   Service: Army

In 1959 at age 15, Nicholas Caruso left St. Catharines, Ontario, with his parents and younger brother and moved to Wilmington, Delaware, because of the economic recession. He joined the Delaware Army National Guard. In 1962 he enlisted in the U.S. Army. From July 1965 to July 1966, Specialist Five (Sergeant) Caruso served at An Khe with the 15th Administration Company, 1st Cavalry Division (Airmobile). He operated in the field with brigade and battalion headquarters to speed casualty reports to the division for proper assignment of replacements. In December 1966 Nicholas became an American citizen. He retired as a master sergeant in January 1982. He then returned to university and in 1988 was awarded a master's degree in public administration. He now works for the City of San Marcos, Texas, as a public works administrator.

Nicholas offers some recollections commencing in the summer of 1965, when he was a personnel management specialist with the 11th Administration Company, 11th Air Assault Division:

The army, in all its great wisdom and understanding, often organizes units in mysterious ways. That was certainly the case in forming the 1st Cavalry Division (Airmobile). The 11th Air Assault Division (Test), at Fort Benning, Georgia, had been in existence for about three years, and had been engaged in testing the use of helicopters for troop transport and close air support. The 11th Air Assault itself was the old 11th Airborne Division activated and reorganized for the test. Even the shoulder patch was similar (the Airborne tab had been substituted with Air Assault).

Specialist Five Nicholas Caruso, An Khe, South Vietnam, early 1966. Hong Kong Mountain is in the background. (Courtesy N. Caruso.)

One day in July 1965, we were asked to bring any portable TVs we had to work the next day. The program of choice was a news conference "starring" the secretary of defence. The good secretary announced that troops were to be deployed to the Republic of Vietnam. The 11th was not mentioned as part of that deployment; however, the 1st Cavalry Division was prominently pointed out as a deploying unit. The Cav was located in Korea at the time. We were not sure any of this pertained to us. Keep your eye on the pea and the shells.

In Korea, the army had the 7th Infantry Division and the 1st Cavalry Division. At Fort Benning, we had the 11th Air Assault Division and the 2nd Infantry Division. The colours of the 1st Cav were transferred to the 11th Air Assault and the colours of the 11th Air Assault Division were retired. The 7th Infantry Division colours were retired, and some of their units combined with units that were part of the Cavalry Division in Korea. The colours of the 2nd Infantry Division were transferred to Korea, and the units there became the 2nd Infantry Division. Members of the 2nd Infantry Division at Fort Benning became fillers and replacements for the 1st Cavalry Division (now Airmobile) at Fort Benning. I'm not sure, but I think the same people who came up with that move are working on our federal budget now!

The pace of training and preparation picked up enormously. We had been armed with the M-14 rifle but our Table of Organization and Equipment called for the M-16. At the time, the only divisions armed with the M-16 were the 101st Airborne and 82nd Airborne. I believe the 1st Infantry Division (deployed to the Republic of Vietnam about the same time) was also rearmed with the M-16. Picture 16,000 men who needed to be familiarized with the new rifle almost instantaneously. The ranges were busy round the clock. An attempt was made to run everyone through an escape-and-evasion course. Additionally, we climbed cargo nets in preparation for loading landing craft — just like in the John Wayne movies. It was the last time we saw cargo nets.

The 11th Air Assault Division had one brigade that was airborne. However, it was a "Phantom Brigade." It contained a brigade headquarters and only one battalion of airborne troops. An airborne brigade needs an airborne artillery battalion to support it. Division artillery contained only one airborne battery. Fillers from the old 2nd Infantry Division took care of most of the vacancies in the Cav, but filling the airborne units was another problem. The problem was solved by transferring folks to the Cav from the 101st Airborne Division at Fort Campbell, Kentucky, and the 82nd Airborne Division at Fort Bragg, North Carolina, and running intensive airborne training courses for volunteers.

During this period, I was assigned to work at a temporary in-processing centre for soldiers being assigned to the Cav. The centre worked 24 hours a day, processing hundreds daily. Two humorous incidents occurred that might indicate the intensity of preparation that was going on. A young SP-4 (specialist four) by the name of John Kitzlik, whom I knew from an earlier assignment in Germany, showed up at the centre asking to be reassigned. I knew he was already a member of the division and questioned him about it. Here's his story. Kitzlik was assigned to the artillery battalion that contained the airborne battery prior to reorganization. That battalion was selected to become the airborne battalion, and they were in the process of receiving airborne replacements, reassigning non-airborne personnel, and running a hard campaign to convince their non-airborne personnel to volunteer for jump training. Kitzlik was not airborne qualified, nor did he have any desire to "jump from perfectly good airplanes." He was an S-3 (operations clerk) in the battalion, patiently waiting for reassignment instructions. One day while waiting for his XO (battalion executive officer) to sign a document, the XO was trying to give Kitzlik a shot in the arm from the "glory gun" and convince him to volunteer for airborne. Kitzlik underestimated the "gung ho quotient" of this airborne major. He finally told the major that he didn't qualify for airborne — his IQ was too high; and besides, he had no need to reassure his manhood. As we all know, some officers just don't have a sense of humour. The major picked Kitzlik up by his collar and belt (Kitzlik is a pretty small guy), and he threw him through a window. Fortunately for Kitzlik the window was open, and all he really went through was the screen. We reassigned Kitzlik to a helicopter battalion.

One of the most flamboyant members of the Cav was the sergeant major from the only "real Cav" in the division. (Each division has only one squadron of cavalry whose modern mission is predominantly reconnaissance and screening. The Cav Division's infantry units carried the colours of old cavalry units, but were definitely infantry. Hence, the confusing designations, i.e., *Company* A, 1st *Battalion*, 7th Cavalry. Cavalry units do not have companies and battalions, they have troops and squadrons. The 1st Squadron, 9th Cavalry, liked to refer to themselves as real Cav.) Sergeant Major Kennedy of the 1st Squadron, 9th Cavalry, became somewhat a legend during the first year of the 1st Cav (Air). This guy pulled more shenanigans than anyone I know and stayed out of jail. He started out stealing *people*. Sgt. Maj. Kennedy didn't believe he was getting his fillers fast enough. He would bring a truck to the inprocessing centre and wait for the busses to deliver troops for processing. Sgt. Maj. Kennedy would stop likely candidates before they even got into the building and ask, "Soldier, do you want to be a door gunner on a helicopter?" If they answered in the affirmative, he would load them on the truck and take them away to his unit. Several of those soldiers were carried AWOL for months before it was realized what he had done. Kennedy and his squadron commander, Lieutenant Colonel Stockton, became famous/infamous (take your pick) before that year was up. Lt. Col. Stockton was rumoured to have taken one of his troops into Cambodia and executed an extremely effective ambush on the Ho Chi Minh Trail. Stockton was a dynamic personality, and it rubbed off on all with whom he came in contact. I'm really not sure the action took place, but the rumours were hot and heavy.

During the Ia Drang Operation in November 1965 (I think it was November), the Cav came into contact with North Vietnamese Army (NVA) regulars for the first time. The tactics used during this operation were very effective, and the NVA did some puzzling things — to our advantage. The Cav would position a platoon or company-sized unit in a good defensive position and do anything to announce their arrival. They would make plenty of noise, fires at night, etc., just to get the NVA's attention. When the NVA estimated the strength of the position, they would attack with the appropriate number to defeat the platoon/company. The idea was to locate the NVA. If it could be done, the platoon/company would be taken out by helicopter; if not, they provided a base of fire while all the fire support in the world rained down on the NVA. At the same time other units were airlifted in to prevent their escape. The Cav continued this for about a month, and the NVA kept coming the whole time. I believe the NVA were interested in testing American troops and their own. Ia Drang (the Drang River) is not far from the Cambodian border. I believe in some places it is the border. The NVA entered the area of operations from Cambodia, where we were forbidden to go. It was a perfect sanctuary for them.

Stockton had apparently reconnoitred the Cambodian side and placed a troop-sized unit in ambush along a major trail. Rumour had it that he destroyed an entire NVA company-sized unit without firing a rifle. They had lined the trail on both sides with Claymore mines. The ambush was a total surprise. A company-sized unit of NVA (about 200) were marching down the trail in a column of four singing when the ambush was executed. There were so many Claymores that the Cav Troop did not have to fire a shot — the NVA were all dead. Of course the Cav Troop was not supposed to be there. Again, I didn't hear it, but there is a radio conversation that reportedly went something like:

> *Major General Kinnard*: God damn it Stockton, you
> violated three orders — two written and one verbal!
> *Lieutenant Colonel Stockton*: Yes sir and I accept full
> responsibility!

A description of An Khe is in order. When the Cav set up its base camp near the village of An Khe, it became the largest population in the area. The village was small and had little to offer. Shortly after we arrived, we were permitted to go into the village to purchase "health and comfort items." Mirrors for shaving, wash basins, gasoline stoves to warm C-rations, etc. It wasn't long before the Vietnamese found a way to make money from the GIs. Initially there were two bars where one could purchase cool Biere 33 and Beer LaRue (tiger piss). One could also purchase a roaring case of VD. Both bars were running about 10 girls each. Twenty girls and 16,000 men made for some interesting scenes. I saw a line of GIs coming from the back room of one bar, winding through the bar, out the doorway, and down the street about 100 metres. In my 20 years in the army, I've waited in line for pay, chow, mail, laundry, ammo, and a host of other commodities and material — but that was ridiculous! A buddy and myself were drinking a beer and commenting on the line, and the funny picture it presented when someone tried to "jump the pussy line." Of course an argument ensued. I though it all very funny until someone jacked a round into the chamber of his M-16. I had immediate visions of my wife receiving a telegram explaining how I was caught in a crossfire in a Vietnamese cat house — I got out of there!

A few months later, a section of town was built solely to house bars and temporary bedding facilities. It was guarded by ARVN (Army of the Republic of Vietnam) military police (MP). The place was named "Sin City" in an article by a reporter from *Time* magazine. The division received complaints, about leading our saintly soldiers to hell, from everybody — mothers, wives, girlfriends, priests — including, God help us, congressmen. I never did have much affection for the press .

Our Home Sweet Home

The 15th Administration Company's home at the "Golf Course" was located at the foot of Hong Kong Mountain, really just a hill, but the only major topographic relief in the area. The first days were taken with setting up general-purpose medium tents for work space, unloading folding chairs and field desks from containers, and generally setting up for work.

Our living quarters during the first few months were pup tents — two men per tent who shared what became known as a "mortar hole." The hole was three feet by five feet and three feet deep. The purpose of the hole was to give protection when and if we were ever subjected to "incoming." There were some early mortar attacks in other parts of the Golf Course, but for the most part we felt removed and unaffected. It's difficult to be concerned with tactical matters when you spend the day carrying out mundane chores such as setting up tents, unboxing typewriters, sorting forms and conducting the army's great administrative mission. Truly, ignorance is bliss.

A communications station was established on top of Hong Kong Mountain. The distance from the top of Hong Kong to our company area was about 500 metres, perhaps a little more. It was there, and we paid very little attention to it. One night the Viet Cong decided to give it a great deal of attention. Sir Charles infiltrated and overran the commo station at the top of Hong Kong, but not before signals alerted the division. The division responded with gunships that alternated between machine-gun fire and rockets on each pass. All this activity was aimed at or near the top of the mountain. And it was spectacular. Low-flying choppers, tracers and the flash of rockets went on for about an hour.

Now it didn't take long for even us adjutant general (AG) soldiers to realize something unusual was going on. This was something we had never seen before. The tourist in us took over. The fact that a firefight and strafing were taking place less than 500 metres away was unreal. The surrealistic visions of tracers in a black sky, the flash of rockets firing and the thump of their explosions, and the noise of attacking choppers appearing and disappearing captivated us. Instead of collecting our weapons and manning our holes, we stood in small groups and watched like children at a fireworks display. Some brought folding chairs from the office tents to view the show.

I've thought about this incident many times since then and wonder at our behaviour and luck. No one in our company was wounded or killed. The only explanation is the good fortune that accompanies naivete and inexperience. Had it taken place later, after a few months of handling casualty reports and body bags, the incident would have been taken far more seriously. The transition from tourist to soldier takes a little longer for AG soldiers than for grunts.

Chairborne Rangers

Most units on the Golf Course were responsible for providing security for a sector on the perimeter. The 15th Administration Company was no exception. The unit was 400 strong and a conglomeration of the most unlikely people to secure anything. We were composed of personnel records clerks, personnel management specialists, cooks, finance clerks, public information specialists, re-enlistment sergeants, data-processing specialists, and more.

For our security mission, we organized into three provisional rifle companies. One would secure division finance and provide a roving guard at night in the company area. The other two companies alternated nights on the perimeter. Every organization needs a name and tradition and it didn't take us long to develop both. Shortly after organization of the provisional rifle companies, we christened ourselves the "Chairborne Rangers" — "Retreat Hell! We Backspace."

"Shower with a Nurse"

After two weeks at the Golf Course the word was out — division engineers had set up a shower point on a riverbank near the village of An Khe. Later, most units would construct showers in their own areas, but early on, this was a luxury. I caught a ride on the first truck to the shower point.

Describing an army shower point to someone is a difficult task. It's akin to explaining the game of baseball to an African. Both have the same result. The "explainee" cocks his head, looks suspiciously at the "explainer" and tries to discern whether it's a joke or the person he's looking at is mentally ill.

A shower point is usually two large general-purpose tents linked together end to end. The first tent is used to disrobe and is a semi-dry place to leave your clothes. It is extremely crowded with dirty, smelly, sweating men trying to undress, and freshly showered and wet men trying to dry themselves and dress.

The second tent is an exercise in masochism. There are four points which are fed water from hoses coming from under the sides of the tent. Each point has four shower heads alternating sprays of boiling hot and frigid water. The only light comes from the doorway to the first tent and that leaking in from under the side flaps of the tent. Showering becomes a nightmare trying to reconcile your desire to get clean with the extremes in temperature, the constant screaming of those dodging the changes in water, and the urging of those in the doorway to hurry. If Dante were alive today he would include an army shower point in his description of hell.

If I had any intention of lingering in the shower it was forgotten when I entered the first tent. My shower was in record time. Struggling through a crowd of naked men trying to find my towel and clothes, I heard a booming voice say, "Well, at least you can write home and tell everyone you showered with a nurse." Try to picture 50 or so men in various states of dress and undress looking around for a woman. I couldn't see a woman so I turned in the direction of the voice that had announced the nurse. There was a very large fellow putting on his fatigue jacket. I noticed his branch insignia. There was a nurse in the tent all right — a male nurse. Oh well, what do you expect in a combat zone.[5]

DAVID S. MITCHELL

Vietnam: August 1965 to November 1965   Service: Army
          June 1969 to June 1970

David Mitchell was born in St. John's, Newfoundland, on 10 July 1944. His father was originally from Scotland but served in the Canadian Merchant Navy. His mother was from St. John's. David grew up in Winchester, Massachusetts. An important influence was his uncle, who had served overseas in the First World War with the 13th Battalion. In December 1962

Staff Sergeant David Mitchell in a UH-1 (Huey) helicopter while on a long-range reconnaissance patrol extraction mission from islands in the vicinity of Nha Trang, December 1969. (Courtesy D. Mitchell.)

David enlisted for three years in the U.S. Army. As a Canadian citizen, he had to go to Montreal to obtain a non-quota landed-immigrant card.

David was sent by ship along with the rest of the newly formed 1st Cavalry Division (Airmobile) to Vietnam, arriving in September 1965. As an SP-4, David fought in the bitter battle of the Ia Drang Valley in October-November. The North Vietnamese attempt to cut South Vietnam in two, from Pleiku to the coast, was averted. In spite of taking an orange malaria pill once a week, David took sick with malaria in late November and was evacuated back to the United States.

David offers a glimpse of his service in Vietnam:

I was a member of Company A, 1st Battalion, 12th Cavalry. Because we still had the draft our company had quite a cross section of society — the college professor who carried the 81-mm tube and the high school dropout who carried the bipod. There were several aliens in our company, including an Ecuadorian who was drafted six months after he arrived in New York City. To the best of my knowledge I was the only Canadian in Company A. With us we had a veteran of Iwo Jima and Korea — Staff Sergeant Harold W. Hambrick. He was the finest soldier I ever served with.

It's extremely difficult to write about my Vietnam experience because, like for a lot of people who fought there, the memories and pain have not diminished with the years. There are many veterans of that Southeast Asian war whose lives were changed forever because of that experience and to an even greater degree as a result of their treatment upon their return. For far too many the real war began on their arrival home.

Not long after being "in country," our company was airlifted into an area that was called "Happy Valley," 40 or so miles northeast of our base camp at An Khe. The entire battalion was engaged in this operation. We were to clear the enemy from this location that they were supposedly using as a training area. Needless to say, we ran into a real hornet's nest, and we suffered our first casualties. I vividly recall one kid whom I knew — Terry Wright. He was in Company B, and only 17. I may be wrong but I believe Terry was the first fatal casualty of the day. He was killed instantly on 10 October by a well-placed rifle shot while getting off the helicopter. I do know that he was far from the only one killed that day because before the sun went down there were more dead and wounded than we knew what to do with. Two platoons from my company operating with two platoons from Company B were hit real hard with heavy automatic weapons fire while caught in a dried-up creek bed. The enemy held the high ground on either side of the creek bed and had a field of fire that exceeded 75 yards. The enemy held their fire until they could get the maximum number of hits. Among a whole lot of others, my buddy Nestor Argenzio was killed with a single round through the top of his helmet. Nester, our "Latin lover" as he was called, was the Ecuadorian draftee. Sergeant Hambrick was also killed at another location during the operation as were several more of our company.

After 60 days out of the army, David decided to re-enlist in March 1966 for another three years. That year he married a girl from Boston whose father was from Pubnico, Nova Scotia. In June 1967 David joined the Special Forces. Two years later, he had become an American citizen and was in Vietnam with the 5th Special Forces as a staff sergeant (E-6) stationed at Nha Trang until June 1970. There he was responsible for administrative matters at the Recondo (reconnaissance/commando) School which had a three-week course on long-range patrolling.

David remained in the army as a recruiter in Boston until 1 November 1983, retiring as a master sergeant. He works for the U.S. postal service in Deerfield, New Hampshire.[6]

GERALD GIROLDI

Vietnam: August to December 1965   Service: Marines

Some Canadian Vietnam veterans had served in the Canadian Forces and wanted to see action. Gerald M. Giroldi is typical of this group. Born in Woodstock, Ontario, in 1941, at age 16 he joined the Canadian Army under an apprentice plan. From 1957 to 1959 he was stationed at Camp Borden, where he received a combination of schooling and training with the Royal Canadian Army Service Corps. He transferred to the Black Watch and was stationed at Camp Gagetown, New Brunswick, from 1959 to 1962. Seeking adventure, he took the option of leaving the Canadian Army in June 1962 and joined the U.S. Marines in October. After boot camp, he married a girl from his hometown, and during his 10 years in the marines, depending on his posting, his wife either stayed behind in Woodstock or lived on various marine bases. While he was stationed in Japan, Jerry's wish to go to Vietnam was granted. He served there from August to December 1965 with the 3rd Reconnaissance Battalion, 3rd Marine Division. Much of Corporal Giroldi's time was spent on patrol six or seven miles outside of Da Nang in the area of Hill 327.

Staff Sergeant Giroldi ended his career as a drill instructor at Parris Island, South Carolina.

Corporal G.M. Giroldi prior to boarding a helicopter several miles northwest of Da Nang, 18 October 1965. (Courtesy G.M. Giroldi.)

While there, recruits, some of whom would be going to Vietnam, had their training period reduced from 13 weeks to 8 or 9 in order to meet quotas. While at Parris Island, he never came across any Canadian recruits. Following his service in the marines, Jerry left the United States. He returned to Woodstock, and when a strike closed down the company where he had obtained employment, he moved to Brooks, Alberta, now his permanent home.

Gerald Giroldi recounts what he remembers about his tour in Vietnam:

En Route

We flew from Okinawa to Da Nang aboard a C-130 so loaded with cargo that we couldn't stretch our legs out straight. This was made even more uncomfortable by the fact that we had gotten a shot of gamma globulin in the ass the day before. Had to climb over dozing marines and cargo to get to the urinals attached to the forward bulkheads only to find them plugged and overflowing onto the deck.

Arrival

Arriving over Da Nang after some nine hours we could see what appeared to be shell craters near the south end of the base. We later learned they were Vietnamese graves. We were then introduced to a "combat-landing" — when the plane went into a long steep dive, then seemed to level off and touch down at the same time. We could feel the heat as the plane taxied but weren't prepared for the blast of hot air that hit us when the ramp dropped.

In Country

When the truck arrived to take me out to 3rd Reconnaissance Battalion command post, I was surprised to see that the driver and co-driver were armed with unloaded M-14 rifles. I later understood when I had to read and sign the "Rules of Engagement." The 3rd Reconnaissance area was named Camp Reasoner after 1st Lieutenant Frank Reasoner, who had been awarded a posthumous Medal of Honor.

On my first patrol I thought I had found a couple of genuine VC (Viet Cong) suspects. The first was a middle-aged man in a hamlet we passed through. He was the only adult to be seen. As I approached him, I could see that half of his face had been blown away. It was obvious that he was of little use beyond baby-sitting.

The second was a man in his mid-20s and he started to run away as we approached. I went after him and captured him. He was very well built for a Vietnamese and in his wallet were macho-type pictures of himself with some good-looking Vietnamese women. We checked out the hootch he said he lived in, but there was nothing in it but a shirt, a big pot and a pack board. To me the whole thing looked suspicious. However, our ARVN interpreter said "No VC," gave him a swift kick in the behind and sent him on his way. During this patrol, we provided security for two teams who were on the Song Cu De (also Cu De) River in rubber boats and were blowing up caves and tunnels dug into the banks.

On 18 October, two companies hiked into a VC-dominated area, 16 miles southeast of Da Nang, nicknamed "Happy Valley." Their mission was to determine the size of enemy concentrations in the hills west of the Da Nang tactical area of responsibility. For a week, 18-24 October, the reconnaissance force prowled the hills. Two VC were killed but five separate enemy base areas were discovered and a vast amount of trail network information was accumulated. This operation, known as "Trailblazer," was the last of the reconnaissance-in-force operations conducted by the battalion. A new trend was in motion. By December, the battalion was concentrating on patrolling, sending out more smaller-size patrols; a company-size patrol was the exception.

Giroldi continues with his recollections of that operation:

Trailblazer

Operation "Trailblazer" took place during the monsoon season. Between the heat and the rain it was impossible to stay dry; ponchos only made you hotter and sweatier. Extra socks and cigarettes got soaked even though wrapped in plastic. We used insect repellent around collars, cuffs, waistbands, flies and so on to repel leeches. However, the rain soaked it through to the skin and caused burns.

On the second night of "Trailblazer" we bivouacked just at the edge of the canopied jungle. The artillery forward observer registered a couple of rounds on the hill in front of us and that was somewhat reassuring. However, a short time later someone in the jungle below started beating on a drum. Word was — "jungle telegraph."

Next day we humped until after dark, the last of it going practically hand over hand up rocks when the word was passed to secure for the night. There wasn't a spot clear enough to lie down, so I decided to sleep sitting cross-legged with my poncho over me. During the night I was awakened when something about the size of a hand started to move across my poncho. It stopped about halfway and I literally froze. Finally it moved on. I never did find out what it was, though somebody did mention land crabs. In the morning I was somewhat unnerved to discover that I was sitting within two feet of a 50-foot cliff!

Later that day we humped up a hill that had a large clearing and beat down the brush to make an LZ (landing zone) for a chopper resupply. Just before the choppers came, a sniper put three rounds into the LZ but didn't hit anybody. Needless to say, the choppers were reluctant to set down after that, but they did come in, and didn't waste any time unloading. Of all the supplies, the ones most appreciated were the boxes of chocolate chip cookies one of the cooks had baked special for those of us in the field. We were like kids at a party.

The next day it was obvious that we were in VC country: hilltops covered with punji stakes; spider traps (VC guerrilla foxholes, often connected to a tunnel network); and bundles of punji stakes alongside the trail. There was even one place on the trail where they had set up a tollgate to collect from woodcutters and other peasants who might use the trail. We hadn't been on the move for very long when the point (lead) was fired on. Being strung out in a column on a jungle trail isn't very good. There is almost no room to manoeuvre at all. Anyway we moved on and as the point approached a VC camp a firefight broke out. This time we could hear a grenade as well. The call "corpsman up" came down the column so we knew we had casualties. Finally we moved on into the camp. The corpsmen (medics) had a black marine by the name of Swift all tagged and patched lying on a stretcher. He looked like hell. He'd been shot in the groin as he stepped over a crevice between two rocks.

This part of the VC camp had a classroom and a factory where they made hewn wooden mine moulds. There was a pile of them in a cave. I tried to break one with the butt of my M-14 but it never even scratched it. I also used an M-34 W-P (white phosphorus) grenade under the ones in the cave but it didn't do much damage either.

Several marines were detailed to carry "Swifty" back down the trail to a clearing about half a mile away for medevac (medical evacuation) by helicopter. In the meantime, "D" Company had moved further into the camp area where they found several more structures and also got into a firefight, killing at least one VC while suffering several wounded themselves. These casualties were brought back to the factory area for medevac. A marine UH-34 helicopter hovered at treetop level but its hoist cable wasn't long enough. Then an air force Huskie helicopter came over. He had 400 feet of cable and it just reached the ground. However, it was enough to take out our casualties. The rest of the battalion then moved on to the upper area of the camp and set up perimeter security. One of the first things we did was drag the VC out of the ravine he'd fallen into, as he was starting to stink already. He'd been shot between the eyes and the back of his head was blown off so his jacket was pulled over what was left of his head. We dug a shallow grave and dumped him in it. Thinking it should be marked somehow, I stuck a stick in the dirt and hung this round thing with a cross in it on the stick. I later learned it was a VC sighting device.

Deciding to answer nature's call, I told another marine to cover me and started down a trail armed only with a K-Bar (combat knife); as I rounded a big rock a pig was coming the other way — well, I don't know which of us was more scared — because I went running back up the trail and the pig went running and squealing in the opposite direction. When I realized what it was, I felt pretty stupid.

We spent the next day and night in the camp and that night myself and another marine were assigned a position at the top of the previously mentioned trail. We were pretty sure that there were VC in the area, as you could almost feel them watching. Sometime after dark we could hear movement on the trail and coming closer to us. Whatever it was it was almost up to me when I realized it was that damn pig again, so I let it come right up then kicked it and it went squealing away down the trail.

We tried a 50 per cent watch, changing off every 30 minutes. The air was so tense that you could feel it and 30 minutes was about all you could stand at one time. About 0200 there was a clatter down the hill below my position. It sounded like somebody had dropped an empty five-gallon jerry-can. I expected some trigger-happy marine to open up but it stayed quiet. We were pretty sure Charlie was moving around but nothing happened.

The next morning some marines from D Company who came by asked me what we were making all the noise about last night. When I told them it wasn't us and that nobody had come through our position, they left with a funny look on their faces.

For some reason it was decided to terminate the operation at this point. We loaded up all the captured documents and explosives, such as Chicom (Chinese Communist) grenades, to carry with us. There was even a piece of marble that looked like a tombstone with Vietnamese writing carved on it. An ARVN lieutenant who was with us said it was some kind of message from Ho Chi Minh to the Viet Cong. We rounded up the pigs and shot them and burned the hootches and rice. As we moved out, Delta Company fell out, set up an ambush in case any VC followed. This left me to be the point man. I moved down the trail, and cautiously into the large clearing that was to be the LZ for our extraction. As the rest of the battalion moved into the clearing to start preparing the LZ, two F-4 Phantoms came on station and circled way above us. Then four Huey gunships came in and circled, two on each side of the valley we were in. After awhile came one of the most beautiful sights I have ever seen — a swarm of 24 UH-34 helicopters. The whole formation circled overhead, guarded by the Hueys and Phantoms, and would land two at a time, pick up their heli-teams and streak for Da Nang.

I often wonder what thoughts went through the minds of the new guys at Da Nang when chopper after chopper landed and all these grubby, grungy, raggedy-ass marines got off. I know that as tired and smelly as we were, we walked a little taller when we passed by them.

Other Patrols

Headquarters and Service Company used to run a daily patrol out through the rice paddies between Camp Reasoner and Highway 1 and then over to "Dogpatch," then take a different route back to the command post. This patrol was called Deputy Dog, the name being derived partly from Dogpatch which was the turnaround point for the patrol, and partly from a popular TV cartoon character of the same name. This patrol was no big deal but it did get us away from the command post and I volunteered for it many times. Mainly we would check IDs and look for anything suspicious. Sometimes we'd go into a hootch and poke around. The Vietnamese would never say anything, just watch. But you knew from their looks that they hated you. Our orders were always the same. "If a gook runs from you go after him and apprehend, but DO NOT SHOOT." Almost every time, peasants would see us approaching, some would run. One day we were approaching a group of peasants in a rice paddy when one took off running. I said I would go after him or her. There was a finger of woods and garden between us and I figured I would intercept by cutting through it. My calculation was correct and I arrived just ahead of the suspect. However, I still had to get over a four-foot fence. Just as I was going over, my foot caught on the top wire and I started to fall. The suspect still hadn't seen me and was right in front of me when I hollered. It was a girl of about 14 and she froze in her tracks when she looked up and saw this 200-pound marine falling, screaming out of the sky. I landed right in front of her and I thought she was going to die. I took her back to the group. It turned out she had forgotten her ID and was afraid of what we would do to her. We gave her a couple of cigarettes, although she obviously didn't know what to do with them. Anyway, we had a good chuckle over the incident.

One time we were ready to go out on a Deputy Dog when they changed the orders. This time if any ran we could shoot. It seemed like the gooks had gotten the same word — because nobody ran. We charged at some of the groups of peasants but couldn't spook any into running. Next time out it was "no shooting" again and all kinds of gooks ran.

On another Deputy Dog we ran across a funeral near Dogpatch and after being somewhat disruptive we went on into Dogpatch. We decided to have a beer before starting back. One of the guys decided he needed more than beer and disappeared with one of the boom-boom girls. We were just finishing when a couple of squads of grunts pulled up on Mules (wheeled transport vehicles). We started to leave when the grunt captain came in and wanted to know what we were doing. The sergeant in charge of our patrol explained that we were just checking out some of the hootches in Dogpatch before starting back. The captain said he'd had reports of digging going on and we told him about the funeral we had seen. He seemed satisfied and left but came back a few minutes later and wanted to know more about our patrol. Apparently he thought we were up to no good. Anyway, he made us go outside and contact the command post by radio. In the meantime, the guy who had been with the whore had heard what was going on and jumped out the back window. He came around while we were radioing in and, trying to sound officious, reported that the rear of the building was secure. The captain eyed him very suspiciously. After radio contact was made, the captain talked to our command post, but he still wasn't satisfied that we were legitimate so he secured our patrol and ordered us to go straight back to the battalion. We really didn't mind as we had put one over on him anyway.[7]

DAVID DEAR

Vietnam: October 1965 to June 1966   Service: Navy

I was born in Parry Sound, Ontario, 27 October 1944. My dad was a captain in the Canadian Army. He took off when I was about two years old. I joined the U.S. Navy on 31 January 1963 for a four-year hitch. After boot camp and hospital corps school, I was stationed at the U.S. Naval Hospital, Great Lakes, Illinois. I married in July 1965, and in September I got orders to report to Field Medical Service School at the Marine Corps Base at Camp Pendleton, California. After graduation, I had 72 hours to catch a plane to Okinawa, where the 3rd Marine Division's headquarters was located. The marines are a

Petty Officer (Hospitalman) 3rd Class David Dear (right) with M-14 rifle at Quang Nai, south of Chu Lai, February 1966. In contrast to the red sand on which he is standing is white beach in the distant background and then some 200 yards beyond the South China Sea. (Courtesy D. Dear.)

part of the navy. So when they needed corpsmen, doctors, dental technicians or dentists, they "volunteer" them from the navy.

I landed in Da Nang on 19 October 1965 and reported to Company C, 3rd Medical Battalion, 3rd Marine Division. This was a BAS (battalion aid station). The army calls them MASH units or field hospitals. This unit was located about 10 to 15 miles west of Da Nang. Casualties were brought directly to us from the field for treatment. Minor casualties were treated, placed in the wards, and then sent back to duty. Major casualties were operated on, placed in recovery until stabilized, then sent to Da Nang for medical evacuation to hospitals in Japan, Guam, the Philippines or wherever, then eventually back to the United States.

Casualties

I arrived at my first duty station on 20 October 1965. I was just feeling my way around and didn't know much what was going on or their procedure. On 27 October 1965 (my birthday) some of us had some time off, so we went up to our club, which our unit had built, to have some beers. In the club, some guys were relaxing with beer, others were reading letters, others playing cards. It had gotten dark and one of the guys went out to take a leak but came back in and yelled, "Look at this!" We all rushed out and looked toward the South China Sea miles away and saw the whole area illuminated by flares. We could hear (even at that distance) many explosions. Then a gong went off. Someone began beating a truck rim hanging from a tree with a hammer. I asked, "What the hell is that?" Someone yelled, "Everyone get your ass to the chopper pad right now!" The club was cleared in three seconds. We ran the 100 yards or so and got there just as the first choppers were landing. I didn't know what to do so I just stood and watched. Just then a chopper landed on the far end of the pad. A member of the crew was frantically waving me over. I ran up and I put my ear to his mouth. He yelled, "Get those men off here, we have to get back!" I looked around and saw a couple of guys by the pile of stretchers and yelled, "Get a stretcher over here!" When I looked to see what was in the chopper, all I saw was a pile of motionless bodies with ponchos thrown over them. I grabbed two teams of two guys and we offloaded them in no time and the chopper was off. In the process of trying to hurry and get this dead weight untangled and off the chopper, I pulled on an arm and it came off. But I just had to keep going — the door gunner was still yelling at us. He wanted to get back. I didn't think much of it at the time but that is one of the images that pops up on me every so often. That and the smell of blood and chopper exhaust. There were enough guys to handle stretchers and the walking wounded on the side of the pad nearest the emergency ward, so we waited a few minutes. Sure enough, two choppers soon arrived and landed on the far side again with more dead.

When all the patients were in, we hustled stretchers around to surgery, X-ray, and a tent for the cleansing of wounds. I worked in that tent for a while plucking "Willie Peter" (white phosphorus) and small pieces of shrapnel out of legs, chests and backsides. Talking to the patients, I learned what was going on. The marine air group on Marble Mountain was hit by a mortar attack. Viet Cong sappers infiltrated and blew a number of aircraft, choppers and living quarters. They had had some gooks helping them in the construction of a new air strip for the marine air wing. It was thus pretty easy for the enemy to pinpoint a mortar attack. One guy I was working on (pulling Willie Peter out of his ass) said he had been on perimeter duty — four guys to a bunker — when a Willie Peter round hit behind them and knocked them all down. Next thing he saw was gooks running around inside the wire. They were stripped nearly naked and wore satchel charges all over. One came up to his bunker, jumped down on his back and proceeded to shoot his friends lying there. He played dead and the gook left. The way his clothes were smouldering from the Willie Peter the gook probably believed him to be dead.

Being with a medical battalion you see some really bizarre things. Here are some examples:

One guy came in and it looked like he had a punk haircut. An enemy bullet had hit the chin strap clip on his helmet, made a few buzzes around inside his helmet, hit the other chin strap and fell out on the ground in front of him. He picked it up and said he would put it on a necklace. He had marks around the back of his head where the hair was burnt off.

Once I was walking back along the helicopter pad when two guys approached me holding a poncho like a garbage bag from the top. One fellow asked me casually, "What should I do with these guys?" I said, "What do you mean?" He replied, "These guys in the bag." He laid out the poncho on the ground and opened it. It looked like ground beef with some pieces of clothing. It was the remains of three of their buddies. I just stood there for what seemed like an hour, finally pointed to the tent in the field and simply said, "Graves Registration."

Another time the bloated body of a sergeant, pulled from the Da Nang River, was brought in. His hands were tied behind his back, and there were multiple stabs wounds in his back. Apparently, he was alive when he hit the water because they found water in his lungs. The doctor noticed his lips were sewed shut with string. Upon cutting the sutures and opening his mouth, the doctor located the sergeant's missing testicles.

We also treated Vietnamese civilians and POWs. We would treat anyone who came to us for help. After a few months at "Charlie Med," I felt I was being given the worst jobs. I was put on kitchen work, perimeter duty, taking chow to the patients, even guarding civilians who came onto the base to dig up their dead ancestors from graves on base and transport them to a place near their village for reburial.

When my friends told me about Task Force "Delta" of which Delta Med (Company D, 3rd Medical Battalion) was a part, I eagerly volunteered for that. Delta Med was a floating medical company which was part of the Task Force. When an operation would come up, we would load up supplies, go to the area of operation, and set up a BAS in the immediate vicinity of the operation. I really felt as if I was accomplishing something in this unit.

My first son was born 5 February 1966 during Operation "Double Eagle." I received a Red Cross notification about three days later by

resupply helicopter. I felt I should give out some cigars so I asked my
buddy who flew in our supplies to see if he could locate some. A
couple of days later he brought in a few boxes of sweets which I
passed out in our unit. At least it was something to celebrate and take
our minds off things for a while.

Friendly Fire

After the first phase of Operation "Double Eagle," we loaded back
aboard LSTs (landing ship, tank) and were ferried up to Chu Lai. It
was dark when we landed, but the whole beach area was lit by large
lights on tall tripods. There were four or five LSTs beached and a
massive operation of offloading equipment was going on. We were
told to spend the night on the beach. The major in charge of the shore
party told us to camp out on the beach to the south at the end of the
vehicle parking lot. We found our jeep with the trailer load of
stretchers. Each of us grabbed a stretcher and moved to the beach at
the end of the line of trucks. Why sleep on the sand when you have
stretchers? I set up and proceeded to heat up some cocoa. The water
was heating up when someone opened up with an M-60 (American)
machine gun — at us! There was an 8- to 10-shot burst and we were
in the sand playing turtle trying to bury ourselves. I lay right on my
stove with the heat tab still burning and burnt my utility jacket. We
then heard the shore party major (we called him Major Bear Tracks)
yelling at someone on the perimeter wire, "Cease fire — hold your
fire!" I couldn't believe it. The beach area was lit up like a shopping
mall and the guy was dinging at us. No sooner had the major yelled
at this guy than he opened up again. He put another 15-20 rounds
just barely over our heads. I heard them snap, and the tracers
couldn't have been more than two feet over our heads. They
slammed into a small rise of sand just feet from us. The major was
really unglued by now, not to mention us, and we heard him yelling,
"Cease fire or I'm coming up there and blow you away." Then we
heard the distinctive sound of a .45 automatic racking a round in the
chamber and ole Major Bear Tracks double-timing up the sand rise
toward the perimeter wire. We never found out what happened to
that guy, but I can imagine he got the book thrown at him. I have
been sniped at a number of times and been near an Ontos (lightly
armoured tracked vehicle) when it was blown by a land mine, but
that incident on the beach was the closest I ever came to getting hit
over there, and by "friendly fire."

Khe Sanh

When I was transferred to the grunts up in Phu Bai near Hue it was a completely different life. We were always out of the battalion area either on operations or on wild-goose chases. I guess they didn't want all the companies in the battalion area at once in case of a major attack. We would be out in the field for a time, come back to the battalion area for a hot meal, shower, get a clean set of utilities, a night's rest, breakfast, and back out again. We never spent more than 24 hours in the area. We went on an operation up in Khe Sanh in early 1966. They told us there was a suspected three divisions of the North Vietnamese Army in the Demilitarized Zone near there. We laid down to the Phu Bai Air Base with a number of other units and waited around. After about two hours (hurry up and wait), they told us to load up. We went up and relieved 2nd Platoon who were guarding supplies. Khe Sanh at the time was just a Special Forces camp. We were told to move out north of the air strip and around the corner to a road which I believe was Route 9 into Laos.

The first night I spent on perimeter duty with a marine and another corpsman. We didn't have a foxhole, just a six-foot-long sandbag wall three or four bags high. There was ahead of us about a 75-yard field of fire cut out of small trees. It was my turn for watch. I'm sitting on the bag wall, my .45 pistol on the bags, making some cocoa when a trip flare went off about 50 yards directly in front of me. I tumbled backwards on the marine but came up with the pistol at the ready. Everyone is awake but our night vision is gone since we are temporarily blinded by flares going off. We wait and then wait some more. Nothing happens. Next morning we went out to check the flares and found the largest set of tracks we've ever seen. A tiger! Good thing he didn't come our way. He would have run us over.

Another time I went with a squad down the airstrip to guard the water purification point manned by two guys with German shepherd dogs. We were bedding in at dusk when the dogs perked up, so we stopped talking and listened. Sure enough we heard some rustling downhill in the brush which was about knee high. Everyone was at the ready. We waited. Then one of our guys spotted movement and opened up with his M-14 on full automatic. We moved down the hill with extreme caution. What we found was a wild boar. We called the Green Berets to let them know it was just a pig. About a minute later a troop of South Vietnamese from the camp came running towards us. We asked the radio operator, "Did you tell them it's just a pig? We don't need help." Too late. The South Vietnamese forces arrived but they weren't carrying guns. They had knives and machetes and whacked up that pig in less than three minutes flat. Then with each carrying a chunk of pork over their shoulder, they departed. As for the pig, there was nothing left but blood in the grass. One of our guys just said, "Amazing." Some of the butchers back home could learn a lesson or two from these guys.

When the operation got under way, it was preceded by a B-52 strike. We then humped all over the hills and around Khe Sanh. This was jungle of the triple-canopy variety that blocked out the light. Little land leeches were all over, particularly in our armpits and crotches. When we got to where we camped, we all stripped and doused the little critters with bug juice.

As we were settling in for the night, our platoon sergeant came over to me and asked if I had a safety pin and some suture material including a needle. Sarge was a big Indian — of what tribe, I don't know. He sat by a little stream that was about one and a half feet wide and about 10 inches deep and caught four little fishes that looked like trout. He made a small lean-to fire and cooked them up. Damn things smelled good too as we sat there eating our C-rations. Sarge wouldn't part with a morsel.

When I was with the grunts, whenever we went out in the field, I never knew where we were. Nobody ever told us where we were going or much of what we were doing. It scares the hell out of me now to realize that if we got hit and I was the only one left, I wouldn't know where I was.

I had no R&R (rest and recreation) during my whole tour. Something always came up. When I got back from "Double Eagle," I was supposed to go to Bangkok. Two days before I was to leave, I was transferred to 3rd Platoon, Company C, 1st Battalion, 1st Regiment, 1st Marine Division. All I ever had were two Cinderella liberties in Da Nang — Cinderella liberty being a "get back to your base before dark."[8]

LORNE SIMS

Vietnam: 1965 to 1967   Service: Marines

Lorne Thomas Sims of Ottawa ended up in Vietnam because he happened to be in the U.S. Marines when his unit was sent there. He did not join the marines specifically to go to Vietnam. His father was a veteran of the Second World War and Korea, and his older brother, Earl, was with the Marine Corps. At age 17, with only a Grade 7 education, Lorne signed for a four-year stint with the marines. (Pa-

Private 1st Class L.T. Sims (left) in Vietnam. (Courtesy L.T. Sims.)

rental consent was required for enlistment of those under 18). Basic training at Parris Island was brutal. Several of his friends had completed basic training just to prove that they could take it and then later deserted, but Lorne stuck to the agreement he had made. When Sims said he was from Canada, the drill sergeant, a mean-looking individual, remarked he must be a spy or someone working for the CIA. During basic training, young men were stretched to the limit mentally and emotionally and were even physically beaten. Unquestioning, automatic obedience was emphasized. In a run of five to six miles, the men learned that they had to finish together. Anyone who could not make it to the end was helped out by the remainder of the squad. It became ingrained that they were a unit. Those who could not conform or take the stress were weeded out. Lorne also took advanced infantry training at Camp Lejeune.

When it appeared that Sims's unit would be going to Vietnam, the men were told the reason for going was to fight communism because it was bad. They had to fight the Communists in Vietnam so that they would not have to fight them in the United States. Most of the young men with him were eager to "kick ass" in Vietnam.

Lorne was assigned to the service company of the headquarters and supply battalion, 3rd Marine Division. In 1965 he was based at Da Nang. He usually drove a water truck to supply marine outposts. He remembers being sickened by the sight of some 200 Viet Cong killed during a suicidal attack on a marine position. Throughout his tour, he never had occasion even to fire upon any of the enemy.

After one year in Vietnam, Sims returned to U.S. Marine headquarters at Quantico, Virginia, but in order to avoid the spit and polish there and the loneliness of weekends, he requested and was granted another tour in Vietnam in 1966-67. There he worked seven days a week, until leave, with little free time on his hands. The major contacts he saw the marines have with the South Vietnamese were through prostitutes or young children, from whom soft drinks and marijuana could be purchased.

While in Vietnam on this tour, Corporal Sims came to the aid of a friend from West Virginia in a serious fight with several blacks. Sims discharged his gun in order to break up the quarrel. There was a court martial. In his defence, it was proven that he was not racially prejudiced. Because he was a volunteer from Canada, Sims's punishment was mild. He was demoted from corporal to private and given a fine.

At the end of another two years, Sims was honourably discharged. He recalled leaving at the time of the riots following the assassination of Martin Luther King. Washington was ablaze and there was chaos in the streets. Racial problems were an important factor in his decision not to settle in the United States. He immediately put the marines and Vietnam behind him. Sims returned to Ottawa, married, had two daughters and is currently employed as a municipal worker, frequently on water emergency repairs, for the Regional Municipality of Ottawa-Carleton. Since his return, he has not watched any movies on Vietnam or read any literature about it for fear of stirring up bad memories.[9] This attitude is typical.

GUY MATHIEU

Vietnam: November 1965 to January 1966   Service: Army

Guy Mathieu was born on 21 August 1942 at Black Lake, Quebec. For economic reasons his family moved to Manchester, New Hampshire, in 1962. His mother, an American citizen, was originally from Laconia, in the same state. Guy tried to enlist in the Canadian Army but was rejected. In 1964 he was drafted into the U.S. Army. Guy served as a private with the 188th Ordnance Company (Ammunition) at Pleiku from 1965 to early 1966. Returning home, he used GI benefits to attend college. In 1967 he took out American citizenship. He resides in Laconia, is unemployed and subsists on a disability pension.

Guy offers a few memories of his brief time in Vietnam:

We left Fort Bragg, North Carolina, by bus to take a boat in Charlestown, South Carolina, for Vietnam. We went by the Panama Canal but we had to change boats at Long Beach, California, because the boat was taking on too much water. On our way to Vietnam, we stopped at Guam. When we arrived on the Saigon River we were confined below deck. Grenades were thrown overboard intermittently to prevent sabotage by enemy frogmen. At Saigon we were allowed to go two at a time for two beers but then had to return to the ship. From Saigon we went to Cam Ranh Bay where we let some troops off and continued on to Qui Nhon. We went ashore by landing craft, then by truck to our base. They let us take our weapons but we didn't have any ammunition. I certainly didn't like the feeling of travelling that way. There was one guy riding shotgun, but if anything happened we wouldn't have been able to defend ourselves. The trip was not that long, but long enough to put you on edge.

For the next few days we were confined to the base area. They gave us a few shots to protect us from disease. Our small unit was divided into two groups with 12-hour shifts each. I was put on the shift from 6 a.m. to 6 p.m. I experienced a lot of problems with the heat and the 1st sergeant.

As an ammunition helper, I remember most of the time we worked with the engineers. I helped load and unload a truck in order to build up an ammunition dump. We had to travel 35 to 50 miles out of camp. In my group there were never more than six or seven soldiers in the back of the 3/4-ton truck and we had only two magazines. Each magazine had 20 rounds so fighting was out of the question. I remember once the 1st sergeant asked me what I would do if we were attacked. I told him I would have no choice but to give up my weapon and surrender.

After each meal our mess hall was turned into a beer hall. In Qui Nhon the only beer available was Black Label. In Qui Nhon we were able to buy two bottles on Tuesday and two on Thursday. Our ration cards were never checked.

There was a lot of drinking going on even when on duty. We usually took a cooler with us and drank. I even remember having to help support those unable to walk because no matter how drunk we had to go out of base camp if ordered.

I don't remember how long I stayed in Qui Nhon. When the company moved to Pleiku we were stationed at Camp Holloway and I didn't have to go out much. I was put on medication and most of my time was spent on the base. One night we were under fire and everyone of us was lined up in firing position and we were waiting for permission to fire but the order never came. As you can see, my story is nothing like that of Rambo.

After Vietnam I returned to work as a machine operator in New Hampshire. There was an opening for a mechanic in the plant and I was successful in obtaining that job. But I had problems with the supervisor. I asked for a transfer. Not long after that I quit and if my memory serves me right, I then had a dozen different jobs. In 1968 I was hired by another company. As a mechanic I helped build heavy machinery until I had a medical problem and in January 1971 my employment was terminated. That was my last job. From 1971 to 1983 I lived day to day; every day was the same. In 1983 I became involved with the Disabled American Veterans in New Hampshire and have held a number of posts.[10]

MICHEL BRODEUR

Vietnam: December 1965 to May 1966   Service: Navy
        June 1968 to January 1969

Michel Brodeur was born 1 September 1945 and raised in Danville, Quebec. Layoffs at the asbestos mine there resulted in the family moving to New Britain, Connecticut, where they still live. In 1964 upon graduation from high school, Michel joined the U.S. Navy. He had to sign a declaration of intent to become a U.S. citizen. Upon completion of recruit training in December 1964, he was assigned to the USS Catamount homeported in San Diego. In late 1965 the ship operated in Vietnamese waters transporting marines from Okinawa to places such as Da Nang and Chu Lai. There were threats over Radio Hanoi of a night attack, but nothing materialized. Michel served on the Catamount until May of 1966. In 1968 he became an

Apprentice Seaman Michel Brodeur aboard the USS Catamount, Long Beach, California, 1965. (Courtesy M. Brodeur.)

American citizen. In his second tour off Vietnam, 1968-69, Michel served with Attack Squadron 147 on board the USS Constellation.

In June 1984 Michel retired from the U.S. Navy as a chief petty officer and has since been employed by IBM in Cincinnati.

Mike offers a few memories of Vietnam:

My ship, the *Catamount*, was an LSD (landing ship, dock) capable of opening its stern gate and flooding its well deck. Once the well deck is flooded, water craft can float in and out.

I served in the "deck" division. The physical appearance of the ship was one of our responsibilities. Special detail included the launching of amphibious craft. The deck division also provided lookouts.

During the transit to Vietnam, I met a marine from Connecticut. His name was Gerry. The friendship was short-lived as Gerry was killed soon afterwards.

During my next assignment in the Vietnam War Zone, I was aboard the aircraft carrier *Constellation*. On it, the flight deck was one of the most dangerous places to work. A young man in my squadron was killed by an A-7 Corsair's intake. Two weeks later another man was killed in a similar accident.

Later, while on a tour with crew members in Yugoslavia, I came across a group of French senior citizens in our hotel lobby and greeted them with "bonjour." An elderly man took my arm and asked me to translate a message.

"I wanted to commend you and your men for your impeccable appearance but most of all I want to tell them that the anti-American demonstrations you see on television do not represent the feelings of all the French people. These sentiments are coming from the younger generation who were not around during the Second World War. We will never forget that we were prisoners in our own country and Americans helped to free us. For that we will forever be grateful."

When I finished, the sailors started applauding the French and the French responded by applauding the Americans. There wasn't a dry eye among us.[11]

WILLIAM BRICKER

Vietnam: March 1966 to March 1967   Service: Air Force

William Bricker was born 15 April 1945 in Vancouver, but was raised in Fernie, British Columbia, after his father's death in a logging accident. In 1961 he moved to California where his mother and brother had settled.[12] Bill continues with his story:

I liked the beach area and soon had a good job as second mate on a charter boat taking parties sport fishing to Santa Catalina for albacore or further south towards Mexico. One afternoon two men in suits come to the marina in Newport Beach. They informed me that I had not registered for the draft and should do so immediately or leave the country. My options were to enlist in the army for three years, get drafted for two years, or enlist in the air force. I chose the latter.

Our group was flown from Los Angeles to Lackland Air Force Base, Texas, in August 1965. Our basic training was five weeks. After graduation very few of us went on to technical school, as the schools were full of Vietnamese troops. We were offered exams without having taken the course and I passed the mechanical vocation exam. After two weeks, the captain handed me orders one morning — electrical power production specialist to Travis Air Force Base, California. My job was servicing power units for runway lights. I was an E-2, pay $79.10 a month. I, along with most of the other people who had enlisted for four years, would be remaining at Travis for our entire stint. At the 18 months' point, Travis became very boring. I asked to go to Vietnam.

After 30 days' leave, I flew back to Travis. My flight overseas was on Braniff Airlines. As I boarded the aircraft I saw mostly army personnel. The route was standard — Hawaii, Guam, Clark Air Base in the Philippines and Saigon. Upon landing we were quickly hustled into a terminal shed building. Our orders were checked and I was told to report to a barracks not far away. An army sergeant told me I'd be going up country the next day to Phu Cat Air Base, near Qui Nhon, in Binh Dinh province. I spent the night in an open bay barracks where there were Korean technicians. They cooked on a charcoal stove; the smell was unbelievable. I ate in the nearby mess hall. They served flour biscuits and a gravy-like substance. The cooks were out back grilling steaks. I had arrived.

The next morning I boarded a Hercules C-130 for Qui Nhon. We made an assault landing and the plane backed into a revetment. Rocks and gravel flew in as the rear door opened. We jumped out baggage in hand. The C-130 was out of there in less than two minutes. I reported to a tent with a sign reading "Sierra Hotel." The airman in charge told me to catch anything heading north. It was 17 kilometres up to Phu Cat. My ride was a mail run in a jeep. The other passenger was a black, technical sergeant. We decided to stick together.

We turned in our personnel folders and went to the Club, a bombed-out Buddhist temple. We were each given a can of warm Korean beer and our choice of a sheet or a blanket. The sarge and I picked the sheets. We walked around a while and settled on a concrete slab for our quarters.

The base was under construction. RMKBRJ were the contractors, a Texas-based consortium said to be associated with the Johnson family of Texas. The top priority was the runway and aprons. Next came facilities for the F-4 squadron personnel. Within three weeks we built over 40 barracks. For sanitation we pounded six-inch pipes into the ground. They stuck out at odd angles. People stood in line to pee in those things. We also built outhouses and burned the waste. People who didn't follow the rules were on the burn detail. I never had that privilege.

Showers were on Wednesday evening for our group. A fire hose was connected to a huge bladder. First we had a turn at jumping on the bladder then our chance to get under the hose. The rest of the week we used the creek. One of our group was killed at the creek one evening by a sniper — we never went back. We built our own washroom by working long into the night.

The place was so hot and miserable, we just worked, ate and slept when we could. The base perimeter was out five miles like a ring. The Korean Army's Tiger Division held the outer ring; the U.S. Army held the inner ring a mile back.

After four months a little village grew up outside the base on the access road. The local Chinese set up little bars and whorehouses. We called it "the Strip." Some guys started stopping there and it caught on. A short walk out of the gate, they could get new uniforms, boots, rain gear, cold American beer for a dollar a can, and hookers in silk dresses. After a few serious gunfights, motivated by too much drinking, the commander shut it down. When it reopened after two weeks, MPs patrolled the area. Our base doctors conducted a weekly inspection clinic there and everybody was happy.

At the seven-month point, five of us were asked if we'd like to transfer down country. My friend Dave from Seattle and I got Saigon. We boarded a C-47 and bid farewell to Phu Cat. As we seemingly inched our way south we saw huge areas of bombed-out tropical forest, defoliation and burn-off.

At Saigon we were met by our new supervisor. As Dave and I walked into a non-commissioned officers' club, people stared at us. We were told to get cleaned up. We needed new fatigues, boots, haircuts, and especially hot showers. Our clothes were falling off, our boots torn and we both had telltale red clay in our hair. Later that night we went back to the club. It was great. They had real vegetables, milk, steak, fish, red wine and even round-eyed women.

Next morning we were assigned to our duties. Dave got mamasan crew — driving a dump truck full of Vietnamese women to pick up trash, sweep and clean. These old women gave Dave a hard time. They all chewed beachy nuts with teeth that were just black stubs. They never stopped complaining except to eat. My days were spent in big diesel trucks moving earth to a landfill.

We were off most weekends. I visited Tu Do Street (night life), Cholon (the Chinese section) and the zoo. Our unit also transported truckloads of cement bags to Bien Hoa. Each trip out there I saw they had a couple of Viet Cong tied to a tree. The Koreans did the interrogation. I didn't stay long to watch.

I requested R&R. Kuala Lumpur was very nice, civilized and clean. Upon my return, I felt strongly about getting out of Vietnam. While up country, I'd been shot at, mortared and scared a few times. But Tet was different. The 122-mm rockets were the real danger. They came in with a roar, like a bus going down a mountain in low gear. One of them can take out an air terminal — which they did. We received many hits during Tet. The base was devastated.

Our perimeter was overrun and the enemy bodies were afterwards buried in mass graves between the runways. F-4 fighters took off on sorties to drop ordnance at the end of the runway. In two weeks it was all over and we rebuilt the base .

In March my Braniff 707 took off for Travis. I cleared Customs and then walked out into the clean night air. My 365 days of duty in South Vietnam were over. My new assignment was Spain. Within 18 months I was married to a lovely lady from Sevilla. I eventually became an American citizen. On 1 September 1985, I retired as a master sergeant from the air force.[13]

A year later Bill went to Saudi Arabia, where he works for an aircraft company.

GRAEME WEBSTER

Vietnam: 1966 to 1967   Service: Marines

The great philosopher Santayana once said, "Read nothing but history and biography, for that is life without theory." If that is true, then the living of a period of history, especially in a war — and how one got there — moulds a life indeed.

I graduated from Fisher Park High School in 1963 and was not exactly what might be called an ace student. I did, however, achieve two things while in school. One was a deep and genuine love of the reading and study of history, the only subject I cared about; and the other was being able to get into the school band playing third clarinet, not a small accomplishment at that time. Mr. Heath, the director of the band, was a strict disciplinarian and wanted perfection at all times. A certain student a couple of years before that time had tried out for the band playing the trumpet, and was disqualified because he had, according to Mr. Heath, "no sense of music appreciation." His name was Paul Anka.

I had worked as a lifeguard during the summers at the Chateau Laurier Hotel — that bastion of old and granite-hard tradition of

Sergeant Graeme Webster, the Citadel, Hue, early 1967. (Courtesy G. Webster.)

accommodation in the heart of the nation's capital. In the summer of 1963, a certain family from Chicago, while staying at the hotel, came down to the pool to swim. He was a lawyer by profession, and soon he and I were talking away about the events of the day and history in general. They left a few days later and I soon forgot our conversation. A few weeks later, I was shocked to receive a letter from this individual asking if I would consider being interviewed by the history chairman of the University of Chicago for possible acceptance to study at that famous institution. Needless to say, I left for Chicago and the appointment was arranged. 1963 was a year in history when the epoch of one period ends and another begins. While in Chicago that November 22, a world ended and I was caught up in events which changed my life. The spirit of the times dictated to do something. Suddenly school didn't seem important any more; action did. But, what to do?

Military history had always fascinated me, and it seemed natural at the time, and in the spirit of the period to, as they say, "join up." I wanted the best, and as everyone knows in the United States, the Marine Corps was the best. I volunteered, filled out the paperwork, passed the physical and in January 1964 found myself in San Diego, California, at the Marine Corps Recruit Depot, under the command of Maj. Gen. Bruno A. Hochmuth. That name would come back to haunt me.

The Marine Corps is more than a military force in the United States. It is an idea, a way of being and thinking and the price of initiation into this order is "boot camp." It is 14 weeks of pure hell where one's sense of individuality and importance is knocked out and the Corps, and only the Corps, matters. Its traditions and history are pounded into you day and night, and when the day comes to graduate as a marine, it is almost like the second coming!

After graduation, my orders were to report to the Marine Corps Air Station at El Toro, California, just up the coast from San Diego and a few miles from Disneyland. It was considered and still is a cushy assignment. After reporting in and being processed, I was assigned to the public works department of the base as a map and topographical specialist for base engineering, and was to report to — of all things, a "civilian"! The squadron to which I was assigned only handled my records so for the most part I had ample free time, most weekends off, no extra duty such as firewatch in the barracks; indeed, it could be said I had it made.

With all my free time, I enrolled in college for night school in history. Indeed, I was able to take a full load of courses with all the time I had to study. One of my subjects was a beautiful, long golden-haired girl who just happened to sit next to me, and it wasn't long before I was being invited to spend the weekends at her home. The barracks became for me a thing of the past. Her father was a recently retired colonel of the air force and had grave suspicions about my intentions towards his only daughter! After all, everybody knows what enters a marine's head at liberty time. However, those magical days of sunlit utopia continued throughout the summer of 1965 and I didn't have a care in the world — until one storm-drenched night.

When it rains in southern California, it really rains! Late one Sunday evening as I was leaving my girlfriend's house, it came in a downpour. As I was only lightly clothed, the colonel offered me his old flight jacket to stay somewhat dry on my motorbike to get back to the base, about 20 miles away. As I drove up to the sentry to show my liberty card, he told me to report to the provost marshal's office a few feet away. The officer in charge asked me where I got a flight jacket with full colonel's insignia on the shoulders! I immediately turned my head and looked. Sure enough, there were the sew-on eagles of a full colonel. I explained the circumstances of how I got the jacket. With a look of disbelief, he asked for the phone number of the colonel to confirm my story. The captain called, the colonel answered, and after a few minutes my story was confirmed. The captain apologized for waking up the colonel at 2 a.m. and hung up. I was ordered back to the barracks with a verbal reprimand on the implication of impersonating an officer. My name was sent to the squadron adjutant as routine MP follow-up paperwork. My cushy days were numbered!

I continued night school through the winter semester, taking a course in modern Chinese history since the Second World War. The sunlit days were disappearing fast. The news from Vietnam was not good; there were even rumours that elements of the Corps might be sent soon. One night in the barracks, a fellow marine and myself were discussing current events and especially the role of China in Vietnam, or whether China should be in the UN. The conversation lasted an hour or so, and then I turned in for the night. At work the next morning around 10 a.m., my civilian supervisor received a call from base security asking that I report to the provost marshal's office at 1 a.m., in full uniform. I was completely in the dark as to why I was to report. At precisely 1 a.m., I reported to the provost marshal's office. I was brought into a darkened office, and told to stand at parade rest until the OIC would see me. Eventually the captain appeared, the same captain as had checked my story a few weeks before about the flight jacket incident. He asked me my views on political matters in general, and then my opinion on China in the UN. It seemed that someone had heard my friend and myself discussing politics and reported our conversation to his office as being "un-American."

After about 15 minutes of grilling, I asked if I was being charged with anything. The captain said, "No." However, he did ask me to sign a typed statement stating that I fully supported the foreign policy of the U.S. and other statements to that effect. I refused on the grounds that I wouldn't have been in the Marine Corps in the first place and secondly, my political views were my own business. I was given two days to think it over and return at that time to sign the statement. After two days, I returned and informed the captain that I would not sign any statement and I was dismissed and told to report back to duty.

The spring of 1966 was dark and rainy in southern California. The mood of the land reflected the events from overseas. I was now a lance corporal, and the weekends at my girlfriend's home somehow didn't have the same golden glow as the previous year. In January of 1966, I received orders to report to Camp Pendleton for refresher training and to report to 4th Regiment, 3rd Marine Division, for assignment overseas. I knew what overseas meant. The body bags were already landing at El Toro on a daily basis, and it didn't take a genius to figure out where I was going. Curious that I had received my orders a little over two weeks from the time of my interview at base security, but I couldn't prove that. In any case, the war was about to become my life.

Sergeant Graeme Webster, Khe Sanh, December 1967.
(Courtesy G. Webster.)

The refresher training at Camp Pendleton consisted of a few weeks of the latest ambush training, and booby traps which the Viet Cong were currently using in South Vietnam. Little thought was given to what would happen if regular divisions of the North Vietnamese Army (NVA) were encountered. As far as the political situation in the country of the time, nothing was discussed. We were there to stop aggression on the part of the North Vietnamese and the Viet Cong to overthrow the freely elected government of South Vietnam.

A combat tour in Vietnam for a marine was 13 months. For a soldier in the army, it was 11 months. That two-month difference could mean a ticket home on a chartered jet or a trip in a body bag. In any case, I boarded the troopship *General W.H. Gordon* in San Diego with 750 other marines, and we sailed to Hawaii to pick up elements of the U.S. Army's 25th Infantry Division. After doing that, we sailed for Okinawa and then on to Da Nang for deployment. Being marines, of course, we had to have a proper beach landing. That meant going over the side in scrambling nets, down the side of the ship into landing craft and, as they say in the Corps, "hitting the beach." My position in the landing craft was the second row from the ramp. The boat hit the beach hard and down the ramp came. Off we charged onto the broad beach and as I looked up at the crest of the beach there were about 15 busses waiting to pick us up! Some of us thought at the time, "What the hell kind of a war is this anyway?" In any case, we boarded the busses and were taken to be issued our combat gear and taken to our respective units. I had arrived at the war. The date was 6 April 1966.

I joined the regiment at Phu Bai, just south of the old imperial capital of Hue on Highway 1, the main road running north and south along the coastal plains. Assigned to the regimental S-3 (operations), I worked for Major Fullum as his operations NCO. My responsibilities consisted of preparing all the current situation reports, overlays, and in co-ordination with the S-2 (intelligence), formulating the battle plans to be presented for upcoming operations.

The early months of 1966 saw anti-government demonstrations spring up in Saigon, Da Nang and, most importantly, in Hue. If Saigon was the political capital of South Vietnam, Hue was the intellectual, religious and moral centre of the upper class. Indeed, even Ho Chi Minh admitted it was his home, and had attended the university there. The 1st ARVN Division HQ was located at the citadel inside the city itself, and it was considered perhaps the best division the South Vietnamese had.

In May, the regiment was ordered to proceed through Hue for search-and-destroy operations north of the capital. The city was divided by the Perfume River, the south side being the wealthy Catholic section, and the north side being the Buddhist section. Our column of vehicles proceeded through the Catholic section smoothly, and advanced across the bridge where we were stopped by hundreds of students, Buddhist monks and even Vietnamese girl scouts. Everything came to a halt. I was in the second vehicle with my major, and we were literally stopped on the middle of the bridge and couldn't move. By this time the Buddhist monks had situated themselves in front of our vehicles. Suddenly, one of them sat down in front of the column, and before anyone knew what was happening, he burned himself alive before my eyes. The situation was becoming desperate. On advice from Marine HQ at Da Nang we were ordered to await the Vietnamese paratroopers being flown up from Saigon.

It took about three hours before the paratroopers reached our position at the bridge. By this time, demonstrations had broken out all over the city and makeshift barricades had been placed around our column. As we watched, the paratroopers laid into the demonstrators with their weapons and clubs. Eventually, a path was cleared for us to advance out of the city. A number of students were killed as well as girl scouts. I remember as I drove my jeep off the opposite side of the bridge, seeing a blood-stained scout bandanna with the scout emblem on it. I thought at the time what would Lord Baden-Powell have said if he had seen this. So much for the theory of a popularly elected government in Saigon!

July of 1966 may be considered the beginning of large-scale operations in I Corps. The "324th B" North Vietnamese Division had begun to move across the DMZ (Demilitarized Zone) into Quang Tri Province. For the first time, we were up against regular NVA soldiers. The 324th was a veteran division, the same division that had beaten the French at Dien Bien Phu in 1954.

During the next few months we were constantly on the move throughout I Corps. Sleep became a thing of memory, and time was measured by remembering to take the big red horse pill for malaria on Sundays. My weight had dropped to 155 pounds from 175. My body was covered with white spots of jungle rot and luxury was considered to be a dry uniform with clean dry socks.

By late 1966 we were at Con Thien when I was ordered back to the Citadel in Hue with my major for a briefing for future operations. A Chinook chopper was sent to pick us up. Just before taking off, the ramp was lowered at the rear of the craft, and a truck backed in.

Filling the back of the truck were about 20 body bags — marines killed in the fighting around the perimeter of Con Thien. I helped load them into the chopper and we took off. The major and I sat together on the webbed seats along the side of the chopper, the only light being the red night light near the cockpit. In the heat and humidity, the bodies began to swell. Not a word was said between us the whole trip. By this time my major and I had become one in thoughts and actions. By the time we landed at Phu Bai and the ramp went down we smelled of death.

Operation "Hastings" grew into Operation "Prairie" and the 4th was spread all over the DMZ, elements being located at all the strategic points along Highway 9, which ran east and west from Highway 1, along the DMZ. While moving to Cam Lo to set up regimental headquarters, our convoy ran into mines. Luckily only one truck hit a mine; however, it happened to be the one truck with all the personnel records in it. My friend in S-1 (personnel administration) was the driver. The vehicle was ablaze by the time I reached it, and records and files were blowing all over the place. We had come under fire from the distance, and mortar rounds began to fall for effect. We established a perimeter defence, and I called for air support. Eventually the fire ceased and we proceeded to the outpost at Cam Lo. It was impossible to retrieve most of the records. I stayed behind with the rear party and put my friend into a body bag and made sure that the toe tag identified him properly for Graves Registration.

By the end of January 1967, the first phase of the operation had ended. In the war of statistics and body count which measured "success," the score was NVA and VC 1,397 killed by actual body count and 27 captured. Final marine casualties were 225 killed and 1,159 wounded.

I was approaching my 12th month in Vietnam. Normal procedure was to send a marine back to the rear 30 days prior to his rotation date in order to stand down, and have a chance to relax before getting back to the "real world." My orders for rotation came while the regiment was located at Quang Tri. By this time my whole world was the regiment and everything that we had done in I Corps up to that point. So much so, that when I received combat promotion to sergeant from my CO, it was more of a family affair than a military award.

In the northern part of S. Vietnam, the climate is very much like the northwestern U.S. — very damp and cold. My weight was now 145. I was down to possessing one good set of jungle fatigues. The major took me to the landing zone (or LZ) for the chopper to pick me up. Neither one of us said anything. The chopper landed and that awful red laterite (soil formed by the decomposition of rock) blew all over us. I turned to my major, looked in his sunken eyes and after a few seconds of thought, I reached for the brown envelope containing my orders — and tore them up. The major walked over to the chopper, my gear was unloaded and we drove back in the rain.

The Corps gave me a 30-day leave anywhere in the world for agreeing to stay in Vietnam. I chose Ottawa. I still remember walking up the long driveway of my parents' home at 3 a.m. and rapping on their bedroom window to let me in. It was winter in Ottawa, and my body was covered with jungle rot. Strange indeed!

Needless to say, my father was shocked to learn that I was to return to Vietnam. Already television reports showed what was happening on a daily basis and casualty figures were recounted nightly.

I returned to the regiment at Con Thien, the uppermost part of the DMZ next to the North Vietnamese border. The next day my major was ordered to report to Hue for briefings with General Westmoreland. I remained in the command post. After the briefing was over, the major left Hue for our location. His chopper was brought down 20 miles south of our position. I boarded the medevac helicopter, and arrived at the site. What was left of the major no sane man should ever see.

Upon returning from Vietnam, I visited my major's widow in San Diego. A gracious lady, she offered me her late husband's service ring. The ring remains on my hand and shall be worn for the rest of my life.

In Vietnam, the remainder of 1967 saw offensive search-and-destroy missions throughout the DMZ. The regiment deployed throughout I Corps from Khe Sanh in the west, to the mouth of the Cau Viet River flowing into the South China Sea. By this time, replacements to the regiment were coming on a daily basis. All of the original marines with whom I had landed were gone. There was even talk that the Corps would have to resort to the draft in order to keep up to strength. To a volunteer, that did not exactly strike the right chord.

In late August, the regiment was ordered to stand down and return to Phu Bai, just north of the old imperial capital of Hue. It was there that my orders for rotation back to the real world came in October. I was now a sergeant and had one set of jungle fatigues to my name. I flew out of Da Nang on a chartered jet in November.

Upon discharge, I received plane tickets, one month's basic pay for unused leave time in Vietnam as well as the routine discharge briefing. I was told not to discuss anything with which I had been involved the past year or so, especially high-level decisions made at briefings where I was present.

As I walked out the gate at El Toro, a demonstration was taking place with students from the University of California protesting the war. One of the demonstrators came up and spat on me. The bus drove up, I boarded and I left.

Wars are fought by men and not technology. The war was lost that day in Hue when the people revolted against what they saw was happening in Saigon. But I had fought as hard as I could.[14]

DOMINIC BILOTTA

Vietnam: September 1966 to September 1967   Service: Marines

Sergeant Dominic Bilotta (right), Dong Ha, June 1967. (Courtesy D. Bilotta.)

Dominic Bilotta was born 4 September 1945 in Niagara Falls, Ontario. He joined the U.S. Marines in July 1965 because he had always wanted to be a marine. During basic training at Parris Island, he was teased by the drill sergeant for being "a dumb Canuck screwing up my Marine Corps." In Vietnam he was based near the Demilitarized Zone. Dominic rose to the rank of sergeant (E-5) and was also an acting gunnery sergeant (E-7). A member of Mike Company, 3rd Battalion, 4th Regiment, 3rd Marine Division, he was wounded three times, including once by friendly fire.

Dominic left the service in August 1968 with a disability pension. He married in 1969. He lives and works in Niagara Falls, New York, but remains a Canadian citizen.[15]

Dominic recounts some of the events of the war as he remembers them:

On the way up by truck with our unit to Camp Carroll — we had the task of protecting the camp's perimeter — a water buffalo rammed and tipped over one of the trucks in the convoy killing a marine. It was the first time I saw someone get killed. We got to Camp Carroll and another incident happened at night. One of the sergeants went to check out a new recruit who seemed edgy and was killed by a shot to the head. After only one week, I witnessed two of our marines killed not by the enemy but through accidents. I myself accidentally got wounded in November by shrapnel from one of our own hand grenades. I spent two months in a hospital ship recovering from the wounds.

We were always about eight miles from the Demilitarized Zone (DMZ). The majority of our larger operations were all basically the same. You are on patrol but battalion-size everyday. You establish a perimeter at nighttime and also set up ambushes. I enjoyed going on ambushes. We did make some hits. On ambushes you are supposed to stay awake but there is always the time you fall asleep.

When you go out on an operation there is always the fear of the unexpected. Even today I still live with that fear. You relive that fear not so much in the daytime but at night.

About March 1967 we went to Okinawa for several months to regroup, train new arrivals and switch from the M-14 rifle to the M-16. But things got so bad they sent us back early. When we returned in May, the enemy initially hit us hard and we took quite a few casualties.

Soon after, we were told we were going on the first multi-battalion operation inside the DMZ. Everything previously had been on a small scale. My helicopter was the first to land in the DMZ but there was nothing. A few guys in our unit shot several water buffalo but that was all there was for us. Others had a more difficult time.

As we withdrew from the DMZ we came across Hill 174. The North Vietnamese had a bunker complex there that was unbelievable. The main bunker was about the size of a house with tunnels leading to many little bunkers. They had everything underground. To reach it, you had to go up the hill then down a ravine. We assaulted their main bunker and also the smaller ones.

We had one man go up to within two feet of the main bunker and was about to throw in a hand grenade but was shot in the head. A corpsman moved up to the body and he too was shot in the head. Others got close to the bunkers and threw hand grenades into the apertures. The bunker was designed with a trench on the inside so that the enemy could obtain protection on the other side of the trench. Our executive officers then advised waiting four or five seconds before throwing in the live grenades, as they usually took eight seconds to explode.

Tear gas was tried but didn't work because it blew back on us. The second day word came down for help from anyone who could fire a 3.5-inch rocket launcher, popularly called the bazooka. But all the people on rockets were either wounded or dead. I volunteered and fired a rocket round right into the aperture causing significant damage.

I remember also pulling back and it was very upsetting. I had tears in my eyes. I said we can't leave the bodies of our men there. The next day they sent in jets with napalm and just demolished the whole complex. We went up the fourth day and the enemy was gone. They had mutilated our dead. In that three-day operation we had 97 wounded and 6 killed — part of Operation "Hickory." The North Vietnamese again showed us they were very good fighters, not like the Viet Cong.

I recall on a platoon-size patrol we had 75 artillery rounds fall all around us. Fortunately, nobody was hurt. When we got back, we found the barrage was from the U.S. Army, who thought we were North Vietnamese on patrol.

We were also at the Rockpile — a mountain that just went straight up. To get on top you needed a helicopter. Guys at nighttime used to shoot their 106-mm recoilless rifles into the side of the mountain. There were wild apes living there and you could hear them screaming.

After the operation on Hill 174, we were based at an old French fort. The fort was built in the shape of a triangle. We had South Vietnamese with us. There were also a lot of rats. There was a trench dug around the perimeter with barbed wire and Claymore mines. We used to wake up in the morning and find the Claymore mines turned around. Then we knew we had North Vietnamese sympathizers among us. The whole time we were there we sent out patrols every day and every night including ambushes. Daily we took casualties but no fatalities. We had guys with feet blown off, hands, etc. We never saw the enemy once all the time we were there. Our morale was very low. If the nearby village had been wiped out, we couldn't have cared less.

Then we moved to Con Thien, a quarter kilometre from the DMZ. There you could see for miles around. We were there from mid-July to September. We were sent there because the previous battalion had been so badly hurt. Con Thien took enemy artillery and rocket fire daily. There was a half battalion at Con Thien and companies around the perimeter. We went on patrol and took casualties

U.S. marines patrol a hill near the Rockpile (in background), November 1966. (Courtesy USMC.)

every day. On 4 September, on my birthday, we went out on a company-sized patrol. About two or three thousand metres away, we got hit by a lot of artillery and small-arms fire. It was a small skirmish of about half an hour. We took some casualties. A corpsman was giving mouth to mouth to one of the wounded and I was pumping his heart for half an hour. Then the lieutenant ordered us to put the body on the tank and the guy died.

We regrouped on 7 September but when falling back we were caught in a L-shaped ambush. Seven of my men were killed outright. I was shot in the hand and also took a piece of shrapnel in the arm. I managed to crawl to a bomb crater and return fire. A pineapple hand grenade blew up very close to me but I only took some shrapnel. After the firefight died down, I could hear the North Vietnamese going around shooting in the head our wounded who were still alive. I still think about it today. I could hear Charlie talking. That's how close they were. Our own artillery came in because it was assumed we were all dead. After that ambush, I was sent back home to a couple of hospitals and recovered from my wounds.

I recall the heat, the monsoons when I couldn't keep dry. I myself had dysentery up at the Rockpile. Above all, I will always remember the guys.[16]

PHILIP HOCKING

Vietnam: November 1966 to December 1966   Service: Army
          December 1968 to December 1969

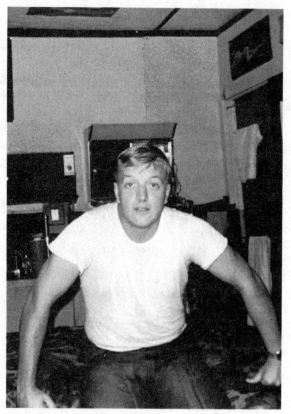

Warrant Officer Philip Hocking in his living quarters at Phu Loi, South Vietnam, 1969. (Courtesy P. Hocking.)

Philip Hocking was born in Hamilton, Ontario, on 29 October 1945 but grew up in Dawson Creek, British Columbia, and Beaverlodge, Alberta. His mother's marriage had broken up, following which she moved back home to the Peace River country. In 1954 she married an American who was a radar technician in the U.S. Air Force. From 1959 to 1964 Phil lived on an air base at Fairbanks, Alaska. He was awarded a scholarship to attend the University of Washington, but the sudden freedom resulted in his devoting little time to his studies. Poor grades brought about the loss of the scholarship.

Out of university and wanting to fly, Phil enlisted in the U.S. Army. From October to November 1965, he took basic training at Fort Ord, California, and flight training at Fort Wolters, Texas, and at Fort Rucker, Alabama. He had to serve three years in the army following graduation.

In Vietnam, Phil was assigned to the 155th Aviation Company, based at Ban Me Thuot. As a result of a truce during the Christmas period, he was sent to evacuate some members of the 4th Infantry Division for 48 hours. For undetermined reasons his helicopter crashed and burned. Several soldiers were killed but Phil was pulled unconscious from the wreckage. He had a broken collarbone and burns. He was evacuated to Cam Ranh Bay and then to Japan, after having flown only about 100 hours in Vietnam.

From March 1967 to November 1968 Phil served in the United States, mainly as a helicopter flying instructor. Rather than go back again to Vietnam, likely as a gunship pilot on the Huey helicopter, he took a four-week familiarization on a larger-type helicopter, the CH-47 Chinook. Still a warrant officer, he flew Chinooks with the 205th Aviation Company out of Phu Loi. After a year he returned to San Francisco and was honourably discharged. As a civilian, Phil worked on Quebec's James Bay power development and then moved back to the Peace River country where he still flies helicopters for a living.

Phil recalls some of his experiences inVietnam:

It's been more than 20 years since I was in Vietnam. I have read most of the books and seen most of the movies about the war. Very few, if any, portray the situation as I experienced it. The general approach seems to be to highlight the moments that were scary. But they were only a very small portion of the total time that a person spent over there. I can't speak for those who fought on the ground, but for helicopter pilots it was accepted as a job. It wasn't that a lot of guys didn't go out with the idea of defending the United States, but in order to cope you couldn't dwell on how dangerous it was. You did the best you could. You couldn't think about the bad press about the war coming from the United States. You had to dismiss it or else you couldn't do the job.

Tonight I had a few pilots over for a few drinks. My wife is asleep and I am talking into a tape recorder. It seems the only time I can even start to talk about that period is after a few drinks. I think back now on how fruitless and how political the whole war was over there. I don't remember very much from the first tour, but I will relate incidents from the second tour when I flew Chinooks. My base was at Phu Loi just north of Saigon. We were a general support company. We got our mission sometime in the late evening and then got up in the morning. We flew 80 per cent for American forces, 10 per cent for Australian forces and 10 per cent for Vietnamese and Thai forces. You usually didn't know whom you were flying for until you went in the operations shack in the morning. Flying for the Australians was always an experience. Their military units were the most professional that I worked for. I recall that all that the Thais ever wanted were Kool menthol cigarettes.

Once on a daylight mission in northern III Corps resupplying bases, we broke off early for lunch. We had been flying by an air strip deserted except for a C-130 Hercules transport aircraft on the side of the runway. I landed and shut down the chopper near the Hercules. There was one air force guy moving about driving a front- end loader. We stayed inside the aircraft and proceeded to have lunch when all of a sudden mortar rounds began coming in. We just bailed out the back and headed for the bunker. We took cover in this bunker but this other fellow was still driving around in his front-end loader. In about 10 minutes, he comes over to our bunker, gets off his vehicle, goes to the observation slits in the bunker, looks down and says, "Sir, would you please kindly move that damn helicopter? It's drawing enemy fire." Well, we got out of there but to this day I can't figure out why the enemy didn't try to bomb that Hercules. My guess is that the enemy was probably using the Hercules as a decoy to entice other aircraft to land there.

As well as night duty, there was the necessity during the day of keeping a Chinook available for recovery purposes. If a smaller helicopter went down, they had a specialized unit to help, which they called "Pipesmoke." They would go out in a Huey, land and rig up the damaged machine. All we had to do was come in, hover, get hooked up and then take off. In the area I worked, the downed helicopter would be brought back to Saigon. If necessary, the damaged helicopter would be sent back by ship to Corpus Christi, Texas, to be rebuilt.

One day, we received this call for assistance. The location was given to me in military grid co-ordinates. I flew out as instructed but grew a little concerned because the location was close to the border with Laos. I flew to the area at 3,000-4,000 feet above the ground. I was trying to contact this Pipesmoke helicopter on FM-radio and finally I heard him very faintly. It turned out we were given the wrong co-ordinates and were more than 10,000 metres away from where we should have been. Just as I realized that, the crew chief came over the intercom and said, "Sir, what are those little puffs about 11 o'clock high?" I looked up and there was flak coming up at us. It didn't take me long to get out of there. One goes out on a mission and here some jerk gets your co-ordinates wrong! But this wasn't typical.

At one time we were in support of an army ground unit commanded by George Patton's son, a full colonel. They had made a sweep up through the Michelin rubber plantation. We were told to make a night resupply to them. Night missions were dangerous because it was difficult to maintain visual reference. I asked for gunship support. This request took place just after the army had received some of the new Cobra gunships. We requested gunship support for this night resupply, as the troops were in desperate need of ammunition. The reply was that no way was the officer in charge sending his new gunships. We argued. In the end, we wound up doing the resupply without any gunship support. Fortunately, nothing happened.

I got a call late one night to go out on medevac. We hardly ever used the Chinook for medevac. Two or three Chinooks were required. There was this unit northeast of Bien Hoa in heavy engagement suffering a lot of casualties. When we arrived they were still in contact. They had set up a landing area for us. We made a night approach. One of the strangest aircraft in Vietnam was an old DC-3 or C-47 called "Spooky." They had a million-watt candle-power searchlight in the cargo door plus a .50-calibre machine gun laying down cover. You could see the tracer rounds of a .50-calibre gun firing with tracers every two or three rounds. It was just like a red fountain coming out of the sky. It was stupid to even try to go into the area, but you knew there were casualties. They loaded stretchers on all three helicopters. I looked back and saw American troops covered in blood. All I wanted to do was get these boys back to the hospital and try to save lives.

It's hard to convey what it was like landing on a hot landing zone. As an example, I recall going into LZ Dot to drop off arms to a Special Forces unit. As soon as you touched down, you got incoming mortar rounds so you take off. But the men on the ground need the ammunition so you make another approach. The crew chief and gunner try to get the load near the rear of the aircraft. As soon as you touch down, the ramp goes down and they kick the stuff out. However, all the time you are taking incoming fire. You look back now and see that you took too many chances. But when you were there what you did seemed like the best thing to do at the time.

Well, that's about all I can think of now. I really haven't enjoyed talking about these things.[17]

MICHAEL MALE

Vietnam: January 1967 to July 1970   Service: Army
December 1970 to December 1971

Staff Sergeant Michael Male in South Vietnam, 1968. (Courtesy M. Male.)

Michael Male was born in London, England, on 21 October 1942. His father, a member of the Canadian Army, and his mother, a British war bride, separated and later divorced. Michael's mother moved to Vancouver, and that was where he grew up. From 1959 to 1962 Michael was a member of the 6th Field Squadron, Royal Canadian Engineers. The training he received as a demolition engineer proved useful.

On 19 April 1962 Michael enlisted in the U.S. Army for three years and volunteered to go to Korea. He was there from September 1962 to September 1963. After a brief stint at Fort Meade, Maryland, he re-enlisted for a three-year hitch. He volunteered again for Korea, where he was kept busy removing old mines and laying new ones from late January 1964 to mid-February 1965. By now a sergeant, he was sent to Fort Bliss, Texas, where he underwent additional training

Staff Sergeant Michael Male (left, wearing glasses) helps tend one of two soldiers wounded when a jeep hit a 40-pound land mine on Route 534, June 1968. Three other Americans were killed. (Courtesy M. Male.)

from February 1965 to January 1967 while his unit, the 39th Engineer Battalion (Combat), was being built up for Vietnam.

When Michael first arrived in Vietnam in early 1967 he was kept busy rebuilding and keeping open Highway 1 from Van Gia to Tuy Hoa. At the time the Koreans were in that area and security was good. As part of Task Force Oregon, in April he landed at Duc Pho and helped in the construction of an airfield, ammunition dumps and the road from Mo Duc to Bong Son until December 1967. For a while he was attached to 101st Airborne Division, then the 196th Infantry Brigade.

During the Tet offensive Mike was in the area between Landing Zone Ross, near Quang Nam, and Landing Zone Baldy. He was kept very busy minesweeping a road going to the Que Son Valley, an infiltration route from North Vietnam. There 40-pound mines were to be found about a foot under the surface. There were also anti-personnel mines and booby traps on the side of the road. All the mines were simple yet effective.

In May 1968 Male found himself in the area of LZ Colt near Thang Binh. Old Highway 534 and other former French roads were being opened to permit road supply east-west rather than just north-south.

Initially, the mines could be spotted because of the different soil that was dug up during the night. This shortcoming was soon rectified. A Viet Cong defector showed Michael and his men where the Communists had planted mines. Sticks and rocks would indicate to Communist forces where mines had been planted. At one time or another, Michael worked on most of the roads in I Corps.

The 39th Engineer Battalion had its headquarters at Chu Lai, but Staff Sergeant Male and four other men he selected from the battalion did reconnaissance for a host of combat troops in the area. None of Male's men were ever lost. This was due to good training, thoroughness and caution rather than just luck.

In July 1970, Michael was sent back to Fort Belvoir, Virginia, as an instructor (E-6). Michael was unhappy there and voluntarily requested another tour in Vietnam. He was sent back again and served from December 1970 to December 1971.

Although he was still a Canadian citizen, Michael was given security clearance and served with the intelligence section of the 39th. Being a Canadian, he was often jokingly referred to as a "mercenary."

Having served a total of four and a half years in Vietnam, Michael was shipped back to Fort Leonard Wood, Missouri. While there he was ordered to do a further tour in Vietnam. By this time Michael was battle weary. Unable to get an assignment at Fort Lewis, Washington, where he would be close to his mother, enabling him to help her work a farm on weekends, he deserted and returned to Canada. But Mike had been out of the country for about 10 years and was unable to get a new Canadian passport. Thus, from 1971 to 1980, he could not leave the country. In 1975 he married a Canadian citizen but still could not get his Canadian citizenship papers until 1980. He remains happily married and settled in Calgary where he lives and works as a paperhanger.

Michael corresponded with the U.S. Army explaining why he deserted and was given an honourable discharge.[18]

WILLIAM YOACHIM

Vietnam: March 1967 to March 1968   Service: Air Force
August 1969 to August 1970

*2nd Lieutenant William Yoachim, Da Nang,
Vietnam, June 1967. (Courtesy W. Yoachim.)*

William Yoachim was born in Cardston, Alberta, August 1943. After moving with his family to Tacoma, Washington, he became an American citizen in 1958. Bill received his commission from the University of Nebraska Reserve Officers Training Course and went through navigator training. During his year in Vietnam, 2nd Lieutenant Yoachim was with the 12th Air Commando Squadron (Defoliation), Bien Hoa, navigating UC-123 Providers. He returned to Thailand for another one-year tour in August 1969 as a captain. There he served as a weapons systems officer in the rear seat of a Phantom RF-4C with the 11th Tactical Reconnaissance Squadron out of Udorn. Bill eventually rose to the rank of lieutenant colonel. He is chief of base operations, Hill Air Force Base, Utah, and resides in nearby Clearfield.

Bill sent in the following account of his tours in Southeast Asia:

My first operational assignment was with the 12th AC Squadron stationed at Bien Hoa, South Vietnam. Until I arrived, only captains, majors and lieutenant colonels were assigned in rated (flying) positions. I was the first 2nd lieutenant to fly with the "Ranch Hands" (the code name for our operations). We sprayed Agent Orange, which is now somewhat controversial. However, it was highly effective. Once on leave in Hong Kong, a Green Beret told me that he estimated our spraying saved at least one American or Vietnamese life per week by denying the enemy cover for ambushes. We usually flew two missions a day and were on our first target as soon as it was light enough to see the terrain. The UC-123 Providers we flew were twin-engine, propeller-driven airplanes with a 1,000-gallon tank of defoliant. Usually we had three to six aircraft on a mission. We would fly in echelon during spray operations at 130 knots only 100 feet above the treetops.

Our squadron took more hits from small-arms fire than any other air force unit in Southeast Asia. The NVA (North Vietnamese Army) and "Charlie" (Viet Cong) were especially unhappy with us when we were performing our secondary mission of crop destruction in remote areas near the border where their infiltration trails entered South Vietnam. I was lead navigator on a mission to take out rice and banana crops near the A Shau Valley. The target was in a bowl-shaped valley and required three passes for complete coverage. On our first pass we came in low and popped over the ridge surrounding the valley. We caught them by surprise and received only sporadic ground fire. The second pass was quite a different story — they were waiting and ready. We started receiving small-arms fire as soon as we cleared the ridge, and near the middle of the run heavy machine guns opened up. Our flight mechanic tossed a red smoke grenade out the open rear cargo ramp (standard practice when we received heavy fire) and I radioed directions and distance from the smoke to our fighter escort for a strike. As we were coming around for our third pass the fighters put napalm on the spot I had given them. It was the only time I saw napalm used, but it was very effective. It obviously impressed the NVA too — there wasn't a single shot at us during the third pass.

I was at Bien Hoa during the big Tet offensive in 1968. Charlie slammed the base hard with 122-mm rockets and mortar rounds. Fortunately, we had been alerted: our squadron sat out the barrage in bunkers. We didn't take any casualties, but one of our hootches was turned into a parking lot. We spent the rest of the night taking turns at bunker entrances looking across a single barbed-wire fence at the dark and deserted South Vietnamese Air Force compound. The attack slated for our side of the base never took place. We learned later that a South Vietnamese ranger battalion had decimated the Dong Ni

Regiment of the Viet Cong which had been scheduled to hit us.

A couple of weeks after Tet, Charlie dropped in a few rounds of harassing mortar fire around midnight. We waited in the bunkers for two hours before receiving the all clear. Incidentally, we were housed in French-built 8- or 12-man hootches which had screened sides with louvred boards so that the air could circulate. When lying on your bunk you could see outside easily. I had just settled down from the mortar raid when I heard a loud whooshing sound followed by brilliant flashes and tremendous explosions. The flashes approached in a straight line. One of my friends made it over to the bunker without bothering to open the screen door on our hootch — as I recall he suffered a broken toe. I rolled off my bunk and got as flat as possible on the floor. We found out the next day that some idiot was worried about possible infiltrators and had requested a photo run by a reconnaissance jet. What we had seen and heard were photoflash cartridges going off — believe me, they are *loud*.

After a short tour back in the States as a combat crew instructor, I upgraded in a new aircraft and headed back to Southeast Asia for my second combat tour in a "Photo Phantom" (RF-4C). From our base in northeast Thailand, our primary area of operations was Laos and the lower part of North Vietnam. Mainly, we flew over the Ho Chi Minh Trail — the infiltration system that stretched from North Vietnam through Laos to the South. We searched for camouflaged truck parts, enemy movement, supply dumps and gun/missile emplacements. We also ran bomb damage assessment following attacks by our fighters and bombers. In Laos we usually went in alone. However, missions into North Vietnam were usually two-ship formations with a fighter escort. Because we were unarmed, our aircraft had much less drag than the fighters and consequently were much faster. Speed and manoeuverability were our defence, and we soon learned not to take the fighters down with us on our low-level reconnaissance runs. Down low they only slowed us up and they themselves were out of position to attack ground defences. By holding high they could keep us in sight plus spot and attack anyone firing at us. To accomplish our mission we carried forward- and side-looking cameras and split vertical cameras that could be mounted with 3-, 6-, 12- or 18-inch lenses and a 500-foot roll of film. We also had a vertical panoramic camera that produced an 11-inch-wide picture from one horizon to the other, and an excellent IR (infrared) system which produced images, day or night, using external heat sources from the ground. In fact, IR could detect truck engine and campfire heat through the jungle canopy. It was used extensively at night; we only used photoflash cartridges on a few necessary pinpoint targets, because, if you released more than three cartridges in a row, you gave the anti-aircraft gunners a tracking solution.

The daytime over Laos was pretty hot too, especially around congested areas like Tchepone and the main routes leading out of North Vietnam (Mu Gia Pass and Ban Ban Valley, Laos). One of the rules of flying combat is to constantly vary your altitude, speed and heading to ruin tracking solutions. A second is to stay away from cloud bases because the gunners know the precise altitude of the base. Another cardinal rule in reconnaissance is not to make multiple passes over the same target. One day my pilot and I were conducting a medium-level route reconnaissance up Ban Ban Valley from the Plain of Jars into North Vietnam. We were looking for targets of opportunity and thought we saw one. Making a wide sweeping turn we realigned and started down into the area. Naturally, this second pass gave the gunners time to get set, and 37-mm crews opened up on us. Anti-aircraft fire is quite pretty to see; 37-mm looks like iridescent orange softballs, and they seem to move rather slowly as they loop up towards you. We made a hard break and got out of there fast.

Perhaps my most exciting mission was bomb damage assessment following a massive strike on two surface-to-air missile (SAM) sites guarding the NVA supply dumps southeast of Mu Gia Pass. To get good reconnaissance pictures we would have to wait 30 minutes or so after a strike to let the dust settle and the smoke clear. Of course the NVA knew there would be a reconnaissance bird following any big strike. We came in extremely low on a different route than the strike force had taken and used higher terrain to mask our approach. As we cleared the last ridge the target was right in front of us. It had been hit hard. There were still several fires raging and lots of smoke. My pilot pushed the throttles up all the way and popped up to photo altitude. As we sped through the smoke and debris at well over 600 knots, I operated the sensors. We were both so busy we disregarded ground fire. On this particular mission we went straight to Saigon to debrief headquarters intelligence directly because of the urgency.

The closest I ever came to "buying the farm" (being killed) was not as a result of enemy action. We had a mission near Attopeu in southern Laos. As we crossed the Mekong River we encountered thick, solid, low cloud cover over the whole country. Nearing Attopeu we spotted an opening near our target area. Since we could see the ground through the hole we decided to go in after the targets. Rolling inverted, my pilot pulled the nose down in a split-S manoeuvre. As we flashed into the hole we passed within a few feet of an Air America light transport using the same hole to climb out. We passed canopy to canopy, and I could see every feature on his face. It is the closest I've ever come to a mid-air collision.

The air war in Southeast Asia was different from the ground war. It was often exciting and sometimes scary.[19]

NORMAN MALAYNEY

Vietnam: April 1967 to December 1968   Service: Air Force

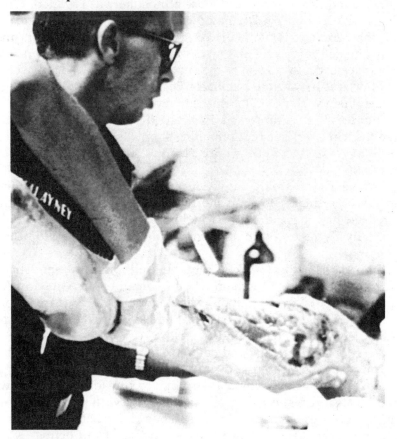

Staff Sergeant Norman Malayney changing the dressing of a wounded soldier, Cam Ranh Bay, September 1968. The wounded man had stepped on a land mine and had a leg blown off. (Courtesy N. Malayney.)

Norman Malayney of Winnipeg spent 19 months, from April 1967 to December 1968, in Vietnam as an air force medic. He recounts some of his experiences:

There were two main embarkation points for U.S. troops shipped to Vietnam: Travis AFB (Air Force Base), California, and McChord AFB, Washington. It was during the evening that my flight left Travis. This was a Pan Am Boeing 707 on contract to move U.S. military personnel to the war zone in Vietnam with destination Saigon. Flights from

McChord landed at Cam Ranh Bay, my assignment area, but for reasons unknown to me the military chose that I go through Travis.

It was a quiet, sombre and tense atmosphere as I waited. First, officers ranking higher than major were allowed to board and claim seats, then down to lieutenant, then non-commissioned officers and finally enlisted privates. Rank has its privileges and the officers had the best seats. As I was one of the very last to board, the only seat I could find was between two colonels. Both were hefty, so I wedged in between them with not much space to move in my seat.

The flight to Saigon was a long one. It took some 26 hours to make the trip over. The first refuelling stop was Hawaii, and then it was on to Wake Island. The entire island was practically covered by runways.

Our next stop was Guam. Several huge black B-52 bombers loaded with ordnance took off shortly after we landed. It seemed the entire base had these aircraft packed in rows on rows. They would eventually fly non-stop to and from South Vietnam to drop their bombs.

The next stop was Clark AFB in the Philippines for another re-fuelling and then on to Vietnam. The descent into Tan Son Nhut Air Base, on the outskirts of Saigon, was steep to avoid any areas con-trolled by the Viet Cong. The base was filled with revetments storing military jets and combat aircraft.

We got off the aircraft and entered the rustic terminal building. An army truck appeared and unloaded our duffle bags in a large mound. Then it was mayhem attempting to spread them out so we could locate our respective gear. A school bus with wire mesh cov-ering the glassless windows took us to our billets to await flights to various regions of the country. I was so tired from being awake during the entire trip that I went immediately to sleep.

Next morning when I awoke I heard some of the fellows talking about the excitement during the night. Unknown to me the VC had possibly probed the perimeter of the base. There was gunfire, and flares lit the sky. A warning was given advising personnel to seek protective cover. Everyone made for the sandbag bunkers except me. Being so tired I had slept through the entire affair.

Eventually, I was provided with transportation and loaded aboard a C-130 aircraft packed with army troops being delivered to various bases. We made several short hops landing to unload men. The inside of the aircraft was literally packed with soldiers lining both sides of the fuselage and in canvas-web racks facing each other. As I looked at the solemn faces I sat silently. I was a stranger among strangers heading for an unknown destiny.

I arrived at Cam Ranh Bay at night. Transportation from the 12th Hospital picked me up and delivered me. I was assigned to the 26th Casualty Staging Unit which was attached to the hospital unit for administrative purposes. My billet was in one of many "hooches" (huts used for housing military personnel).

I awoke in the morning to find myself in what can be considered the middle of a small desert. Cam Ranh is a peninsula that juts out from and parallels the coast of Vietnam helping to form a beautiful turquoise-coloured bay which provides excellent harbouring facilities for ships. The entire peninsula is rock and sand. The heat reflected by the hot sun off the white sand raises the temperature year-round to the 90- to 100-degree range. The army had a huge logistics complex at the southern end that supplied troops with ammunition, fuel and any other wartime material. The navy had two areas. One was along the seaside where boats were located to patrol the sea coast. Near the northern end were two 10,000-foot runways, one made of concrete and the other of steel matting. U.S. Air Force Phantom and Caribou aircraft were revetted on the east side of the runway, while the navy had patrol aircraft on the west side. The army's 7th Convalescent Center was located at the northern part of the base.

The entire hospital complex had a thousand beds. Wounded troops who required less than 30 days to recover stayed at the 12th Hospital. Those with wounds requiring more time to heal were temporarily held at the 26th, then loaded aboard transport aircraft for air-evacuation to Japan or the U.S.A. The 26th was a holding area where wounded were triaged or sorted according to the extent of their wounds. Severity determined whether a casualty would be sent to the 12th Hospital or evacuated to Japan.

It was around three in the morning on 31 January that everyone in our hooch was awakened and notified a red alert was on. In the distance explosions could be heard. Unknown to us the Communists had launched a nation-wide attack which became known as the Tet offensive. Tet is a traditional Vietnamese holiday. It celebrates the beginning of the lunar new year. It had been customary during the Vietnam War to observe a cease-fire during the Tet holidays. The Communists caught everyone by surprise.

So massive was the Communist attack that all out-country air traffic was closed down. All except Cam Ranh Bay. The South Korean 9th (White Horse) Division protected its approaches and managed to blunt any Communist hope of inflicting damage on this installation. With wounded from the field hospitals building up and with air traffic closed out of other major installations such as Da Nang and Saigon, the wounded were boarded on C-130 and C-123 aircraft to

Cam Ranh. During the first 48 hours our unit received 500 casualties and they kept coming and coming. As fast as they arrived, the wounded had their dressings changed, were fed and washed, then loaded onto C-141 aircraft for safe transport to Japan or else onto C-130 aircraft for the flight to the Philippines.

All the badly wounded brought on stretchers were handled by us, while walking wounded were temporarily housed at the 12th Hospital. The 12th, in turn, set up portable cots in storage hangars to house their walking wounded. Upon arrival of air-evacuation we would empty our wards and haul out the wounded from the 12th and load them onto aircraft. At the same time as unloading was taking place, in-country aircraft landed and their wounded were loaded onto our field ambulance and litter carrying buses, and brought to the 26th for immediate care and treatment. This went on around the clock.

The 26th was like a butcher shop with tons of open meat uncovered during the dressing changes. It was a hectic pace with many of the nurses working 24 hours non-stop. The lights stayed on all night and the work never ended. No sooner were wounded transported out of our unit than the doors opened and more flooded in.

It is difficult to describe the activities at our unit except that I never want to go through Tet again with so many wounded. The wounded talked about where they came from and what they saw. We learned from these eyewitnesses of the massive assault launched by the Communists throughout the country. It was only later, as the U.S. forces repelled the attack, that the full extent of what had transpired became known.

From 31 January to 11 February 1968 the Communists lost some 30,000 dead. By the end of February estimated Communist losses were 40,000 dead. The U.S. had close to 1,000 dead. By this time, some two or three weeks after the offensive began, the U.S. Marines were still fighting in Hue to root out the Communists in house-to-house fighting. We received plane load after plane load of wounded marines who provided graphic details of the fighting taking place. The Citadel was held by Communist forces and this was slowly being blown to pieces by ground and aerial bombardment while marines slowly cleaned up the areas having pockets of resistance. Then we heard all kinds of stories of mass graves that were found with dead Vietnamese civilians the Communists executed when they took control.

During the Tet offensive, besides battle casualties, we had men with self-inflicted wounds. The easiest way to get out of action was to shoot yourself in the leg or have someone shoot you. These were desperate times when all hell broke loose and death appeared imminent.

During the month of February one of our male nurses was sick from the carnage passing through our unit and went to the psych ward for a rest. But things became so bad that in order to handle all the wounded flowing in, we had to haul him out and put him to work in his pyjamas. Such was Tet.

In combat freak wounds occur. One fellow suffered an injury which resulted in all four limbs being amputated. Only six-inch stumps remained of each limb. He was once over six feet but was now reduced to a torso with a head. The medics and nurses were traumatized by this horrible disfigurement such that most were afraid to approach him.

The most massive wound I witnessed was one soldier with wounds to his back. The nurse assigned to redo the dressing removed the burn-pack dressing that covered the entire back area and nearly fainted when the extent of the wound was revealed. You could see every single muscle that glistened white and blue just like in an anatomy textbook.

I will always remember my first combat casualty die. It is forever part of my being. He was 23 years old. He had suffered a chest wound in a firefight and was not found until 48 hours later. The army mobile hospital tried their best to keep him alive and shipped him to us. The doctors gave him antibiotics with intravenous fluids and blood, but it was obvious that we were losing him. I never felt so helpless in my life. His breathing became more and more shallow until the medical staff pronounced him dead.

I assisted one of the medics pack the body, a task I had not done before. Both hands and legs were crossed and identification tags attached. Then one of the metal dog tags was removed from the leather strip to which it was attached around his neck. The dog tag was placed inside the mouth against the cheek and the mouth closed. Should somehow the identification tags be lost, at least the dog tag inside the mouth would still help to identify the deceased. We then wrapped the body in a plastic shroud and slipped it into a body bag. We transported the remains to a portable reefer until arrangements were made for shipment of the body to either Saigon or Qui Nhon where a civilian U.S. organization had embalming facilities prior to its transport back to the United States.

In our unit many of the posts at the heads of the beds were bent and twisted out of shape. This came about because the patients would grab on to the rails when their dressings were being changed. The guys would never utter a word or cry but just grimace from the excruciating pain as we removed their soiled dressings and applied new ones.

One patient who had lost a leg pulled out a little matchbox to show me. In it he had a human ear from the enemy all packed away with salt. A huge, soft-spoken black pulled out of his bag a necklace consisting of shrivelled-up human ears, each one spray-painted different colours and placed them around his neck. The different colours signified the various ways he had killed each person such as shooting, torture, or stabbing with a bayonet. He seemed the kindest, gentlest, most considerate person I had met. He had lost a lot of his friends early in his tour.

Another fellow in our ward was brought in from the jungles with massive wounds to his foot. Apparently a tiger had grabbed him by the foot while he slept at night and was dragging him off until his screams wakened his buddies who rescued him.

Wounds ran the gamut, including a South Vietnamese soldier with no lower jaw, a young Vietnamese girl with almost no face and three Americans with 80 per cent burns to their body.

One patient would continually go to an open latrine, deliberately get dirty and then wash himself off with cold water and return to bed all wet. I guess he was washing away his sins. It became necessary to transfer him to the psych ward where they tied him to his bed with leather straps and shipped him out.

I was stationed at Kontum in September 1968. A few American patients recounted seeing in the field a dead black and a dead white whose heads had been switched by the enemy. Other patients told of witnessing a dead comrade whose genitals had been sewn into his mouth by the Viet Cong. Early one morning a nurse discovered a Viet Cong POW patient decapitated. The culprit was never found.

I spent several days in Saigon. During the daytime along the street there were vendors under colourful tarpaulins selling food as well as black market goods taken from the American PXs. It was hot and muggy. The humidity just stuck all over you. You could never get rid of it once your fatigues were damp with sweat. All the trees in Saigon were dead, apparently as a result of the exhaust fumes from vehicles, mainly motor bikes and motor scooters. At night air force fixed-wing gunships nicknamed "Puff, the Magic Dragon" fired their machine guns into suspected Viet Cong positions around the perimeter of Tan Son Nhut Air Base. Bars were loaded with prostitutes trying to get GIs to go in.

After a year, most of the guys I was with rotated back to the States but I was still there. I had extended my tour for another six months. There had been a great esprit de corps and camaraderie among the first group.

Day after day we would send out patients and then get new ones. It got to me. I saw every imaginable form of human disfigurement. More stretchers, more wounded; there was always something new and terrible. It was carnage.[20]

JAMES M

Vietnam: 1967 to 1968   Service: Navy

James M, who wishes to remain anonymous, enlisted in May 1966 in the U.S. Navy. He took his basic training at the Great Lakes Naval Training Center at Waukegan, Illinois. As well as military drill, there were tests to determine his abilities. He showed an aptitude for radio work but would have preferred working in shipping and receiving. However, he ended up going to Newport, Rhode Island, beginning in July 1966, for eight weeks' training as a cook. At Groton, Connecticut, Jim took additional training at submarine school but dropped out. He was reassigned to Vietnam. Was this a reward or a punishment? At Norfolk, Virginia, there was more training. All the instructors were Vietnam veterans. Prior to going to Vietnam, Seaman M was posted to the naval air station at Imperial Beach just south of San Diego. He would be going to a naval helicopter squadron in Vietnam as a cook.

Why did the navy use its own helicopters in Vietnam? Initially, air cover was given to the navy by the army. It quickly became evident to the navy that their requirements were not being met; thus, they created their own helicopter unit to give support to their river patrol boats.

On 15 June 1967, Seaman M arrived in South Vietnam. He was sent to a naval helicopter combat support squadron at Vung Tau. He was kept occupied cooking for 150 sailors who were within the base of the 765th Transportation Battalion of 1,500 men. Although Jim worked in an army mess, he tried his best to satisfy the navy personnel who were accustomed to the better navy food.

The following observations provide some insight as to what Vietnam was like for Jim:

I left San Francisco 15 June 1967 in dress blues, 100 per cent wool, because California was not in summer uniform. Tan Son Nhut Airport, Saigon, was about 120 degrees Fahrenheit in the shade at 10:00 — but there was no shade. Upon arrival, we were sent to Military Assistance Command Vietnam (MACV) headquarters for welcoming, uniforms and finally weapons. We were informed that if we managed to stay alive throughout our first 30 days in country, we would probably live until we had reached our last 30 days and if we didn't get careless, we would probably make it home....

The Annapolis Hotel, Saigon, was owned and operated under the auspices of Naval Forces, Vietnam. What a hole! Plaster fell everywhere when Saigon was under attack. The safest place was in the doorways between rooms. And stink! No running water. The water closets were enamelled holes in the floor with small pads to use as foot rests. You just squatted, did your job and got out.

During the next two to three days at "welcome aboard" lectures, we were cautioned. Helpful hints like never drink from a bottle that is opened out of sight, that soda pop may be battery acid. Don't accept packages from sweet, smiling kids. They may be carrying live grenades.

Although I got my orders to report to Helicopter Attack (Light) Squadron Three, in Vung Tau, I got sidetracked at Can Tho for 32 days. This was a SEAL (navy special sea, air, land warfare force) and river patrol boat-operating base. I stood a lot of guard duty here. Pointing a loaded M-14 at a dirty-faced, smiling five-year-old begging for food made me sick. About the damnedest thing I ever saw at Can Tho was this old Vietnamese who drove up to the garbage cans behind the mess hall every night about sundown in a pony cart to dip up enough slop for his family's next day's meals.

I finally arrived at Vung Tau. The squadron's personnel officer asked how long I had been in the country. I said 33 or 34 days and asked why? He said he thought I had become eligible for promotion because of the time I had spent in country already. Six months later, I became a petty officer 3rd class for the same reason.

One incident really changed my attitude toward the use of the word military and intelligence in the same sentence. We, who were being shelled almost daily, were told to crate our weapons for shipment to Saigon for reissue because we were in a "safe" area. Two days after we complied with this order, we were surrounded by the enemy in battalion strength and spent the next two weeks running for the sandbagged bunkers almost nightly until the army blew away Uncle Ho's troops.

At this time there was a study being done by the U.S. Air Force as to the reality of unidentified flying objects. The conclusion of the study was that they did not exist. The navy printers made up some decals which read "UFOs are real, the USAF does not exist." They were stuck on several air force vehicles. In retaliation somebody teargassed the naval barracks. Some guys just have no sense of humour!

To me the war was, well, not a hot firefight, not long-range reconnaissance missions or the usual shooting war that was televised on the six o'clock news, but it was more a year of living with the idea that there are people out there who want to kill me and I don't know who they are. I can't kill them because my orders don't allow me to return fire unless I have a clearly identifiable target. But the rockets keep coming in, so maybe I won't see tomorrow....

At last my DEROS (date eligible for return from overseas) had arrived! I don't think I kissed the ground good-bye, but I felt like it.[21]

About July 1968, Jim arrived at Argentia, where he spent some two years working in the mess hall. He met and married a Newfoundlander in 1969. Jim experienced flashbacks and nightmares. This problem and extended naval service contributed to the breakdown of his marriage. After serving a total of 10 years in the U.S. Navy, he was honourably discharged as a petty officer 1st class in 1976 and returned to St. John's, Newfoundland.

THOMAS HILL

Vietnam: September 1967 to April 1969   Service: Army

Thomas Hill of Ohsweken, Ontario, was born on 22 May 1945. He joined the U.S. Army in Buffalo, New York, in April 1967 for a three-year stint. Tom arrived in Vietnam in September 1967. Most of the time was spent in III Corps area around Saigon. Specialist Four Hill performed a wide variety of duties, mostly bulldozing brush. In spite of hitting mines or collapsing tunnels, he was never injured. As well as tearing up the jungle, Tom was kept busy building and repairing roads and landing zones. Following Vietnam, he completed his service in the U.S. Army at Fort Hood, Texas.

Tom tells his story:

For my three loving children — Andrea, Sean and Tyler

There were about two inches of slush and snow already on the ground on 17 April 1967 and it was snowing as I left Buffalo to begin my service in the U.S. Army. When I arrived in Atlanta, it was 75 degrees. Right off the bus which took us to Fort Benning we were given haircuts and then uniforms. Every move was at double time.

After eight weeks I graduated from basic training. I was loaded on a Greyhound bus and taken to Fort Leonard Wood, Missouri. The engineers' school there was more relaxed than basic training. I started the first week of orientation on the D-7 tractor (dozer), the next week it was a Caterpillar 12 heavy road grader, the third week a front-end loader, and the fourth week I trained on a rather new type of scraper the army had started using. This was called the 290M all-hydraulic scraper (Caterpillar 4x4 wheeled tractor). The tractor part weighed approximately 25 tons, the scraper part maybe 18 to 20 tons. When fully loaded it weighed about 65 to 70 tons. I became quite proficient at operating this piece of equipment so they gave me advanced individual training for the next two and a half weeks. Then I received orders to go to the 90th Replacement Battalion, Long Binh, South Vietnam.

I came home for 15 days' leave, then I reported back at Fort Dix, New Jersey. From there I went to Anchorage, then Wake Island and, finally, Tan Son Nhut Air Base in Saigon. It was near the monsoon season, September 1967. As we approached the air base in a thunder storm at three o'clock in the morning, the plane began rocking and bouncing around with lightning flashing outside. The plane had all its interior lights off to make it a more difficult target. It was very stressful for a few new arrivals who began shouting that we were being fired upon because the blue flashes from the lightning made eerie patterns inside the aircraft.

We landed and were transported by bus from the air base to near Long Binh. Armed jeeps escorted us up the highway. Nothing happened to us along the way, but we could see flares off in the distance along with tracer rounds from the mini-guns on the helicopter gunships.

After a quick head count, we were issued combat helmets and flak jackets and shown bunkers where to run or crawl in the event of a mortar attack. There was no such attack but I slept for awhile with my helmet and flak jacket on. That afternoon I was assigned to the 92nd Engineer Battalion (Construction). I arrived at 5:30 p.m. in time for chow, but found it hard adjusting to the food. Everything was dehydrated to powder and the taste was different.

After being around the 92nd headquarters at Long Binh for a couple of weeks, I went to a small camp. We were widening a road for a shortcut to the 25th Infantry Division. The camp itself was under the control of the 1st Infantry Division. I stayed there for about three months. While I was there, a cook got his leg blown off by one of the kids he fed with leftovers from the cook tent.

Making this road wider took tons and tons of fill. Every morning the road had to be cleared for land mines. Sometimes we handled our own security but mostly the 1st Infantry Division would do this so that we could go on with our construction.

We were all transferred back to Long Binh a couple of days before Christmas. We worked on repairing our equipment and coordinating our defences. We were told that in all probability our area would be a target area. We made more sandbags to protect our tents and reinforce our bunkers but the attack never happened in my area.

The Viet Cong did mortar a supply area and started huge fires. I was assigned to drive a five-ton tractor with a 5,000-gallon water tanker. I would haul water to a pumper to pour on the fires. The hardest hit area was the north side of Bien Hoa Air Base and the supply area.

After things cooled down a bit, our unit was assigned to the 1st Infantry Division at a place called Di An. I operated a 290M scraper and a D-7 dozer. With the D-7 I cleared jungle along the road.

I remember once I was highballing at about 40 mph when I sideswiped a water buffalo on the road. It cost the U.S. Army about $200 to replace the buffalo. They didn't know who hit the buffalo because I didn't stop. The risk of ambush or of a sniper was too high.

At Di An we got new D-9 dozers. They really had power and they were huge. From Di An, I moved along with my unit to Phu Cuong. There a couple of spans of a new bridge had been blown by underwater sappers. When we arrived we helped put in a pontoon float bridge. Mortar attacks were consistent almost every night between 2 and 3 a.m. It would be a few rounds and then end. During one mortar attack, they blew up part of our tent and killed the guy next to me who had only been in Vietnam a month. After that a few of us moved under the bridge.

I came home in September for some 30 days. It was rather uncomfortable for me at Oakland army base because there were protestors outside the gate. I felt angry because they called us "killers" of so-called innocent Vietnamese. There were six of us GIs. Together we came out of the gate to catch a taxi to San Francisco airport. Spontaneously these 10 or so protestors were given a few good lumps before we jumped into taxis and were gone.

I came back to Buffalo and tried to relax but I found I was pretty jumpy. I remember the food was good after a year of dehydrated potatoes, eggs and milk. After leave, I headed back for the six more months of duty which I had requested.

Upon my return I was sent to Bear Cat where the Royal Thailand Army was stationed. Our unit cleared jungle around their area. While there a Thai soldier was shot in the back of the head by the sergeant of the guard for sleeping on guard duty in a combat zone.

I rotated home for the final time in May 1969 before heading for Fort Hood. I was assigned to a maintenance unit supporting the 1st and 2nd Armored Divisions. My adjustment was a bit uncomfortable for the first three or four days. It was like starting basic training over again. I stayed only about three weeks with this unit and got a

Tilling a paddy in I Corps, South Vietnam, 1966. (Courtesy K. McVeigh/CVVO.)

transfer to 664 Ordnance Unit. I would have reached the rank of SP-5 (specialist five) if I hadn't beaten up two recruits in a bar in Temple, Texas. My promotion was rescinded but I got an honourable discharge.

I next went to work at construction on a steam power generating station at Stony Point on the Hudson River. I found construction workers were more supportive than any other working-class type of people. But after work I would make a mad dash to the local bar to relax.

I got married in 1973. The marriage didn't last long — about two and a half years. My wife couldn't understand my unacceptable behaviour. My attitude, boozing and smoking were blamed on my Vietnam experience. I would have stayed married had I sought help but I just ran away and came back to Canada.

I stifled my feelings about Vietnam for a long time. I had guilt feelings because I survived and I had a lot of anger and hostility. My way of earning respect was to drink more alcohol and smoke more pot than the other people with whom I associated. I have been charged in several American states and Canada for assault. There are quite a few punch-outs that were never reported. I now have had counselling for my guilt feelings for being a survivor and also for the angry, hostile attitude that caused my unacceptable behaviour. A drug-abuse recovery program is now working for me.[22]

HOWARD WALKER

Vietnam: October 1967 to July 1970   Service: Army

Staff Sergeant Howard Walker and a Vietnamese family, 1968. (Courtesy H.W. Walker.)

Howard Walker was born in Verdun, Quebec, in 1939. He enlisted in the U.S. Army on 13 June 1966 for the purpose of going to fight in Vietnam. There he was with the 1st Battalion, 6th Infantry (Regiment), 198th Brigade of the Americal Division, from 4 October 1967 until 10 July 1970. Walker served in the southern part of I Corps. He was battalion ammunition chief and later on he became a platoon leader in Delta Company. Some of the letters he wrote from Vietnam to his sister, her husband and their son follow.

17 October 1967
mid-Pacific Ocean

Dear Jean, George and Randy,

Before boarding the USS *Upshur* in Oakland, we were met by the Red Cross and given coffee and doughnuts.... Fourteen days have gone by and still no land. Tomorrow we are due to arrive in Okinawa.

Our accommodations are not the very best, in fact, they are pretty bad. The food tastes awful. The first five days most everyone was sick, and I mean sick. I am sitting on the foredeck writing this letter and the wind is pretty strong and the boat is rocking and rolling. Four more days and we'll be in Vietnam.

The weather is in the high eighties at night. There is now a shortage of shower water which makes my compartment smell sweaty. The water is getting rough now so I'll close. Thinking of you all the time.

Howard

31 October 1967

Dear Jean, George and Randy,

Since leaving Chu Lai I have been part of an advance party for my battalion. We were airlifted into a place just a few klicks from Duc Pho. It is a very mountainous region with a lot of rice paddies. The weather gets real hot and it usually rains during the night. We are being kept busy with the ammunition. We are not getting too much sleep as our guns are harassing us, although, as you know, they are supposed to harass the enemy.

We are getting two C-ration meals and one hot meal but we also get plenty of goodies what they call a Sundry Packet — cigarettes, candy, razor blades, writing paper, pens and just about everything you can think of. Each day we take malaria pills and so now I am wondering if they do any good as I am being bitten by mosquitoes.

I just gave myself what is known as a steel pot bath. I took off my helmet, put water in it and bathed myself. It must be damn near one in the morning so I thought I had better get this letter off before I retire for the night.

Howard

10 November 1967

Dear Jean, George and Randy,

Yesterday I was confronted with one of the saddest experiences in my life. In the afternoon of yesterday a helicopter set down on the heliport and exploded. The cause has not been determined. It had five people on board. Since I was in the closest tent to the area I saw two men being hurled in the air on fire. When I ran out the machine guns that are on the copters were firing by themselves as the heat from the fire was so great. The gunner of the copter ran toward me yelling for me to help him. He was covered in gasoline and was bleeding terribly. I got him in my arms to help him lie down. I noticed that he not only was burnt bad but also had four bullet holes in his chest and was bleeding from his mouth. A medic came to give him some morphine and moments later he died. There were as I said before five people and in less than five minutes I saw three of them die.

That night when I got ready for bed I couldn't sleep and I kept hearing that young boy asking me to help him and I couldn't. It choked me after so much that tears came to my eyes.

Not all the time sad things happen. Today the captain introduced me to another captain and a warrant officer from the Australian 2nd Division. They were as glad as I was when the captain told them I was their only Canadian. Boy, they shook my hand and started talking about Canada and brought ice-cold beer out and we had a damn good time. They went off later to join their Vietnamese battalion in which they act as advisors.

I am in charge of civil affairs in the village area near our camp for our battalion. Each morning I go into the village and gather a dozen or so workers. I put them on the truck and take them to wherever they work and then stand guard on them all day. I have to see that they don't get to see too much that is going on in my base camp as the peasants could be friendly during the day and hostile at night....

I hope all are well.

Howard

23 December 1967
Nouc Mau

Dear Jean, George and Randy,

Yesterday the children, about 40 of them, from a village north of Nouc Mau, raided our perimeter and looted a building. They ran off with a movie camera and a still camera, army clothing, cigarettes, soap and just about anything that a soldier has lying around. My men and myself gave chase and we had to fire a couple of shots over their heads before they would stop. They were so frightened that down deep I felt sorry for them. We caught a woman who had some army clothing in the rafters of her house so we took her back to the base for questioning. She later revealed to us the whereabouts and hiding places of stolen things.

I told about 20 of them that for each day that my men went without their cameras an ear would fall. Boy, did they ever listen to me! They all started to squeal on one another and turned in a whole pile of stuff that didn't even belong to my men. They have a terrible fear when they die if all the parts of their body are not with them, they will not go to heaven.

Two more days and it's Xmas time. A cease-fire will be observed by us and I hope the VC will honour our holidays and we will honour their holiday next month. They have a four-day holiday for the New Year starting at the end of January — around the 29th to the 3rd of February....

Howard

26 February 1968

Dear Jean, George and Randy,

Today I went north on what I thought was going to be a search-and-clear mission. But it turned out to be security for a mine-sweeping team clearing Highway 1 north to a Korean Marine camp south of Da Nang. The minesweeping team found some wires and Charlie opened up. After lying prone for five minutes we decided to move out. Another Charlie fired a shot that cracked over my right ear. Boy, did I move fast for a 28-year-old. Then we moved in closer and a single shot whistled off to the right. Into the mud I went for the third time. Then the lieutenant decided that there wasn't enough of us so we called for armoured personnel carriers.

This action took place outside a village. While going through the village a Viet Cong shot at us again. I ran so fast trying to get cover for myself that I ran right through a fence and into the main room of a cement house as there was no front door. There were Vietnamese in the house but all were lying on the floor. Not knowing if these people were VC sympathizers or not I told them that the first person who moved towards me would get crocodiled. All Vietnamese know this word means killed. I no sooner got the table turned over and put it across the door, so I could rest my weapon to shoot across the rice paddy, when I heard a baby crying. So I jumped over the table and scooped him up and jumped back into the house hearing bullets whining all around me. The baby ran over to a man hiding in the open part of a fireplace which was used as a bunker. I cursed that individual for leaving the little kid outside while he had sought shelter. The whole family caught on what I was trying to say and they all started pointing their fingers at him and shouting to him in Vietnamese what I had just said in English.

If I were scared, I would worry. But I am not scared. Frightened yes, but not scared.

Your brother

Howard

Hat worn by Staff Sergeant Howard Walker, Vietnam, 1969. (Courtesy H.M. Walker.)

13 May 1968

Dear Jean, George and Randy,

Last night one of my squad leaders was throwing some garbage in a bomb crater to the left of my bunker. He noticed a little air hole in the ground and saw an AK-47 (Chinese Communist automatic rifle). He yelled to me that he found this weapon. Then he saw a hand come up and grab the weapon. My bunker was close by so I grabbed a machine gun, stuck the barrel in the hole and let go with 50 rounds. Then my radio telephone operator came up and threw two grenades in the hole. After the smoke cleared we dug the roof off this guy's hiding place. We pulled this guy out and he was one hell of a mess. We discovered a large tunnel complex. The 1st platoon are checking it out.

We figure that this guy was hiding in the hole for at least five days and was waiting for us to move out. I don't know how they do it. He must have been starving or dying of thirst. I am going to close for now.

Howard

P.S. Thanks for the hockey book. I read it and showed it to guys with me from Chicago. I've got to keep reminding them who has the best hockey team.

23 May 1968

Dear Jean, George and Randy,

I am now, believe it or not, platoon leader which is a 2nd lieutenant's position. I am glad that it is only temporary and within a couple of days a lieutenant will be out to command my small force. Our company used to be 153 and now we number a little over 70. My platoon is down from 35 men to 18. Yesterday my platoon joined the 3rd platoon who are down to 13 men. I was put in charge of our move to another landing zone. Everybody else was airlifted but orders were changed and we had to walk.

My point element hit a booby trap, knocking down seven men. Two might not walk again. You should have seen the trouble I had controlling the men. Half of them went hysterical. One grabbed a machine gun and wanted to kill us all. I had to get a helicopter in to take the wounded out. The helicopter finally came but I had to carry the wounded to a landing zone more than 100 metres away. Everybody was screaming and I had to hit two men to quieten them down. I had a lot of guys who said they wouldn't go further on foot. The colonel reconsidered his orders and sent in helicopters to get my men out.

This mountain smells so bad from death that I feel like putting on my gas mask. I'll be OK and home soon.

Howard

3 June 1968

Dear Jean, George and Randy,

For the last two weeks we have been living in the jungle. It rains every day and writing paper is scarce. Today is the first day that we stopped and that is because we are so wet. We are suffering from exposure. I just cleaned my weapon and thought I'd drop you these few lines.

Two nights ago I got nicknamed John Wayne because I charged up a hill firing my M-16 killing a few North Vietnamese who were dug in in what was supposed to be our night laager (a place to camp). But they got there before us. I jumped into one of their trenches and captured an AK-47 but had to retreat as there were too many of them. I was deaf for about 12 hours as grenades landed near me as I attacked their forward position. I guess they were surprised to see me get up the hill so fast because four of them stood up firing their automatic assault weapons at me and, luckily for me, they missed. I assure you I won't do this again.

My point had been leading and when we got into action, we had to drop our rucksacks to manoeuvre better and faster. When we saw that the rest of the company was having difficulty getting up to where we were, we had to beat it leaving behind, of course, my rucksack with my food, your tape, cigars (40), letters, plus my Canadian flag that I always carry.

I can see those damn North Vietnamese reading my letters, listening to my tape, smoking my cigars, eating my rations and using my air mattress. By the way, my M-16 jammed up on me at one time when I found myself in a crossfire from the ginks higher up on the hill so I used the AK-47 on them bringing one of them down.

Howard

20 June 1968

Dear Jean, George and Randy,

Remember me telling you not long ago about the point men and four stepping on a booby trap. Well, I received a letter from one of the men and he tells me he is bad physically but will pull through in time. The other man is mentally disturbed but will also pull through in time. The others are well and are back in the field.

This is not one of my best letters as I'm physically and mentally tired. Walking all night leading the men is taking a lot out of me. Fourteen hours a day walking in the jungle searching for the enemy is nerve-wracking but I have only 110 more days left to do. Sure will be nice to close both my ears, both my eyes and sleep for a few silent hours.

Howard

23 June 1968

Dear Jean, George and Randy,

Last night the patrol caught an old man in the outskirts of his village fiddling with a drainage pipe for irrigating the rice paddy. Because we were a little more cautious, this man is alive today. He doesn't know how lucky he is because the new rules of engagement during the hours of darkness are to shoot to kill any moving object outside the village. The man was so scared when I questioned him that he just fell down shaking. I feel good I didn't shoot an old man just because he had to get his water running into the rice paddy. I guess he never thought we would come back through his village as we had passed through it about four hours prior.

Howard

28 June 1968

Dear Jean, George and Randy,

This morning while on patrol I asked and received permission to take a few men and search out a village near my area of operations. I ended up capturing 18 young men, half of whom are hard-core VC, the other half sympathizers. I didn't even have to fire a shot. We broke into the village just as it was getting light and caught half of them sleeping. This doesn't happen too often. I marched them back to my company commander and you should have seen his eyes — just like Eddie Cantor. He radioed the colonel and he came out with some local police and took them away for questioning.

I must look mean because when I look at these people they seem to tremble. It must be my Alpine hat with my red handkerchief tied around my neck. My tone of voice must have something to do with it also.

Keep me a cool beer. Boy, could I go for one now. Haven't had a beer in so long I don't remember what it tastes like.

Howard

3 September 1968

Dear Jean, George and Randy,

The VC blew a bridge to our north which is used extensively along our supply routes. This bridge was guarded by South Vietnam's Popular Forces — a group of men forced into the army. They are not good-disciplined soldiers but when the going gets hot, they sure can run fast (the other way).

Yesterday we reached a top of a mountain that is well over 2,100 feet above sea level. On this hill was a little bombed-out clearing which not long ago belonged to the 2nd NVA (North Vietnamese Army) Division. Today it is ours. But my platoon paid for it. I lost two men yesterday. They paid for this lousy piece of jungle terrain that took us three days to climb — one and a half days without food or water.

It was yesterday afternoon that they got killed as my platoon was walking along a trail. The NVA cut us up bad. The rain and clouds would not permit us to medevac them. Today they lie beside my bunker. My eyes are full of tears and my heart is broken....

Staff Sergeant Howard Walker stayed in the U.S. Army after Vietnam. Upon his return to the United States, Howard was assigned as an instructor to the Allied Officer School at Fort Knox, Kentucky. He trained Cam-

bodians and Laotians in anti-tank warfare. During a field training exercise he suffered permanent hearing damage as a result of being caught in the back-blast area of a 106-mm recoilless rifle. He was assigned to the medical field. While a non-commissioned officer at Fitzsimons Army Medical Center, Aurora, Colorado, from August 1977 to January 1986, he fell in love with the area. On 1 February 1988 he retired as a master sergeant. He lives in Aurora, where he keeps busy as a recreational fisherman most of the time. Howard remains a Canadian citizen and proud of it.[23]

TIMOTHY LABUTE

Vietnam: October 1967 to November 1968   Service: Army

Tim LaBute was born in Windsor, Ontario, on 14 May 1947. When he was age 10, his family moved for economic reasons to the east side of Detroit. As their house was getting too small for six other brothers and sisters, they moved to Mount Clemens, Michigan, where Tim attended high school. In August 1966 he received a draft notice. Still being a Canadian citizen, he could have moved back to Canada but decided not to. Rather than serve two years as an infantryman, he signed up for three years in the hope of getting into the aviation branch.

In September 1966 Tim was sent to Fort Knox, Kentucky, but because there was no room there, he was sent along with many other new recruits for eight weeks' basic training at Fort Lewis, Washington. He was able to fulfil his wish for the aviation branch when he was sent to Fort Rucker, Alabama, in November. There he had line maintenance training on the 0-1 Bird Dog observation plane, the CH-47 Chinook helicopter and especially the UH-1 Huey helicopter. During the Christmas holidays and while on leave, he visited family in Canada, where he could have remained.

In February 1967 Tim was sent to Fort Carson, Colorado, where he joined the 195th Assault Helicopter Company, part of the 12th Group, 1st Aviation Brigade, for service in Vietnam. While at Fort Carson, the FBI checked his security, even extending its questioning into Canada. Being an alien, Tim had to sign a waiver like all other foreigners, agreeing to serve in the Vietnam combat zone. He received additional training until October. Then he was crammed aboard a troopship along with 3,200 others bound for Vietnam. After a slow trip across the Pacific to Vung Tau, his unit was moved ashore by shallow boats and thence by Caribou aircraft to Bien Hoa. His UH-1C Huey helicopter, nicknamed the Raped Ape because it moved quickly, sometimes carried a Canadian flag, courtesy of Tim. He served as a helicopter crew chief, which meant among other things being a door gunner, and was with the same helicopter throughout his tour.

Corporal Timothy LaBute in Vietnam, January 1968. (Courtesy T. LaBute.)

The citations for the medals he received provide an indication of Tim's missions. Shortly after he arrived, Tim earned the Soldier's Medal for "giving assistance to the victims of an airplane crash. He utilized his own clothing to extinguish the flames on one victim who was attempting to crawl from the flaming wreckage, and removed him to safety. He then found another victim pinned to the ground by the ship, and with assistance succeeded in freeing the victim. His courage throughout the hour long rescue operation was instrumental in the saving of five human lives."

Tim, along with another crew member, was awarded the Army Commendation Medal with "V" device for heroism for "valorous action while serving on an armed UH-1C helicopter gunship during the extraction of a besieged six man reconnaissance team under intense fire and in danger of being overrun. Departing Dau Tieng (1 August 1968) under adverse weather, they assisted the aircraft commander in clearing the aircraft to prevent a possible mid-air collision. Flying at tree top level to the area of the imperiled team, they kept constant vigilance on the jungle floor for enemy ground fire. Arriving on location they spotted several enemy positions and silenced several of them with their machine guns. Despite furious enemy fire, they leaned outside of the aircraft and drove the enemy to flight with devastating fire. As a result the team was safely extracted."

Tim recalls the most strenuous period of his tour — the Tet offensive:

During early 1968, the Communists had been building up their forces. The evening of Tet on 31 January was quiet until about 3 a.m. Then we began getting heavily mortared. Our helicopter was one of the first in the air. As soon as we took off from our encampment, which at this time was at Bien Hoa, the helicopter was hit five times and forced to land. At eight o'clock that morning, about a mile away, the enemy blew up the ammunition dump. At first there were several small explosions followed by a big mushroom cloud. One could see the aftershock heading towards us. It shattered the windows and even moved our building over six inches.

Amidst the fighting I was trying to help repair our helicopter. I jumped on another helicopter in order to do some gun runs (strafes) in the area. When I got back to the base about five hours later, my ship was in working condition. I then carried on flying. When I stopped, 52 hours had elapsed from the first mortaring.

During the Tet offensive the enemy was very much in evidence and could be easily identified by flags flying. Prior to Tet, we were always firing at treelines and were never sure who was the enemy. Initially, we flew missions around our camp area for half a day and then we were called down in support of the Australians at Ba Ria near Nui Dat mountain. The town of Ba Ria had been completely taken over by the enemy.

We were doing gun runs when we saw a group of the enemy in black pyjamas running for a Buddhist pagoda. It was a forbidden target, but our rockets somehow strayed into it. We had 10 confirmed killed from that incident.

Soon after we were called to Saigon because the Viet Cong were trying to take over the American embassy. We went in and scattered people. Then we did four or five gun runs to help out some MPs held down by enemy fire.

We made our way back to our home base when we noticed muzzle flashes from mortars firing into our base. I guess the enemy didn't notice us. We had a few rounds and a couple of rockets left which we fired, silencing that position, and headed back to base.

By this time we were all almost zombies from exhaustion. As part of our landing procedure on this helicopter the mini-guns had to be rotated and a rod put through so that the unexpended rounds wouldn't fire. My wingman had forgotten to do that. After we landed and pulled into our revetment, he pushed his mini-gun down and one of the unexpended rounds went off wounding him in the heel. He didn't feel it because of utter fatigue. In a calm manner he informed me what had happened. After bandaging him up, we sent him to first aid. In due course, he was sent home.

For much of my later tour, my company was stationed in the central highlands with the Green Berets. We usually flew missions along the Ho Chi Minh Trail two or three hours a day, just moving people — often two Americans and three counter-insurgents, normally Thais or Cambodians. If they got in trouble, we went in to extricate them. I remember once we flew into Cambodia and were chased out by a MiG piloted by a Russian.

After completing his tour in Vietnam, Tim was assigned to Fort Benning, Georgia. For three months he was crew chief of an air ambulance retrieving injured, including those hurt in parachute training. He was reassigned as a lifeguard at a swimming pool for the rest of his time in the service, thanks to a former officer in Vietnam who was also now at Fort Benning.

With the help of GI benefits, Tim went to university and graduated with a degree in aviation technology. After graduation he moved back to Michigan and worked in aviation. Not feeling at home in the United States, he returned to Windsor in 1971, where he continues to work with aircraft.[24]

DAVID SAVAGE

Vietnam: November 1967 to August 1968   Service: Army

David Savage was born in Toronto, 20 September 1945. In 1965 he moved down to Pasadena, California, where an aunt resided. David enlisted in October 1966 for three years in the U.S. Army. He ended up with the 173rd Airborne Brigade. As a member of Company D, 16th Armor, he was wounded by shrapnel in the face in March near Tuy Hoa. David returned to his unit and saw further action, but his condition worsened and he had to end his tour. Sergeant Savage was sent for treatment in September to Chelsea Naval Hospital, near Boston. He recovered and made his way back to the Pasadena area, where he married. That marriage failed, as did a second marriage. Dave has become an American citizen and lives in Sedona, Arizona. His brother, Jack, retained the following selection of letters sent from Vietnam:

Early November 1967

Hi Jack,

I'll bring you up-to-date on what has been happening. First I left Fort Dix, New Jersey. Our first stop was Anchorage, Alaska, then Yokota, Japan. Next, we flew into Bien Hoa located about 30 miles northeast of Saigon. I received my orders for the 173rd. The 173rd is located at An Khe which is about middle Vietnam. After a week of classes I was assigned to Tuy Hoa with the armour on the coast. The majority of the fellows with the infantry are going to Dak To.

Last evening our company opened an entertainment club. Five hours later the place was closed down. A near riot developed amongst all those smashed GIs. They didn't even put on the stripper as planned.

Two of the un-nicest diseases one can catch here are the clap (leaky water pipe) and malaria. They say the doctors can treat these diseases but not cure them. There are some men who can't go home because they have the clap so bad.

Good bye for now,

Dave

30 November 1967

Hello Jack,

Impressions of Vietnam are quite varied. The first day I arrived at D-16 Armor we took off down the coast to wash the APCs (armoured personnel carriers). We did spend 15 minutes cleaning up and the rest of the afternoon swimming and surfing on our air mattresses in the South China Sea. Then we proceeded to have a beer party and target practice. We blasted the hell out of everything in sight. It cost the taxpayers a few grand that afternoon. Oh, by the way, swimming is off limits here.

Our duty falls in the evening hours escorting convoys from the coast through the mountains and across the plains (rice paddies) to our base. The convoy usually carries munitions. Last evening there were no convoys but we went out on patrol over the same road. We struck at likely VC ambush positions — ammunition.

About midnight our platoon stopped for a few hours across the road from a local whorehouse. Well, you could say we put the inside of the APCs to good use. You name it we did it last evening.

Dave

P.S. A lot of the things I mentioned is the sort of stuff you don't broadcast to the general public. A lot of people would get upset if they really knew what their boys were up to. This is one of the basic effects of any war — waste and corruption. In fact, we have Vietnamese girls in our barracks (not whores) screwing about. They are just an accepted part of life around here. They also wash clothes, sew, and things like that.

17 December 1967

Dear Jack,

Well D-16 has a new commanding officer. This last week he has been dumping all over us with ridiculous regulations. The way some of us feel the old captain better not get near us in the field or he just might get a few rounds in the back.

Reports were getting to the general that D-16 vehicles were always broken down. Yesterday the general paid us a visit and couldn't believe what he saw — all the vehicles were in good order. From now on he will use us more.

The grunts are back from Dak To and some of their stories are fairly hairy. The worst fate a VC could have would be to have his head cut off. To them the head is sacred. The battalion's grunts did cut off a few heads and put them on poles. This shocked me at first but in war one has the basest emotions. One cannot really moralize until one has been through it.

Keep up the work at school and let me know what's happening back in the world.

Your brother,

Dave

1 January 1968

Hello Jack,

Well, man, here it is 1968.

In my last letter I mentioned about the practice of our grunts cutting off the ears and other things from dead gooks. Apparently Charlie started this practice a few years ago. The then general of the 173rd stated that if the gooks wanted to fight this way, we would as well. A newspaper reporter happened to see one of the 173rd with a set of ears and raised a big stink. The grunts are not supposed to mutilate the gooks. But it is done in an unofficial way. For example, on one of our sweeps the grunts killed a gook, cut off his ears and proceeded to blow off his head to prevent anyone from knowing. Apparently a set of ears brings $75 or more back at Tuy Hoa. Some of those in the rear have never been outside the front gate. With a set of ears they have an instant war story. A few years ago the gooks tried to send a captain's head to San Francisco by mail but it was discovered. The package was addressed to his parents. That is why one burns all mail in the field, especially the return addresses.

New Year's Eve was a blast. We weren't allowed any passes but with the "tail" in town no one could stop us. After wrecking the beer hall, dancing on the tables, fighting and numerous other incidents, we headed into town. After getting relieved the MPs picked us up. There were four of us and one of him. After getting quite mouthy, the MP let us off at the gate. One guy then threw a grenade at the departing jeep. That MP will think twice next time about giving us hell.

At midnight the whole sky was lit up with hundreds of flares and quite a few rounds of tracer ammunition. This is New Year's Eve Vietnam style.

> Your brother,
>
> Dave

15 February 1968

Hi Jack,

Last week we burned down a village for selling the VC food and giving them shelter. The people were airlifted out of the area to a refugee camp where they were questioned. All the guys on top of the track were having a blast setting all the straw hootches on fire. I got a few kicks myself though driving through numerous houses. Great sport.

Did I mention I'm writing another girl back home? I met Lynn at Dianne's reception last fall. She wanted to write someone in Nam. Lynn is in first year University of Toronto (Victoria College). Stuff over here is as cheap as hell. The camera I bought over here for $40 is worth $110 back in TO.

Charlie killed one of our laundry girls. She was eight months pregnant. These VC don't play games.

Say hello to everyone for me.

> Love,
>
> Dave

5 March 1968

Dear Jack,

Well man, the war finally caught up to our outfit yesterday. An estimated 300 North Vietnamese Army regulars dug in just outside Tuy Hoa in a few villages. Our mission was to help root them out. About 10 a.m. the second platoon got on line and started a sweep into a suspected enemy-held village. We were about 100 yards into the village when we came under heavy rocket, machine-gun and automatic weapons fire. Of the three men on my track I was the only one unhurt. Air strikes were called onto the enemy and Charlie disengaged.

We continued to sweep all day. Our last sweep got us suckered in real bad. We started to sweep a finger of land jutting into the rice paddies. Halfway down the finger Charlie hit one APC with a rocket. It was shortly after this that I was hit in the left cheek with a tiny metal fragment. However, it felt like a big chunk had been ripped out and the wound bled for about 20 minutes. Within this time I was on a chopper and into a hospital at Tuy Hoa. The medical people at Tuy Hoa were so busy that they sent myself and some other men down to the coast to Nha Trang for medical attention.

That's the word from here.

Dave

16 March 1968

Hi Jack,

One of the first things I did on my return to the company was check out the five destroyed APCs. Man, did those rockets do a job! When I got hit in the cheek I scrambled out the back door to an APC just to our rear. It was none too soon. Within minutes my track was burning like hell. Most of my gear was destroyed including my camera. All this about my track was unknown to me for a few days. I was inside the other APC heading to a chopper and was oblivious to what was happening outside. Two guys burned to death inside one track. It is a weird feeling finding pieces of a man who was alive just a week ago.

Out of the 20 men in our platoon (2nd), there were five men walking at the end of that Monday. We had five killed in action and ten wounded in action. One always reads about something happening to the other outfit. When one finally does get into the thick of it, there is an air of unreality because everything happens so fast.

Well baby brother, take care and give my best to our clan down in California.

Love

Dave

22 April 1968

Hi Man,

Charlie hit us again on a road clearing mission but our superior firepower saved us again. One of the sergeants just came off an extended leave. He said I've aged about four years since the last time he saw me.

We don't have to worry about high-priced whores where we are. The going price is one dollar but a slick guy can get it for chop chop (food). The women are not the best but when did a GI ever get particular? Most just lie there and giggle.

Along with our camp comes a few disadvantages, kids to be exact. Hordes. From dawn until dark they hang around for chop chop. They trade some scrawny fruit for C-rations. Even now I have three of these little monsters hanging on every sentence I write.

Take care and all that stuff.

Dave[25]

WALTER MULLANEY

Vietnam: November 1967 to December 1968   Service: Air Force

Walter Mullaney was born in New York City on 7 February 1921. Joining the RCAF in Toronto in August 1941, he served with Bomber Command, notably in No. 429 Squadron of No. 6 Group. On his 16th mission Walter was shot down over northeast Belgium. He escaped capture for 28 days. With the help of the Belgian underground, he made it to Paris, where he was betrayed and turned over to the Gestapo. As a result of his attempts to escape, Walter was transferred from one prisoner of war camp to another. He was successful in escaping from a camp near Leipzig in April 1945.

In October 1947 Mullaney joined the United States Air Force and served with them for 27 years. He was posted to Vietnam from 27 November 1967 to 3 December 1968. His assignments were to the 12th Tactical Fighter Wing at Cam Ranh Bay and the Vietnamese armed forces language school in Saigon. Although Walter is an American citizen, his Second World War service gives his story a Canadian connection.

I suppose there is a parallel between an American joining the Canadian wartime services when the United States was not at war and a Canadian joining the U.S. wartime services when his own country was not at war. As to their motives, one must bear in mind that no one takes such a serious step for one reason alone. Their reasons run

Technical Sergeant Walter Mullaney, Cam Ranh Bay, South Vietnam, December 1968. (Courtesy W. Mullaney.)

the gamut from high-minded idealism all the way to self-serving materialism. In my own case, the self-serving reason was my desire to fly, and the RCAF looked like the best bet. I was highly unimpressed with the collegiate, juvenile nonsense that the U.S. Army Air Corps was full of at that time. I reasoned that since Canadians were being shot at they might be expected to be more adult. I was right about that. But there was another reason, perhaps not so self-centred. It had come to my attention that some very nasty events were happening in Europe. What could I, one young, untrained, half-educated, high school boy, do about it? His country seemed to be rather unconcerned, but just across the border a whole people was doing something about it. I thought about it for over a year, and finally decided to apply for a position with those people.

The Second World War was everyone's war. There was never any question about the necessity of fighting the war, nor was there ever any question about the honourable nature of our cause or the dishonourable nature of our opponent's cause. There were no such clear-cut feelings about the Vietnam War. It might be described as a war that was badly managed and never adequately explained. Millions in the United States and around the world opposed the war and many of those condemned the warrior as well as the war itself.

When I returned to my home in 1945 I was not met with brass bands but I was treated with respect. When I returned from Vietnam 23 years later in 1968, and this time wearing the uniform of my own country, I was treated with scorn. On my way home I was spat upon in the face in a bar in Sacramento, California.

A few words about those Americans who sneaked off to Canada during the Vietnam War. I can admire a man who stands up and says, "I won't go," and is prepared to stand up and take the consequences of his actions. I can admire a man who says, "I will go," and is prepared to take the consequences. But I have nothing but contempt for those who were not prepared to accept the consequences of their actions.

A few words about my tour in Vietnam. My home base was Cam Ranh Air Base. I was assigned as an aircraft maintenance supervisor on F-4 Phantom aircraft. Not long after arriving President Lyndon Johnson paid us a visit. He made a speech, visited the base hospital and was gone. Just before Christmas Bob Hope and Raquel Welch paid us a visit. She was a lot better looking than Lyndon Johnson.

A little over a month later the Viet Cong paid us a visit. This was one visit we could have done without. It was a definite downturn. This was the Tet offensive of 1968. There followed two smaller offensives.

During the May offensive I was reassigned on temporary duty from Cam Ranh Bay to the Vietnamese armed forces language school in Saigon. This was supposed to be a temporary duty. In fact I spent the rest of my tour in Saigon. I only returned to Cam Ranh in November 1968 to turn in my M-16 rifle, my .38 Smith & Wesson revolver and re-enlist for another four years in the USAF.

While in Saigon I was shot at a few times, taught English and took rest-and-recreation leave in Darwin and Sydney, Australia. As always, I found the Australians to be a warm and friendly people. This came as no great surprise since serving with them in Canada, Britain, Germany and Vietnam.

It is my belief that everyone carries with him the values and mores of the society that formed him. The societies of America and Canada, though diverse in many ways, at the same time have many basic similarities. This is not to say that the two countries are rubber stamps of each other. There are differences. We must never forget that each country does its own thinking.[26]

ROBERT CREPEAU

Vietnam: February 1968 to December 1968   Service: Army

Sergeant Robert Crepeau of Montreal after a night ambush, Di An, South Vietnam, 1968. (Courtesy R. Crepeau.)

Robert Crepeau was born in Montréal on 27 February 1932. In 1948 at age 16, he quit school, and with a false affidavit stating that he was 18, he joined the U.S. Army. During the Korean War, Bob served some seven months in Korea from August 1951 to early 1952. He had accumulated a certain number of points and was thus rotated out. A member of Fox Company, 7th Regiment, 3rd Infantry Division, he was in several major battles, including one on Hill 355. After Korea, he left the army as a corporal. It was not until 1962 that he took out American citizenship.

In 1967 Bob re-enlisted. He was sent to Vietnam in February 1968 and assigned to the 1st Battalion, 18th Regiment, 1st Infantry Division. He

spent much of his tour as an infantryman on ambushes but ended as a
sergeant (E-5). Bob was discharged in January 1969 and became a civilian
once more. In 1971 at age 40, he again re-enlisted, finally retiring as a
staff sergeant (E-6) in 1986. Bob currently makes his home in Columbus,
Georgia.
   Bob offers his recollections:

My unit main base camp was Di An. I spent most of my time at Di
An, Lai Khe, the water plant in Thu Duc, the Michelin plant and
Phuoc Vinh. My unit worked the III Corps area and was on the move
quite a lot. When I arrived in the country, the '68 Tet had started.
   The Korean War fighting was generally more intense than Vietnam. I remember the cold weather, poor resupply and the human
wave attacks. In Vietnam I remember the drug problem. It was a big
one. I wasn't impressed with our leadership. I don't think that the
troops lost the Vietnam War. It was the politicians, and the American
public exemplified by Jane Fonda. We called her "Red Jane." But to
sum it up I blame it on this lazy generation. All they want to do is
party and make a fast buck.[27]

THOMAS DAVID HORNELL

Vietnam: February 1968 to February 1969   Service: Air Force

Thomas David ("Dave") Hornell was born in Toronto, 30 May 1940. He is
a cousin of Flight Lieutenant David Hornell, who was posthumously
awarded the Victoria Cross in the Second World War. Dave served in the
Royal Canadian Ordnance Corps as an officer cadet from September 1957 to
September 1958 and with the Royal Canadian Air Force as a leading
aircraftman from November 1959 to June 1961.

I left Canada in 1962 to join the USAF, and after tours in Maine,
Missouri, Newfoundland and Arkansas, I was attached to the 101st
Airborne Division, at Bien Hoa, in the III Corps area of Vietnam.
   Each U.S. Army division has a complement of USAF weather
personnel attached to it under the operational control of the G-2
(intelligence). These USAF "operating locations" were divided into
four CWTs (combat weather teams) attached to each brigade and
commanded by a company grade officer (USAF).
   I spent February and March 1968 with the "division rear" at Bien
Hoa, while the main contingent went north to assist in the action at
Hue. Late in March I flew up to Da Nang Air Base and drove through

the Hai Van Pass on up to Camp Eagle (the base camp of the 101st Airborne Division) to join my unit.

Dave recalls the first convoy after the Tet offensive through the Hai Van Pass:

During my stint in the Canadian Army, I participated in a couple of convoys near Ste-Thérèse, Québec. These manoeuvres were always preceded by a series of briefings wherein the officers, NCOs and drivers were all briefed on convoy discipline (spacing, speed, defensive manoeuvres, air attack tactics, etc.) We all knew where we were bound, how to get there, who was in charge and things of this nature. When the convoy was on the road, members of the Provost Corps would direct traffic through key intersections and race about the convoy like sheepdogs herding the flock. The U.S. Army, and specifically the 101st Airborne Division, had a different approach to matters.

The 101st Airborne Division was deployed piecemeal to I Corps during and after the Tet offensive: initially, as I recall, the 2nd Brigade, then elements of the division headquarters, then the 1st Brigade and, late in 1968, ultimately the 3rd Brigade. As mentioned, each brigade had its little cadre of USAF weathermen (two or three) who were there to take weather observations (for relay to the weather team at division headquarters and, ultimately, the central data collection point in Saigon) and assist the brigade S-2 (intelligence officer) with whatever meteorological information he needed for presentation to the brigade commander. The 101st saw quite a lot of action in and around Hue during that time. Division headquarters was relocated from Bien Hoa (northwest of Saigon in III Corps) to Camp Eagle, a location just southwest of Hue straddling a major infiltration route from Laos.

I was assigned to the division weather team and tasked, no doubt due to my experience as an ex-Ottawa taxi driver, to drive a one-and-a-half carryall from Bien Hoa to Saigon (where it was to be loaded into a ship) and then from Da Nang to Camp Eagle (some 90 kilometres up Highway 1, "Street Without Joy," through the Hai Van Pass). When the vehicles were offloaded at the navy port south of Da Nang, I managed to "steal" our truck away from the troops who were tasked with parking it in the convoy marshalling area and, instead, I drove off to Da Nang Air Base with it to await orders to move off some four days down the road. The quarters at the air base were far and away better than those offered the paratroopers at the port, and besides, that gave me four days with my own personal trans-

*Sergeant T. David Hornell, Camp Eagle, South
Vietnam, May 1968. (Courtesy T. David Hornell.)*

portation to see the sights of Da Nang and environs (which included China Beach).

The convoy was to form at 0600 on the fifth day so I gassed up "my" truck, HQ41, courtesy of the United States Air Force at Da Nang the night before and struck out in the pre-dawn darkness through a shantytown just outside the air base called "Dogpatch." Dogpatch was supposedly a hotbed of VC sympathizers. Despite my daylight reconnoitring, I promptly got myself lost and, without another GI to be seen, got the queasy feeling that unless I got unlost damn quick, I and my truck and its cargo of whiskey, C-rations and weather paraphernalia would turn up permanently missing. Just when I was sure I'd passed the same narrow intersection for the fifth time, the dawn filtered through the gloom, the route to the navy port presented itself, and I roared off to safety.

When I arrived at the marshalling yard my tardiness, like my four-day absence, had gone unnoticed. The place was a real circus. Troops and vehicles were milling about to no apparent purpose in response to shouted directions and counter-directions for those "in charge." I diverted through the supply yard by the dock and came up in the rear as though I'd been part of the parade all along and dutifully waited for the G-2 representative to find me. Find me he did as I knew he must because I was to haul one of his trailers behind me. Actually, I was "found" by a fellow USAF weatherman assigned to the 101st (S. Sgt. Paul Roodben) who had been sent down from Camp Eagle to ride "shotgun" with me.

The convoy sorted itself out like a Venezuelan traffic jam. I received my "briefing" which consisted of the instructions, "Follow that guy!" and, a little after 9 a.m., we lurched out of the marshalling yard heading north. It was a fairly impressive sight with vehicles before and behind me as far as the eye could see, helicopters swooping like swallows overhead: everything but bagpipes. It wasn't long though before things began to come unravelled. About 30 vehicles ahead of me I saw the convoy split! I, true to my "briefing," followed the guy ahead as did all those behind me and I watched as the new lead vehicle took us off to the west on a road which became a track and then little more than a dyke between paddies. All came to a stop as the first truck approached dense jungle. The driver got out and worked his way back along the convoy replying to queries, polite and not so, with the same song, "I don't know, man!" After a half-hour or so of watching our helicopter escorts losing patience overhead, we were directed to turn around (no easy chore on a single-track rice paddy dyke with a trailer behind) and, in reverse order, we rejoined the main body around noon in a huge, sandy cemetery somewhere on the outskirts of Da Nang. Here it turned out that only HQ41 had a full tank of gas, the rest of the gaggle having overlooked the necessity of fuel for the journey.

While waiting for fuel trucks we set into a C-ration luncheon, topped off with cold cokes purchased at a dime a can from refrigerator trailers sent out courtesy of the Army/Air Force Exchange Service. As the convoy was fuelled by hand, hundreds of Vietnamese children emerged to beg cokes, candy and whatever. We rewarded the kids amply and, after a couple more wasted hours, commenced to form up in earnest. When we began to show signs of more purposeful activity, the kids disappeared and I was approached by a paratroop major whose helmet sat squarely over his eyes. As I saluted him he pointed a stubby finger at me and my shotgun and announced, "You're in the air force." I agreed and he relaxed slightly and gave me my second convoy briefing. He explained then that we were to be the first convoy through the pass since Tet and that we should "have our weapons locked and loaded and be ready to fight!" Having weapons that we'd never fired and only four clips of ammunition between us didn't put me or my shotgun in much of a mood to fight — particularly given the lack of organization we'd seen so far on the part of our comrades.

We set out somewhat grimly but in only one direction this time and gained altitude rapidly. The sand and heat quickly gave way to clouds and greenery as we slowly ground our way up a series of switchbacks into the mountains north of Da Nang. After about an hour in the densest of forests and gloomiest of clouds, the convoy stopped. Suddenly, coming at us from out of the foliage were dozens of black pyjama-clad types we were warned about. I figured that this was it. Not so. These folks were peddling flags of the Confederacy, skin books, sunglasses and warm cokes. These were the parents of the kids to whom we'd given the cokes down in the valley. While we were relieved that the "attack" was solely commercial, most were not a little put out that they'd try to sell us the same sodas we'd given to their children to enjoy.

Just before dusk we rolled into Camp Eagle, a 90-kilometre trip in only 12 hours, mostly driven at speeds of 80 or more kilometres per hour. No doubt we won some hearts and minds back in Da Nang when we gave away the cokes.

I spent April through September at Camp Eagle providing weather service to the 101st in support of various operations throughout I Corps. In October, I spent two weeks back down in III Corps at Phuoc Vinh and thence to R&R in Hawaii. On return I took over duties as NCO in charge of the weather team in support of the 4th Infantry Division at Camp Enari (Dragon Mountain — near Pleiku in the II Corps area) and, ultimately, ended my tour in support of the USAF 366th TAC Fighter Wing, Da Nang Air Base, until rotation back to the U.S.A. in February 1969.

Queries made over the first 10 years of my service in the USAF relative to return to Canada and employment opportunities were never very encouraging. I became a U.S. citizen in '74.[28]

After serving back in the United States and the territory of Guam, first as a weather technician, then as a weather superintendent, Dave retired in 1984 as a senior master sergeant. He now works as a weather forecaster at the weather station at Plattsburgh Air Force Base and also does the weather on WPTZ-TV whenever the regular weatherman is absent. He resides in West Chazy, New York, not far from the Canadian border.

JOHN RIDOUT

Vietnam: March 1968 to December 1969   Service: Army

Sergeant John Ridout (centre), Nha Trang, South Vietnam, 1969. (Courtesy J. Ridout.)

John Ridout was born in the east end of Toronto in 1936. He attended Roden Public School, then Danforth Technical School. After graduation from high school in 1955, he worked for Colgate Palmolive until 1959, when he married a girl from Toronto. John and his wife moved to Detroit that September in search of a new life and a good job. In January 1960 he found out that since he was an alien, he should have registered at his local draft board within 30 days of arrival in the United States. Soon after, he learned he was about to be drafted for two years, but he instead volunteered for three years in order to be eligible for American citizenship at the conclusion of his service.

After basic training he enrolled in the jump school at Fort Bragg, North Carolina, and ended up as a staff sergeant (E-6) with the Golden Knights Parachute Team as the company clerk and announcer. He became a U.S. citizen in 1964 and then volunteered for the Special Forces. After about three years in Germany, he went to Vietnam in March 1968. While he was in Vietnam, his wife gave birth to a son. A birth announcement in a Toronto paper, which mentioned that her husband was in Vietnam, resulted in her receiving anonymous, insulting phone calls and hate mail from anti-war extremists. After Vietnam, John returned to Fort Bragg and the Special

Forces. Other assignments included a tour in Korea in 1972 and seven years in Germany.
John describes the memorable first two weeks of his tour:

The First Time, The Last Time

Like most Canadians and even more Americans, I had not heard of Vietnam when I volunteered for service in the U.S. Army in 1960. It was not until I had completed Special Forces training in 1965 that the rumours of a far-off country receiving military assistance in the form of "advisor teams" became known to me. Personal friends would be missing from the usual happy-hour formations at the NCO club. When asked about the absence, others would simply shrug and say "TDY" (temporary duty)! Enough in that statement is understood by those assigned to operational detachments, or "A Teams," that one does not ask further about who, where, or for how long the temporary duty will last. It was in May of 1965 that I received orders assigning me to duty with the 10th Special Forces Group in Bad Toelz, Germany. After a very challenging, educational and, overall, very enjoyable tour of duty in Europe, it became clear to me that I should apply for Officer Candidate School (OCS), not necessarily to better serve the U.S. Army, but because I was becoming more aware of what officers actually did for their pay.

It was with a broad grin that I reported to the headquarters personnel office after being called on the telephone to come to pick up my orders. Upon reading them, all questions were answered. Report to Fort Lewis, Washington, for further movement to the Republic of Vietnam, March 1968.

We decided that my wife, Fran, and daughter, Michelle, would travel with me to Toronto to be close to our parents while I was off to fight the "Cong." Very few individuals can share the feelings and emotions one has when boarding an airplane in Toronto to fly off to the great unknown to the west. Several rye and gingers got me to the West Coast where I was met by my brother-in-law, Richard, at my hotel overlooking the beautiful fountain in front of the government building in downtown Vancouver. This after the departure of the fire engines who were called to flush the fountain after some "love person" had thrown a box of Tide laundry soap into it, causing a four-foot wall of suds to spew forth into traffic.

My arrival in Nam was uneventful. Arriving in Cam Ranh Bay after a 20-hour flight from Seattle, Washington, and stepping from the aircraft into 110-degree heat and 95 per cent humidity gave one the overwhelming urge to crawl and gasp for breath.

The reception centre for all incoming army personnel at Cam Ranh was deceiving at first — situated on a peninsula in the South China Sea, beautiful white sand beaches, palm trees, sail boats skimming the crystal blue water. Then one's attention is drawn to the triple-strand concertina barbed wire, machine-gun emplacements every 30 metres, the sandbagged bunkers and minefield warning signs.

I had made the acquaintance of two other Special Forces sergeants and we decided to wait for our final assignment orders together in the club over a couple cold ones. These turned out to be warm beer in a paper cup with a six-ounce chunk of ice. Not bad ice, anyway! The three of us reported to the orderly room the next morning for our assignment. The two others were assigned to Nha Trang, Special Forces headquarters, for replacement assignment to a Special Forces camp somewhere in the central highlands, but no orders for me. Next day — assignment to MACV-SOG-CSD-PRU. What does that mean? Someone would telephone me here sometime, was the reply. The phone call came that evening on about my fourth chunk of ice. "Be on the Air America flight tomorrow and wear civilian clothes." My civilian wardrobe at the time consisted of a sticky nylon short-sleeve shirt and a pair of wool slacks.

I was met at the Saigon airport and whisked off for several briefings and orientations on several ongoing aid, assistance and relocation programs sponsored by the U.S. government. This sounded great, but what was my job? I was told that I was to be the PRU (Provincial Reconnaissance Unit) strike team leader in Khanh Hoa Province, with headquarters in Nha Trang.

Upon settling into my new surroundings in Nha Trang and receiving a brief overview of what I was going to be doing for the next year, I was off to meet my unit — a group of 54 repatriated Viet Cong and North Vietnamese defectors whom I was supposed to lead on operations targeted against the Viet Cong cadre operating in my province. Our unit would gather intelligence on Viet Cong activities throughout the province and attempt to intercept the VC teams as they moved from village to village.

Came the time for my first operation with the unit. We had planned this operation for a week, having infiltrated team members into villages in order to gather information from VC sympathizers on when and where the VC team would be active. This was no simple task, as all planning and coordination had to be done through my translator, Trinh.

The operation began on schedule, moving some 20 miles by truck to a drop-off point at dusk, then moving to the rice paddies we must cross to reach our intended ambush position some six miles further on. Our movement across the paddies went well. Several changes in direction were made to confuse any observer. This was probably a waste of time because nobody could see more than 10 feet in front. I was the ninth man in line as we walked, with Trinh in front of me. After moving for about two hours I wanted to call a rest halt. I reached forward for Trinh and felt nothing but air and the paddy dike under my feet. I made an abrupt stop and, as if in a cartoon, felt several bumps as the man behind me and the man behind him, and the man behind the man behind shunted into each other. I sent a man forward to halt the front portion of the patrol. He returned a few minutes later. Trinh had moved to my side by now. I asked what happened to the front of the patrol. I then discovered that the lead member of the patrol had stepped off the paddy dike and allowed the rest to pass and then followed the last man as he passed. This was done by each member of the patrol in turn, including Trinh.

It was a month or so later that I met Trinh while in a beach cabana having a couple chunks of ice. He had found new employment with another agency after a hasty separation from the PRU. He was rather cool toward me and his conversation was guarded. He did give me a good piece of advice, though. His advice was to leave the cabana now, which I did. The cabana was destroyed by a bomb later that evening. Thank you, Trinh.

I often look back at my tour in Nam. There were some good times along with the bad. I'm thankful for the experience gained and the friends made. It wasn't until I returned to Canada, my wife, Fran, my daughter, and newly born son, Eric, that I heard of the hate mail and nasty phone calls my wife endured while I was in Vietnam. But that is also something I can look back on.[29]

MALCOLM SYMONS

Vietnam: May 1968 to May 1969   Service: Army

Malcolm Symons was born near Winnipeg on 10 March 1942. His father served overseas with the RCAF. Mal married a girl from the Winnipeg area in August 1964. He was a good football player and sought to pursue a college education with the help of football. After obtaining their visas, the Symonses moved to Dallas. While his wife worked for the Great-West Life Insurance Company, Mal entered North Texas State University. He tried to continue his studies as well as play on the football team, but finding the load too heavy, he left school and, about to be drafted, joined the army. Basic

Malcolm Symons in Phu Loi, South Vietnam, 16 May 1968. (Courtesy M. Symons.)

training at Fort Benning, Georgia, was followed by advanced individual training at Fort Sill, Oklahoma. Figuring the artillery offered a better chance of survival, Mal took artillery officer training at Fort Sill. He was successful and went on to flight school at Fort Wolters, Texas, then to Hunter Army Airfield, Georgia, where he received a good deal of training on the Huey.

Mal offers a few memories of Vietnam:

I was assigned to the 23rd Artillery Group (Field Artillery) stationed at Phu Loi and then on down to the 1st Battalion, 27th Artillery, based at Dau Tieng. My job was to fly intelligence officers, the battalion commander and others to the various batteries within the battalion.

Our colonel was an avid handball player. He even had a handball court built. The colonel learned that I was interested in the game and as a result I would regularly be ordered to be at Phu Loi about 4:30 in the afternoons. It became embarrassing after a while when I would be ordered in the middle of my duties to fly to Phu Loi. Eventually, I had to ask not to be called on a regular basis from my duties in order to play handball.

I remember once a camp was under mortar and rocket attack. We were asked by a senior officer to fly in ice cream for the evening meal.

A few of my friends were killed as a result. After that, the officer in question was never high on my hit parade.

During Tet in early 1969 some of the Viet Cong tunnelled into our base at Dau Tieng. They began setting off satchel charges. Unforeseen by them, the base was also used to train killer dogs such as Dobermans and German shepherds. The dogs were let loose and the enemy was quickly found and killed.[30]

Following his tour in Vietnam, Mal returned to Hunter as an instrument instructor for helicopters. He was going to do a second tour in Vietnam in 1971 but the army was cutting back. After becoming an American citizen in 1972, Mal went at army expense to university, graduating in 1974 with a B.A. in aviation management. The previous year he left active service but continued in the reserve. As a civilian he has flown helicopters servicing oil rigs in the Gulf of Mexico and, as well, engaging in air ambulance work. He currently resides in Galveston, Texas.

EDWARD BOWES

Vietnam: 1968 to 1969   Service: Army

Edward Bowes of Dorchester, New Brunswick, was a sergeant in South Vietnam in 1968. Two letters he composed after his return follow: the first gives his reason for enlisting; the second describes an unforgettable incident.

Ottawa, Canada: Summer, 1967

Strolling through centre-town on a pleasant day, I chanced upon a demonstration protesting the war in Vietnam. Wellington Street in front of the United States Embassy was jammed with hippies, yippies and draft-dodgers raising hell. I circulated among the "great unwashed" and, feigning stupid, inquired what it was all about in the parlance of the times: "Hey man, what's happenin'?" This intentionally gave those self-righteous, self-appointed moral guardians the opportunity to pontificate and vent their slogans of Peace and Love and Dope. Particularly vociferous were the shrieking Jane Fondas who would never have to go there anyway. Some of the braless flower-less "flower children" didn't even know where they were, let alone where Vietnam was located.

So I decided to go and find out for myself. I journeyed to Bangor, Maine, enlisted in the United States Army, and volunteered to serve in the Republic of Vietnam. It seemed like a good idea at the time.

*Sergeant Edward Bowes calling artillery strikes near Da Nang, summer, 1968.
(Courtesy E. Bowes.)*

Marble Mountain near Da Nang, South Vietnam: Summer, 1968

It was 3 a.m., blacker than the hobs of hell. I was huddled in the sandbagged firing point, peering out through the tangle of concertina wire that encircled our perimeter. I strained my eyes to detect any movement, any change in the dismal battlefield in front of me. "Charlie" liked to probe us around this time of night, just to see if we were awake.

I sensed something over to the left. I whirled and saw a figure waving a rifle, outlined against the side of the hill.

"Hey, GI," someone called out.

Was it a ruse? A suicidal Viet Cong wrapped in "plastique" trying to breach our wire by blowing himself up? Was Charlie taunting us? High on marijuana, or the taste of death, or whatever made them into savage guerrilla fighters, those little devils sure knew how to die.

Here we go again, I thought. But before I could bring my M-60 around, there was a long burst of machine-gun fire. A stream of tracers went through the figure. It dropped without a sound.

Flares went up, spreading an eerie wavering light over the landscape. Nothing moved on that desolate scene.

That ambush was a good idea, I thought. I had watched before dark as four GIs had dug a hole and set up a machine gun — outside the wire!

The communications phone started ticking; I grabbed it and said, "Post 10."

"What's all the racket out there?" It was my old pal Bum in the command bunker, secure under a small mountain of logs and sandbags.

"Just a stray gook, and he's deader'n hell," I said with a chuckle.

"Good." Bum came back, "Keep an eye on 'im; they may come for the body." Rumour had it that the Vietnamese did not believe that the spirit would join their ancestors if the body was not properly buried.

"Roger." I hung up.

My two partners in the hole were awake and we spent the rest of the night watching, anticipating an attempt to retrieve the corpse, or the weapon. The night passed without further incident. As the dawn slowly picked out the details of our field of fire, I began to see that something was wrong. I took a closer look through the binoculars. Jesus! I said to myself, that's the first gook I've ever seen with blond hair!

I rang up the command bunker, "Bum, you better send out the roving patrol to take a look at that enemy casualty."

Daylight arrived as I watched a jeep bounce out to the scene. The sergeant-of-the-guard jumped out to look at the body.

He yelled up to me, "You'd better come out here. I'll send the jeep around for you."

It was Mike. He had 14 bullet holes in him. He was dead.

The day before had been his birthday. He was 20 years old. Even in a combat zone you can wangle a day off on your birthday. Mike had celebrated. He had apparently slipped out to see his girlfriend in the village adjacent to our camp. That was during the daylight hours. His last mistake was to come back after dark.

Later in the day, the company commander asked me, "Do you want to take your buddy home?"

He was offering me what we crudely called a "stiff flight" — an early return to "the World" accompanying the body of a soldier to his home. I saw myself knocking on the door of a suburban home, and saying to a middle-aged couple whom I had never met: "Hello, I've brought your son home — in a box."

I declined the offer.[31]

Edward Bowes is happily married, has a young son and daughter, and resides in Saint John, New Brunswick, where he teaches high school. He has contributed articles on local history to scholarly publications and newspapers. His life is back to normal.

JOHN LAURIN

Vietnam: August 1968 to April 1969   Service: Army

John Laurin was born in Montreal in 1942 and grew up in the suburb of Verdun. About 1964 he felt like joining the military. He first applied to the three branches of the Canadian Forces, then the U.S. Air Force, Navy and Marines, but the waiting lines were too long. He tried the U.S. Army at Albany, New York, and was accepted for a three-year hitch. Basic training at Fort Dix, New Jersey, was followed by 12 long weeks at Fort Belvoir, Virginia, where he learned maintenance of heavy machinery for construction. That fall, John took airborne training at Fort Bragg, North Carolina. In 1965 he re-enlisted for three years from that date and received different training. He attended the helicopter school at Fort Eustis, Virginia, for six months, mainly studying maintenance. He next went to Fort Lewis, Washington, to join the 4th Infantry Division. There he applied for the Officer Candidate School at Fort Eustis, but he did not complete the course. Following a tour as a crew chief in Germany in 1968, he returned to Fort Eustis for training in helicopter quality control. As a staff sergeant he received orders for Vietnam in that same year. Based at Freedom Hill, Da Nang, he served with a maintenance battalion as a quality inspector for the CH-54 Sky Crane helicopter.

John sent in a few memories of Vietnam:

The first day in country I learned a lesson. During our briefing we were all told that if we heard incoming rockets in the middle of the night to get down on the floor of our hootch, as the sandbags piled around the building would protect us from the explosion. That night, feeling sorry for myself, I had a few too many beers at the NCO club. Some time after midnight, I was awakened by the sound of rocket fire. I remembered the briefing but forgot I was in the top bunk. I rolled out of the bed and fell to the floor cutting my chin wide open on a steel pot. The guy in the bunk asked what the hell I was doing. I answered, "The rockets are coming." He laughed and said, "Don't you know the difference between incoming and outgoing?"

Freedom Hill was really a good assignment. Everything I had heard about the 478th Aviation Company was true. I got to share my room with another staff sergeant (E-6). We had a TV, electric fans and a hootch girl to clean up. But the weather was hot. Sometimes it rained so hard you could hardly see in front of your face.

At least twice a week we would have a rocket attack. When I lay down to sleep, I used to wonder whether I would see the next morning.

At night I could look out beyond our perimeter and watch the action right in front of me. I could see the Viet Cong firing up at the American aircraft and the return fire back at them. The gunfire from the aircraft looked like a lazer beam because of the tracer bullets. It was some show.

Christmas and New Year's was the worst time for everyone. We all counted the days left to go. I only spent nine months over there but it felt like nine years.

I saw so many dead people that I got used to it. I hope that we never have a war again. It is such a waste of lives.[32]

As an alien serving in the American armed forces in Vietnam John was offered, along with others, the opportunity to become an American citizen. Periodically, aliens in the U.S. forces in Vietnam were flown to the Honolulu Hilton Hotel where mass swearing-in ceremonies were conducted. John was among a group of some 500 aliens who were asked such typical questions as who was the first president of the United States and what president freed the slaves. He then took the oath of allegiance and received his U.S. citizenship. In April 1970 John's period of enlistment in the service expired.

After Vietnam, John went to aviation school in California, taking advantage of the GI benefits. He worked for several years for Northrop Aircraft as a quality control expert for fighter aircraft until he moved to Boeing Aerospace. With that company at Houston he heads a team of 26 other inspectors responsible for quality control.

ROBERT JOHNSON

Vietnam: September 1968 to September 1969   Service: Marines

Robert Earl Johnson, a Mohawk, was born near Brantford, Ontario, 5 September 1946. His father had served in the American army during the Second World War and worked for a time in Buffalo. An aunt and uncle lived and worked in that city. Partly because he wanted to mature and become a man, partly as well because he sought action and adventure, and partly to fight communism, he went to Buffalo in March 1968 and enlisted in the U.S. Marines for a three-year hitch. In January 1968 he applied for and obtained an American alien registration (green) card. From Buffalo, he was sent to Parris Island for basic training. From there it was on to further training as a rifleman at Camp Lejeune. In early August he was posted to Camp Pendleton near San Diego, California, for more training, including map reading and conventional and jungle warfare tactics. Then he was sent via

Corporal Robert Johnson (left) checks for weapons in a rural area of Vietnam, southwest of Da Nang, 1969. (Courtesy R. Johnson.)

Okinawa to Da Nang. Johnson was assigned to Company C, 1st Battalion, 7th Regiment, 1st Marine Division. He arrived apprehensively in the dark while rain poured down at his company's forward observation post on a hill. What followed was a routine of innumerable patrols both at night and in the daytime through rural areas. Both the marines and Viet Cong kept busy trying to ambush each other.

During a halt in the bombing, there would be increased enemy activity as enemy supplies moved unhindered. On patrol, Johnson did not particularly care for dogs being used, for if they or their handlers were even slightly injured, a helicopter would immediately be called in to evacuate them. Helicopters attracted the attention of Viet Cong in the vicinity, and enemy fire inevitably produced more casualties. Air support was welcomed, although friendly fire did account for a considerable number of casualties. Johnson felt the marines' field discipline was good. He remembers a search-and-destroy operation when his unit was surrounded. A call by the enemy in English to surrender only increased the men's will to resist and they successfully broke out with the help of artillery fire.

On 3 September 1969 Ho Chi Minh died. One week later Corporal Johnson's tour was over. Taking advantage of President Nixon's efforts to cut back on American troop strength in Vietnam, Johnson elected to leave the service a year early. He was honourably discharged 6 March 1970. Johnson is now employed by the Department of Health and Welfare and is involved in the administration of the health-care needs of people on the Six Nations Reserve. Johnson married a co-worker in 1972 and has two sons.

Bob Johnson became a close friend of Michael Skoumbros from Stamford, Connecticut. Both were riflemen in the same squad. They fought together, were wounded by the same booby trap and saved each other's lives. Johnson rescued his friend during an ambush, and Skoumbros in turn rescued him — weighed down with weapons and ammunition — from drowning when he stepped into a deep, water-filled crater during a night patrol. After the war, they remained best friends. Each attended the other's wedding. They continue to keep in touch and visit regularly.[33]

ERNEST NEVILLE

Vietnam: September 1968 to September 1969   Service: Air Force

Ernest Neville was born in Detroit on 4 July 1931 but grew up in Canada. His father's roots go back to Ross Township near Renfrew, Ontario. His mother was from Mayo, near Buckingham, Quebec, and that is where Ernest received his early education. The Nevilles moved wherever work was available, including Kapuskasing, Cochrane, Temagami, Peterborough and finally Windsor, where Ernest attended Assumption High School.

A dual citizen, Ernest registered for the American draft during the Korean War and decided to voluntarily join the U.S. Air Force in October 1951. From Detroit, he was sent to Sampson Air Force Base (AFB), Geneva, New York. Then it was on to Central Missouri State College at Warrensburg for training to enable him to do administrative work. In March 1952 he was sent to Travis AFB, California. His application for navigator training was accepted in 1954, and he went on to Lackland AFB, Texas. In August 1955 2nd Lieutenant Neville received his wings as a

Captain Ernest Neville (left) about to have some refreshing coconut milk at a village in Thailand, 1969. (Courtesy E. Neville.)

navigator and then married his girlfriend from Windsor. In 1958 Lieutenant Neville received his pilot's wings. In 1959 he took advanced training at the helicopter school at Stead AFB, Nevada. There, Captain Neville flew the Sikorsky H-19 helicopter. He was posted to Thule, Greenland, in 1962-63 with the Air Rescue Service. It was at a subsequent posting at Incirlik, Turkey, that he learned he was going to Southeast Asia. During Ernie's year overseas, September 1968 to September 1969, his wife and children lived in Sacramento, California.

Ernie was sent to Saigon and from there to Muang Ubon in eastern Thailand, where he was a member of the 38th Air Rescue Squadron. Flying HH-43 Huskie helicopters within a 100-mile radius of Ubon was not easy. Their rescue duties at Ubon kept them busier than air force helicopter pilots based in South Vietnam. For "his personal bravery and energetic application of his knowledge and skill," Ernie, now a major, was awarded the Distinguished Flying Cross. After his tour, Ernie taught flying at the USAF helicopter pilot school, Sheppard AFB, Texas. Upon retirement from the force in 1971, Ernie enrolled at Ferris State College, Michigan, graduating with bachelor's degrees in business administration and data processing. He frequently returns from his home in Tecumseh, Michigan, to Ottawa and vicinity to visit relatives living there.

Ernie offers some memories of his tour in Thailand:

In retrospect I would have to say that, had I been able to choose where to be stationed while serving in Southeast Asia, I could not have made a better choice of countries, simply because of the people. The Thai people were the happiest and friendliest that I have witnessed. Even in the rainy season, which could be a depressing time, they had a festival dedicated to cleansing, making it a fun time. Needless to say, everyone moving about during that period became a little waterlogged. The climate, overall, was hot and humid.

Our work schedule consisted of a 24-hour shift followed by a day off when manning was adequate. Other duties took up our hours whenever we were not on alert so there wasn't much time for other daytime activities. For instance, I was a functional check-flight pilot and therefore flew the test flights whenever maintenance of any nature required a test hop. I was also a flight instructor involved in the training and upgrading of other aircrew members.

Being in the rescue business and supporting an extensive flying operation kept us busy around the clock. The pilots were also responsible for the administration of the various tasks which made up the overall operation. Additionally, our flying requirements included not only those in support of other base units, but also incorporated the direct medical support of 10 outlying villages. Whenever a village was some distance from the base, we would remain in the village rather than making two long round trips. In consequence, we shared some of the duties like cleaning instruments for reuse by the dentist of the medical team. We also were provided with drink and food by the villagers. After taking care of our helicopter chores we were sometimes given green coconuts, sliced open to provide us with something to drink.

But Ernie's main job was search and rescue. He recounts a routine incident:

We had already scrambled with our fire suppression kit in response to an inflight aircraft emergency and were orbiting a short distance off to one side of the approach end of the runway so as to be available when the distressed aircraft landed. The F-4 pilot radioed that he was having engine difficulties and would be maintaining altitude until over the airfield so the helicopter crew was alerted to try to spot him early. On reaching the field, he began a left turn to bring him around to the runway for landing, but part way through his turn the engine failed, and he and the other pilot on board ejected. The impact of the F-4 momentarily lit up the night sky in the distance and gave us the general direction of the crash site. I immediately flew back to the alert pad, deposited the fire suppression kit and two firefighter crew members, picked up my crew chief, and departed. Also on board was a medic and my co-pilot.

With the base behind us, we were now engulfed in total darkness with no outside visible reference for guidance. Fortunately, one of the downed pilots was able to give an emergency beeper signal which we were able to receive. We flew for what seemed an eternity, taking offset readings from their signal and making adjustments until we arrived in their general area. Our next problem became apparent when I turned on the floodlights and landing lights and found the terrain to be extremely irregular. I chose a spot that seemed large enough to get into, but even it had a slope steep enough to prevent a safe landing. I inched the helicopter until I felt us touch down on the uphill side. Having to keep power in order to maintain our position, I dispatched the medic and my co-pilot to locate the downed aircrew somewhere in front of our location.

All other local conditions were unknown to us so the most beautiful sight at that time and place was seeing my crew members emerge from the darkness accompanying the two downed pilots. After everyone was safely aboard, we headed directly back to the base and a medical team which was standing by to recover the injured survivors. What seemed like forever to accomplish that night had been completed in less than 30 minutes.[34]

EDWARD LAMOUR

Vietnam: December 1968 to December 1969   Service: Army
December 1973 to September 1974

Edward Lamour (Lamoureux prior to a change of name in 1971, when he became a U.S. citizen) was born in Winnipeg on 15 December 1944. As a teenager he served in the Canadian militia. About 1960 he became interested in going to Vietnam. In December 1962 the tall skinny youth crossed the border to Fargo, North Dakota, where the U.S. Army deemed him fit for military service. In April 1963 Ed enlisted for three years. After basic training at Fort Ord, California, he was sent for advanced individual training in military accounting to the finance school at Fort Benjamin Harrison. Ed was next posted to Fort Hamilton, Brooklyn. While there, he applied to go to Vietnam but was unsuccessful. Ed was next posted to the finance office at Fort McArthur, San Pedro, California, and then received an overseas assignment to Germany, where he worked in supply (1964 to 1966). After a brief stint at Fort Sill, Oklahoma (1966 to 1967), Ed briefly returned to civilian life working in a warehouse for the International Nickel Company

Sergeant Edward Lamour in Nha Trang, Vietnam, 1969. (Courtesy E. Lamour.)

at Thompson, Manitoba. In January 1968 he re-enlisted and was sent to Fort Ord. After a thorough investigation of his past, he was given top-secret security clearance and went to Vietnam as a staff sergeant.

Ed describes his tour in Vietnam:

I arrived in Vietnam on 21 December 1968, was processed, then sent to Nha Trang to the 1st Field Force Headquarters (IFF), II Corps Tactical Zone (II CTZ), that is, the central military region of South Vietnam.

My very first night in Vietnam, I lay on my bunk listening to machine-gun fire and off in the distance I could hear Bob Hope giving a performance. This Bob Hope show really drove home the fact that I had finally arrived in Vietnam and I was prepared to do my best in whatever assignment was to be thrust upon me.

I travelled via C-130 from Saigon to Nha Trang. My travelling companions were pigs, chickens and many Vietnamese civilians. When I arrived at IFF headquarters, I found out that I was to be assigned to CORDS (Civil Operations and Rural Development Support). Orders were issued to that effect and I was picked up and taken to CORDS headquarters. The headquarters was located in what was an old two-storey hotel. Personnel then assigned me to the Chieu Hoi Division. This was a part of the pacification program that was set up to entice the Viet Cong to defect to the South Vietnamese government.

The division chief was an Australian by the name of Richard Armstrong Ashley Riddle. I believe Mr. Riddle was from Sidney, as he had me hand deliver a letter to an attorney in Sidney when I went on my R&R. Mr. Riddle was a former Aussie officer and he reminded me very much of the British type of officer with the British handlebar moustache. A Mr. "Fajhardo" was a former Philippine officer who was also on a personal contract with CORDS. There were also three foreign service officers from the U.S. State Department and two Vietnamese specialists, whose primary job was interpreting for the division. (The two Vietnamese specialists I suspected of being VC then and still do to this day.)

I was the only military person assigned to Chieu Hoi and I suppose that I was supposed to do whatever I was told by any of the action officers. As it turned out, my responsibility was only to the chief, Mr. Riddle. The Chieu Hoi Division was really a bastard unit that did not get along with the PSYOPS (Psychological Operations) Division which was located in the same office as Chieu Hoi. There was a constant battle going on with the U.S. Army officers for power over the Chieu Hoi personnel. There was a colonel over at the PSYOPS Division who tried to subordinate Mr. Riddle at every opportunity.

My mission was to reform the Chieu Hoi Division from a USAID- (U.S. Agency for International Development) type correspondence to a military one. I hired two females as typists since it was much too time-consuming for me to type correspondence in Vietnamese. I taught them military correspondence which I also required the two area specialists to learn. This task took only about four months to accomplish and the only duties I had were supervision and correspondence — secret and above. I had a great deal of time on my hands after that.

The Chieu Hoi Division needed a logistics officer and had an authorized position for one, but one had not been assigned while I was in country. The division had a unit known as an APT (armed propaganda team) consisting of over 900 ex-VC. Most of the team had no uniforms, much less equipment in order to accomplish their mission in the field. I was bored with very little duties and as much as I enjoyed running the young women and the bars, I asked for and received permission to try my hand at the mission of the logistics officer that we didn't have. There was a SP-4 Richard Smith assigned to the PSYOPS Division whose heart was with the mission of Chieu Hoi. Richard was from Circleville, Ohio. He had been served a draft notice and then skipped to Montreal. He spent about a year there then was finally persuaded by the FBI to return and submit to the draft. When he found out that I was Canadian and from Winnipeg, he and I became real close friends. I was living in a hotel when one day he and I decided to rent a house together, since he was unhappy with barracks living, along with another fellow by the name of PFC Woo Fang Hue You, half Chinese and half black. Hue You's mission in life was to rewrite the Bible. I wonder if he ever finished. Anyway, we all moved into this nice little house and the owner of the house lived in the back part and became our cook and laundress. Mamasan also made sure that all of our neighbours got to know us and we soon became part of the neighbourhood.

I asked Smitty if he would take care of my classified duties whenever I was out of town as I had planned on attempting to equip the APT and had to start from scratch. Smitty jumped at the opportunity and allowed me to hit the road. At the time I was a sergeant but on my first trip to Cam Ranh Bay I put on PFC insignia, checked out a real nice 1966 Ford sedan from the USAID motor pool, and headed south to the Cam Ranh Bay Support Command. I arrived at Cam Ranh about 7 p.m. and went directly to the enlisted men's club. There I met a few guys that worked in Support Command and told them that the food, drinks and women would be on me, no strings attached. The fellows had a real great time and I made friends.

The next morning I gave them a copy of Chieu Hoi's authorization for equipment and asked them how to go about getting the junk. They rattled off a bunch of forms that needed to be filled out and signed. I told them I did not even know how to order the forms that I needed to order the equipment. They told me that they would help me when they finished work. I thanked them and told them I would be back at six o'clock and picked them up for supper, on me. I returned to the town outside of Cam Ranh, located a very fine restaurant and made arrangements for a very fine meal of lobsters, French wine, etc. I then found the brothel where the officers and gentlemen spent their leisure time and arranged for 10 very beautiful and talented women to entertain during and after supper. At six o'clock I returned to fetch the fellows, but they had already prepared hundreds of little IBM-type requisition forms for my signature. My supply system was already in place.

Upon returning I found that it was next to impossible to arrange transportation among the U.S. military transportation units. Even the practice of starting at the lowest rank and working my way up did not work. I ended up borrowing one truck and moving the stuff myself one truckload at a time.

One day, I was carrying a load of metal — the stuff was used to make temporary landing strips — when I stopped along the road for a beer. While I was there a Republic of Vietnam (RVN) convoy pulled up and the NCO in charge, a Sergeant Ahn, came up and sat down with me. He asked me where I was stationed and I told him Chieu Hoi in Nha Trang. Sergeant Ahn told me that he was stationed in Nha Trang and the VC had a price on the head of all Chieu Hoi personnel. I laughed and told him that if the VC was willing to pay enough I would turn myself in to them. He enjoyed my sense of humour and he sent the convoy on ahead and we stayed for more beer and rice. The owner of the little roadside shop came up to us and asked in Vietnamese if I would be willing to sell one of the bunches of metal I had on the truck. I told him that he was welcome to a bundle. However, as we were leaving he insisted on paying something for the bundle and gave me some piastres. Technically I suppose that was wrong but I considered it partial reimbursement for the money that I had spent to get this system going. Sergeant Ahn asked me whether I was worried that my unit would notice it was missing. I told him no — that the unit was me — and it was all for the Chieu Hoi program. He rode with me back to Nha Trang and during the ride he told me that perhaps his commander could help the Chieu Hoi program since he was a commander of an RVN transportation company. I met with the commander the next day and he advised me that he had many trucks that were not operational for need of batteries. I told him I would see what I could do. Cam Ranh told me that I was not able to order batteries for vehicles and all of our logistics for vehicles had to be handled through USAID. This I already knew, but it was worth a try. I then went on the local economy to see what they had. There were plenty of batteries to be purchased and I put the idea into the back of my head. One day Sergeant Ahn called me and told me that he had a few trucks with drivers that I could use that day if I needed them. I needed a lot every day and took him up on it. While we were loading metal, rubber, uniforms and the like he asked me if they ever gave me more than I ordered. I explained that the guys in the office were just going down the list of authorized supplies and issuing me the stuff as fast as I could move it from the depot.

That question did arouse a little curiosity in my mind as to just how they were charging my authorization, so I told the fellows that if they could get away that weekend I would like them to come to visit Nha Trang and they would have a real great time at our house. Two of them took me up on the offer. During the weekend I asked them how they were charging it to the Chieu Hoi and they told me that they were not charging it to anybody, just giving me the stuff that was on the authorization. They were just making sure that it would be allowed if anybody ever questioned it. It seems that Chieu Hoi's requests were supposed to go through the 1st Logistics Command in Saigon. With this knowledge I thought that I had better jump on an Air America flight to Saigon and see what was going on down there.

When I got there I felt somewhat sick. It was just like being stateside. I felt real sorry for the Saigon fellows. While walking the halls of the 1st Logistics Command I ran into an old sergeant with whom I had been stationed in Germany. I told him I was with II CTZ Chieu Hoi and I needed to order supplies. He told me that he could help and all that I had to do was just send my requests directly to his office and he would take care of it for me. Now I had a second supply system in place. However, the 1st Logistics Command had a great deal of power and it was soon arranged where construction equipment, badly needed by the Chieu Hoi program, but not authorized, started to flow.

One day Sergeant X called me and asked if I could use any cement. Cement was a very scarce and hard-to-come-by material in II CTZ. I told him yes. "OK Eddie, I have 30 tons for you. You must arrange shipment to wherever you need it."

Down the beach was a very high class restaurant, off limits to military personnel, where I decided to go and have a quiet supper with a young friend of mine. When I entered, the first thing I noticed was a colonel in the place with a young friend of his. He immediately got up and asked me what I was doing in there. I showed him my MI (military intelligence) credentials and asked him what he was doing in there. My first Mexican stand-off in Vietnam. The colonel got up and left, hardly waiting for his young friend. That was my first of many uses of the MI credentials after that. However, it also caused me a great deal of trouble with members of the 272nd MP Company.

One day I was driving down the main street that ran along the beach and I was pulled over by the 272nd MPs for speeding. I let them know that I found it silly that they would be sitting alongside of the road checking the speed of vehicles during a war. They issued me a speeding ticket. A few days later I got a call from the 1st sergeant from the MI detachment asking me to come and see him. This was to be my first of two visits to the detachment. The 1st sergeant had the copy of my speeding ticket and he also advised me that I had not ever signed into the unit. I told him that I did not know that I needed to sign into the unit and I was very sorry that I had gotten the ticket but I was on an important run at the time. In fact, I was just going to visit a young friend at the time. He growled a little as all 1st sergeants do. I offered him some cement, as I noticed that the unit's personnel only had a dirt basketball court. The speeding ticket was forgotten. I told him that the cement was still in Saigon, as I was having trouble obtaining transportation for it. He told me that he had a friend that was stationed in Taiwan that was a crew chief on a C-130 and if I returned later in the day he would introduce me to him. I met with his friend and he introduced me to a navigator who, in turn, introduced me to the pilot. The pilot invited me to fly with him that evening, which I did, and during the flight we made a deal. He would arrange air transport for my cement in exchange for Communist weapons and uniforms and all of the other goodies that the U.S. military so much enjoyed. Now that I had shipments coming from both Cam Ranh and Saigon I found that I was constantly getting duplication. I had a lot of trading materials. I told Sergeant Ahn's commander from now on one out of every four truckloads of anything was his. I now had convoys of trucks, anywhere from 30 to 60, going around the II CTZ. I became a travelling man. I visited with all of the provinces in II CTZ and all the other three Chieu Hoi divisions throughout the country.

On one visit to Saigon I was arrested at a USO (United Service Organization) club for having a concealed weapon and they made me go to the MP station even though my orders clearly stated that I was authorized to carry a concealed weapon. They released me but left me without transportation back to the club. I began to hate the U.S. military with a passion.

Meanwhile, back at my office, the U.S. military and Mr. Riddle were having a battle. One day he got fed up and leased a very large villa in the city, miles away from CORDS, and moved the office into it. When that happened I left Smitty and Woo Fang and moved into the villa with Riddle. The foreign service officers didn't like it much but they had no choice. It was great living with Riddle. His contract was of such a nature that it gave him the same rights and privileges as a general officer and access to the general officers' mess — the only place where one could run into American, Australian and other non-Vietnamese women. A very nice place indeed.

Sergeant Ahn and his commander must have been making a killing on the black market. Sergeant Ahn bought himself a little truck, the kind that were used for taxis. I swapped vehicles with him once for a week. Nha Trang had a crime problem, where GIs would be knifed and robbed while a passenger. I took that taxi out at night and I would wear the straw and black silk and drive in the dark, making like a taxi. Very, very seldom did any of the GIs or Vietnamese know that I was driving. On a few occasions an attempted robbery would take place in the back of the truck. You should have seen the expressions on the GIs and the Vietnamese criminals when I would stop the truck. I hoped that the GIs realized just how close they came and took more precautions after that but it just kept continuing.

One day when we were not home the MPs raided Mr. Riddle's and my home and arrested our friends and placed them in the local jail. Mr. Riddle got furious. He called his counterpart with the Nha Trang police and told him he was going to the jail to get his friend and he had better meet him there. Mr. Riddle ended up liberating about 50 friends that evening.

The Chieu Hoi was in a position now to begin to help the community. There were more items being delivered such as refrigerators, food, everything you could think of. I then began to start a community chest. I would find a need in the community and take care of it. The Chieu Hoi Division had the opportunity to obtain generators for a Catholic priest who had no electricity at his church and school.

In my neighbourhood I had the privilege of attending a Buddhist party in memory of a dead son. I dined on barbecued mouse, and it was good. A great deal of food. The only one I did not ever repeat again was partially formed chicken in the egg. On that occasion the 272nd were trying to catch me for some infraction. As I rounded a corner, on foot, there was a group of old ladies squatted down and candling these things. I was dressed in black silk and straw hat and squatted down with them. They giggled and the MPs came around the corner and parked right there beside us. One old lady candled one, smiled and handed it to me. I ate it, they didn't tell and I didn't vomit — saved myself another round with the 272nd. One night I was real drunk and the 272nd got me placed under arrest and into the back of a jeep. There was a second MP company in Nha Trang — I can't recall the unit. One of their jeeps came by and I managed to get them to give me to them stating they have been trying to get me for months and they would appreciate it. That was one of the units that benefited from the Chieu Hoi supply system.

SP-4 Smith did a great job in keeping my administrative duties going. It got to the point where I only had to take care of the top secret stuff and that was it. That happened only on occasion and it gave me a free hand to do whatever.

Mr. Riddle tried to get me promoted, going through the chain of command at CORDS. The colonel stated he would not recommend anyone for promotion that did not wear his uniform. Riddle tried to reason with him that it would be a hindrance to the Chieu Hoi program to have a military person involved in my doings. He would not budge. Mr. Riddle took up the problem with headquarters directly. I was promoted to staff sergeant.

One day I was driving back from up north when I ran into a Korean unit, a unit of the White Horse Division, having lunch on the side of the road. They had an elaborate defence position taken to prevent an ambush and I drove up along in a Ford. They asked me if I was crazy driving the highway alone. I told them that I had a .38 pistol in my pocket and an M-14 rifle in the trunk and that I could hit anything within a quarter of a mile. I told them that if I were attacked and not killed I would go home and get my 105-mm howitzer and blow up the entire bush. They asked me where I got the howitzer and I told them I had paid a reward to a Hoi Chaun (returnee, ex-VC) for it. They asked me if I wanted to sell it. I told them I did not sell any equipment but I would trade it if they had anything. They told me that they had a lot of wine at Cam Ranh they would trade for. I told them I would tag along with them to Cam Ranh. When they got there they showed me a barge loaded with thousands of cases of wine. I made the deal. At the time we were dropping little yellow radios all over II CTZ on little parachutes. I added wine bottles to the drop and had the APTs leave cases of it all over II CTZ. I hope some of it made it to the VC. It was truly the worst wine I ever tasted.

I suppose it will not shock you that there was a lot of drug use going on in Vietnam. I will admit that I used pot. Mr. Riddle had a friend running around Vietnam named Derek. What Derek's mission was in Vietnam I never learned. He did not work for any government. He was a lone soldier. He had his own arms and equipment. Air America was his transportation to anywhere he wanted to go. If he worked for the CIA I was never able to find out. He did not work for Phoenix (pacification program). Anyway, one day I was in a brothel that was next door to a Hoi Chaun Centre. I was high and heard a commotion going on outside in the yard at the Hoi Chaun Centre. I went outside and saw Derek browbeating a couple of Hoi Chauns. I went into a rage and jumped Derek. I was going to kill him, when suddenly I realized what I was doing. I apologized to him and never used the stuff again. However, I suppose that I was justified. Derek had no business that I knew of to be questioning anyone in the Centre. I know that he was a good friend of Riddle's but even Riddle stayed out of it. Anyway Derek and I still remained friends up till I left the country. Sorry Derek, I'll never forgive myself.

The problems that I had with the 272nd MP Company came to an end one day when I entered a brothel looking for a female VC that was going to defect and low and behold there was a high-ranking member of the 272nd with her. I placed him under arrest and told him that I caught him in bed with a well-known VC. I released him and from then on when the 272nd saw me they went the other way.

Smitty wanted to throw a farewell party at his house and asked my assistance. He was introducing a lot of U.S. military and their Vietnamese counterparts and figured a party would be the best way to do it. I obtained cases and cases of T-bone steaks from the depot. We tried to lay on baked potatoes and ended up having to trade T-bones pound for pound for potatoes, lobster, fish, and fine French wines. The party was great. I actually got to meet my commander for the very first time. He kept looking at me most of the evening and finally told me he thought my name sounded familiar. When he told me what unit he was in I told him so was I and that was when he told me he was the CO. I felt a little apprehensive for I knew that Smitty was going to serve pot joints for dessert. I took the CO aside and let him know that I had nothing to do with the dessert, only the main course. He gave me a bewildered look but understood and that large bowl of pot was brought out. My discomfort ended when a U.S. brigadier general lit one up. It was great, brigadiers on down, mayors, politicians, CIA, everyone having a great time. I kind of wish the 272nd MPs would have come around that evening.

Following his year in Vietnam, Ed was a documents clerk from January to October 1970 at Fort Leavenworth, Kansas, and from November 1970 to March 1972 at Fort Sam Houston, Texas. It was at about this time that he met his wife, Mary. They were married in April 1972. Ed remembers the last three draftees coming through the door for processing. The next day the draft was to be abolished. The paperwork was quietly put aside except that concerning one obnoxious draftee who was inducted.

From December 1973 to September 1974, Ed, then a staff sergeant, was in Thailand. Ed was the last Canadian to serve in the Vietnam War Zone. He recalls his time there during that period:

Thailand, that was a strange assignment. One of my dumb jobs was one that a modern-day computer could have done. I was assigned to the United States Special Activities Group (USSAG), which was made up mostly of the 7th Air Force. There the air force ran the whole thing. Army and naval personnel were there mostly as a way of obtaining personnel who had top-secret, special intelligence clearances. I was very unhappy in my job.

Air force types were not my type at all. They, of the unit, were considered the cream of the crop and assignment to USSAG was the ultimate. Well, I hated it. As soon as my day was done I headed for the town, Nakhon Phanom (the military just called it NKP). The Joint Military Resolution Command was also located there. That unit is now based in Hawaii and is the unit that is responsible for identifying the remains of troops coming out of Vietnam. Theirs is a grisly mission. In my search for a new unit I was getting ready to accept an assignment with them when out of the blue I found a position at Sattaship, located at the very south part of Thailand. The Joint Military Resolution Command would have been an interesting assignment but NKP was a terrible place. January 1974 was the worst month I ever spent. It was *cold*. I called home for long underwear and a wool robe. The barracks were built for the tropics. Cold air would blow through the walls and screen. Some poor GI lit a heater and took it to bed with him and killed himself. There was a fuel shortage at the time and they did not let us have diesel fuel to heat water for showering. Later I found out that beneath NKP was a huge fuel storage facility for fuel. So when Sattaship offered me a job I took it.

Thailand is a beautiful country, once I got down south. There I was assigned to the deep-water port where all the cargo coming into or leaving Southeast Asia was handled. My job was that as a contracting officer of the United States, a glorified title that simply meant that when I signed a document the identified vendor would be paid. A simple job. I would report to work at 8:00 a.m. and in just a few weeks I would be done by 8:20 and be home by 9:00 a.m. The staff of my office were entirely Thai civilians who were all jealous of one another. With that type of environment it was quite a simple task of diplomacy to keep the office honest and on its toes. Any type of fraud or dishonesty was quickly detected by one other staff member and promptly reported to me.

Thailand turned out to be one extended vacation. I travelled by motor car every day to somewhere. My only responsibility was to be at my office each day at 8 a.m. and work until I processed the prior day's work — process being signing the vouchers. I could sign 200 in 20 minutes. I would be extremely upset on a day of hanky panky for I would be there about 12 hours continuously.

My wife was teaching in Amarillo when I was assigned to Thailand and had planned to visit Thailand during June and July. By June I had found us a very nice two-storey house with the bath and two bedrooms upstairs, kitchen and the biggest living room you ever saw downstairs. The house was located across the street from a compound that was made up completely of GIs and their "tealocks." (A tealock is a temporary wife that most of the military personnel took while living in Thailand.)

My wife was in the country perhaps 10 days when my grandfather died. So there she was just recently in the country and I go off to Winnipeg. I was given 30 days' leave for the funeral and in three days it was over. Mary had everything she needed and there were a lot of people from the deep-water port where I worked living right across the street from us. After the funeral I decided to hitchhike across Canada to Vancouver. My Uncle Bob Lamoureux gave me a lift just west of Winnipeg's perimeter highway and we said goodbye. My first ride pulled over before my uncle could cross the highway and turn around. A soldier based west of Winnipeg picked me up and was full of questions about Thailand and Vietnam. He was confident that Canada would have given a good account of herself had she gone. I agreed, letting him know that the best training that I had received was with the Canadian militia.

While I was gone, my wife had made up her mind that she was going to skip teaching in the coming year and just stay on with me for the rest of my tour. She has never told me if it was the charm of Thailand itself or the custom of tealocks that she worried about. In any event she had already established a school for the dependant children of military personnel at the Utapao Air Force Base and a missionary's children by the name of Givens. When I landed at Bangkok I stopped at the commissary and for some reason, I don't know why, I bought a turkey. These missionary friends of my wife seized the opportunity to create a Thanksgiving dinner in July. Missionaries are a weird group.

So there, things had really changed. The bottom floor of our home was now a schoolhouse. I had nothing to do each day so to speak. I would be home by 9 a.m. each day wanting to go riding and my wife had to teach. We finally agreed to go on at least a four-day school week so we could continue to travel around south Thailand meeting the people, finding the most beautiful beaches you could possibly hope for.

A fellow by the name of Cham Long was a PX taxi driver who had become a friend and we all chipped in and bought him a Toyota so he could have his own taxi. Cham Long became my semi-private chauffeur. My wife had to renew her visa each month and the graft that we had to pay each time kept getting more and more expensive. So finally we decided to go out of the country to renew it. Since Cambodia was the nearest country, a few hours' drive, that is where we went. When we got to the border, Mary had no problem crossing since she did have a passport. I didn't and I just told her to go ahead, get her visa and I would wait right here at the border. She left and went into the town. After about an hour, a Cambodian fellow came

over and asked me why I did not go into town with my wife. I told
him that I did not have my passport with me and I would have to
wait. He went over and told the customs official about it and when
he returned he said for a few baht (25 baht = 1 dollar) the official
would let me into Cambodia. I sent Cham Long over to talk with the
Thai people and they couldn't care less. I would not be bothered
when I returned to Thailand. I crossed, got a cyclo cab and went
looking for my wife. The first place I looked, I found her — the
shopping bazaar. I called to her very loudly numerous times. Finally
I caught up to her and asked her why she did not turn around. She
said she heard her name being called but since she did not know
anyone in Cambodia she was sure that it was for someone else. We
shopped and she got her visa. I sure was happy to get back as I knew
it was illegal for the U.S. military to be in Cambodia.[35]

*After some two years at Fort Ord, California, Ed was assigned to Fort Lewis,
Washington. A daughter had been born in 1975 and Ed decided it would be
best for the family if he settled down in one place rather than having to move
all the time. Following the end of his tour at Fort Lewis in October 1976, Ed
retired to Lubbock, Texas, the spot he now considers home.*

SHANE POLLOCK

Vietnam: December 1968 to November 1969   Service: Marines

Shane Pollock was born in Maple Creek, Saskatchewan, 5 September
1950. His parents separated and were divorced when he was little.
He then moved out to Osoyoos, British Columbia, where he lived
with his grandparents on their ranch. When his grandparents retired,
Shane, then about 12, moved back with his father who had remarried. In 1960 Shane's father and stepmother moved to Tonasket,
Washington, and Shane went with them. He retained his Canadian
citizenship, however, and never gave it up.

Shane's teen years proved to be most unhappy. He dropped out
of school and became a delinquent. Shane wanted to join the navy
but he was rejected for lack of education. As boot camp for the army
was only three hours' drive from his home, Shane decided to enlist in
the U.S. Marines in order to get farther away from his parents.

The induction centre for the marines was at Seattle, where Shane
signed up on 7 July 1967 for four years. A flight took him and others
to San Diego for basic training. Although he stands over six feet,
Shane remembers being overwhelmed and scared by the drill in-

Private Shane Pollock in South Vietnam, December 1968. This photo was taken the first week he was there. (Courtesy S. Pollock.)

structor upon arrival. Basic training followed in the heat of July and August. After some eight weeks in San Diego, it was on to Camp Pendleton (near San Clemente) for further infantry training. After Shane reached his 18th birthday, he was ordered to Vietnam. Departure in December 1968 was through El Toro, California, then to Hawaii, Wake Island, and Okinawa for final vaccinations. Next stop was Da Nang in the central highlands of Vietnam.

Private Pollock was assigned to Company G, 2nd Battalion, 7th Regiment, 1st Marine Division. He was sent along with six other new arrivals as replacements to a marine outpost in the A Shau Valley in Quang Tri Province. Shane's first assignment outside the base camp was with a force responding to a patrol that had made contact with the enemy. His very first job was to pick up the pieces of a marine killed by a booby trap. He remembers vomiting as he gathered up the pieces of rotting flesh. He cannot forget the heat or the humidity.

During Pollock's tour, and it was an action-packed tour, he clashed with the Viet Cong and North Vietnamese regulars on numerous occasions. He especially remembers the first time he saw action. He and his comrades were on a road sweep when Viet Cong snipers quickly killed three or four and wounded several others of the patrol. In reaction, Shane and a machine gunner, another new arrival, expended vast amounts of ammunition only to later discover plenty of damage to the terrain but no enemy casualties.

To Shane, the fighting consisted of a hit-and-run guerrilla war conducted by an enemy who knew the country intimately. It seemed more or less an accident when a patrol encountered an enemy force. There were sweeps into Cambodia and arduous 30-day operations through rugged terrain. Prisoners or villagers sometimes gave helpful information. Shane remembers hours spent crawling up a hill or sitting in ambush at night as mosquitoes attacked him. He recalls many hours spent in the rain.

The war took its toll physically and mentally on the combat troops. Towards the end of Pollock's tour, his unit was ambushed near Dong Ha. Shane was among the wounded, hit in the leg by a ricochet. He was evacuated eventually to Okinawa, where he recovered. The remainder of his tour with the marines was spent in Honolulu, Hawaii, mainly doing office work.

As a result of President Nixon's decision to cut back troops in Vietnam, it was possible for those with a tour in Vietnam and three years' service to obtain an early discharge. Shane Pollock took advantage of this program. When he returned to Tonasket, Washington, he could not settle down or even find work. His military service was of no account when it came to the job market. Unable to get along again with his father, Shane returned to the only home he had really known, Maple Creek, Saskatchewan. There he worked at various jobs. He was a cowboy for a while, then worked in a meat-packing plant until he finally obtained a job with Parks Canada. Shane works as a mechanic at Prince Albert National Park and is a happily married man with two children, a boy and a girl.[36]

DWIGHT ANDERSON

Vietnam: January 1969 to January 1970   Service: Marines

A western Canadian who enlisted to fight communism in South Vietnam was Dwight Anderson, born in Wadena, Saskatchewan, in 1949 but raised in Lynn Lake, Manitoba. His efforts to join the U.S. Marines began in February 1968 and were completed in May. Anderson served as a rifleman in Vietnam with the 2nd Battalion, 5th Regiment, 1st Marine Division, from 6 January 1969 to 1 January 1970. Of the 32 who came as replacements with him, only 6 survived for the full tour. Of that 6, all received the Purple Heart at least once for being wounded in combat. Apart from four

years as a civilian (1970-74), much of Dwight's adult life has been spent in the military. He remains on active duty in the U.S. Army.[37]
The following is a selection of some of the letters he wrote home:

7 or 8 January 1969
Place: just west of Wake Island

Dear all at home:

Left Marine Corps Airbase El Toro (south of Los Angeles) at two o'clock this morning. Landed in Honolulu, Hawaii, about five hours later — 5:55 their time. We had half an hour there. The weather was nice and warm but very humid, not like southern California which is dry. We pulled out of there after refuelling just as the sun was coming up. We just passed Wake Island about 15 minutes ago. It was very clear to see even though we were 50 miles from it, as the water inside the coral reef is a turquoise blue compared to the sky blue of the Pacific. The trip from Hawaii to Kadena, Okinawa, is 10 hours. I don't know if we have crossed the date line yet.

The plane we are on just got back from Vietnam before we got in with men coming home. Let me tell you they were a happy bunch. I even saw a couple crying they were so happy. At the same time the wives of some of the men on the plane now were bawling because their husbands were going back. Some of them have kids as well who are old enough to know what is happening and I sure felt sorry for them....

11 January 1968
An-Hoa, South Vietnam

Dear all at home:

Greetings from this side of the Pacific. As you can tell by the address above, I am in Vietnam. Let me tell you, it has got to be the most different place I've ever been and probably the worst. It is hot and very humid, but I should get used to that very soon. Half of the country is mud, ankle deep. To be truthful, the country is very pretty.

13 January 1968

Dear all at home:

We have been pretty busy getting all our gear issued to us. Today we were out most of the day firing so we could get our weapons sighted.

We live in tents. All around us is barbed wire covered by machine-gun bunkers in case the gooks try to get through. There is artillery around us on all sides, firing support for the men and in the field on patrols. This bangs away all night and illumination rounds from 81-mm mortars are shot up so the sentries can see the gooks if they are trying to get up to our wire. In the daytime the civilians are all around the area outside our wire. Some of the trusted ones are allowed in to work. I personally don't trust any of the slanted-eyed, slope-headed, rice-propelled bastards myself. One minute they can be your friends and the next they might try to kill you. Three marines were killed here yesterday by some little boys (7-8) who threw a grenade at them. We fool around with them and tease them, give them smokes and C-rations.

One kid about six came up to me when I was guarding the road to the range where we were firing today and says, "Hey, No. 1 GI, gimme smoke." So I gave him a smoke and he started smoking. He even had his own matches. There were all kinds of people going by. The women, both young and old, carrying heavy loads in baskets hung on the ends of poles. (The men carry as little as possible.) I don't know how they can carry so much, they are so small and skinny. They are about four feet five inches tall.

It has been raining all day and everything is all mud again, what little had dried in the couple days of sunshine. We are expecting the shit to hit the fan here in this area pretty soon, with the coming of the Tet lunar new year. A regiment of NVA soldiers has been spotted about two miles from here. We could get mortared anytime but they don't have the rounds to waste except for an attack. We should be going to the bush (jungle so thick it is fairly dark even in the daytime) in about a week to ambush, find, and fight with the gooks to try and keep them offbalance so they cannot mount a very effective attack.

Where we are is about 30 miles south of Da Nang. I am in the 5th Marine Regiment, 2nd Battalion, Fox Company (part of the 1st Marine Division). This place is called An-Hoa (pronounced an-wa). Excuse the writing but it is getting dark and we have no electricity in our tent. We have no real mess hall here, just a tent where they serve whatever they can get. For a plate I have a canteen cup, which is four inches high and five inches wide (some plate). My cup is a Black Label beer can with one end cut out. The only eating utensil I have is a plastic spoon (so I use my fingers mostly). The living conditions here are best described as revolting but I am getting used to them. Believe me, if I ever live through the 13 months and get back to the world, I'll never be fussy! This place is bad but it is an education just being here and worth whatever I have to go through. Must close as it is getting too dark to write....

Lance Corporal Dwight Anderson writing home from "Arizona Territory," South Vietnam, April 1969. (Courtesy D. Anderson.)

26 January 1969

Dear all at home:

From the mountain we are on top of we can see the lowlands (rice paddies) with the South China Sea way in the background. On the other side we can see nothing but mountains and jungle; about 10 miles or so over is Laos. About 35 feet from me is a crashed helicopter. The gooks shot it down two days ago as it was bringing us in supplies. No one was killed but one of the crew members was awfully busted up and they didn't think he would live. I was lucky; I was out on patrol when it happened as it crashed close to where I sleep.

The VC have little or no artillery and no air power. Our artillery is shooting constantly. This morning we watched for an hour as jet after jet came in dropping napalm and bombs and shot rockets on a hill about one mile from here.

I've only been fired on once last night. As we were going on patrol, two gooks opened up on us. They fired about 25 shots but as they were firing uphill at us and it was thick bush, the rounds went over our heads hitting on the trees above us.

The weather has really been nice the last 10 days, so no rain and the temperature has been in 80-90 degrees area. I will almost hate to go back to Canada where it is cold after being here. In the summertime here, it gets up to 120 degrees. It is now the winter or monsoon season. One thing this country crawls with is bugs, every shape and form. I have seen earthworms two feet long almost as thick as my little finger.... We have to take malaria pills every week. This climate is good for one thing. All my pimples have cleared up again....

25 February 1969

Dear all at home:

Hope you all aren't too worried about me as I know with this outbreak of VC attacks you are probably seeing all kinds of stuff on TV. Right now I am not in An-Hoa but out of it about two miles. It got rocketed and attacked last night. From where we are I could see it real good. It looked like a big fireworks. I got in my first real good fight the other day. We were down in the lowlands and were crossing an open area which was nothing but sand. It was 200 yards across. I was walking sixth man from the last. We were just about across it when the gooks started shooting at us with automatic weapons from the other side. As soon as I heard the rounds, I hit the deck. The guy next to me got hit in the back. I saw the round hit him. He was lucky his pack and flak jacket stopped the round. We just lay there for 10 more seconds while they shot. They stopped firing to reload and we took off into the tall elephant grass about 30 feet from where I was laying. I am the assistant gunner for a machine gun as they are short of machine gunners right now. I was right behind the gunner, a guy from Texas. His name is Tommy Byrd, so we call him T-Byrd. Once in the grass, everyone on the trail was pinned down and had to get out, so me and T-Byrd had to stay and give protective fire for the men. We stood up and started firing. T-Byrd firing and me feeding the rounds on a belt into the gun. When we fired, the guys would get up and get out of the danger area. Every time we got down to put in a new belt of ammo into the gun, the gooks would fire at us. They were trying to get me and T-Byrd the hardest. The rounds were hitting all around us. Man, I don't know how we never got hit. They were hitting the dirt around me and singing through the grass not more than six inches from me sometimes. When everyone was out, me and T-Byrd stood up and started firing, ran 15 feet, stopped, fired some more and ran some more. They fired back like crazy. It was a good fight but we got the best of them even though they were set up in ambush just waiting for us....

5 March 1969

Dear all at home:

We only had a short patrol today. Tramped around out in the muddy old rice paddies stopping gooks on the way to market or wherever they are always sneaking around with their junk on their back. We stop them and check their IDs. Most of them have IDs but the pictures on the cards don't usually look like the guy carrying it. We have an ex-NVA soldier attached to us as a Kit Carson Scout. He goes along and talks to any we pick up. He can usually tell if they are lying to him and if they are he starts squawking and jabbering and kicking stuff around, hits and beats on them until they talk. He is only about five feet high. He is a cool little dude, wears fancy sunglasses, gold teeth, watch, radio....

12 March 1969

Dear all at home:

Just a short letter with some gook stuff I captured. I took them off a dead gook. He fired at us from a clump of trees and we got close and returned fire. When we did, he got up and started running across a small paddy to another clump of trees. I jumped up and fired a magazine full automatic at him. He went down so I know I hit him. We fired in some more rounds where he went down and then waited a few minutes before going in after him. We found him with six rounds in his legs and back, dead as a doornail. I was the first one to reach him, so frisked him and found his wallet with this stuff and some papers I could not keep as they are to be sent in to be interpreted by intelligence. I wouldn't say for sure but I am certain I killed him. It didn't bother me too much though as he tried to do the same thing to us, so he got what he tried to give out....

14 March 1969

Dear all at home:

Received your letter yesterday and Auntie Eva's package. Thanks a lot Auntie. The chocolates were a little battered but still good.

Not too much news over here. Life goes on pretty much the same. Patrols, night ambushes, sleeping on the ground, eating C-rations. I must smell something awful from tramping around in the rice paddies. They use human waste to fertilize them with, so that smell is in everything.

The weather here the last few days has been kinda miserable, cloudy and drizzling off and on. I sure wish they would take us into the rear pretty soon. We've been out 25 days now. It's been a pretty rough 25. So far 11 guys have gotten killed including one of my best friends, a guy from Billings, Montana.

I have a fire team now, that is, three men plus myself, of whom I am in charge. One of them, John X, gave me quite a bit of trouble when he first got here. He was scared of mud for some reason. As soon as we hit a muddy paddy he would get scared and couldn't go anywhere until we took most of his gear and carried it. We were moving after dark one evening to a real big muddy paddy we had to cross. He went about a 100 feet and fell down saying he couldn't go any further. The squad leader and I had to go back and get him moving. We got left behind from everyone else out there in the dark. He would go a little ways, maybe 10 feet and fall down again bawling that he couldn't make it. We started beating him. He still wouldn't go. We could have easily got killed out there by ourselves if any VC had been around. Finally, I told him I would drown him in the mud and leave him if he didn't move. He didn't, so I pushed his head in the mud about 15-20 seconds and he came up more ready to move. I know that if he pulls any of that stuff again where he could get someone hurt, I'll beat him so bad they'll have to medevac him. He tries a lot harder now and seems to be getting over his fear of mud. I hated to be so rough on him. He's not that big but it's no game we're playing over here. It isn't just "bang, you're dead" and you get up again, you don't. I've seen enough dead marines to know that....

27 March 1969

Dear all at home:

We just got back in off patrol and it is hot as can be sitting here under the shade. Patrol today was pretty well routine. We went a long ways and saw no enemy. All we did was go out into the villes surrounding the area we are set up in. We go to all the hutches and crawl in the bunkers they build to protect themselves from artillery and check them. Poke around in all their property and make sure they aren't hiding anything that belongs to the VC. I like getting to the personal gear they have which belonged to their ancestors. They put it in woven baskets and store it away neatly. I hate these bastards. They are all two-faced. In all villes it is the same thing. Old women and a few young ones and piles of kids. The only men are the ones too old to be any good to the VC.

In the ville we were in this morning, there was one guy about 35. The interpreter asked him a bunch of questions but all he said was "Khongbiet" which means I don't know. I got sick of hearing him so I went over and kicked him in the ass. Another guy slugged him in the jaw and flattened him. When he got up he was sure talking.

This whole area we are working in now is nothing but VC and VC sympathizers. The ones who weren't VC have all been pulled up and moved close to An-Hoa where they are safe. There is a large CAC-ville just outside An-Hoa and the people in it live real decent. A CAC-ville is one where the Combined Action Company teams stay and work with the people.

We've been out now for 36 days, so they should be taking us in the rear pretty soon I hope....

23 April 1969

Dear all at home:

Since I got back to the bush they've been running us ragged. This is the first day we've had off in a long time. Yesterday we had a patrol which was about seven miles long. When we have to go on patrols that long we get mad, so we take our anger out on these slimy Vietnamese. One guy hit a booby trap which shattered the bone in his leg and tore him up pretty good. Another guy hit one they had put up in a tree and he got hit in the back of the neck and head. The people just sit in their hutches like nothing happened, when it was about 50 yards from their hutch. They know the booby traps are there. I about did one old bat in with dirt lumps. The guy hit a booby trap close to her place and then she comes out and tries to beg food....

24 April 1969

Dear Grandma:

Just a short line to let you know how I am. We didn't have a patrol today so I was just thinking of everyone back there. I wish more people could see this place. I can safely say it must be the closest thing we have to hell on the face of the earth. The people live in rundown hovels that most people back home would probably use as pigpens. When you look in their faces, it is really a pity. They haven't had much and don't expect much out of life. Their whole life revolves around simply getting something to eat and staying alive from day to day. In areas where the grip of the VC is broken it isn't like this. The people look happy, are well dressed, and fed. If we could win this war and get out of here and let the people start running this country, they would be a well-to-do nation. The soil in Vietnam is reddish, it is very rich, and they could grow more than they would ever need. I'm just happy I don't have to live here and at the end of my tour I can get out....

7 May 1969

Dear all at home:

Today at two o'clock my whole company leaves for China Beach in Da Nang for a three-day in-country rest and recreation (R&R). This is a gesture from the commanding general of the 1st Marine Division for the beating we gave the gooks in the last three months. The whole 2nd Battalion, 5th Marine Regiment, gets to go, one company at a time. Boy, when we hit the beach, it is going to be the biggest party to ever hit that place....

11 June 1969

Dear all at home:

Received your letter today Mom with Grandma's in it. That crazy grandma saying I should get my alien discharge. She doesn't understand that I started this and I intend to stick it out and take my chances over here even though I could get killed and messed up.

I signed up and took an oath that I would stick it out for my three years, the same as anyone else over here. Just because I'm a Canadian doesn't mean that if the going gets rough I could put my tail between my legs and run home. Sure I'd love to get out of here, everyone here would, but that isn't the honourable thing to do.

We had a blast at China Beach in Da Nang. We had all the beer we could drink, a band, hamburger, steaks, grilled down on the beach and went swimming in the South China Sea. We all got drunk as skunks and had a beer fight. Everyone dumped beer all over each other. The only bad part was we had to go there and come back by truck convoy over these damn dusty roads....

5 July 1969

Dear all at home:

They took us off the bridge and put us back in the bush. The second day out, my platoon got ambushed coming across an open paddy. The point men in each squad were almost to the trees when they opened up. Boy, bullets were going everywhere. They were to our direct front and left flank. I am pretty sure I killed one on the left flank as I was the only one to put fire out to the left and we found one body there but no weapon. He must have had some buddies close who grabbed it. They opened up from the front first and then the left. I was about 10 people or so from the front, so I didn't fire up there right away. Then I could pick out the sound of a rifle about 30 yards to my left. At first I was scared, as I couldn't make out just where he was. I was flat on the ground and crawling and praying like crazy. I could just feel his eyes on me and thought for sure I would be dead any second. All this happened in about five seconds but it seemed like a lifetime. I got turned around and began firing semi-automatic all back and forth across the treeline in clumps where I thought he was. I fired two magazines (20 rounds in each), couldn't hear him still firing, so got up and ran to the front of the ambush where the front guys were pinned down. I started working rounds back and forth across that treeline. While this was going on a helicopter was diving them, shooting rockets and firing in at them. Altogether, it lasted about 20 minutes of steady shooting. They finally broke contact and started running off. They left three more dead behind. We had four wounded, none too badly, all in the arms and legs.

It was pretty hairy while it lasted, but when it stopped, we were surprised as they had had the advantage but we fouled them up with our firepower. In all, I fired 12 magazines. It's so hard to describe a firefight. It's a great deal of fun while it's going on. I like them, but I'm scared all the time. Yet, I've done some crazy stuff. Everybody seems to. I've caught myself standing shooting from the hip and swearing at the top of my voice at them as I'm shooting, then running out of rounds and just standing there shaking my fist and swearing before getting down and putting in a fresh magazine. It seems whichever side is the craziest is the one that wins the fight. One guy that was beside me fired out his rounds and then got down and calmly asked me for a cigarette like nothing was going on. It just seems that one loses one's sense of values temporarily and doesn't give a damn. Then after it's all over and you start thinking right again; you say to yourself, damn, I could have gotten killed and it scares you then. But you try not to think about it or you will lose your nerve and that could be worse than having too much nerve. I think it's better to be brave and shoot back at them, as it gets their heads down and puts off their aim. If we just lay there, they'd shoot us like fish in a barrel.

Don't worry about me. I'll be alright if the heat doesn't get me or the mosquitoes don't carry me off at night....

17 July 1969

Dear all at home:

We never stay in one place more than a day and run patrols or make night movements all the time. I hate these night movements. On the last one, a guy in our platoon hit a box mine and lost a leg and a half-hour later another guy, a second platoon lieutenant, hit and lost both legs. About five days before that, two guys got killed and five wounded by booby traps. They are what cause most of our casualties. I hate them. You never know where they are so you have to be on the alert all the time for them. It is especially bad at night when you can't see them — they are hard enough to spot in the daytime. Most won't kill you but take your legs off. If you die, it's usually from going into shock. They are especially hard on your nerves because of the constant danger....

9 August 1969

Dear all at home:

Right now I'm back in the mountains and we've been busy moving around trying to catch the gooks and pin them down so we can hit them with air strikes. I've already been on R&R and it was the best time I've had in my life. Hong Kong is fabulous. While I was there I had a girl for five days and nights. I just stayed happy the whole time I was there. At night we would go to a movie or a night club or bar, somewhere where they had a band and I just drank all kinds of booze. At night we would go back to the hotel about two in the morning and not get up till about two the next day and then I'd go down to the bar in the hotel, eat and then sit and drink and listen to the stories and stay nice and mellow the rest of the day. It was so nice I just never thought about this place at all. The day I had to come back though I felt like the world was coming to an end, knowing I had to come back to this hell hole....

21 September 1969

Dear all at home:

For about five days since Ho Chi Minh died we couldn't hardly get any sleep. We had firefights that would go on all night. My very best buddy, Byron Canada, from Flint, Michigan, got messed up by a gook grenade. He has been medevacked out of country and is probably in some hospital close to his home by now. If anything were to happen to me, I want you to tell him. He's the best friend I've ever had.

I finally made up my mind to get my discharge. I'm getting the papers I'll need. I can't see doing 16 more months in the Marine Corps when I leave here. Besides I never joined the Marine Corps for any real reason but to come over here so when I'm through here, I want to be finished with the Marine Corps. I can't see 16 months of spit and polish, stateside duty, and for sure I'm not coming back here for six more months so I can get an early out. So, in about 135 days, I'll be a civilian and out of here. [Dwight became a civilian from 1970 to 1974.] The monsoon is on now so it's rain, rain, rain, from now till I rotate.

Somebody up there is looking after me. I know it. Since I've been here, my battalion has been getting its ass kicked out in the "Arizona Territory" (Quang Nam Province)....

26 October 1969

Dear all at home:

It won't be too long now till I'm out of here. I'll be so glad. My feet have about had it. They are all blistered and half rotten on the bottom. It is so seldom I get to put on clean socks or even take my boots off. My nerves are about shot. I pop up all the time at night to any little noise. I've never been this scared since I've been here. I can't get along with hardly anyone. I'm so irritable. I'll just have to be this way for the next 50 days or so and then I'll be out of here. I'm going to come home and just relax. I don't want anyone to bug me at all. Just put up with me for the first while. OK....

10 November 1969

Dear all at home:

Today is the Marine Corps birthday so we're all going up to Hill 65 for free beer and a USO show. I got the package today. Thanks for the rain clothes. They sure are a lot better than the marines' issue.

The weather sure has been miserable lately. It just rains off and on constantly. It wouldn't be so bad but it swells up the rice paddies and patrols are so damn muddy. It will take 5 to 10 days processing till I get out and then I'll be coming straight home....

*Lance Corporal Dwight Anderson at "Football Island,"
South Vietnam, June 1969. (Courtesy D. Anderson.)*

16 December 1969

Dear all at home:

Inside a gook hutch writing this. This morning was the best day the platoon has had since I've been here. We trapped a bunch of NVA on a long sandbar in the river. It was all overgrown with elephant grass. The NVA were down here trying to gather rice, as we have been starving them out by tearing up their rice paddy beds before the farmers can plant them in the paddies. We spotted two of them running over to the sandbar and went after them. As we did, they threw a couple of grenades at us out of the grass. So we fired into the grass real good and they went across. I've never seen so many NVA in one place. They were trying to hide in the grass. Some were trying to hide in the water. We started throwing grenades in the water. Boy, did that make them come out fast! In less than one hour we killed 20 and captured 29. Seven of them were young NVA nurses. Everyone is still excited. They say that CBS is going to send some cameramen out here tomorrow to go out and film us while we are on patrol. Maybe you'll get to see me on TV!

See you all soon. Love,

Dwight[38]

ERIC WALSH

Vietnam: 1969 to 1970   Service: Army
          1971 to 1972

Specialist Five Eric Walsh in the door of a Chinook helicopter, Phu Loi, South Vietnam, 1969-70. (Courtesy E. Walsh.)

Eric Walsh was born 19 May 1950 in Ottawa, the middle child in a family of two girls and one boy. While he was in primary school, his father died. Eric attended St. Patrick's Separate School and Glashan Public School in Ottawa. He went on to Ottawa Technical High School.

Eric became fascinated by the adventure aspect of the Vietnam War and decided to join the American forces. Following receipt of his alien registration card from the American consulate in Montreal, Walsh enlisted at Buffalo and along with others, mostly draftees, was sent to Fort Dix near Newark, New Jersey, for basic training. There, he experienced the sweltering hot American summer of 1968. He had never encountered such hot and humid weather for such a long period.

From Fort Dix, Private Walsh was sent on to the Transportation School at Fort Eustis, Virginia, where he was trained on Chinook and Huey helicopters. His mechanical skills quickly brought him to the level of SP-4. On 20 December 1968 he was told that as an alien he had not received the necessary security clearance for a combat zone. After one month of frustrating kitchen duty, he lodged a complaint. His case was investigated and it was discovered a clerk had made an error. Security clearance had been given upon his induction. Walsh was at last able to go to Vietnam.

From McGuire Air Force Base in New Jersey, Walsh flew to San Francisco and then to Hawaii, stopped at Guam and then landed at Tan Son Nhut Air Base, Saigon. What struck him most when he landed on 17 March 1969 in Vietnam was the heat and then the smell. He was sent to Phu Loi, a helicopter base, and assigned to the 11th Aviation Battalion, 1st Aviation Brigade. Within a short time, he was sent to the 205th Assault Support Company at Phu Loi, where he served with the ground crew. By May 1969 Walsh was with a flight platoon, and he became a crew chief on board a Chinook (CH-47) helicopter. (The Chinook usually had a crew of five.) Following the end of his first tour in Vietnam on 17 March 1970, he took leave and was granted the six months' extension he had requested.

After 18 months in Nam, Walsh was sent to Fort Sill, Oklahoma, but found it boring. His job was to help ferry junked vehicles to an artillery range to give gunners an opportunity to practise. As an industrious, hard-working individual used to the excitement of combat missions, he found it difficult to readjust to the dull routine of an army post.

Walsh's second tour as a crewman in Vietnam was from 16 August 1971 to 16 August 1972. At Phu Loi, he was with the 213th Assault Support Company, 11th Aviation Battalion of the 1st Aviation Brigade, and rose to platoon sergeant. He requested and received a second extension to 29 March 1973. Eric became quite excited when he learned that Canadian peacekeeping troops would be arriving. He wanted his American friends to be impressed by the military bearing of the Canadian troops. Instead, Walsh was deeply disappointed when what appeared were middle-aged men in shorts, many overweight. He was slightly embarrassed by the Canadians' obsession with sex, particularly their lack of discretion or discrimination in the prostitutes they openly patronized. A member of a crew of four, he helped fly Canadian members of the ICCS (International Commission of Control and Supervision for Vietnam) on Huey helicopters as they began setting up inspection sites. SP-5 Walsh ended his military career at Fort Campbell, Kentucky, on 27 March 1974.

Eric has managed to turn his Vietnam experience into something positive. Having lived through and overcome that espisode, he continues to call upon the inner resources which helped him survive there.[39]

DAVID ROSS

Vietnam: May 1969 to May 1970   Service: Army

Warrant Officer David Ross in Phu Hiep, South Vietnam, 1969-70.
(Courtesy D. Ross.)

David Ross was born 11 November 1947 in Toronto, Ontario. In 1965 his father, an engineer, accepted a job offer from an aircraft company in San Diego. Dave moved there. He attended school but in 1967 decided to return home to work. A draft notice was forwarded to him in Pickering, but Dave just ignored it. Early in 1968 he moved back to San Diego and was drafted. In April Dave joined the army with the aim of learning how to fly a helicopter. After basic training at Fort Polk, Louisiana, he was sent to Fort Wolters, Texas, for primary training, then for a similar period to Fort Rucker, Alabama, for advanced training. Upon successfully completing the course, he agreed to serve a few more years in the army. Soon after graduation Dave received orders for Vietnam.

With the rank of warrant officer, Dave was assigned to the 134th As-
sault Helicopter Company based at Phu Hiep, which was on the coast
halfway between Nha Trang and Qui Nhon. Dave flew "slicks," that is,
Hueys used primarily for transport. Following his year in Vietnam, Dave
was sent to Fort Hood, Texas, where he served some five months. As a result
of the scaling down of the Vietnam War, the U.S. armed forces were being
reduced, and taking advantage of an early-out program for helicopter pilots
who had served a year in Vietnam, Dave obtained an early honourable dis-
charge in January 1971. Still a Canadian citizen, Dave resides in Denver
with his wife and two children and works as a financial manager.
The following are his recollections of his Vietnam tour:

When I first arrived at the 134th, I really wasn't made to feel welcome. New guys weren't readily accepted. I just seemingly stumbled
about the first few days. My first mission was with a hunter-killer
team consisting of a helicopter flying low with a heat-seeking device,
an observation helicopter flying high at 3,000 feet and a pair of
gunships in the middle. Each time we flew over an area the aircraft
commander of the ship with the heat-seeking device would call "hot
spot." Then the gunships would shoot a couple of rockets into the
area. Near the end of the mission, the high observer ship spotted an
elephant with a person on it. The gunships quickly hit that Viet Cong
before he could escape. I couldn't believe that anybody could so
coolly kill another human being or an elephant. Most of the ensuing
missions were of the routine local resupply variety in the II Corps
area of Vietnam.

After about two weeks, I was sent up to Dak To, which was in the
northwestern area of II Corps, called the tri-border area because that
was where Vietnam, Cambodia and Laos all come together. We
landed at a fire base just before noon. The aircraft commander shut
down our chopper and went into the operations hut. I was just sitting
in the chopper along with the crew chief and gunner when the North
Vietnamese began pumping rockets down the runway. Because I was
new, I didn't know what to do. Once you shut down a Huey, you
can't restart the engine until it cools down. This usually takes 10 to 15
minutes. So I just sat there. The crew chief and gunner finally hollered at me to take cover with them in a bunker, which I eventually
did. For the next few months I continued flying as a Peter pilot or co-
pilot on combat-assault, resupply and other hunter-killer missions.

The 134th was a general support company. Usually most helicopter companies in Vietnam were attached to a unit such as the
101st Airborne Division or the 4th Infantry Division. We were not
attached to anyone. We handled the overflow. If there were compa-

nies with not enough aircraft, we would be sent to support them. We got to fly for a lot of different units. We flew Koreans, Vietnamese as well as Americans. I found that the Koreans were excellent soldiers. For example, we would put them into an area for 15 to 30 days. We would bring in and out medical supplies, weapons, etc. One thing we found that was noticeably different about the Koreans — we never brought out prisoners.

After two and a half months in Vietnam, I was made an aircraft commander. There are a number of incidents I remember in that position. I recall once I was the number two ship on a flight. We had a relatively new major who was leading the flight into a cold LZ (landing zone), which means they had not received any fire recently. The gunship strafed the area but no enemy seemed around. It was a small LZ and the troops were to be landed by a scattered formation. The lead ship would go in, drop its troops, take off and then be followed by the next helicopter. The lead ship went in and let out three men, of a total of about six, then quickly took off without a word to anyone. I made the assumption while coming in to land that he must have had some type of mechanical difficulty. While touching down, I saw that the three men on the ground were taking small-arms fire. I had to let my troops off to help the other three and then took off. The gunships were no longer present to support us. There ensued a lot of screaming over the radio as to why the major hadn't said anything. It took us the rest of the day to try to extract those who managed to survive.

One night while on stand-by, a fire base just north of us was being overrun. They called us for help. The gunships were unable to take off for some reason. We went in to try and rescue the Americans and Vietnamese. We took a lot of fire. When we took off we had people desperately clinging to the sides of the helicopter in order to get out.

We lost a lot more crews and helicopters through pilot stupidity than we did through combat. I can remember seeing helicopters coming back without any skids because they had been ripped off flying low over a rice paddy. In fact, my room-mate crashed into a rice paddy. There were pilots who crashed into trestles trying to fly under them. Not all was the pilot's fault. I remember going to the pad and you couldn't see 20 feet in front of you, yet the army expected us to fly.

In November 1969, I flew an ass and trash mission which was just a resupply of the grunts out in the field. It was my 22nd birthday. I was just a little nervous flying that day because my mother's twin brother, a Spitfire pilot during the Second World War, was killed on his 21st birthday. About 5:30 p.m. a flight of three of us took off from the fire base to fly home. Still maintaining radio frequency, we were about 10 minutes away from the base when all hell broke loose and they requested support from us. The weather was very bad, the ceiling extremely low and we were in a mountainous area. There were no gunships available. There was nothing we could do but try to bring more troops in. We flew back to the fire base, picked up troops and ammunition. I was the middle of the three ships. Again this was a one-ship LZ — only one ship could land at a time. One had to go over a ridge then land. The first helicopter took extremely heavy fire, both .50-calibre and small weapons. The aircraft commander received a .50-calibre wound. The bullet hit his chicken plate (chest armour) and ripped off his bicep. The crew chief who was sitting in the back took a small AK-47 round in his heel. It travelled up and around his leg and came out his butt. The co-pilot, who was up looking out the window, had a .30-calibre round come up through the fuel gauge. Had he been sitting at the controls the round would have gone through his head. That aircraft crashed into the LZ, making it even more difficult to get in there. Somehow we got in, dropped off our troops, took out the wounded and the dead, and made it out safely. The third helicopter that went in received heavy small-arms fire, and made it back to the fire base, but was so badly damaged that it could not be flown anymore. That night I flew back into that LZ about two or three more times but amazingly did not receive a single hit.

One of the things I found in Vietnam was that I became very hardened to death and to people. After you are there for a while you avoid making friends. That is one way you try to avoid getting hurt. When someone is killed, there would be a memorial service of about 10 minutes. At the service would be a pair of boots and a helmet. Following the service, everyone would go to the bar for a drink. That was it.

About once a month I had to be officer of the day, which meant having to stay up and check on the guards. If there was an attack, you had to make sure the pilots were ready to go. Once when I was officer of the day, one of the men came down and said there was a fellow in the enlisted men's club who was threatening to commit suicide. I told him to take away the fellow's gun and put him to bed. I figured he was just drunk. A second, more desperate appeal brought me to the club. When I went in the door this guy put an M-16 on full automatic and pulled the trigger, blowing his head off in front of everyone.

Because we were a general support company we flew all over II

Corps, which included An Khe, Ban Me Thuot, Dalat and Pleiku. Dalat was a city in the southwestern part of II Corps. It was where the South Vietnamese had their military school like West Point. It was an absolutely beautiful city that seemed so out of place in Vietnam. I only got to down there three or four times but it always amazed me that they had gas stations just like in the United States. The people there seemed so much healthier than the rest in Vietnam. Most of the Vietnamese that we worked with were very slight. They didn't have, for example, the physique or good build of the Montagnards around Pleiku and Dak To.

Every once in a while I would fly with people I had known from flight school. On one huge combat assault with the Koreans due west of Cam Ranh Bay, I flew along with an ex-classmate. He was a flight lead on one flight and I was a flight lead on another. We were going to put in troops simultaneously in this area. The LZ they had picked out for him was almost vertically on the side of the mountain. On the first go, he got the troops in alright; the second time, an attempt was made to land the troops a little higher on the hill. When he went in, he tried to get the toes of his skids on the side of the hill and one of his blades hit the side of the hill and the other blade came around and went through the cockpit and decapitated him. That really sticks in my mind even though I saw an awful lot of death and destruction over there, especially because I was talking to him on the radio just before. It seems strange that I could be talking to him one second and the next second he was gone. We also did a lot of support for the 101st Airborne out of LZ English. I recall this vibrant young kid new to Vietnam. I remember taking him out to the field and then bringing his body back the same day. That really shook me up. He seemed the type of person that nothing could ever happen to.

I recall another incident when we were flying a lieutenant colonel around and he had a couple of prisoners with him. He was going to throw one of the prisoners out of the helicopter and I wouldn't let him. Regardless of rank, as aircraft commander, I was in charge of that helicopter. He said he was going to report me. By this time we had a new major who was a good guy. I told him about the incident and he supported me. That meant a lot.

There was a place called Ban Me Thuot. There was a company in that area called the 7 of the 17th. One day we were down there supporting them. It was the only time when I was in Vietnam that I saw gunships and air force jets, F-4s and F-100s primarily, firing at the ground and receiving more fire than they were throwing down. We were supposed to do some insertions or combat assaults, as we called them, and we never did because they couldn't get the area sufficiently clear. A number of aircraft and gunships got badly shot up that day.

In the company there were 30 helicopters — 22 slicks (helicopters used for transport) and 8 gunships. There was always someone getting shot or something happening. But during the period between Christmas and New Year's, I recall that it was absolutely quiet.

While in Vietnam I had an offer to go to Hawaii for about 10 days to become an American citizen. I certainly would have liked to go to Hawaii, but I chose not to as I did not want to become an American citizen.

One of the biggest disappointments was my R&R. I picked Sydney, Australia. Everything I had heard about that country was fantastic. I failed to realize, however, that a lot of GIs in Vietnam had been going there previously. Sydney was certainly unique, a very pretty city, but I found the people there trying to take advantage of the American GI. Although I was glad to get out of Vietnam for a week, I really didn't enjoy myself.

Upon my return to Vietnam from R&R I only had about 60 days left in country. I was getting a little bit nervous. Going back was really difficult. I also made two three-day trips to Udorn, Thailand — about a 45-minute flight on a C-130 aircraft. There it was like an entirely different world. You could walk the streets and do what you wanted without fear of the Viet Cong.

About a mile north of us was Tuy Hoa Air Force Base. In contrast to what we had, theirs was very elaborate. They actually had paved streets, stop signs, air-conditioned buildings, a movie theatre showing first-run movies, an officers' club with a huge sunken bar right on the water. It was only a mile away but a very rough mile to travel at night. If we had been drinking to the point that we didn't care, we would borrow a truck and drive over.

With only a few weeks left to go, I flew down to Cam Ranh Bay and had a heck of a time with those with whom I had gone to flight school. Most were no longer flying but I was still flying because I hadn't yet received my new orders. In fact, I was flying a mission when my orders came in. They replaced me with another pilot, flew me to Cam Ranh Bay where I stayed for about an hour and a half, and then I was on a plane home.[40]

GEORGE TISSINGTON

Vietnam: 1969 to 1972   Service: Army

Sergeant George Tissington at Phu Bai, South Vietnam, 1971.
(Courtesy G. Tissington.)

The American draft dodgers and deserters George Tissington came across in
Canada motivated him to volunteer to go to Vietnam. George was curious to
see what these people wanted so much to avoid. Born in England in 1936, he
moved to Edmonton in 1949. For three years he served in the Canadian
Army with the artillery and later the airborne. Following his discharge, he
worked for the Alberta Forest Service.

In 1967 he enlisted in the American forces. His wish to go to Vietnam
was realized in May 1969, when he was assigned to the intelligence section

of the 101st Airborne about 10 kilometres northwest of Hue. He acted as an observer for artillery strikes. Sergeant Tissington's second term was as an air observer in a light fixed-wing observation aircraft with the 101st at Phu Bai from March 1971 to March 1972. In October 1975 he left the U.S. forces because of diabetes and returned to Edmonton.

George recalls some memorable incidents:

20 June 1969. It was 1730 hours on the first day of a search-and-destroy mission when our squad of 13 decided to set up a night defensive position. This consisted of digging in and setting up a perimeter. Two men were assigned to each foxhole with a 50 per cent alert status (one man awake while the other would sleep). Twelve Claymore anti-personnel mines were set up on the best enemy infiltration routes around the perimeter, which was located 12 feet from each foxhole.

Dark fell at 1900 and it was during this time that we chowed down and performed other routine duties. Just after midnight, one of the Claymores went off. Suddenly, the jungle woke up with monkeys screaming and a thrashing coming from the area where the mine detonated. Even though the thrashing lasted only two full minutes, it seemed like hours. We immediately went to full alert. We were certain that Charlie was paying us a visit. Our adrenalin was so high that you could hear your buddy's heart pound. The waiting lasted for two hours with no sign of the enemy.

At 0645 we wanted to get out of the area in case Charlie came to investigate what the ruckus of the previous night was all about. The fellow closest to the Claymore went to investigate what had tripped it. When he reached the area, he found a python with a one-foot section missing. He estimated its length to be 32 feet long. [*The Guinness Book of Records* lists the longest python as being 32 feet 9.5 inches.] Without a doubt, this snake, who interrupted our sleep, was the topic of discussion for days to follow.

10 August 1969, approximately 1400 hours. My squad of 13 men had been airlifted into a jungle clearing about two miles from the Laotian border. Our mission was to set up an ambush along a trail well used by enemy troops entering South Vietnam, skirting the Demilitarized Zone from North Vietnam.

We had worked our way to within a half-mile of the proposed ambush position when suddenly we were confronted by a force of 200 North Vietnamese. I told the men to get the hell back to the pickup zone and we all took off like striped gazelles. SP-4 Eric Frank and myself thundered off in the general direction of the pickup zone with what we were sure was the whole of the North Vietnamese

Army on our tails. After crashing through the jungle approximately 500 yards, we were too winded to go any further. We decided to make our stand behind a hollow, rotted tree six feet in diameter. The tree and particularly the entrance to it were shrouded in vines. Parting the vines, we dived headlong into the sanctuary of our stronghold.

We discovered we already had uninvited company in the form of a well-decomposed North Vietnamese Army soldier, with the personality of a dial tone — the corpse literally humming with flies. Clutching our weapons with one hand and our noses with the other, trying our best not to gag, we awaited the arrival of the enemy. They were not long in coming. As they charged around the tree, Eric and I opened fire, killing all 11 that had been following us, both of us emptying one clip of ammunition (28 rounds per clip).

Cautiously we exited our haven, took a quick look around, and "di di mau'd" (hightailed) it back to the pickup zone. All the other 11 squad members had made it safely and had accounted for another 30 North Vietnamese killed in action.

One night in April 1970 I was sergeant of the guard at LZ Sally. I had five bunkers in my section of the berm; each was manned by four troopers. The bunkers were approximately 150 feet apart. Weapons in each bunker consisted of one M-60 machine gun, four M-16 rifles, one M-79 grenade launcher and about 30 fragmentation grenades.

The weather was lousy. Rain was coming down as it could only in Vietnam. I was soaking wet, cold, but in good spirits. Only a month or so to go and I would be on my way back to the World. The way I figured it maybe one more trip into the boonies for a few days and that would be it. At 34, I was getting a bit too old to be crawling around in jungles and rice paddies.

By 0100 hours I had made a half-dozen trips to each of my bunkers. I slogged through mud over my boot tops and spent a few minutes chatting with the "Screaming Eagles" of the 101st Airborne on guard duty in the bunkers.

At 0130 hours all hell broke loose. First to hit us were the 122-mm rockets quickly joined by mortars and B-40 rocket-propelled grenades. Luckily for me, only a few moments prior to the incoming explosives, I had reached the relative safety of another bunker.

The 122s were falling to our rear, in the company area. The mortars and B-40 rounds, however, were landing almost directly on our positions.

The field telephones in each bunker began clattering. It was the officer on duty passing word to fire a "mad minute" on his order. Simply put, every man on the line was to fire his weapon continuously for one minute, sweeping the area immediately to his front with devastating effect on the enemy. Within a couple of minutes from the start of incoming enemy rounds, other things began to happen very quickly. More GIs, rudely awakened in the middle of the night, tumbled from their cots and made their way to their pre-assigned fighting positions. Artillery units at Camp Evans, 10 kilometres to the northwest, and Fire Base Bastogne, 16 kilometres to the south, began lobbing 105- and 155-mm and 8-inch shells around the perimeter of LZ Sally. These friendly incoming rounds, known as defensive targets or simply "Delta Tangos," may be fired each night at any time. Hopefully if Charlie was attempting to sneak up on us, he would change his mind and withdraw, or better still, the fire would catch him in the open and kill him.

At last the order for the mad minute came through. Every man on the line opened fire. Our small arms, combined with the artillery, turned our front into an invader's nightmare. To describe the scene is almost impossible. Torrential rain, the thunder of exploding artillery shells, the cracking sounds of small arms, shrapnel whizzing by, the smell of cordite and hot steel, the eerie glow overhead provided by flares — all this gives anyone a first-hand glimpse of what hell must really be all about.

After what seemed like hours, but was in fact only a minute, the "cease fire" order was called. We gradually and reluctantly stopped blazing away blindly at the unseen enemy until only the steady beat of the rain could be heard. Charlie had pulled his disappearing act again.

Throughout the remainder of that long night, we fired a couple more mad minutes at possible targets and Camp Evans along with Fire Base Bastogne dropped more Delta Tangos around our perimeter. One heart-breaking piece of news reached us a few hours later. Thirty-four men of the 101st Airborne had died when the enemy rockets crashed into their hooches.

At first light, a sweep of the jungle line 400 metres to our front revealed their half-dozen mangled, pyjama-clad bodies. The rain had effectively erased any blood trails. The Viet Cong had come out ahead of us in that fight.

A few days later we were out on a search-and-destroy mission. This time we could see and get at our enemy. Even on his own ground with a greater number of troops Charlie was annihilated. Revenge was sweet.[41]

These three incidents represent only a small fraction of what happened to George while in Vietnam. A manuscript he had completed was destroyed by his wife, whom he subsequently divorced. With the encouragement of Marion, a new lady in his life, he began rewriting the book, but he died in 1989, having only completed 20 pages.

REID FELTMATE

Vietnam: June 1969 to December 1970   Service: Army

Reid Feltmate was born in Timmins, Ontario, in 1948. He grew up there and in Gagnon, Québec. Reid completed Grade 11 in Quebec and in 1965 continued with his schooling at the University of Utah, Salt Lake City.

Rather than obtain a student visa, he took out a permanent resident's card in order to enable him to work in Utah during the summer. When Reid found out he was going to be drafted, he enlisted for three years in the army in October 1967. He hoped the war would soon be over.

Reid took basic training at Fort Lewis, Washington, then instruction as a medic at Fort Sam Houston, San Antonio, and finally airborne training at Fort Benning, Georgia. Reid had a choice of joining the 82nd Airborne or flying a helicopter, and chose the latter. Thus, from September 1968 to May 1969, he received instruction on the UH-I and reached the rank of warrant officer 1. Then Reid went to Vietnam.

After an honourable discharge from the army, Reid rejoined some close friends from his unit at Columbus, Ohio, where he spent January to May 1971. That summer he moved to Red Lake, Ontario, and worked as a labourer at an iron-ore mine before enrolling at Carleton University, Ottawa. In 1976 he graduated with an honours B.A. in English literature. Then he worked for a year in the registrar's office.

Reid moved back to Columbus in September 1979 where he worked in the registrar's office, this time at Ohio State University. He met a girl from Bangor, Maine, doing graduate work at the university whom he married. Around this time he also joined the army reserve, and this work eventually led him to pursue a permanent career in the army. As with other aliens who had served their year in Vietnam, Reid was still eligible for citizenship, which he took out in 1982. He has reached the rank of chief warrant officer 4 and remains with the aviation branch of the U.S. Army.

Reid most clearly recalls one individual from Vietnam:

The WOPACABANA (Warrant Officers Protection Association), as our bunker was called, stood at the end of a square surrounded by four rows of clapboard and screened hooches. It shared the space with a concrete slab, a telephone pole and a basketball net. This structure stood 10 feet high, was about 15-foot square and had a makeshift ladder to its top which served as a dandy place to sit and drink beer. We spent a lot of time in and on the WOPACABANA.

Invariably, evenings on the WOPACABANA were first-rate bull sessions. The new guys received their unofficial briefings, the co-pilots suffered their status and the old guys reigned. One day, an individual occupying a separate niche arrived at the unit. We called him Shakey. He was a chief warrant officer, an experienced gunship pilot, but possessed by a haunting emotional deformity. A youngish man around 21, he hardly ever spoke, rarely left the WOPA-CABANA day or night, and was seldom sober. He had been trans-ferred to our unit simply to bide his time prior to going home and being discharged. Normally, we would have resented the presence of a non-contributor, but somehow in his shaking, drinking and mo-roseness we sensed a certain "there but for the grace of God go I" feeling. Our initial tolerance became affection, and before he finally left we were able to piece together his story.

Shakey had been the aircraft commander of a helicopter gunship in a team of two, and they had been covering an insertion by a single helicopter. It was a routine mission except that it was over by the Cambodian border in northern II Corps. After the helicopter had touched down, it came under murderous small-arms fire and was destroyed within seconds, all aboard being killed or seriously wounded. The gun team, in the course of covering this event, came under the same fire. Shakey's aircraft had gone down, he being the sole surviving crew member. Now he was on the ground, sur-rounded by his dead and dying buddies, and the enemy. His only hope was the remaining gunship circling warily overhead, providing cover and ducking the best it could. He was relatively safe for the moment.

The NVA (North Vietnamese Army) regulars were particularly adept at springing this type of trap. The American soldier would not leave comrades behind, and sooner or later someone would come for the bodies and survivors. These would also be attacked, and as the NVA slowly became outnumbered or outgunned, they would melt away into the bush. But Shakey wasn't analyzing tactics at this point; all he knew was that he was surrounded by the enemy and his only hope was his wing-mate circling overhead out of harm's way. He was still hanging on.

The surviving wing-mate radioed he was running out of gas. His initial MAYDAY had been answered by both army and air force aircraft in the area and the expected help was coming. Two Huey helicopters and three Cobra helicopter gunships were inbound, as were a pair of F-4 Phantom jets from the coast, but they wouldn't arrive for 15 or 20 minutes. The cover gunship stayed on station until it was absolutely void of fuel. The rescue formation was visible on the horizon and minutes away. The wing-mate handed over the battle to the Cavalry commander and gunships and departed.

Shakey saw that helicopter depart and his rope snapped. It was his last rational realization and he remembers nothing after that moment. Now, sitting on our bunker, drunk, shaken, he was agonizingly waiting to be captured and shot. Through the alcohol, I guess, he saw us as friendly, but the mind we saw through his wide, teary eyes was far away in that incident on the border. Shakey eventually left us and the WOPACABANA and we never heard from him again.[42]

PETER LEMON

Vietnam: 1969 to 1970   Service: Army

The most highly decorated American citizen from the Vietnam War having an association with Canada is Peter Lemon. He is the only individual born in Canada to be awarded the Medal of Honor during the Vietnam War. He was born in Norwich, Ontario, in June 1950. His mother was a war bride from England married to a former member of the RCAF. When Peter was quite young, the family moved to Alabaster, Michigan, where his father worked as a mining engineer with U.S. Gypsum. Peter became a U.S. citizen at age 12. He attended high school at Saginaw and volunteered for the infantry at East Tawas City in February 1969. He went to Fort Knox, Kentucky, for basic training and took advanced jungle warfare training at Fort Polk, Louisiana. He was sent to Vietnam in July as a member of Company I, 75th Infantry (Ranger), 1st Infantry Division, and was with them until December. For the second part of his tour, he was transferred to Company E, 2nd Battalion, 8th Cavalry Regiment, 1st Cavalry Division (Airmobile). It was in an engagement near the Cambodian border on 1 April 1970 that he won the Medal of Honor.

For conspicuous gallantry and intrepidity in action at the risk of his life above and beyond the call of duty. Sgt. Lemon (then SP-4) distinguished himself while serving as an assistant machine gunner during the defense of Fire Support Base Illingworth. When the base came under heavy enemy attack, Sgt. Lemon engaged a numerically superior enemy with machine gun and rifle fire from his

*Medal of Honor recipient Sergeant Peter Lemon, 15 June 1971.
(Courtesy U.S. Army.)*

defensive position until both weapons malfunctioned. He
then used hand grenades to fend off the intensified enemy
attack launched in his direction. After eliminating all but 1
of the enemy soldiers in the immediate vicinity, he pursued
and disposed of the remaining soldier in hand-to-hand
combat. Despite fragment wounds from an exploding
grenade, Sgt. Lemon regained his position, carried a more
seriously wounded comrade to an aid station, and, as he
returned, was wounded a second time by enemy fire.
Disregarding his personal injuries, he moved to his position through a hail of small arms and grenade fire. Sgt.
Lemon immediately realized that the defensive sector was
in danger of being overrun by the enemy and unhesitatingly
assaulted the enemy soldiers by throwing hand grenades
and engaging in hand-to-hand combat. He was wounded

yet a third time, but his determined efforts successfully drove the enemy from the position. Securing an operable machine gun, Sgt. Lemon stood atop an embankment fully exposed to enemy fire and placed effective fire upon the enemy until he collapsed from his multiple wounds and exhaustion. After regaining consciousness at the aid station, he refused medical evacuation until his more seriously wounded comrades had been evacuated. Sgt. Lemon's gallantry and extraordinary heroism are in keeping with the highest traditions of the military services and reflect great credit on him, his unit, and the U.S. Army.[43]

Peter was honourably discharged on 4 December 1970 and returned home. A year later, President Nixon presented him with the Medal of Honor at a ceremony in Washington, D.C., with several other recipients. After working as a carpenter in Colorado, he returned to university. Four years later he graduated with a master's degree in business administration. Since graduation, he has worked in insurance.

Peter married in 1978, settled in Colorado Springs, and has a girl and boy. He keeps in touch with his relatives in Canada and England.[44]

JOSEPH EDWARDS

Vietnam: August 1969 to August 1970   Service: Marines

I am a Canadian Vietnam veteran and I read your request in the veterans' newspaper my cell partner had. You see I am at present a guest of the Texas Department of Corrections.

My name is Joseph Edwards and I was in the United States Marine Corps for three years. I joined in April 1968. I went to boot camp at San Diego and then I went to Camp Pendleton. That was my infantry regiment training. After that, I went to the truck drivers' school at Pendleton for my MOS (military occupational specialty) in the marines. I was assigned to the Field Maintenance Battalion, Hawaii. I did some driving on the island of Oahu until I turned 18. Then in 1969 I received my orders for Vietnam.

I got to Nam in mid-August 1969. I was assigned to the 5th Communications Battalion Motor Transport Company of the 3rd Marine Division. Our job was to provide transportation and part of the supply line to marine outlets north of Da Nang. I was stationed in Da Nang but spent a lot of time on the road. My 2.5-ton multi-fuelled truck had a brass ring with a .50-calibre machine gun mounted on it. We provided light armour support for the convoy.

I don't like to recall nor really remember my tour. To me it was a waste of some fine men I called brothers. I don't have any more nightmares. They stopped after I'd been back a couple of years. I am not a loony case nor do I see myself as anything but a survivor, plain and simple.

I was born in the Grace Hospital in Windsor, Ontario, 6 March 1951. I used to have a landed-immigrant card but in 1972, when I decided to go back to Canada, the people on the Canadian side of the Ambassador Bridge cut it up. I have never been naturalized so I still retain my Canadian citizenship. I am proud I am a Canadian. I consider Canada my home and never want to be an American.

I am a journeyman meat cutter. I've always wanted to open up my own meat market. Yet, my GI benefits of a business loan aren't worth a damn in Canada. So I tried to work over here and save up so I could return to my home and set up my business.

I only have one problem that stems from Vietnam and I truly believe it is what got me here in this prison. You see by losing three close friends to snipers I was left with the rage and anger of wanting to get back or pay back. When I returned, whenever someone hurt me physically, I didn't let them get away with it. I know this may sound rather wild to you but it is the truth, plain and simple. I am not a rough tough hard guy but when someone gave me pain, I snapped and I usually ended up in big trouble for my actions.

On returning from the war I found myself doing three jobs: attending an institute of meat cutting three or four days a week, working with my dad at an independent meat market and, on Friday, Saturday and Sunday night, helping as a floor guard at a Detroit roller-skating rink. That is where I met Kathy. We were married and moved to Amherstburg. Things were tight financially. I broke the law in Chatham, Ontario, and got six months. At the proceedings my attorney told the judge that I was an honourably discharged marine and Vietnam veteran. The judge stated that I was now in Canada and in Canada Vietnam was merely an opinion so he'd give me his. He said the United States had no right being in Vietnam so I knew where that left me!

When I was on the outside this guy I'd met at the Guelph Correctional Centre asked me for a lift to a mall where he had some applications for work he needed to hand in. So I took him in my car. He said he'd be back in five minutes. It turned out he was inside writing bum cheques. I had no knowledge of it yet I got nine months for conspiracy to commit fraud!

When I got out, my wife had run around town and was seven months pregnant. I didn't abandon her immediately. I set her up two blocks from her oldest sister. I got a job with a carnival so I didn't have to stay at the house. You see, carnie people work and sleep on the site. I hung around until she could get around after the birth. Then I left. I didn't think of myself as running away. Marines never retreat; it's drilled into us. During the Korean War, when the general in charge was asked how it felt to be responsible for the first Marine Corps retreat, he replied: "We are not retreating. We're just attacking in a different direction." That's what I felt I had to do.

I headed to Florida, found a job, and stayed in Tampa until I bought a 1951 Harley-Davidson motorcycle. When it was road-worthy, I took off. My travels were many, as were my experiences. I passed through Texas countless times until 7 November 1978, when I got into big trouble. I have done seven and a half years now on a twelve-year sentence for aggravated robbery.

The United States is a great country and I have family and friends in all parts of it. Yet still I have a bitterness towards it that someday will find me living back in Canada with pride in my heart for my own country. To me, there's no place like home.

Joe described his tour in Vietnam in a subsequent letter:

I spent two weeks in Okinawa getting my shots all updated. Then 7 September 1969 I was put on a military plane at night and me and 50 other marines were flown to Da Nang. I arrived at night and once there, 16 of us were told to put our gear on a "deuce and a half" (a 2.5-ton multi-fuel truck) with the yellow 5th Communications shield on it. I later learned this stood for the 5th Communications Battalion. I was assigned to the motor transport part of the battalion of the 3rd Marine Division. The base, as I was later to learn, was situated between Marble Mountain and Monkey Mountain. Army compounds or camps surrounded us. Our camp had the beach to our rear and an orphanage on one side of our perimeter.

There was lightning and thunder as we boarded the truck. It was man-made. It came from artillery fire off in the distance. The place we landed was called Freedom Hill.

We were taken around the camp to check at various places. The armoury was first and there we were issued our "sweet 16s" (M-16 rifles). After lunch, we went back to the motor pool for assignments. Nine of us were drivers; the others were mechanics. Names were called out assigning each of us to our vehicle. As I was the only private my name was last. I was sent to the fifth bay.

My truck had no canvas top over the cab, just one large brass ring, two square armour plates with slits in them for windows and for the side windows armoured plate squares.

I found the fifth bay and there was a real grease monkey mechanic with the name Mac written on the back of his shop coat. I said, "Hey, Mac, where the hell is this truck going?" Mac replied: "This here vehicle is light armour support for convoys." Just then the driver came up, whom I called "Slim." I learned he was from Kentucky and had twin sons. He had been in the country four months and had nine to go. Then I helped him mount the .50-calibre machine gun. A friendship was made right off as I recall even before we hit the first road run together.

The captain told us we'd be spending a lot of time on the road and would usually be sleeping in other camps. Our job was to go to the docks, get loaded up at FLC (Force Logistics Command), just this side of the Hai Phong Pass and wait for the lead jeep to move out and head the convoy. If a truck was disabled we would be notified via the ham radio we carried. The tow truck or wrecker with its twin 60-calibre machine guns would pull up in front of the disabled vehicle, while our truck would help lay down covering fire. That I might not see the end of the 13-month tour hit me right then.

The captain told us our first convoy run was Friday so we had two days to get ready. That night we hit the only watering hole, the EM (enlisted men's) club. There I drank Budweiser and listened to a slant-eyed female singing "Stand by Your Man." I was amazed at how much she sounded like Tammy Wynette. When I handed her a beer she smiled at me and told me "You Number One GI." I got really drunk that night.

Well the day of my first convoy finally came. Our vehicle was placed fifth from the front. In total we added up to 18 trucks and 4 jeeps. We eventually found out that most convoys were much smaller.

I recall the first trip was much more resembling a sightseeing tour. We drove to one base at a time: from Forward Logistics Command to Quang Tri, Dong Ha, Con Thien, Phong Dien, Hue, Phu Bai. The major areas that got the most supplies were Con Thien, Dong Ha and Quang Tri. These three were within 15 kilometres of the Demilitarized Zone. The total trip took usually two to two and a half weeks depending on the amount of repair the radio technicians who came along had to do.

As well as ambushes there were other hazards we had to contend with like mines in the road. There was also the occasional herd of water buffalo crossing the road. Then the largest concern was theft by the Vietnamese as we drove. They'd drive up to a truck from behind

— two men on a small motorcycle or scooter. The passenger would hop up in the truck and start tossing out whatever was in the back.

The further north we went the greater the night shelling. Con Thien, Dong Ha and Quang Tri were the roughest in that regard when we stayed there. We never drove at night.

My first night at Dong Ha we got shelled. I saw a man run over to a hole just as a round went off. As soon as the blast had passed I ran to the same hole. The man was laying in a heap. I saw a rather huge piece of steel protruding from his left thigh. I grabbed his first-aid packet and out fell a dozen skinny rolled cigarettes. He said, "Brother, put a tourniquet on my thigh and fire me up a doobie [marijuana cigarette]," which I did. After two joints, he pulled the hunk of steel out himself. Then I put a pressure bandage on the wound and sat on it for pressure until the siren told us the shelling was over. Slim helped me get him to the sick bay. Slim and I became best friends. Not only did he call me "little brother" but watched over me like a real big brother would.

Once a month there were the larger supply runs. Sometimes convoys only numbered seven or eight trucks and the convoy commander's jeep. The smaller runs hit those heavy-shelling areas. We called them Charlie's playground because it was in his front yard to the north.

The fourth or fifth return trip back from Dong Ha heading south I was the last truck of 11. Truck number 10 was a new driver. He couldn't keep the same distance between himself and the next truck in front of him. Suddenly he increased his speed to prevent some water buffalos from crossing in front of him. I had to stop. One buffalo just stood there in front of my bumper. I hit the air horn and the damn thing put its horn though my radiator. Hot water practically cooked the animal's head as he jumped up and down trying to dislodge its horn, causing the truck to bob up and down. Slim then put three or four 50-calibre bullets in it and the shaking stopped. "Didn't you say you were a meat cutter?" said Slim. I answered in the affirmative. I got the animal's horn out of the radiator as the wrecker drove up to tow us. I grabbed an entrenching tool and K-bar knife and went to work cutting off the hindquarters which I put in the back of our truck. Slim tossed the kid herding the animals a carton of cigarettes and a case of C-rations.

I held up the first sirloin for Slim's approval, the muscle still slightly quivering and he said, "Hope when I bite into it, it don't bite back." We made one bag of weed (marijuana) and 19 bucks selling meat to the guys in the wrecker. At Phu Bai, Slim gave one of the cooks the price list we had devised and he passed us $55.

After four months, Slim took his R&R and went to Bangkok. I got a needed seven days on our base camp. In Bangkok he got himself two ladies at the Happy Happy Massage Parlor, and later posted their pictures in the truck.

I think it was my sixth month, 21 February 1970, and we were on a small convoy trip back from Phu Bai. The heat was scorching. We were roughly 75 miles from our home base when a call came over our radio: "Truck hit, needs support and wrecker, snipers in the tree-line." So I pulled up behind the vehicle and Slim started his routine covering fire as the wrecker backed up to the other truck. Finally, the job was completed and the wrecker driver said, "O.K., let's split, gang." I got in my truck, put it in gear and the next sound I heard was a blown-out front left tire. I told Slim to "melt the barrel if you must but I have to change that tire." I replaced that flat in record time.

Slim was coming down into the cab from the ring mount when I heard a sickening sound. A round hit the brass ring and tumbled from Slim's right shoulder down across his belly and tossed his kneecap on the gear shifter knob and various other parts mostly blood and torn-up intestines all over the cab. He just held himself together at his chest and said: "Catch up to the medic truck quick, little brother." I drove for it seemed like forever till I finally caught up with the convoy. I passed all the trucks till I was even with the medic's vehicle and blasted the SOS in Morse Code on the horn. But Slim's eyes were closed. He appeared as though sleeping only his eyes seemed slightly deeper somehow. When the medic opened the door Slim about knocked the medic off the truck as his body slid toward him. When I had become part of the convoy again, the medic said, "He's dead." In the back a marine giving cover had caught one in the throat, killing him instantly. The medic noticed I had been slightly hit and pulled a stringy piece of something off my face. Hell, I hadn't even felt it. I then vomited in the seat.

We finally got back to the motor pool and they took off the two bodies and I just sat in the driver's seat. The convoy commander opened up my door and asked if I was O.K. I said I needed to be by myself for a while. I was left alone and started to cry like a baby. When I emerged from the truck I passed the main office and heard the captain ask me to step into his inner office. I saw him grab a large glass and in this he poured some Bacardi rum. Never having had rum before I just drank it like a glass of water. That was the last thing I remember until I awoke and noticed officers all around. I was to report back to my captain at the motor pool after I got showered and fed.

When I made it to the captain's office, he called me in and told me to have a seat. He explained that he had me carried to his bunk when I knocked myself out from the rum. Then he said he noticed I'd been in country six months and he did strongly recommend I take my seven-day, six-night R&R. I replied that I needed to be away from this place for a while. "Any idea where you'd like to go?" I said, "The Happy Happy Massage Parlor in Bangkok."

The loss of my friend left me really angry as did the loss of two other gunners killed. One received a round in the head while giving covering fire. The other was killed by a fragmentation grenade thrown by a kid among a group of drivers who were handing out candy to kids while the trucks were being loaded.

This is as much as I chose to relate. When I finished (writing) this story I cried and cried. Tears have not fallen since I was 18.

Finally, it was time to return. I was part of the redeployment of American troops from South Vietnam. I was aboard the USS *Denver*. There was, I believe, 1,650 marines aboard for the 18-day trip at sea. We went south of India, south of Africa, south of South America and then for three days we were anchored off Del Mar Beach in California waiting for orders to go ashore. The big day came and all the landing craft were loaded and us marines hit the shore in one wave. On a high spot directly to our front stood a general at a microphone. He called us to platoon formation and started to recite a speech. Someone in our platoon interrupted with "We want to go home." The general cut his speech short after that comment.

Some 650 of us were to be discharged within a few days. I remember getting on a bus headed to the Los Angeles airport. There were four buses loaded that day with discharged U.S. Marine Vietnam veterans. Our arrival and our subsequent departure for the airport was reported in the local media.

When we came to the airport, protestors were gathered in front of the doors of the terminal. They were yelling "war mongers," "baby killers" and other insults. Eggs were being tossed on us and a pretty young girl spat on me as I passed her by. It made me feel like hell.

In my list of mistakes I've made, my biggest mistake was going to Vietnam. The shame is not ours (Vietnam vets) to bear. The blame for the disgrace and treatment we received lies with the U.S. government. We could have won independence for the South Vietnamese but those in charge wouldn't let us.

> Sincerely,
>
> A Canadian
> A Vietnam vet
> An Ex-Marine
> Ellis I Unit
> Huntsville[45]

MARSHA JORDAN

Vietnam: 1969 to 1971   Service: Air Force

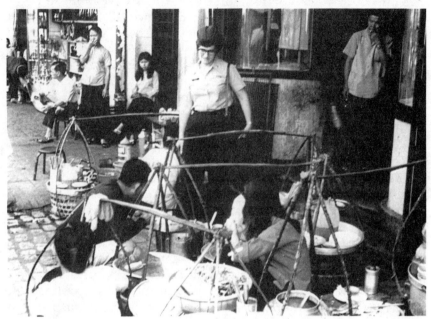

First Lieutenant Marsha Jordan, downtown Saigon, 1970. (Courtesy M. Jordan.)

Of the some 7,500 military women who served on active military duty in Vietnam, over 80 per cent were nurses. All nurses were officers and had to be at least 21 to serve in the combat zone. Their tour of duty was generally a year. Like all military personnel, the nurses were rotated in and out of Vietnam on an individual basis. Eight women are listed on the Vietnam Memorial. There was very little Canadian female involvement in the Vietnam War. One case I came across was Marsha Jordan, born in Sydney, Nova Scotia, in 1946. When she was 16, her family moved to Boston, where her father worked as a shipper and receiver. While she was in high school, Marsha worked part-time as a nurse's aide in nursing homes around Boston. She enjoyed being with people and preferred nursing to being a secretary or teacher. In 1964, at 18, she entered nursing school and graduated three years later. She became an American citizen and joined the air force in April 1968, hoping to be trained as a flight nurse. Marsha wanted to serve aboard an aircraft flying casualties out of Vietnam because of the challenge of the work. On these flights, there were usually two flight nurses and three medical technicians.

Marsha took basic training for three weeks at Sheppard Air Base in Witchita Falls, Texas. The course included a simulated air accident with casualties. The nurses had to do triage and care for the casualties. Next was six weeks of flight school at Brooks Air Force Base in San Antonio. Training there was intensive, ranging from loading patients onto and unloading them from an airplane to learning the effects of altitude on the human body.

Two squadrons of C-141 aircraft cargo planes converted to transport the wounded, one based at Clark Air Force Base in the Philippines, the other at Yokota, Japan, flew patients into and out of Vietnam. The same aircraft would take the patients, if they were stable enough, on to the United States. Marsha was assigned to the 56th Air Evacuation Squadron based at Yokota. She flew into and out of Vietnam from August of 1969 to August of 1971. She has retired after 20 years' service in the air force and lives in Tampa, Florida. Marsha has a sister and other relatives in Nova Scotia and returns periodically to visit.[46]

DANIEL CUNNINGHAM

Vietnam: October 1969 to October 1970   Service: Marines

I was born in September 1947 in Hamilton, Ontario. I left when I was 21 to join up. I was sworn in on 17 December 1968. I went through basic training at Parris Island, South Carolina, the only boot camp for the east half of the U.S.A. I was given an MOS (military occupational specialty) for computer sciences and went to infantry training at Camp Lejeune, North Carolina, as a non-combat marine — a 12-day wonder. It is hard to believe our training was so short. Anyway, after this, I was sent to Quantico, Virginia, for schooling in computers, but I got out of it and was reassigned to infantry rifleman (MOS 0311), but never went back for the full training that infantry receive.

Then I got "staging" at Camp Pendleton in California for two weeks. This special training for Vietnam was cut short too because I was among those chosen to go to Vietnamese language school in Monterey.

In Vietnam I was initially with Mike Company, 3rd Battalion, 26th Regiment, 1st Marine Division. Then, for a couple of months, after the 3/26 left, I was with Kilo Company of the 3rd Battalion, 1st Regiment, 1st Marine Division. Then I was with India Company, 3rd Battalion, 1st Regiment. I guess this is what is referred to as my unit. CUPP refers to Combat Unit Participation Program. Unlike the bet-

Daniel Cunningham at Ap Quan Nam, South Vietnam, 1970-71. (Courtesy D. Cunningham.)

ter-known CAP (Combined Action Platoons) we "combined" with the South Vietnamese Regional Forces, as opposed to the Popular Forces with the CAPs. Administratively, we were part of India Company, which was located on Hill 190, commanding the Cu De River. But the CUPP was located in the village of Ap Quan Nam. We referred to the CUPP as our unit. As for the division, there was only the 1st Marine Division in Vietnam at that time. It may be just marine arrogance that we do not usually refer to the division as soldiers do.

I got to Vietnam October 1969 with the rank of private 1st class (E-2) at the age of 22. I made corporal (E-4) in Vietnam.

From the dates I gave, you will know that I missed the big battles and name operations. With the 3/26 during my first months in country I have vague memories of helicopter rides to blasted hilltops, truck convoys going somewhere, loading up and getting off, and getting lost, humping forever up those hills, falling down hillsides, carrying the M-79 grenade launcher with 70 rounds plus grenades and poncho, etc., and very little food and water. I remember walking along the terraced rice paddies and stinking swamps, and jungle rot on your feet; earth-shaking artillery fire as those huge rounds screamed overhead; mosquitoes that used to fight over me; an ambush and two marines killed; the mud, fear, rumours of attacks coming every night; one Brother shot off his trigger finger by accident with an M-16 rifle; a white dude, demonstrating how to set up a Claymore mine, set off the "hell-box" and injured himself; both medevacked back to the World.

25 December 1969. Hill 124, Quang Nam Province. The afternoon of Christmas Day. Clouds billowing in the cold, damp wind. Mike Company of the 3rd Battalion, 26th Regiment, was saddling up for our night activity.

On the radios playing we could hear Bob Hope at Da Nang, which we could almost see through the clouds and fog, a few miles west of us.

Mike Company was slotted to send a few people to the USO show in Da Nang. The corpsman, from the navy, went. I don't think any of the marines wanted to leave the rest of us.

Old veterans from "up north," at the DMZ (Demilitarized Zone), were saying, "See you in the morning," and other words of encouragement to friends in other squads.

As "blupe man," I carried the M-79 grenade launcher, with a vest of rounds. But I felt strong with the weight, ready for action. After two months in country I still hadn't really seen any action.

Well, one night the whole company went out and linked up with some other marine unit and some ARVNs (Army of the Republic of Vietnam). I almost shot at them when I first saw their Oriental faces in the moonlight, columns marching back and forth, to whispered orders and radio commands. We had surrounded some village and one of us was the blocking force, the other the sweeping force, I guess. Anyway, two Viet Cong were killed. I was not close to the scene. I was confused at the village women crying over their bodies.

Another time, on Hill 10 (wherever that was) I was on the OP (observation post) with three other marines. During my watch, two men ran by within a stone's throw of our position. I woke up one guy and he started shooting his M-16 in the direction I pointed. Tinch, the squad leader, came down the hill to our foxhole and wanted to know what the hell was going on. There was nothing to see. So why hadn't I shot first and asked questions later? I didn't know they weren't ARVNs.

Back on Hill 124, on Christmas, during the truce, we walked and slid down the slimy clay hill and through the fields and to our ambush site. Then we went on and stopped and waited for full dark to set in. Then we went back to the designated site.

We set up in a regular L-shaped ambush: the CP (command post), consisting of the squad leader, the lieutenant, the radio man and one rifleman, at the apex; two fire teams, or three or four riflemen each, along one line; and one fire team at right angles to the CP position. I was with Stacey's team; him, me, Jenkins and Neal.

We stayed on full alert until midnight and then took turns at watch, one man awake in each of the four groups at all times. After my watch, I woke Jenkins to take over. Then I fell into dreams, probably about Pat, back in Monterey, her long blond hair, her silky smooth skin.

"Crack, crack, crack!..." sounded the AKs (AK-47 assault rifle), so close I though they went off inside my skull. One Chicom (Chinese Communist) grenade went off too. I was up immediately with my gun and ready to fight.

But where were they? There was no one to be seen. Stacey and Jenkins were hit. One was moaning. The other was silent. Tinch ran to us to see what he could do. There was nothing he could do.

What time was it? Whose watch was it? Stacey's. Had he fallen asleep on watch? Or had Jenkins gone to sleep and not awakened Stacey? Little Jenkins's guts were spilled on the ground. The casings from the AK-47 were within feet of the bodies. The moaning had stopped.

A marine swore and slammed his rifle on the ground. It fired and everyone wondered what happened. Tinch calmed him down. "Be cool." There was no one to shoot at. They called me to the CP. I crawled there with my blupe gun. They had me fire rounds into the treeline — "reconnaissance by fire." At least I had something to do.

We waited.

The medevac chopper came in with a roar and rush of wind. Four of us carried the dead marines to the chopper. I had Stacey's legs or were they Jenkins's?

The chopper was blowing and shaking my bones. It took off and roared away into the darkness.

With the sunrise we went back to Hill 124. We climbed up the 124 metres. I took off the vest with the M-79 rounds in the pockets. But I still felt weighted down.

Over C-ration coffee and hot chocolate, we shook our heads and talked about them. How could it have happened?

Then with Kilo Company, 3/1, on Nam-O bridge, guarding this crossing of the Cu De River on Highway 1 between Da Nang and the Hai Van Pass. We dropped one-pound charges of TNT into the water hourly at night as protection against sappers. We were crazy with boredom. We would attach the TNT to something to make it float and shoot at it. The explosions would shake hell out of the old bridge and splash water all over it and bring the corporal running and a report would have to be filed.

At night sometimes I would go to the OP on top of Monkey Mountain and get stoned on marijuana and speed and rap all night. And we would get a whore to spend the night with us. And we would see the tracer rounds from the firefights down in the valley of the Cu De. Red tracers for us and green for the enemy. The veterans who had been up at the DMZ with the 3rd Marine Division would jump at the sound of gunfire.

At the Hai Van Pass we went on daytime patrols and night ambushes or spent the night guarding some position, watching for gooks in the fog. We went on two-day or three-day operations, climbed Hill 11?- something. Got stoned and watched the fog, clouds tumbling through the pass, and fighters screaming through the pass, only hundreds of feet away and not believing it. We would watch the tiny pinpoints of lights from hundreds of lanterns on the boats in the bay of Da Nang, winking on and off in the fog; the flashes of rockets taking off from China Ridge (?) and landing sometimes in Da Nang, thinking it was better those people in the rear with their cold beer and washed women and live music were getting it. Watching the Dusters (nickname for M42 tracked vehicles mounting twin 40-mm anti-aircraft guns used as ground support in Vietnam) firing at the hillsides at night.

But no combat — just occasional rifle fire in the distance. I finally got transferred to India Company in April or May to be in the CUPP unit in the village of Ap Quan Nam so that I could see some action.

There was a squad of marines (basically three fire teams of four men each) plus a navy corpsman, an extra machine-gun team, radio operator, and a lieutenant. There were over 20 marines when I arrived, along with 55 South Vietnamese. These marines were veterans of the 26th.

Early morning patrol in the village of Ap Quan Nam, Quang Nam Province, I Corps. I was leading my fire team — four men of the reinforced squad of marines, that, with a company of Vietnamese Regional Forces, formed a CUPP unit.

The village surrounded the CUPP compound on three sides, but all the trails from the compound led into the village. Hill 190, to our northeast, dominated the landscape, and on the side of the hill the words "INDIA CO" were formed in whitewashed rocks. Impressive. Anyone could see this was India Company of the 3rd Battalion, 1st Marine Regiment.

Yeah, I was hungry. I was getting hot. We had called in our last checkpoint on the radio and were returning to our compound and breakfast of C-rations.

Beside the trail there was a large house with plastered walls. A crowd was gathered. We stopped, curious. I went inside. A little boy was lying on the bed, very still, surrounded by chattering, clucking women. There was nothing we could do. So we went back to our compound and informed the corpsman.

The radio man turned in his gear and Hill 190 acknowledged our return from patrol. I took off my flak jacket. Even with most of the plates missing from the vest and not wearing a shirt underneath, I was just breaking a sweat, and the sun had not been up very long.

In my hootch I was about to make some breakfast when Doc stepped in and said he was ready to go see the kid and did I want to go along as escort? "Sure."

The boy's sister was inside our compound, waiting — the gunnery sergeant would have a fit if he knew we let Vietnamese civilians in the compound. I slipped my flak jacket on and we put a magazine into our rifles and donned our bush covers and we left.

At the house, I introduced the corpsman. They used the word "Bac si," which means doctor, rather than the word for medic. There was little I could do to help, so I sat outside and flirted with the teenage girls. The corpsman came out and said he couldn't do anything for the boy. He needed a doctor. We couldn't call in a medevac chopper for a Vietnamese kid who was sick. After a lengthy discussion among the Vietnamese — boo coo yak-yak — it seemed there was a Vietnamese doctor in a village just up the road from this village.

I cut the conversation short and told the mother of the boy that we would go to the doctor. Now. The two of us set off across the fields to the marketplace. But mama-san was lagging behind me. Her son was a toddler, not a baby, and he weighed more than my M-16, 7.6 pounds. I handed my rifle to her and I took the boy. What was she going to do? Shoot me, with her child in my arms, even if she knew what to do with a rifle?

What worried me, walking across those rice paddies, was the gunnery sergeant up on Hill 190. He could see us plainly through his field glasses if he happened to be watching. Kind of a creeping feeling, so vulnerable, something like the feeling I got crossing the rice paddies at night when VC might be watching me. But there was nothing I could do about it now.

At the marketplace, fortunately, there was a cyclo-cab, one of their pickup trucks with a tiny two-stroke engine, waiting for a full load of passengers and freight before it would leave. I commandeered the cyclo, giving the kid one dollar in military pay certificates for the ride. Without a load of people, and chickens, and goats, and vegetables, the cyclo made good time.

The village was only six or eight kilometres down the road, and when the villagers saw the child a crowd gathered and led the woman to the doctor's house. Since I wasn't needed, I left.

Days later, I was again on the morning patrol near the house where the sick kid was. I stopped at the archway into the yard. A toddler scampered away.

An old man was working in the yard. I asked about the sick kid. He pointed to the child now hiding behind a water buffalo, peering between its legs. I laughed. I guess that answered my question. The man went on to thank me profusely, saying everyone was grateful that I saved the boy.

From January until about April or May 1970 when I went to the CUPP in the village, I was not in combat. We lost a lot of blood to leeches and cuts from elephant grass, some accidents. One marine was wounded by a short mortar round of ours, but I didn't see any Viet Cong.

During daytime patrols and night ambushes, we played cards with village elders in their houses and taught kids how to fish in the stream with grenades. We'd meet prostitutes in the fields, or smuggle them into our compound. It was in the village that I got into the war.

We got to know the villagers to some extent. These were Buddhists, but some of them were from the North, refugees from the Communists of 1954. Other villages nearby contained a lot of Catholics, who were very strictly anti-Communist. I was the only marine who had gone to language school, so I had the fundamentals of the Vietnamese language. The other marines communicated with many of the kids in a barbarous pidgin language. Teenage girls would talk to each other and giggle and shriek with embarrassment when they discovered that I could understand a little.

One night I was sleeping on my cot, inside the big CP tent. Sandbags were piled around the tent, two or three feet high. I awoke to machine-gun rounds whizzing through the tent just above me. I rolled off the cot onto my hands and knees, alert and ready. I grabbed my rifle and a bandolier of magazines, slipped on my Ho Chi Minh sandals and went into action. Now, 20 years later, people don't understand why a sudden noise, like my dog flapping his ears, makes me wake in the middle of the night and come up fighting; why a sudden touch, like my woman's hand on my face, causes me to panic and defend my life. If that machine gun hadn't missed me then I wouldn't be having these problems now.

Outside machine-gun rounds were splattering across the pathway into the compound. We should have made a second entrance to the compound. A couple of rockets came in. One rocket-propelled grenade hit a Regional Forces hootch. One of the occupants was out on ambush, the other was home on leave. The rocket hit a metal stake that supported the tarpaulin roof. It exploded and shrapnel put holes in the tarp and clothes, etc. A piece of shrapnel penetrated a footlocker, exploding a can of shaving cream, ruining the man's clothes. A Regional Forces soldier was huddled under his bed crying.

I wanted to creep out under the fire and flank that machine gun, maybe. But cooler heads prevailed and we just sat tight and returned fire towards the gun with our M-60 machine gun, rifles, and the Regional Forces' mortar tube. After all, the enemy were not going to overrun the compound; why be a hero? The gunnery sergeant on Hill 190 would have a fit if I got killed wearing sandals and cut-off shorts.

Lieutenant Tan of the Regional Forces was standing on top of the embankment, drawing fire and directing fire. To make fine adjustments on the mortar tube he would tap it with his foot. I remember hearing about the Vietnamese officer who adjusted his mortar by kicking it. Now I was seeing it.

We had no casualties from all the firing. During my five or six months in the village, we did not have casualties inside the compound.

Next morning we walked out to where the machine gun had been set up. In one of the small, ubiquitous graveyards we found fresh machine-gun marks from our M-60. But none of the villagers had seen or heard anything.

On hot summer days we would take a rope and bucket and go to the village well for a bath. We would soap down and throw buckets of cool water over each other. Sometimes we would smoke pot and watch the water turn colours as it splashed, and laugh like hell. The villagers thought we were crazy. They used one-gallon paint cans to draw water to fill their containers that they carried with a bamboo pole across their shoulders. So we would fill their containers with a couple of buckets of water. They thought we were so strong.

One night I had to carry the PRC-25 radio. I was not accustomed to talking on the radio, or to balancing it on my back on the slippery rice paddy dikes.

There were at least three men firing at us from across the little stream in the paddies. I started firing my rifle, like everyone else. I called India Company and directed in the mortar rounds of illumination. The bright flares floated down lighting the fields with the weird, moving bright light, and shadows chased each other across the paddies. The return fire stopped. My heart slowed. We (marines) got up to sweep the area. We walked round and round to find a place to cross the stream. I had to keep asking for more illumination. Unaccustomed to the balance of the radio on my back, I kept falling off the slippery dikes. The enlisted men listening to the radio were busting up at the sound of me curse. The captain wondered what the hell was going on. Why didn't he come down and see for himself?

We reached the site where we had seen the monsters. One man appeared suddenly, sitting up from behind a bush. We fired the M-60, M-16s, and the sergeant fired his (illegal) shotgun.

Later, by daylight, we pointed out the bullet holes in our kill. The big holes from the machine gun and the shotgun pellets were clearly evident. The innocent-looking little M-16 holes were less noticeable.

I have always lived with this memory: the enemy had not made a sound; he had just suddenly sat up with his hands over his head, his rifle beside him on the ground. I loaded my magazines with all tracer rounds. I had seen my tracers go through his body. Later, two more bodies were found downstream somewhere. We claimed them as our kills.

There was a German reporter at India Company then. She stayed on Hill 190 the night of that firefight. In daylight she came to the site. And she visited our compound to talk with us. As a warrior, I accepted the responsibility of explaining the anatomy of a firefight to her.

She discussed political science with the marines. Did we not understand that we were fighting in a people's war? All the people, by definition, were behind the cause. We could never win unless we killed all the people.

If she loved the Communists so much why didn't she go live in East Germany? Why didn't she interview the refugees from the North — especially the Catholics? What about the church with the Browning automatic rifle on the steps to protect the Catholics from Viet Cong? That would be a story. But nobody was writing about that side of the story in 1970.

Lieutenant Tan himself had told me that he had been with the

Viet Minh against the French. But he had become disillusioned with them and joined up to fight against the Communists. The old mama-san who brought us beer and prostitutes had lost two husbands to the Viet Cong. What did she think of the Communists? What has become of her since we left?

How could I be a crusader fighting for a cause that was not just? I knew it wasn't true that we were baby killers. I know we don't deserve the vilification of society today. But who cares?

Danny sent in some observations about difficulties after the war:

As for problems since Vietnam, I think in the stories that I have written there are foreshadowings of troubles to come. Sometimes I find it encouraging to think that some of the physical problems — apathy, lethargy, susceptibility to diseases — have an identifiable cause. Sometimes it gives me an excuse. I can blame the war, the administration, for my problems. I can feel sorry for myself and feel that someone owes me. This leads to depression.

I, like many Vietnam veterans, feel that to find peace I have to get away — find a cave or a mountaintop where the system cannot get at me and there are no people to lie to me and let me down. It is not easy to make your way back into the system and get in tune with society when you feel so strongly that you have been betrayed.

Other veterans have told me stories of getting into fights with cops or losing patience with a clerk at a ticket counter of an airport and jumping on him. They wake up with their hands on their wives' throats.

I remember students at college running off at the mouth about Vietnam. I shook and could not speak, but I wanted to kill. On occasion, I have been startled from my sleep by a girlfriend and I attacked to defend my life. I swung, but just pulled back in time. Once when my woman woke me from a violent dream by touching my face, I bit her. I find this funny, but scary.

Like others, I have not often stayed long in one job or one place. Part of it stems from my feelings inside. Part of it is the prejudice against us by employers and co-workers.

There exists a belief that a man who has gone through combat is ever afterwards immune to fear. He has faced the ultimate and will always react properly with cool competence and courage. I say this is a myth.

There are certainly many Vietnam vets who live in a world of violence as police officers and security guards. But I think these men are the exception. Most Vietnam vets have been shocked by their own vulnerability.

Out of paranoia some keep strong locks on doors, loaded weapons and big watchdogs. We fear anything can happen at any time. We are nervous when people come up quietly behind us. We often react like dogs who have been beaten too much.

The sense of being alienated and rejected goes deep. It keeps me from trying to cultivate new friendships. There are organizations that tend to glorify war, express their patriotism and heroism. This makes me sick. Elements of society ostracize the Vietnam veterans, but not those of other wars which are viewed as heroic.

When you don't have a close network of friends, wife or family for support (some married vets often live in a shell isolated from their wives and children), you are less tied down to life. You have strong feelings about Vietnam which have never been put into perspective. Friends have been killed and you think maybe you should have died instead of them. Your sense of value as a human being, your importance, is often very low. It is not easy to be a Vietnam veteran.[47]

After Vietnam, Danny attended university in the United States, graduating with a master's degree in library science. In 1977 he became an American citizen. He is now employed by the State of California at the Inmate Library, Sierra Conservation Center, Jamestown.

FRANK KETT

Vietnam: May 1970 to May 1971   Service: Air Force

Frank Kett (better known in Canada by his adopted name, Peter Edwards) was born 4 July 1944 in Detroit, but both his parents were Canadian. He was raised in Ottawa, attending Ashbury College and Rideau and Fisher Park high schools. He served with the Cameron Highlanders of Ottawa from 1959 to 1962, not only with the militia but on active duty as an instructor with the civilian readiness program. In the winter of 1962 Frank, having been laid off from the Canadian National Railways and with his wife pregnant, crossed the border and joined the United States Air Force in December 1962. In view of lack of economic prospects in his home town, he re-enlisted in the USAF in 1966.

In 1969 Frank received orders for Udorn, Thailand. His family returned to Ottawa while he was overseas. As a medic and public health officer, Staff Sergeant Kett was involved in the Medical Civic Action Program (teams of military doctors and medics sent to treat the locals in villages that lacked

Staff Sergeant Frank Kett in front of his bunk, Udorn, Thailand, 1970. (Courtesy F. Kett.)

medical facilities) in Thailand and Laos. Frank wore his own uniform, including a maroon field jacket with "Canada" on one sleeve and a Canadian flag on the other. His Canadian status was accepted because it "offered a unified appearance against the Viet and Thai Cong, and it allowed [him] access to places forbidden to Americans." After his tour, the USAF gave him a chance to return to school. His family came down from Canada but marital discord set in and ended in divorce.

In 1981 Frank returned to Ottawa but was still not impressed with the available opportunities, although the city had grown beyond his expectations. Having graduated from university, he retired as a captain from the USAF in 1985. He has remarried, now works for the Veterans Adminis-

tration Medical Center in Houston, and is completing his master's degree in business administration.[48]

Frank recalls some of his experiences:

The Departure

I was stationed in Albuquerque, New Mexico, when I received my orders. This was not the first set of orders. Six months earlier I was headed to Saigon and the orders were revoked. Now it was Thailand. I wanted my family to be in Canada in case anything happened to me. My now ex-wife had a sister and two brothers who lived in Ottawa. She also owned a share of their house, and presumably was guaranteed a place to live. It was early April 1970 when we left New Mexico in our 1967 Volkswagen van. This van had been in an accident and retained many of those dents and contusions; it looked like a "hippie" car of the decade. I kept wondering how many people thought I was going to Canada and not going to return. I was told to hand-carry my golf clubs and ship my clothes on ahead to the port in California. (I'll come back to the golf clubs later.) I stored the van on blocks in front of the house. Its image was befitting the group sharing the house; but at least for the time being the family was situated in a city my wife knew and she was with her family. I took the night train to Detroit.

In Detroit, my cousin, after saying good-bye with a few beers, took me to the airport, and I proceeded on to Los Angeles. This was a stopover to see my old boss and pick up my clothes. We went to the warehouse, and to our bewilderment, there was a strike. Here I was going to Southeast Asia (SEA) to fight a war and I couldn't cross a picket line in the States to get my uniforms. The next day I arrived at Travis Air Force Base (AFB) in my only uniform. I was told that we had a short delay (12 hours) prior to take off at 2 a.m. The only place open was the bowling alley. Since the plane trip was going to be a long dry run, I had several beers. Sometime in the early dawn we boarded the plane. There was this sign stating that no one would be allowed to board intoxicated. Somehow I doubted its integrity. We rapidly made friends on the plane; we played cards and complained about the skimpy box lunches. Several hours later we had our first beer break in Hawaii. The major question was how many beers could you consume in one hour? What seemed like days later, but was in fact only a few hours, we encountered severe weather. The plane rocked and rolled as the lightning flashed. The pilot decided to take a rest stop at Clark AFB in the Philippines. It was nine o'clock in the evening, so we found the NCO club and drank the latest batch of San Miguel beer. Four hours later we poured ourselves back on the plane. We were awakened to be informed we were flying over South Vietnam and would soon reach Bangkok. It felt like a tropical island, hot and sticky. Even worse, it was only 4 a.m. My plane going up country left in three hours. The airport had a 24-hour bar. I boarded a C-130, which is an aircraft with four noisy props and a back-loading door. While in flight, they kept the back door down. I climbed up on a pallet and lay down. Between the heat, the beer, the jet lag and the ride, I thought I was going to die, and then fall out the back door.

My base was the last one on the route. I must have been something to see! A dirty, unkempt, rather anxious sergeant, in dress blues, with a golf bag slung over one shoulder and reeking of stale alcohol. My new boss, and luckily an old friend, met me at the airport with a jeep. This was a rarity, since there were very few sections with jeeps; everyone else took the bus. He said, without any hesitation, the first priority was to get me a uniform and cleaned up, prior to checking in. In a whirlwind tour, I picked up a set of camouflaged fatigues, exchanged American dollars for Thai baht, checked in my golf clubs, and was dropped off in the middle of a strange city at something resembling a hotel.

I shared my room with a huge black airman who disappeared when I crashed into a deep sleep. I awoke in the early evening, hungover, hungry, hot and very nervous. I was 30 kilometres from Laos, warplanes flying overhead, the street sounds of high pitched Oriental voices echoing in my ears, while an odour that I will never forget permeated my nostrils — pungent dried squid. I took a shower, put on civilian clothes and began to wander around. Within a few blocks, I found a restaurant and a massage parlour. I tried both. Full, relaxed, but still very anxious, I returned to the hotel and dozed off to sleep again. I was aroused around midnight by a hammering on my door. My room-mate had returned with a handful of squealing young Thai girls. I awoke the next morning, a golden brown body lying next to me; I threw on my clothes, counted my money and ran to the base bus. "Welcome to Udorn Royal Thai AFB"; at least that's what the sign said as I drove through the front gate.

Udorn

This base was the home of the Commander 7th/13th Air Force, who controlled all aircraft based in Thailand operating over Laos and North Vietnam. It supported the Royal Laotian Government and both Royal Laotian Army and neutralist troops.

Room-mate

I was asked if I wished to live on or off base. After my first night in the city, my nerves suggested that I live in the barracks. Next to my bunk was a rather elaborate set-up, with mosquito netting, a large fan (worth a small ransom) and a storage box (another coveted item). When I asked who slept there, I was nicely informed that the individual was away. Talk about an understatement. My room-mate was in a Thai jail awaiting execution for murder!

Visit to Vientiane

Officially, there were no Americans in Laos. Actually, we supported SOS (Special Operations Squadron) throughout northern Laos. This was needed to provide air support to our aircraft bombing north of the DMZ. Forward air controller sites had to be established and maintained. In addition the CIA and the USAF supported the Royal Laotian Government and friendly ground forces. The major force of concern was around the "Plain of Jars." This area was guarded by 5,000 Meo tribesmen trained by the CIA. My first trip to the north was a little bizarre. I was told to dress in civilian clothes, leave all forms of military identification behind, and proceed to Continental Airlines. I boarded a small, four-passenger, single-engine prop Cessna. Within a few minutes, after a very fast takeoff, we landed in the back of Vientiane airport, Laos. No customs, no immigration, just an unmarked station wagon waiting. This visit was to check environmental conditions at the U.S. Embassy. I was given a tour of the city, including a look at the Communist headquarters. I was told to buy gold for my next visit. My return to Udorn was a little more ominous. I flew back on an unmarked Air America C-123 cargo plane, once again with the back door down, this time I would swear at 10 feet over the treetops. This was my first exposure to ground fire. I learnt that if you hugged the trees on short runs, rather than at a higher altitude, you received less damage because they couldn't see you coming. Too bad they weren't deaf.

Chiang Mai

This is one of the most beautiful spots in Thailand: forests, rolling hills, rivers and the most pleasant of all ... escape from the heat. It is the heart of the Golden Triangle of the opium trade. You could buy a mistress or a harem, an opium pipe, woodcarvings and furniture for a few American dollars. Located in these mountains was a USAF communications site; its exact duties remain classified. I will always remember an offer made to me by a Thai border patrol officer. He asked me if I would like to go on a flight to the Chinese border in a helicopter. I declined; somehow I didn't relish the thought of fathering blond-haired, blue-eyed children for the Chinese. I sometimes wonder if I should have gone, but no second thoughts that day.

VD & Col. Hein

In the spring of 1971, the Royal Laotians suffered massive casualties from the Communists. They brought these victims to Udorn. In order to care for those thousand-odd patients, the air force brought in the reserves from Clark AFB. We established a tent city. The reserves were restricted to the main base area by the hospital commander, "Colonel Hein," where he worked their buns off. VD was at a peak in Udorn. They painted a sign on a bedsheet and hung it on a fence for all to see. It read: "God, VD, and Col. Hein." If one didn't get you, the other would.

Hallway Amputations

Col. Hein was a surgeon, a very good surgeon. At times we thought his hands were permanently stained with betadine. Like the MASH units of TV fame, he stayed in the OR (operating room). Sometimes wounded arrived in such numbers that the patients would pack the OR. We triaged in a small ER (emergency room). One day, a casualty was brought in, his right leg hanging on, bone sticking out, his lifeblood held back by a tourniquet. The ER was full, the OR backed up. In a flash, with a sharp set of bandage scissors, Col. Hein cut through the remaining tissue, ordered the stump dressed and the mutilated leg destroyed. That night we ate roast beef.

Cobra Pets

In the veterinarian office, we had a large wooden box with a glass front. In the box we kept a king cobra, alive. We told everyone that we kept it as a training aid and for venom research. We lied. It was a pet. We loved to see it rise up and spit on the glass or devour live rats. We especially loved to see one of our group, a little black man as black could be with great big white eyes, stare at the snake. He would get that thing mesmerized and when the snake would awake it would spring forth spewing gobs of toxin. It dripped down the glass into little pools at the bottom of the cage. For some reason no one volunteered to clean that cage. After I left, I heard the snake disappeared one night and was never seen again.

Walking Catfish

Speaking of snakes, when I lived off base I lived in a Thai-style condo. This was a long huge room in the middle of a tin-roofed building, composed of many similar rooms. Each room had separations approximately 10 feet high. In the front was a steel expansion gate that opened onto the street; the first area was mine. It housed a sitting area with bamboo furniture and a TV and a large bed covered in heavy mosquito netting. You went through a door to the back where there was a cooking area (a table and Thai fireplace), a Thai bed (a wooden platform), and at the very back a small enclosure that housed a large water barrel and a trough that served as a toilet bowl. Outside was a sewage river or canal that ran between the buildings, and God forbid if you fell in. One night I had to use the john. I knew the way. As I was creeping by the cooking area I stepped on a wet thick soft round object, about the size of a cucumber. It moved. I screamed! I jumped, I ran! When the lights came on I was embarrassed. I had stepped on a slimy little fish. In Thailand they have walking catfish that will survive out of the water for hours. They have learnt to crawl on their fins. My house girl had brought some fish home for dinner and they had escaped from their basket. I hate fish!

Poolside Axe Murderer

One block from my house was an American-style hotel. All American forces personnel had to be off the streets at midnight, and if you returned to the base after midnight you would be punished. There was a hole in the fence behind the hospital. I snuck in one night with friends only to find out the next day that the guard had shot someone coming through the fence the same night. From then on I found an alternative. That alternative was renting a hotel room. One hotel, the "Princess," had a large outside swimming pool surrounded by a huge patio. After the bars closed, everyone would settle in around the pool, it never closed. One night a samlar driver (a Thai taxi which is a bicycle with a carriage behind, the opposite of a rickshaw) ran up the steps of a swimming-pool area. He brandished an axe and proceeded to chop off an American soldier's head. It seemed the American had a fight with his girlfriend and she had hired this killer. He died. The pool action remained quiet for a week, and the samlar drivers were removed from the general area, then the all-nighters started again.

Baht Bounty

One of my jobs was VD control. This included raiding the bars. I would have an entourage of U.S. military police, Thai police, and a Thai public health official. When we hit the bars of my choosing (the ones with the highest VD rate that week), we barricaded the doors then counted all the females or those who looked female (another story). The military rules stated that every female who entered a bar frequented by Americans had to be signed in or present a valid health card at the front door. The numbers counted had to total the signatures, employees and VD cards. If the count did not match, we would place the club off limits. This would basically close the club. For the first offense it was a week, the second two, the third a month, and then forever. You could walk in some bars and get high on the smoke. You can imagine the power I had. Yes, I was offered bribes, but it was not worth the risk to accept one, which really irked some of the most powerful bar owners. It also affected the small bar owner. There was one dive on the strip that I closed. The owner was outraged that I dare threaten her marvellous establishment and decided to buy a contract on my head. She figured she could hire a samlar driver for 50 baht. That's about $2.50. In all honesty, I did have a long-standing bounty for a 1,000 baht; however, it was never initiated because of my honesty and fairness in regulating the bars. I also had a bodyguard supplied by one of the bars and my Thai girlfriend. It was her brother, the biggest Thai I ever saw, a sumo wrestler who also rode a Harley.

Winston Salems and Jim Beam

American cigarettes could be emptied and refilled with hashish laced with opium. When combined with menthol they smoked cooler and the menthol hid the smell. You could buy anything for a carton of Salem cigarettes. This was a subtlety of the war not well recognized. The drugs were sold not for the money, but to destroy the morale and efficiency of the airman. The cigarettes would hook the men into drug use, either making them an object of blackmail or military justice. This was a very cheap weapon. The price of a pack of the laced cigarettes was less than five dollars, but on the street in the U.S. over a hundred. Today, we still see the addicts first hooked back then in SEA. That part of the war continues.

American whiskey was taxed at an outrageous price. A bottle of $2 whiskey on base would sell for $20 to $50 on the black market. If you wanted a good time all you needed to do was buy a bottle (the preferred was a decanter in the shape of a bowling pin) of Jim Beam and head downtown.

Golf

Remember the golf clubs. I did play a round but only once. The course was 10 miles out of town, tightly guarded by police. You were surrounded by water, jungle and cobras. You had to drive through the trees and in the middle of the course the worst hazard of all ... the police hut. If you hit the hut, a $10 fine. If you made it to the green, you had to scrape off the elephant dung and never, never reach in a cup. Remember what I said about snakes — that's where they lived.

The Food

The pungent smell of drying squid will always be etched in my memory. Chicken, complete with head, the body split down the centre and opened in the front — pierced by two sticks and somewhat cooked over two lumps of charcoal — was only edible after large quantities of Mekong whiskey. My water buffalo steaks seem to have come only from completely dead, very old, worn-out animals. Pig in the market is not uncommon, but the only thing not sold or cooked is the squeal. On the other hand, there could also be found delicious Kobe steak sautéed in brandy or creamed chicken inside a pineapple. The most famous Thai dish is "cowpat" — the best fried rice in the world — mixed with an egg and served with a twist of lime. Singha beer made with formaldehyde goes well with the food, but too many will get you pickled.

Going Home

My on-base house girl gave me the most beautiful lei. I shall always look back on that heavy perfumed object; it had scent that lingered for days. I came with squid and left purged by flowers. I also left much more sober than when I came. I had almost quit drinking. It was too dangerous. That last night in Bangkok, I met an old acquaintance from Albuquerque. The last time I saw this guy, he was going to commit suicide by jumping off a water tower. They brought him down, gave him counselling, and sent him to Vietnam. Military Justice.

I will always remember hearing that one special song whispering in the breeze as I departed, "I'm Leaving on a Jet Plane."[49]

MICHAEL X

Vietnam: May 1970 to May 1971   Service: Army

Michael X was 18 when he went to war in Vietnam as a medic in 1970. He was wounded in action and still has pieces of shrapnel in his chest. As a result of his war experience, Mike decided to become a physician. The following are some of his recollections:

I joined the army on the day of my 17th birthday (23 October 1968). This was the youngest age the military would allow. I joined the army to grow up and out of a difficult family and personal situation. I went through three months' basic training in Fort Lewis, Washington, and three months' medical training in Fort Sam Houston, Texas. The majority of my friends that took medical training with me were shipped to Vietnam. I was still under 18 years so I was sent to Germany. Participating in peacetime activities in Germany was disturbing. War games (NATO exercises) seemed superficial and our roles insignificant. In addition, by this time I found the rigours of military life and being on my own had given me a certain maturity I had needed. Due to my three-year commitment to the military I felt I still had a debt to repay. I decided to go where I could do the most good as a medic. By now I had turned 18, so I volunteered to go to Vietnam! Needless to say they accepted my offer and at 18 years old I found myself in Vietnam determined to be the best medic I could.

I was assigned to a field engineer group. This engineer group used Rome plows (large tractors with enormous blades) to clear out the jungle and dig up enemy bunker complexes. We usually travelled with the infantry units and so unofficially I became a combat medic. There are several events that are still vivid in my mind.

When I first arrived in the country, another medic and I were sent to a large emergency station for pre-jungle training. During our first hours of orientation a busload of Vietnamese civilians who had been bombed were brought in. My first patient was a young Vietnamese woman whose hand had been partially blown off. I held her hand while a doctor pulled out loose bone fragments. After things settled I went to look for my friend. I found him out back vomiting. He later told me his first patient was a dead American soldier. A fragmentation grenade had gone off at close range and he was covered in small holes. Those killed in Nam were placed in large green bags and tagged for the U.S.

I received my Purple Heart for being wounded in Cambodia and still have shrapnel in my chest. The evening before I was wounded the North Vietnamese had broken into our radio frequency and had told us we would all be killed. Nothing happened that evening. The next day we moved camp. That night it almost happened: we were nearly overrun. Unfortunately, unknown to us at the time, we set our base camp on top of an underground North Vietnamese supply post. We had just set it up, dug our bunker positions and filled our sandbags for protection. I was sitting on a cot treating someone for a minor injury when the first mortar came whistling in — it knocked me flat and shattered our tent. I gathered up my flak jacket, helmet and aid bag. Calls for "Medic" were piercing the night, and more mortar shells were landing. I began my usual process of low crawling to reach the wounded. I had gotten about 20 feet when the next mortar shell landed nearby. The blast and shrapnel lifted me off the ground and flipped me on my back. The blood was squirting across my chest. The last thing I remember was placing my hand over the area. I went into shock. I experienced an out-of-body awareness common in near-death situations. Later my medic friend told me he was unable to move my hand. While lying on a stretcher waiting to be evacuated by helicopter I became conscious for a moment. I heard someone pleading for a medic, I tried to move, to say something, to get up, to be of help, but I couldn't. I lost consciousness again. My next memory is being thrown onto the medical evacuation helicopter. As I bounced on the floor, the shrapnel in my chest felt like a searing knife. I remember screaming out in pain. Later my friend told me the helicopter I was on was nearly shot down by a sniper. The evening I was wounded the majority of individuals in my unit and the infantry unit (Armored Cavalry) I was with were also wounded. In one tent some men in our unit were found dead — still hanging to their tent poles with large holes in their bodies from the incoming mortars. I still think they died because their reflexes were slowed from smoking dope earlier in the day. Who knows? Out of six medics there that evening only one was not wounded. I was operated on, sent for rehabilitation, and was back in the jungle in six weeks.

I received a Bronze Star and several Army Commendation medals, including one for bravery for other episodes. One I recall vividly. A black American soldier from the infantry unit we were tending was shot through the upper neck. He was unable to breathe and the call went out for medics. When I arrived people were standing around and he was not breathing and had gone into cardiac arrest. I performed a cricothyroidotomy (cut open his neck) with a scalpel and inserted a tracheostomy tube below the bullet wound. Then my partner and I administered cardiac massage and respiratory support for 15 minutes while on a helicopter flight to an emergency processing centre. I recall my friend stating our legs were hanging out the helicopter the entire way. I don't even remember. When we arrived the emergency room staff took over. The soldier lived. They told us we had truly saved his life. They gave us each a purple popsicle and told us we would have to sleep out back till morning when a helicopter would take us back. We had saved a life, and on a hot, humid evening covered in mud and blood we found a popsicle as great a reward as any. There was no sleep that night. We were pretty proud. When we returned we found the other black soldiers were surprised that "white guys" would make such an effort to save their black brother's life. We were heroes.

Another episode was different — not everyone lived. During a mortar attack, an inexperienced lieutenant had ordered my squad to the perimeter. A good friend was shot by our own men by mistake. When I finally found him he was dead. His skull had been shattered by a bullet. I still tried to revive him. When I realized I couldn't give him back his life I held his head in my arms and cried. They had to pull me away. Just hours before he had talked about his family and friends, about his girlfriend who was waiting — what did it matter now? — he died. The lieutenant left the next day under threat of his life for having given an inappropriate order. Later when I returned from the jungle there was a funeral service. My sergeant refused to let me go. He threatened me with court martial. At that point it didn't matter. I went. Nothing happened. His parents never did learn how their son really died. That's probably just as well.

These were a few of the episodes that stand out in the flood of memories. The entire experience of war and Vietnam has left me angry. I've learned to deal with this constructively. Each of us is responsible for "violence" in our lives, relationships and society. The path to peace and ending wars starts with each of us. I now have an intensity of purpose and desire for peace. There are multiple areas of my life that I try to put this into practice. I won't forget my friends, Vietnam or the importance of peace.

Vietnam has left Mike convinced war and violence have no place in this world. Having survived the Vietnam War, Mike has dedicated himself to peace and changing the way we accept violence, both personally and politically. That is why he has participated in actions to encourage taxes to be used for peace (Peace Tax Fund) and in actions against war toys (War Toy Boycott). On a personal level he is a vegetarian, married to a feminist and is trying to raise his son as a non-violent male. He has worked within his community in such fields as male violence, abused women, peace, disarmament, and human rights. He hopes others will act both personally and politically within their communities for peace![50]

HUGH HARGRAVE

Vietnam: July 1970 to June 1971   Service: Navy

Lieutenant Commander Hugh Hargrave and his wife Sharon, Saigon, September 1971. (Courtesy H. Hargrave.)

Hugh Hargrave was born 26 August 1939 in Trail, British Columbia. Hugh grew up there and graduated from Grade 13, the equivalent of first-year college. In 1958 he enrolled in the Faculty of Pharmacy at the University of British Columbia. After two years, he applied to medical school. Hugh graduated in 1964, took his internship in Harrisburg, Pennsylvania, then studied and practised in both Canada and the United States. He moved to live to the United States in 1969. As a permanent immigrant he was subject to the draft within six months of his arrival. Physicians were eligible for the draft until age 36. Rather than get established in practice as an anaesthetist and then be drafted, he elected to enlist in May 1970 and get his military obligation out of the way. He chose the navy: "I hoped I wouldn't be sent to Vietnam — they had the least number of men in country. I did (I think) take the oath of allegiance, although at the time I was (and still am) a Canadian citizen." (Normally, it was necessary to be an American citizen in order to become a commissioned officer in the U.S. forces. But this qualification would be overlooked if one's skill was needed.) Hugh entered and left the U.S. Navy with the rank of lieutenant commander.[51]
Hugh recounts his story:

When we arrived at three in the morning at Tan Son Nhut Airport, Saigon, it had been raining previously. The tarmac was wet and it was very muggy. After collecting my baggage thrown on the ground, I had to stand in line and change any American money I had into military payment certificates. It's a court martial offense here if you are found with any American currency. We then boarded a bus to the Annapolis Hotel for use by incoming navy personnel. We checked in at four in the morning. It is as dirty and smelly a place as I have ever seen in my life. That morning I stood outside and there were thousands of motor scooters, three-wheeled vehicles, and big buses all jammed with people. Everybody seemed to be honking their horns. However, we were not located in downtown Saigon, but an outlying area.

The messes for officers and men were about a block from the hotel. We were warned to beware of Vietnamese cowboys — these are guys who come whipping along on their motor scooters about 10 to 20 mph and grab the watch off your wrist, especially if you have an expansion bracelet. They will also jump you and try to get your wallet. Sometimes they use a razor blade to slash open the button on your hip pocket in case your wallet is buttoned in there. On one guy who went to breakfast, they missed his wallet and got his ass instead, resulting in 14 stitches. If that wasn't bad enough, a bunch of cowboys jumped him at supper and broke his collarbone. We usually walked in groups of at least two or three for our own protection.

We were taken on a bus tour of downtown Saigon. This is where you get the impression a war is going on. There are barbed-wire barricades and, in front of the most important, a bunker with an armed guard. Usually, the guard, a Vietnamese, was asleep or reading. The only Vietnamese guards who were alert were marines in front of the presidential palace. Motor scooters seemed as plentiful as clouds of locusts. Another thing that strikes you are the piles of garbage lying around. Due to the war and uprooting of villages, the city is overcrowded. Around downtown Saigon, there are many little booths and stalls for selling. Most of the items for sale are those for which the military exchanges are always out of stock. The prices, of course, are outrageous. There is anything you might want — even a complete set of monkey wrenches. The stench of the many little food booths mixed in with fumes and garbage is overpowering. An interesting law is that whenever two people ride a motor scooter, the passenger has to ride sidesaddle. This is to discourage shootings and grenade attacks by keeping the passenger offbalance.

My service in Vietnam was in the MILPHAP (Military Provincial Health Assistance Program). These were groups of military health-care personnel loaned to USAID (U.S. Agency for International Development), a civilian agency with the objective of assisting the South Vietnamese civilians in various aspects of civil development (e.g., health, education, agriculture, etc.).

The vast majority of Vietnamese physicians were on active duty in the armed forces, leaving a small number of civilian doctors to look after civilians. We were to serve as consultants to those Vietnamese medical personnel who were in place before our arrival, and to those who had been trained by MILPHAP teams. We were also to teach the Vietnamese physicians and medical personnel newer medical techniques so that they could more effectively treat their own people.

My particular MILPHAP Navy 9 Unit was composed of two physicians (myself a fully trained anaesthesiologist, and my immediate CO, a fully trained cardiothoracic surgeon) and four to five medical corpsmen. Our initial station was the town of Chau Doc, capital of Chau Doc Province, in the Mekong Delta, almost three kilometres from the Cambodian border just south of the Parrot's Beak. The facilities and equipment were very primitive by U.S. and Canadian standards, the majority of health-care funds being utilized by Vietnamese military hospitals. The surgical patient workload was approximately one-half civilian war casualties, one-half routine surgical procedures, i.e., hernias, gallbladders, etc.

MILPHAP 9's billet was a late 1880 French Foreign Legion fort assigned to us and a construction battalion detachment, also working with the Vietnamese civilians. An adjacent U.S. Army military advisory team was responsible for our mess and security, although we were supplied with our own weapons and stood our own watches. Many times, rather than eat at the army mess, we would chip in and buy food on the local economy and cook it ourselves over charcoal — much superior to army chow. The hospital was located approximately two kilometres from our base — a five- to six-minute jeep ride through town. Since our fort had the nearest chopper pad to the hospital, we triaged all incoming wounded Vietnamese military personnel at our base prior to transferring them to the nearby Vietnamese military hospital.

Within three months it was apparent that having an anaesthesiologist and cardiothoracic surgeon at a small provincial hospital was "over-kill," so to speak. Therefore, we were transferred to a larger hospital (Can Tho) in the central delta where we had access to somewhat better equipment and facilities than in Chau Doc, and accordingly, could do more complex cases.

Not infrequently, as the Vietnamese civilian hierarchy became aware of our presence, we would be flown around the delta to do surgery on some local Vietnamese official who otherwise would not have access to the type of service we could provide. I was never (knowingly) under hostile fire. Rightly or wrongly, we MILPHAP team members felt reasonably secure travelling the delta in a marked jeep. We, undoubtedly, treated some VC in the civilian hospitals where we worked and felt the VC would not harm the people giving them the best medical care they could get.

My wife, who flew to Saigon shortly after I arrived in country, found a job in a Seventh Day Adventist hospital. This hospital, administered by U.S. civilians, but staffed by Vietnamese, cared for Vietnamese civilians. Out of necessity my wife became quite proficient in the Vietnamese language, while I was supplied with an interpreter.

Following this interesting but relatively uneventful tour of duty, my wife and I left Vietnam within a few days of each other, and I spent the rest of my military obligation at the Oak Knoll Naval Hospital in Oakland, California. Since leaving the navy I have been in private practice in anaesthesia for the past 17 years in Lancaster, Pennsylvania.

Hugh's wife, Sharon, sent in additional information to supplement her husband's account:

The Seventh Day Adventist hospital where I worked was an old French mansion located on a very busy intersection in the northern sector of Saigon. It was literally a teeming mass of humanity with people jamming the first floor waiting for clinic time to see the doctor.

Once the public health service wanted to install resident cats along with poison traps to rid the place of huge rats. But local hospital personnel objected. They claimed that the resident rats were kept well fed with garbage, but if they were killed, other hungrier rats would move in and attack those patients who were helpless.

What we did have in abundance were tiny grey-green lizards called "cheechucks" because of the tiny squeaks they made if alarmed. Mostly they would climb the walls and ceilings without ever bothering us, so we left them alone. Any control would have been useless anyway. What we did constant battle with, however, were the ants. Traps were everywhere and food containers tightly sealed. Perhaps the most amazing sight was the size of the cockroaches — they measured two to three inches long with a wingspan of one and a half inches on some.

This hospital of 39 beds usually had 75 to 100 patients. Because of the cramped quarters and too many patients, there were two to three patients per bed. A child might be found lying on a bed with a middle-aged woman and an old man — one might have a communicable disease, while the others might be surgical patients. In addition to the patients on the beds, family members were present to help. My first experience of seeing nursing young children at breast as a means of comforting was when I saw grandmothers nursing children as old as four years.

Hugh and I had been married for five years at this time and had no children. The Vietnamese could not comprehend the situation. They were positive that we didn't know a thing about the birds and the bees and their question was always, "Why not?"

One of Hugh's duties was to teach Vietnamese nurses to give anaesthesia. This was complicated by the fact that the Vietnamese language is very primitive and lacks most words for technical and medical terminology. Add to this the fact that most nurses were very resistant and did not want to administer anaesthesia because they thought that exposure to the gases and fumes rendered one "dink-a-dao" (crazy).

The Vietnamese civilian hospitals lacked money for the more modern drugs and equipment to which Hugh was used. Occasionally, ether was the only anaesthesia available, which he had to be taught to use by some of the Vietnamese nurses, as this technique has been outmoded in the U.S. for approximately 30 years!

One night in a small village near Can Tho a six-year-old girl was asleep in her family's hut when a stray bullet from an M-16 penetrated the wall of the hut and entered her abdomen. During the exploratory surgery being performed by Hugh's CO, the cardiothoracic surgeon, the bullet accidentally dislodged and travelled to the superior vena cava. It was necessary to stop the abdominal bleeding and take an X-ray to locate the bullet. It was shown to have lodged in one of her pulmonary arteries, making it necessary to surgically enter her chest wall to remove the bullet. This was successfully completed without the necessity of administering blood. Incidentally, because blood was in such short supply, the surgical team was not allowed to use more than two units per patient.

Coming face to face with the difference between Eastern and Western cultures and values was, sometimes, rather shocking to Americans. One of these times involved a 10-year-old boy who was brought into the Vietnamese hospital with his intestines exposed and laying on the stretcher beside him — a result of a shrapnel wound. Because it was lunchtime, the Vietnamese covered the wound with saline soaked dressings until after their two-hour lunch break. After lunch they took him to the operating room. Fortunately, the youngster recovered and went home.

In addition to their hospital work, the MILPHAP 9 team travelled into the bush occasionally to hold small open clinics for the villagers. These visits consisted of treating simple infections, worms, stomach upsets, respiratory infections, etc., which plagued the populace.

To close on a slightly amusing note, there was the evening the American doctors were being treated to a restaurant dinner by the Vietnamese physicians. In his best Vietnamese, Hugh asked the Vietnamese waitress for ice in his beer. (The beer was served warm due to a lack of refrigeration.) After the poor girl turned three shades of red and fled in a fit of giggles, one Vietnamese informed Hugh that he had actually asked the waitress to pee in his beer![52]

BRIAN LEWIS

Vietnam: October 1970 to September 1971   Service: Army

Brian Lewis was born in Winnipeg on 3 December 1949. He moved to England as a child and to the United States at age 12. He attended high school in Dover, Delaware, and on scholarship attended Delaware Technical and Community College from 1967 to 1969. He received a draft notice for October 1969 but chose to enlist in September. After eight weeks basic training he was assigned to the job of cook's assistant. In June 1970 he volunteered for Vietnam. Because of his Canadian citizenship, Brian would not be sent to combat unless he volunteered. In Vietnam Brian was a cook with the rank of corporal assigned to the 326th Engineer Battalion of the 101st Airborne Division.

The following are some of his memories of Vietnam:

I arrived in Vietnam at Cam Ranh Bay and was processed over two or three days. I remember being told to look at a map to determine my destination and was surprised to see I was approximately 25 miles from the Demilitarized Zone. I was very naive. I enjoyed being there, felt needed and was proud to state I was Canadian. The negative points were that I became dependent upon beer and at 10 cents a can I drank every day. I smoked grass but not regularly. I never tried heroin or LSD as many others did. I did delve into the black market once and was almost trapped and alone in the city of Hue. I managed to get out and link up with my buddy who had been told by the locals to leave the area. I never attempted that again.

Some racial problems developed. I noticed the changes in attitudes as the year went on. Generally, morale was poor and demonstrations back home didn't help. I volunteered for assignment in February 1971 and was conveyed to Khe Sanh. The 101st Airborne

Corporal Brian Lewis (second left) and fellow cooks at Camp Eagle, I Corps, Quang Tri Province, Vietnam, June 1971. (Courtesy B. Lewis.)

Division (Airmobile) and the 1st Brigade, 5th Infantry Division (Mechanized) had reoccupied the abandoned U.S. Marine base at Khe Sanh as an assault position for the South Vietnamese forces in early 1971. This was the beginning of Lam Son 719 — South Vietnam's attempt to raid the Ho Chi Minh Trail in the southern Laotian panhandle.

The operation was a disaster. When I was not working, I travelled around the base and witnessed the South Vietnamese troops clinging to helicopter pads hundreds of feet above ground. Pilots reported that they went in with South Vietnamese troops — only they would not disembark. Wounded were left behind. Panic and chaos took place. Basically, the Vietnam experience was excitement, risk and adventure, but there were also feelings of loneliness and despair.[53]

After an honourable discharge from the U.S. Army in 1971, Brian attended Delaware State College but he could not adjust. He left Dover and worked as a carpenter's helper at various jobs. Most of his brothers and sisters were living in Canada by then and convinced him to move back. As a Canadian national, he only had to confirm his citizenship at the border. He has remained in Canada since 1974. He currently lives in Hamilton, Ontario, and works as a supervisor for Canada Post.

VINCENT DeROSSI

Vietnam: August 1971 to April 1972   Service: Army

Corporal Vincent DeRossi at Phu Bai, Vietnam, October 1971. (Courtesy V. DeRossi.)

Vincent DeRossi was born in Montréal on 10 June 1951. A slump in the construction industry in Montréal forced the family to move to New York City in 1961. In 1970 Vincent enlisted in the U.S. Army for three years. His aim was to go to Vietnam to help win the war.

Private DeRossi landed at Cam Ranh Bay in August 1971. Before he arrived, the ammunition dump was blown up, and there were several rocket attacks while he was there. Vincent mentioned to the sergeant that he thought he had made a mistake in volunteering for Vietnam and wondered if he could be sent back home, since he was still a Canadian citizen. The sergeant suggested that, if they were attacked, Private DeRossi should stand up and tell the Viet Cong not to shoot at him because he was a Canadian citizen.

Shortly thereafter, Vincent was assigned to Company A, 504th Military Police Battalion. Most of his time was spent in I Corps on convoy escorts, guard duty or at observation posts. The U.S. Marines had pulled out of the area and the U.S. Army had taken over.

After Vietnam, Specialist Four DeRossi spent a year at Fort Carson, Colorado, as a driver with the 4th Infantry Division. When his military service was completed, Vincent returned to New York City. It was not until 1980 that Vincent finally decided to become an American citizen.

Vincent offers a few memories of Vietnam:

I remember being away from my family and friends and waiting for letters from home. There are many incidents I could tell about Vietnam. However, most of them are better left unwritten. I have a difficult time recounting what I saw.

I can recall, one time in hospital, there was a boy about 12 years old who had both his legs amputated. He was a Viet Cong prisoner. South Vietnamese soldiers questioned him and found out he had helped to move supplies down the Ho Chi Minh Trail. When they finished interrogating him, they shot him. This was a boy almost as old as my own son now. No words can express the anger I felt.

You would think that prejudice had no place among soldiers, but it did. No whites wanted to share their hootch with a militant black soldier, but me. I saw no colour, only a fellow soldier. We became friends. Some of the other white soldiers didn't share my feelings. They called me "nigger lover." In battle, however, we were as one with no prejudice. We all had one thing in common — we wanted to return home, safe and sound.[54]

KENT MALCOLM

Vietnam: December 1971 to December 1972   Service: Air Force

Kent Malcolm was born of an American mother and a Canadian father in St. Louis, Missouri, in 1951. When he was six months old the family moved to Toronto, his father's home town. He grew up in Newmarket and graduated from high school there in June 1969. Although he is an American citizen, his two brothers and sister are Canadian citizens.

Kent enlisted in the U.S. Air Force in December 1969 and became an F-4 (Phantom II) aircraft maintenance crew chief. He was assigned to Da Nang Air Base in December 1971 as a member of 421st Tactical Fighter Squadron, 366th Tactical Fighter Wing, "The Gunfighters," as an F-4E crew chief. Kent left Da Nang in July 1972 to finish his tour in Takhli, Thailand, as the 366th was pulled out of South Vietnam. He completed his tour at Udorn, Thailand, with the 432nd Organizational Maintenance Squadron, 432nd Tactical Reconnaissance Wing, as a staff sergeant. After he came back from Vietnam, he married a girl from Newmarket. He continued

Sergeant Kent Malcolm behind a 2,000 pound bomb, Udorn, Thailand, November 1972. Crew chief Malcolm's F-4E Phantom is in the background. (Courtesy K. Malcolm.)

with his air force duties but also attended university, graduating with a bachelor's degree. He thus was able to receive a commission in 1981. He is now a captain managing logistics matters for the USAF F-111 fleet at Tactical Air Command Headquarters, Langley Air Force Base, Virginia.

Kent describes "A Day in the Life of a Crew Chief":

Our F-4s were usually employed in close air support of troops or interdiction of enemy supply lines. Most of the flying was done during the day and early evening. Maintenance went on 24 hours a day. We worked 12-hour shifts, four days on, one day off. Each plane had a day and night crew chief who was responsible for its airworthiness whether or not he did the work himself. Aircraft were inspected before and after each flight. All maintenance was done in each aircraft's steel/concrete revetment. It was hot and humid all the time. When it rained it was short and torrential. That didn't cool things off any. It just felt more hot and humid.

There was some relief from the heat after the sun went down, but that was when you started to worry about rocket attacks. Da Nang was called "Rocket City," and for good reason. It was a favourite Viet Cong target after dark. The VC used 107-mm and 122-mm Russian-made rockets with a 18-kg warhead. These were fired from the surrounding hills in the general direction of the airfield. During my tour at Da Nang I endured 26 rocket attacks. (I know it was 26 because I etched a stroke into my helmet for each one.) The intensity and frequency increased significantly after the spring offensive got under way in April 1972. Your only protection was your helmet and flak jacket. There usually wasn't any warning of a rocket attack (consisting of anywhere from one to a dozen or so rockets) until it was upon you. After the first couple of rounds, the base warning sirens would wail. Depending on the impact distance from you, the explosions sounded like "whoomps" and claps of thunder. Not too accurate, the rockets caused significant damage only three times while I was there. One damaged part of our post exchange store. (Everyone thought they should have hit the chow hall instead.) Another destroyed an AC-47 Spooky gunship parked on the other side of the airfield. The third struck closer to home. It was about 10 or 11 p.m. when the rounds came in. I remember hearing the first one or two impact, not too far from my part of the flight line. I was driving an aircraft-towing vehicle at the time, so I pulled over close to a revetment wall and jumped out and hit the ground. I remember I was so shaken that my knees buckled and I just fell from the vehicle. Then I heard a terrific "whoomp" followed by a louder explosion. I thought they hit one of our aircraft. I looked up and saw an orange glow at the end of our revetment row. Something was burning furiously. Having regained my orientation, I got up, jumped in the tow vehicle and started towards the fire, about 100 yards away. I was stopped by one of my buddies who told me a parked fuel truck was hit and flaming jet fuel was working its way down between the double-rowed revetments. While firetrucks arrived to tend the blaze we worked at getting our planes out of the revetments closest to the fire and relocating them into others, lest another rocket attack claim them. It turned out that the burning fuel wouldn't have reached our jets anyway but we didn't know that at the time. It was too confusing and chaotic for us to know for sure what was really happening. The next morning they hauled away the destroyed gas truck. The top of its 6,000-gallon tank was blown off. The impact point of the rocket in the concrete about 15 feet from the truck was clearly evident. It hardly dented its surface. However, the shrapnel from the rocket tore into the truck tank, causing the explosion. Luckily no one was hurt in the whole episode. That was the closest I came to being involved in a really dangerous situation brought on by enemy action.

I worked the noon-to-midnight shift the whole time I was in

Vietnam. Once work was done for the night it was usually off to the chow hall or straight to the barracks. There wasn't any going to bed just yet. The time was passed writing letters home, drinking beer and listening to music. We had a lounge area called "The Swamp." It wasn't very large but had a makeshift bar, fridge and TV. Sometimes someone would bring down a tape-recorder and we'd listen to mostly rock and country & western. We didn't knock anyone's taste in music, we just all got along, being in the same boat as it were. The barracks themselves were two-storey, wooden, with plywood walls halfway up and screen the rest of the way on each floor. The first floor had concrete slabs to protect it. We were cautioned not to remain on the second floor during a rocket attack because if a rocket hit close to the barracks, the shrapnel would travel upwards and tear into the second floor. I always thought the best place to be caught during a rocket attack was in the shower, since the walls were concrete on three sides.

The barracks were originally "open bay" but plywood was put up to make individual rooms where two or three people could live in relative privacy. We had a locker each, and slept in bunk beds surrounded by mosquito netting. The walls were usually wallpapered with *Playboy* centrefolds and similar types of pictures. One guy had his ceiling covered with *Time* covers going back several years. We had mama-sans and papa-sans do general housecleaning chores and do our laundry and shine our boots for 50 cents a week. Our socks usually got lost in the shuffle but it worked out all right for the most part. I never completely trusted them though. They were always asking you to get them stuff at the post exchange. They'd ask for things like hand soap, cigarettes, toothpaste and cassette and eight-track tapes. I know the stuff ended up for sale downtown on the black market.

I'd like to close with a few words about the people I worked with during my tour. The hours were long and living conditions could have been a whole lot better. Many of the guys I worked with joined the air force so they wouldn't get drafted into the army. Four years in the air force made a lot more sense to some than two in the army with a pretty good chance of a Vietnam tour of duty. And even if you ended up in "The Nam" it was a much better existence in the air force, relatively speaking, than what the army had to face. That point was never lost on us. Most of the guys just wanted to do their time and get back to what they were doing before: school, work, etc. Mind you, some decided to stay in. I've met a couple over the years who did just that, after swearing up and down they wouldn't stay in for a million dollars. Such is human nature. Anyways, despite the constant bitching, the people I worked with were among the finest I have ever met. There was a job to be done and it was done in a professional manner. We all realized that the lives of the aircrews were in our hands and if our aircraft couldn't get off the ground that meant close air support couldn't be given to those on the ground who might desperately need it. I personally worked on my airplane as if I were going to fly it and I know most everyone else had that same attitude. "It's my airplane and I let the pilots borrow it" was a common saying (and still is today with the new generation of crew chiefs). It's a sick feeling to lose an airplane you've worked on for any period of time. First you pray for the aircrew and hope they got out OK and then you hope you didn't fail them by having something mechanically go wrong with your aircraft. I lost the first plane I crewed in Vietnam after three months working on it. The crew and plane were lost to enemy fire on the Plain of Jars in Laos. (I was spared the memory of being the crew chief to have strapped the crew into their seats, as the plane was launched on the other shift). There was pride in work-manship and accomplishment and although the Vietnam War was ultimately "lost," I don't think many of the guys felt their effort was wasted. The effort was for the present and by that measure it was unselfishly given and thought worthwhile. It was, however, as I re-call, not much appreciated by the American public, or at least that part catered to by the media. Only now are the sacrifices known and emotional amends being made by a seemingly guilty public that may or may not remember those times. Whether the war was right or wrong, the American fighting man should not have been condemned for orders carried out in the name of the government's foreign policy. Should anything less be expected from a military member, whatever country he or she is sworn to defend?[55]

BROCK McMAHON

Vietnam: Sept. 1972 to Sept. 1973   Service: Air Force

Brock McMahon was born in Thunder Bay, Ontario, on 11 June 1949. His father served in the RCAF during the Second World War. Looking for a change, Brock joined the USAF on 23 September 1970. He became a U.S. citizen in 1979.

At the time of his posting to Thailand, Brock was a sergeant. He recalls the highlights of his tour there:

Sergeant Brock McMahon, Korat, Thailand, 5 February 1973.
(Courtesy B. McMahon.)

I arrived at Korat Royal Thai Air Force Base (150 miles northeast of
Bangkok) 15 September 1972. I had been in the United States Air
Force for exactly two years and had been trained as an aircrew egress
systems technician, or in simpler terms I was an ejection seat technician. I was responsible for removal and inspection of all explosive
items used on the ejection seat and also would remove the seat from
the aircraft whenever other technicians had to do maintenance in the
cockpit area.

At Korat, we had several types of aircraft, F-4 Phantoms that
were real workhorses and flew all kinds of missions, F-105 Thunder-
chiefs that were used to attack surface-to-air missile (SAM) sites, and

EB-66 that were flown ahead of B-52s to jam radar sites, enabling the B-52 to penetrate hostile airspace toward their targets. About a month after my arrival the air force also stationed two squadrons of A-7 Corsairs at Korat to provide close air support. Korat also had C-130 Hercules and EC-121 Constellations but I did not work on them since they did not have ejection seats.

We worked 12-hour shifts — 6 a.m. to 6 p.m., and 6 p.m. to 6 a.m. We would work three days on, one day off, then two days on and one day off, then back to three days on and so on. At times we would continually work longer schedules, depending on current shop manning and mission requirements. With this type of work schedule, you easily lost track of days of the week, so you had no idea if it was a Tuesday or Saturday unless you looked at a calendar. Every 60 days we would get a three-day pass. The USO at Korat was well managed and always had excellent three-day tours available. I went to Bangkok several times, also to see the bridge over the River Kwai and up to the northern part of Thailand to the city of Chiang Mai. After six months in the country, you received a six-day leave. I spent mine at Pattaya Beach in southern Thailand.

The barracks we lived in were comprised of four-man cubicles with central latrines. There was no air conditioning, but ceiling fans kept air circulating, making the conditions more bearable. I remember my first morning there; I was stretching my arms above my head to put my shirt on and got my fingers rapped by the overhead fan. That was the last time I did that. Each barracks usually had a dozen mama-sans, Thai ladies who would come in the morning to do our laundry, polish our boots, make our beds and do regular clean-up. The cost to us for this service was $9 a month, so they were getting 30 cents a day for each person that they took care of. To the Thais, this was excellent pay. The clothes washing machine consisted of one 50-gallon drum of soapy water and another of rinse water; then they would beat the clothes with rocks to get the water out and hang the clothes up to dry. Needless to say, your clothes would have that well-worn look in no time.

Since we were on a Thai air force base, the Thais provided most of the base security supplemented by our security police. If we were ever attacked, it would come at nighttime, so there was usually a C-130 Spectre gunship circling our base whenever we went on Red Alert (when intelligence felt some type of attack was possible). Usually the infiltrators were captured or killed before getting on the base. I personally found myself to be more terrified of the many poisonous snakes in the area than to worry about some Viet Cong sapper attack.

The weather was very comfortable, about 60°F during the night and 80 during the day, humidity was high, and at 4 p.m. every day we would get a 15-minute rain shower; you could watch it coming over the foothills and almost set your watch by its arrival time.

Our aircraft flew missions every day of the week and at all hours. Whenever one of our pilots had shot down a MiG or it was his last combat mission, he would fly across the base at low level and break the sound barrier. If you were not prepared for the sonic boom, it was quite a shock to your system.

The busiest and most exciting time of my tour was December 1972. The North Vietnamese had taken measures to repair and replenish their logistics network and rebuild their forces that had been damaged by LINEBACKER I missions in May 1972.

To persuade the North Vietnamese to continue more meaningful peace negotiations, President Nixon ordered Operation LINE-BACKER II (18-19 December). This was the hardest-hitting campaign of the entire war. The targets were all military, and over 700 missions were flown by B-52 heavy bombers supported by KC-135 refuelling tankers. In addition there were over a thousand fighter-bomber sorties. Most of their targets had not been hit previously because of political restrictions. Among these were transportation facilities, airfields, power plants, docks, petroleum and ammunition storage areas.

During this operation, I volunteered to ride the launch truck, which was a van positioned at the departure end of the runway. It contained one of each type technician that might be needed to quickly repair an aircraft system prior to launch. It was very impressive to see over 30 aircraft at a time lined up down the taxiway waiting to take off. Some of them were so loaded down with bombs that they used up every bit of runway gaining speed to take off and carrying just enough fuel to get to the KC-135 refuelling tanker circling overhead. On Christmas Day we only had to work six-hour shifts each.

By the end of December we had gained complete control of the air. The North Vietnamese Army had expended all their available SAMs and the North Vietnamese Air Force had flown away to bases in China. In January 1973 the North Vietnamese and the United States moved forward with the negotiations for total U.S. withdrawal.

If I had to sum up my time in Southeast Asia, I would say that it was an experience that I can never forget. During my time there, the only way that I could get a restful sleep was to mentally transfer myself back to Loon Lake near my home town of Thunder Bay, Ontario. I had spent many happy summers there growing up, and reliving those memories helped me maintain my sanity during very difficult times.[56]

CONCLUSION

At the Joe Louis Arena in Detroit on 15 January 1987, Edward Wilby of Mississauga, Ontario, dropped the puck for the ceremonial face-off between the Detriot Red Wings and the Toronto Maple Leafs. Wilby was introduced to the audience as representing some 30,000 Canadians who fought in the Vietnam War with the American forces. Wilby was there because of his desire to make Canadians and Americans aware of that participation and to gain recognition and appreciation for that effort. His introduction at centre ice brought an enthusiastic burst of applause from the some 19,000 hockey fans, most of whom, like most Canadians, had been unaware of that contribution.

In 1963, Edward Wilby, at the age of 17, decided to follow the example of his father (an American who served in the RCAF during the Second World War). He left his home at Fredericton, New Brunswick, and crossed the border to enlist at Bangor, Maine. In 1965 Wilby's tour of duty with the 173rd Airborne Brigade took him to Vietnam. There he saw friends ripped apart by a grenade thrown by a child into one of the troop carriers. "At any moment you could lose your life by stepping on a land mine or walking into a booby trap. Believe me, I was no John Wayne. I carried my rosary around in my pocket all the time." The activist for veterans' rights summed up his message: "It is only recently, like our American counterparts, that Canadian Vietnam vets are coming out of hiding. They are troubled, confused, frightened and crippled and unable to get back in the mainstream of life. The Canadian veterans' attitude has been, keep Vietnam out of your resumé — don't tell anyone you served in Vietnam because they'll think your head is screwed on wrong and they won't hire you." Mr. Wilby added, "I am telling them you don't have to hide it any more."[57]

After more than 20 years some Canadian Vietnam veterans have decided to come into the open. Their stepping forward follows in the wake of the general recognition and acceptance by most Americans that their soldiers in Vietnam were instruments of American foreign policy. The culmination of the acceptance by the American public of the Vietnam veteran came with the dedication in November 1982 of the American Vietnam Memorial in Washington — a black granite wall listing the names of those serving in the American forces killed during the war.

Although incomplete, the stories of those Canadians who enlisted provide some insight into who they were and why they went to Vietnam. It is hoped that other Canadian Vietnam veterans will come forward and be more outspoken. If those who have given their stories here receive a sympathetic response, other Canadian Vietnam veterans will be encouraged to talk more openly about their experiences.

Several Canadian Vietnam veterans march in a Veterans' Day parade in the United States, 11 November 1989. (Courtesy H. Walker.)

COMING HOME

Alexander Mills of Port Credit, Ontario, and his wife at the Wall, Washington, D.C., September 1986. (Courtesy Leatherneck.)

INTRODUCTION

Canadian Vietnam veterans, in general, did not participate in the anti-war movement or become political or social activists. Most came back believing in the cause for which they had fought, but they did not take part in demonstrations or publicly defend their actions. They tended to look inward, often longing for the closeness and sense of belonging that they had experienced in Vietnam.

On their return home from a losing war in Southeast Asia, many of Canada's Vietnam veterans had to struggle to readjust to civilian life. For almost all it was a difficult transition, especially the first year or two. There was the problem not only of trying to find employment but of fitting in socially. For a considerable number the battle to reestablish themselves has been even more difficult than the fighting.

Once back, some of Canada's Vietnam veterans were treated with contempt. Others became objects of curiosity. Most concealed where they had been or what they had done. Even now, many of those who served are unwilling to mention their war service for fear of a negative reaction.

Charles Murray was an officer with the Americal (derived from the phrase "Americans in New Caledonia" during the Second World War) Division in 1970 in Vietnam, and now lives near Ottawa. On seeing the movie *Platoon* for the first time, he objected to one particular line of dialogue. A soldier remarked that if he could only make it through his tour alive, the remainder of his life would be "gravy." Because of his own experience, Murray sees this idea as unrealistic. It was an idea the men might have had while in the field, but they would soon become disillusioned once home. Some returning Canadian Vietnam veterans discovered that for them the war was by no means over. There were both immediate problems resulting from their having served in Vietman as well as problems that would arise in the future.

While the demobilization process during the First and Second World War and Korea was gradual and gave veterans the opportunity to readjust, the transition process during Vietnam was too rapid for many veterans. A soldier in the Vietnam jungle whose term of service was coming to an end might find himself back in the United States after a day's flight across the Pacific.

All Vietnam veterans remember certain things in particular about their tour of duty. Some continue to have flashbacks. Helicopters, the smell of diesel fuel, the odour of Asian food cooking, rainy days, refugees, the smell of mould — all these can trigger flashbacks. Veterans remember their arrival in Vietnam and none can forget their departure from that country. There would be loud cheering as soon as their flight lifted off safely. Then there was a tremendous letdown for a good number when they arrived back to an empty welcome. A largely anti-war sentiment prevailed in Canada at the time, and those who identified themselves as Vietnam vets often faced a hostile reception.

For many of those discharged from the forces, the first problem was finding employment. With large numbers of baby-boomers entering the job market, this was not always easy. Others sought to further their education using their veterans' benefits. Some could not quickly adjust and immediately find a place for themselves. Most discarded their past just as they had their uniform. Many felt alone, rejected and lost.

In Canada there was no place where Canadian Vietnam veterans could go to feel a part of a veterans' group. Only recently have they begun to seek one another out. The comradeship is still there, as is concern for those who may still be held prisoner. The stigma of being a Vietnam veteran, though diminishing with the years, has not gone away completely — the support they can give one another helps.

Part III covers the aftermath of the war: the personal problems veterans must face (the struggle for benefits, post-traumatic stress disorder); the prisoners-of-war issue; the effects of Agent Orange; Vietnam veterans' groups and their relations with other veterans' groups; and the pain of remembering those lost, symbolized by the Vietnam Veterans Memorial.

THE STRUGGLE FOR EQUAL BENEFITS

Canada's Vietnam veterans are eligible for only some of the benefits available to American citizens. They have the right to educational assistance and medical benefits for service-related injuries, but those living in Canada cannot obtain, for instance, a Veterans Administration mortgage, since regulations require that the property purchased be located inside the United States. As a result of the often difficult process of obtaining compensation from the Veterans Administration, a few Canadian Vietnam veterans have given up trying to obtain help, choosing instead to go on welfare.

Since May 1988, as a result of a new American law, Bill H.R. 2616 (Public Law 100-322), it has become possible for Canada's Vietnam veterans to receive free medical services, drugs and hospital care in Canada for any service-connected disability whether or not the veteran has become a U.S. citizen. The American Veterans Administration will pay all the costs. This came about as a result of the intense lobbying efforts by the Canadian Vietnam Veterans Coalition, which was formed after a pilgrimage to the Vietnam Veterans Memorial in Washington in September 1986. That trip first drew the attention of American legislators to their plight.

Under a previous reciprocity agreement between the two countries, Canadians who were wounded while fighting for the United States in the two world wars or Korea had their medical treatment paid for by the U.S. government whether it was obtained in Canada or at a veterans' hospital in the United States. That agreement, however, did not apply to Canadian Vietnam veterans because the Vietnam War was not a conflict involving Canada as a nation. Bill H.R. 2616 will do much to help those living on the poverty line.

The American Legion in Canada worked behind the scenes to help muster support. Hildred Rena Chaplin of Montréal, a former member of the Women's Division of the RCAF during the Second World War and a member of the executive of the American Legion in Canada, was one of those who helped lobby the executive of the American Legion. Unlike the Royal Canadian Legion, the American Legion has worked to help Canada's Vietnam veterans.

The American Legion in Canada dates its existence from November 1919, when it was established in Montréal to help promote good will between the United States and Canada. Its first members were American ex-servicemen residing in Canada and Americans who had been in the Canadian Expeditionary Force. Membership across the Dominion jumped from about 275 members in 8 posts prior to the Second World War to over 1,100 in 15 posts in 1943.[1] In 1989, the American Legion's 10 posts in Canada totalled 500 members, including Canadian Vietnam veterans.

POST-TRAUMATIC STRESS DISORDER (PTSD)

Introduction

As well as the physical casualties of battle, there are the psychological wounds suffered by soldiers. These range from mild cases of battle fatigue to more extreme psychological problems. They may be described as battle neuroses. Most of those who exhibited obvious psychological problems stemming from the Vietnam War were successfully treated at the time. Some combatants, however, who had suppressed the unpleasant, found that a traumatic incident in later life could trigger the return of haunting images from past battles. Post-traumatic stress disorder, which is a reaction to extreme stress, can suddenly erupt like a cancer, often requiring psychological assistance. Centres for PTSD were opened for American Vietnam veterans facing this problem. Many Canadian Vietnam veterans have had to go to the United States for help.

For Vietnam veterans, PTSD is usually a delayed reaction to combat experiences. Denial or a sense of numbness during battle had allowed many to maintain their composure in order to survive. The condition can be treated, and the patience, understanding and support of families and even employers are usually essential for good results. Since a family is an interdependent system, the wives and children of a PTSD sufferer bear much of the burden.

Some veterans refuse to admit they are in bad shape. If their condition is left untreated, they may find it difficult to hold a job or remain happily married. Recurring nightmares and flashbacks are not uncommon.[2] Memories of the death of friends, the abuse or killing of enemy prisoners, the fear of being taken prisoner, and the killing of civilians have haunted a considerable number of Vietnam vets who suffer from PTSD. Some, who had managed to cope in Vietnam by suppressing emotions of fear, guilt or horror in face of what was occurring, have found such feelings unleashed in the years after the war. Although they were not casualties of the war then, they have since become casualties.

To some Canadians, PTSD seems a mere excuse for anti-social behaviour by Vietnam veterans. Although some individuals may have used it to justify misdeeds, for most it is a genuine disorder. Anyone can fall victim to PTSD; it should not be left untreated.

Historical Background of PTSD

Some Vietnam veterans who do not have PTSD think that their comrades who now have it had previous psychological problems. Other vets believe PTSD serves as a blanket term for various emotional and psychological ailments caused by service in Vietnam. There are also those who do not believe PTSD is genuine at all, viewing it instead as an excuse for other problems such as alcoholism, drug addiction, unemployment and marriage breakdown. The following historical account may help verify its authenticity.

Post-traumatic stress disorder stands for a set of disorders common to people who are reacting to severe trauma, with the reaction occurring or continuing after the stressful event. It is not found only among war veterans. Survivors of personal traumas, child abuse or social catastrophes may experience PTSD. For the purposes of this book, however, only combat aspects will be discussed.

Before the First World War, psychological problems associated with combat were usually attributed to cowardice or poor discipline. With the heavy concentration of artillery barrages of the Great War, the term "shell shock" was coined. During the Second World War psychiatric breakdown due to combat stress or battle fatigue gained greater recognition. In Korea the number of cases dropped dramatically. This may be explained by a rotational system initiated in early 1951. To qualify for rotation home, an American soldier had to have nine months of service in the combat zone or 36 points; each month at the front was worth 4 points and service elsewhere in Korea was valued at 2 points. Regardless of the progress of the war, American servicemen were rotated home after accumulating so many points. Unlike during the two world wars, they did not have to remain for the duration of the war. There was also better on-site medical treatment so that men could return more readily to the front.

A tour in Vietnam was usually 12 or 13 months. By this system, the incidence of psychological breakdown as a result of protracted combat could be lessened, and in fact reached an all-time minimum level in Vietnam.

A phenomenon that was found to have taken place among veterans following both world wars was recurring nightmares, especially about combat. Such cases were relatively few in number. With the end of direct American troop involvement in Vietnam, the proportion of veterans with such neuro-psychiatric disorders began to show a tremendous increase. As a result, since 1980, the term PTSD came into official use.

There are several types of PTSD: acute, chronic and delayed. In the first, the symptoms occur within six months of the event and last for less than six months. In the second, the problem is ongoing. In the third category, it is delayed for at least six months after the trauma and lasts more than six months.

Vietnam veterans who undergo therapy for PTSD need the support, not the scorn, of fellow veterans and other citizens after treatment. The incidence of PTSD among Canadian Vietnam veterans is now generally higher than among their counterparts in the United States. This has been due to the lack of awareness about the disorder and its treatment here and, until recently, a lack of support groups. There is still a need for more information about the treatment of PTSD in this country.

Some Vietnam veterans not suffering from PTSD have been known to use it as an alibi for infidelity, poor productivity and incapacity. Adds George Crockett, a U.S. marine from Vernon, British Columbia:

> Ever since some vets have found out that there are dollars to be had, it seems like everyone has it. Many veterans could have PTSD but it is hard for me to understand how someone in supply could be totally disabled with PTSD. The only thing I can add is that I am glad that such a person wasn't in the bush with me.[3]

While it was not easy for the contributors to this book to relate their military experiences in Vietnam, it was even more difficult for individuals to publicly admit that they suffered from PTSD. It is hoped that the following accounts will provide the general reader with information and afflicted veterans with the willingness to face their problem and seek help to overcome it.

JOHN EDWARDS

John Edwards was born in Essex County, Ontario, 2 February 1954. He lived for a few years in Nova Scotia, returned to Amherstburg, Ontario, and then moved to Detroit. At age 16, he joined the U.S. Marine Corps and served from 2 August 1970 to 2 August 1974. He spent much of his time in the Vietnam War Zone on board the USS Fresno. He became an American citizen in 1976.

His wife describes his service in the Vietnam War Zone:

While aboard ship, John was constantly harassed and was almost always on guard duty, mess duty or trash detail. One day he fell asleep on guard duty due to exhaustion. His commanding officer threatened to have him shot for falling asleep in a war zone. At his court martial on board ship, they asked if he had any last words before they passed sentence. John replied they had better contact Queen Elizabeth because he was a Canadian citizen. He was dismissed and the next morning it was announced over the P.A. that any Canadians wishing to become U.S. citizens should report to the flight deck. One man responded.

John was fined and placed on bread and water for 4 days and spent 14 days in solitary confinement in a cell no bigger than a small closet. This incident is public record.

Mrs. Edwards continues with John's post-service life:

He was hospitalized twice, for breakdown in 1986 and 1987. In the first breakdown John insisted the ARVNs (Army of the Republic of Vietnam) were here. It was a very difficult time. When we were first married he did have nightmares, talked in his sleep and woke up in a cold sweat. This was in the early 1980s. Those nightmares seem to have stopped and I trust that the Lord has cured him. John denies that he did have two breakdowns, probably out of embarrassment. Did it affect me? Those incidents were very frightening, yet strengthening in character, plus they brought me back to our strong tower, the Lord. I feel John had to release some of what was inside during that time and he came out a better person for it.[4]

DAVID DEAR

I have PTSD. I never knew I had it, but when articles began appearing about it I realized that I fitted the description. All those years I just thought there was something personally wrong with me. I had bouts of depression, sometimes severe. I had a drinking problem. I had fits of rage where I'd fly off the handle for the slightest reason. This would upset my wife (now ex-wife), who went along with my problems and tried to understand. Loud or sharp "unexpected noises" set every nerve in my body on end. I don't have severe flashbacks or nightmares but sometimes events just come into my head while I'm awake. They just pop up and I can't shake them off. I'll just sit there quietly and everything seems as if it just happened yesterday.

I can feel the heat and being dirty. I can hear the noises and I can smell the odours. Odours like the Vietnamese cooking fires that smell like incense, rotting vegetation, and the God-awful smell of chopper fumes and blood combined. I also can clearly see the bodies of gooks that were cooked to a crisp by napalm.

Even at the ripe old age of 45, I am amazed at how uncanny my senses still are. The old eyes aren't what they used to be, but I can pick up any unusual movements very quickly or things that don't seem right. I can smell blood from the smallest cut and my hearing is so sensitive that my cat has awakened me by jumping from my bed to the hardwood floor. I dislike crowds because I have to know what's going on around me at all times. I also have weapons stashed all over the house and I carry a handgun with me if I'm working in the garage at night. With all the crime going on these days, drugs, and all the goofies walking around, it's just about as dangerous on the streets as it was in Nam. I don't trust people (except vets) and it takes me a long time to make friends with someone. I guess people think I'm stand-offish at first, but it's just my way.

I became an American citizen 1981. I was divorced in 1983 and have a house in the country northwest of Port Huron on one and a half acres. I'm alone now and sometimes I think that is the way it was meant to be. I tried a few relationships with women but they didn't work out. I guess it's my guarded condition. I like my privacy, my home and my few possessions. I'm protective of them. I just go to work, come home, and tinker around the house.

Sometimes I break down and cry uncontrollably. Then I feel remorseful and guilty for about two or three days afterwards. I don't want to see anyone or talk to anyone. Just be by myself. I hate to go to work at times like that. Guys want to come up and talk and I really can't say anything.

When it is raining at night, sometimes I'll take my beer and cigarettes out to the garage and just sit there by myself watching the rain and thinking. One time in '72 or '73, I was driving back with the wife and kids from a camping trip. We had just passed Holland, Michigan, I believe, and off to the right about 100 yards away was a train on fire — lots of flames and black smoke 100 feet or so in the air. About 10 to 15 miles down the road a wave came over me like getting hit with a bucket of water. It was severe depression or depression and anxiety combined, I don't know. I felt terrible. I just knew I had to stop. I couldn't drive anymore. I pulled into a motel parking lot and told the wife to drive. She asked what was wrong, I told her I didn't know. I just felt funny, like I wasn't there. It scared the hell out of me. I crawled in the back of the station wagon, curled into a ball, and covered myself with a blanket trying to go to sleep and make it go away. It took an hour or so. I just lay under the blanket with my eyes wide open trying to hide from the kids and everyone I guess. My wife kept asking me what was wrong, and I'd just say, "Nothing, just leave me alone for a while." I finally got up and sat in the front seat, but was so exhausted, I fell dead asleep for another hour. I didn't even hear the kids. It really scared me. I've had minor flashback attacks before and after, but nothing like that. It's strange how things that you do at the time don't bother you that much because it's your job and you do it but come back to haunt you so badly later on.[5]

JOHN EVANS

To be in a state of shock after witnessing the violence and destruction of war is not abnormal. There is a normal recovery process usually helped by sleep, rest and the passage of time. One theory for PTSDs seeming prevalence among Vietnam veterans concerns the nature of the war: the need to be on constant alert because the Viet Cong could strike anywhere or anytime, and the forced suppression of feelings by individuals so that they could carry on with their tour. One day in January 1988, John Evans of Hamilton, Ontario, who had served as a flight engineer, slipped on some ice at work and banged his head. That incident brought back memories from Vietnam. While on an aircraft evacuating dead and wounded, he had hit his head inside the aircraft and had awoken amidst body bags, some open and leaking. The bad memories of Vietnam that the incident in Hamilton rekindled, continued to bother him. In the summer of 1988 he entered the combat stress unit at the Veterans Administration Medical Center in Buffalo for treatment of PTSD. His assessment of the treatment program follows:

This PTSD program is for vets who still live the nightmare of Vietnam, who see, smell and taste the death, fear and pain. I pray that one day soon I will be free. The PTSD program at Buffalo is good while we are there because in some way we are all back in the service, safe, cared for and surrounded by our own understanding peers. We are checked physically and mentally. We are programmed and

Airman 1st Class John Evans on the way to Khe Sanh, Vietnam, 1968. (Courtesy J. Evans.)

de-programmed all at once. A lot of good and zero bad. Where it seems to have failed me is I needed at least a year of follow-up but to date have none but should start soon. The good of the PTSD program far outweighs the bad and if it works for anyone at all, that person is worth it all.[6]

FRANK LANDRY

Frank Landry of Robichaud, New Brunswick, joined the U.S. Army for a career in 1963. In Vietnam he served from February 1967 to September 1968, mostly as a member of the 4th Cavalry (Armored), 1st Infantry Division. He saw temporary duty from July to December with a Long Range Reconnaissance Patrol (LRRP) unit.

In Vietnam, there was plenty of killing and sometimes he enjoyed it. He brought back with him a heavy burden of guilt. When he returned to Canada in 1969 it seemed there was a demon inside of him. He carried on with his life but remained troubled. Twenty years after Vietnam, he found himself divorced, an alcoholic, unemployed and contemplating suicide. In 1988 he too began treatment for PTSD at Buffalo. The program has helped him immensely. Frank urges other Vietnam veterans genuinely affected with the disorder to make use of the program offered by the Veterans Administration in the United States.[7]

ROBERT WHITE

*Petty Officer 3rd Class Robert White at Cam Ranh Bay, South Vietnam, 1971.
(Courtesy R. White.)*

*Robert White of Petrolia, Ontario, left the Royal Canadian Navy as a result
of cutbacks caused by integration. In October 1968 he joined the U.S. Navy
in Port Huron, Michigan, for four years' active service. During the winter
he took his basic training at San Diego, California. Airman White served on
the USS* Bennington *as an aircraft mechanic. Much of the time he was
based at Long Beach, California. Tired of the monotony of repairing aircraft,
he volunteered to serve on a covert operation in Southeast Asia. White saw
action on Operation "Apache Snow" in the spring of 1969, serving on the
Laotian side of the border until hurt in a helicopter crash in May. White
recovered and again was in Vietnam from March to August 1971 with the
naval air arm at Cam Ranh Bay. He saw considerable duty servicing and
flying P-3 Orion aircraft which patrolled the coast. White ended his naval
career as a petty officer 3rd class at Pensacola, Florida, and returned home
to Canada.*

*In late 1981 Bob collapsed and was taken to hospital suffering from a
flashback dream. He recounts what happened while at work in a manufac-
turing factory:*

"Delta One"

I was standing beside the desk. The crate still wasn't filled. The noise seemed louder than normal. You had to shout just to hear yourself swear at the stupid machines. The noise became a physical force pushing against me. It was pulsating, changing to another sound I'd heard long ago. A deep vibrating roar that eliminated all other sound except the steady pop of the door gun. It's happening again. O God, please not here, not now!

"Delta One, Delta One, this is Ridge Runner."

"This is Delta One, go ahead Ridge Runner."

A parachute flare explodes high above my chopper. I close my eyes to keep my night sight, "Go ahead, Ridge Runner."

Damn it, this is a factory, not a fucking war zone!

The flare is still there though. Why is the light so bright?

Something explodes to the starboard side of the slick (helicopter). I feel myself fading. Somewhere in the distance I hear a voice, "Fuck him, he's just fooling around!"

A new voice says, "No way, man. He's really out. Get the foreman and an ambulance!"

"Delta One, Delta One, this is Ridge Runner, come in Delta One."

"Delta One here... What's happenin', bro?"

"We got our ass in a world of shit down here, Delta One. We need a dust-off (medical evacuation) right fucking now!"

"Rodger that, Ridge Runner. We're coming down. Show us some smoke now."

"Copy, Delta One. We're showing red smoke now."

I'm in the middle chopper, a reclaimed Sea King borrowed from the navy for this mission and painted black. We have two door gunners, a radio operator, corpsman, and me, the observer. I see the red smoke and tell the radio operator. We start down. The lead chopper, a gunship, is firing everything he's got into the bush. Ridge Runner is in the LZ (landing zone), waiting for us. Most of them are dead — the rest are wounded. Mike on the starboard door gun keeps up a steady cover fire into the bush on the edge of the LZ. Suddenly the bush starts firing back. AK-47s and heavier shit tear through the LZ. Doc is down! The rest of Ridge Runner is down! Mortar shells start walking in across the LZ. Mike screams to the pilot to get us the fuck out of there — and half his face comes off! I look at the radio operator. He is dead, his chest full of holes, his back missing, blood everywhere. Jon, the other door gunner, is down screaming and bleeding. Neither door gun is giving covering fire. The chopper leans heavily to one side and tries to lift. I grab Mike's gun and open up as

Charlie starts into the LZ. I think I'm screaming. Charlie wants the chopper to prove we were there.

The co-pilot is leaning backward over his seat. The pilot is fighting the controls and trying to pull him off the pedals. We lift off and fly straight and fast back to the base. I use the radio to call in Arc Light (a B-52 bomber strike) on the LZ. The co-pilot is dead. So are the radio operator and both door gunners. Jim, the pilot, is wounded, but he says he is all right.

The lead gunship must be coming back. I see a white light coming in from the south. It looks like three lights. I can hear someone in the distance saying, "Just hold his legs tight. I'm going to insert the needle now." I open my eyes and see a doctor. He tells me not to move. He starts to insert a needle into my back. He hits a nerve and I kick the nurse. He draws a fluid sample and then leaves. The nurses tell me I have to stay flat on my back for 12 hours. They leave the room. My sister and my dad and mother come in. They tell me I passed out at work and that I'm going to be all right. I don't know what the hell's happening to me.

The nurse comes back and gives me a shot. I feel myself start to fade. I hear a voice, I think it's the nurse, telling my dad that I'm going to be fine. Somewhere in the distance I hear a chopper and my voice saying, "Home Plate, Home Plate, this is Delta One."

"Delta One, this is Home Plate. Go ahead."

"Home Plate, Delta One is coming in on one wing."

"Rodger, Delta One, we are standing by."

I see the base out the door. Jim is struggling with the chopper. We are now over the landing pad and the chopper is coming down too fast. Ten feet off the ground, Jim seems to regain control and then we drop. The world becomes fire, pain and blackness. I hear a voice say, "This one's still moving." I feel a world of hurt in my right hand. I can't move my legs. They are jammed up under my seat to the knees. The crash crew slowly removes me. One says, "Lucky bastard, got a ticket home. I don't think they'll save the hand." I'm put on a stretcher and carried to an ambulance. I see them put the pilot in a body bag.

They take X-rays of my hand and set my little finger. The equipment is old and the doctor is tired. I can't move any part of my hand. At least the pain is killed by morphine.

They load me on a medevac (medical evacuation) chopper and fly me out of the base. On the way, I get a look at Ap Bia Mountain, Hill 937, our diversion fight. The crewman on the chopper tells me that they are calling that place Hamburger Hill. Nobody knows why we're fighting for it. I close my eyes and try to sleep. I don't want to talk. The spook who conned me into this mission told us why they are dying down there, but I don't think the 101st wants to know they are just a diversion. I can still hear the chopper but it seems strange as it starts to fade in and out.

I open my eyes and the nurse tells me my dad will soon be here to take me home. I look at my right hand and it is fine. I'm scared.

Dad comes and we go back to the plant to get my things. I tell the foreman that I won't be in for the rest of the shift. On the way home Dad tells me that it is my sister's daughter's christening today, but I don't have to go. I'm not even sure where I am but I go anyway. After the service we go back to my dad's place for a party. I'm sitting on the stairs in the back room trying to watch a football game. The TV starts to strobe. Someone is shaking me and telling me we have arrived at Cam Ranh. I figure that I must be on a bad trip. The sister whose baby was christened is only 10 years old. I don't know what's happening to me.

They reset my hand in the hospital at Cam Ranh. A sky-pilot comes in to talk to me. I tell him about my dream and he tells me that I don't have to worry about that. There is a door at the end of the dorm that I can go through and never have to worry again. When I ask him what he means, he just smiles and leaves.

After the sky-pilot leaves, an officer comes in to tell me I'm going home and I'm going to get a Purple Heart and a Bronze Star for my part in this little show. It seems that the report from the two gunships said that without my running the door gun and calling in the air strike, the chopper would have been captured and Charlie would have had his proof that U.S. troops were in Laos. Of course, the officer tells me that it really "don't matter" because all of this does not exist, not officially anyway. He tells me that I'm going back to San Diego and my family has been notified that I've had a motorcycle accident in Torrance, California. The doctor comes in and gives me a needle. The officer is telling someone to load me up as I fade away.

I open my eyes. I'm in a hospital room and my former mother-in-law is sitting by my bed, talking to me. I wonder to myself why I think of her as my former mother-in-law when I'm not even married. My right hand is immobilized. What is she doing in California anyway. My dad comes in and is obviously really pissed off. My former mother-in-law leaves, and Dad says that my estranged wife and her mother had a lot of nerve coming here like that. My right hand is free now. I want to scream ... I try to tell Dad what is happening to me, but I see that same door that was in the dorm at Cam Ranh. I reach out for it; the room starts spinning and I fade away.

I open my eyes. The world is still moving. Everything is grey and cold. A small noise draws my attention. A friend of mine says, "Come on, let's go, the division officer wants us in the ready room right fucking now!" Now I know where I am. This is like déjà vu. I've been here before. I know what's going to happen but I can't stop it. I'm back on the aircraft carrier. There are about 20 of us in the ready room. Somebody yells, "Attention on deck!" Everybody stands up. This is for real! It's starting all over again! There he is — the Green Man. I still don't know his name, rank or branch of service — he probably doesn't have one. I figure out later that he's a spook. He tells us about this special mission to put a stop to the supply route through Cambodia into South Vietnam called the "Ho Chi Minh Trail." Most of the weapons and supplies for the "68 Tet offensive" came down the trail. Well, he has a plan to stop the trail in Laos, where it won't be expected. A battle will be staged at Hill 937 as a cover for the large amount of troops and choppers in the area. We are told that no mail can be sent, no one is to know where we are. To accomplish this we are sent to survival and escape school and then in country via Guam and Cam Ranh under tight security. All of us sign an "Official Secrets Act" form to make sure we don't talk.

The mission is launched. The only one who is surprised is the Green Man. We get our asses kicked. I make three runs in a flying body bag to pick up KIAs (killed in action). They give me a three-hour stand-down. I close my eyes to sleep. When I open them, I am in a small room that is lit but I can't tell from where. In the room is the door. A voice tells me if I just go through the door, then all my memories, my anxiety, my nightmare will be over. It tells me that beyond the door is total oblivion. I reach for the door. Someone is calling me. I open my eyes and my doctor is sitting beside me in my hospital room. There is a lady with him, who, he tells me, is also a doctor. We talk a long time. I tell them about my nightmare. She tells me I'm having an anxiety attack brought on by my marriage break-down, my dead-end job and my stress. She says I need to talk to someone to get my anger and frustrations out in the open. I tell her about the door. She says that is my mind's way of telling me I'm on overload. If I open that door, all that I am and all that I could be will cease to exist. The two doctors leave. I think about what she said. I think about where I've been and where I would like to go. I decide that I don't need the relief that comes from opening that door. What I had been and what I now am is worth the hassle. I didn't survive Nam just to check out on my own. Slowly I drift off to sleep and like a friend come to visit a sick man, it begins again.

"Delta One, Delta One."

Postscript

I wrote this story as I remember it to have happened to me in late 1981. I can sleep now. It took the collapse and the time in hospital to help me realize that to hold in my emotions and feelings out of fear is not healthy. I've told my story to a few of my closest friends, most of it anyway. Finding other Nam vets and getting involved with them trying to help them, you help yourself.

Bob is remarried now to Linde, the daughter of a former Canadian soldier captured in 1942 at Dieppe. Happily married, they live and work in Petrolia, Ontario. Bob is now president of a Bluewater chapter of Vietnam Veterans of America in his area.[8]

PRISONERS AND ATROCITIES

Introduction

From earliest times prisoners have been taken in battle. Their treatment has varied. Some prisoners of war have been killed or abused, others treated humanely. The Geneva conventions of 1929 and 1949 re-established certain norms of behaviour towards prisoners. The latter developed standards for the treatment of prisoners that stipulated, for example, adequate feeding, delivery of relief supplies and no pressure on prisoners to supply more than a minimum of information.

During the First World War, although there were atrocity tales, both sides generally treated prisoners humanely. During the Second World War, the rules were often abused by some belligerents, especially the Japanese and the German SS. Canadians themselves were not totally exempt. There were cases of German prisoners being shot, especially in Sicily and Normandy.[9] Such incidents, however, were the exception rather than the rule. During the Korean conflict, there were many instances of the North Koreans executing prisoners.

Canadian Vietnam veterans have reported that many Communist prisoners in Vietnam were treated reasonably well under the circumstances. There were, however, accounts of Viet Cong prisoners being killed by the Americans and South Vietnamese. The American standard of behaviour in the treatment of prisoners was lower in

Vietnam than in Korea, but the Communist side was at least equally guilty of killing prisoners.

One Canadian Vietnam veteran recalls that when his unit came across a Viet Cong hospital in a cave, one of the Vietnamese nurses was raped. Like a spectator at a horror movie, he witnessed other acts of brutality during his tour. Villages would be warned that if any hostile fire was encountered, they would be destroyed and they often were. If non-commissioned officers in charge of a patrol condoned violence against the civilian population, the men's behaviour would generally be worse. Who would complain? It was shocking for my Canadian informant to see his buddies commit atrocities. If war is hell, living with horrendous memories of that war can also be a form of hell.

To castigate only American troops for their behaviour would be wrong. The Viet Cong readily used terror and torture tactics to intimidate the opposition. However, their acts of brutality were not as well publicized. The unfortunate victims on both sides of that terrible war remain mute testimony of man's inhumanity to his fellow man.

On the other hand, the Americans performed numerous acts of mercy and saved many South Vietnam civilians at the risk of their own lives. A civic action program assisted villages with medical supplies, agriculture and schools.

While most of the Canadian deaths in Vietnam came about as a result of enemy action in many different engagements, some were due to accident or disease. A few, such as that of Lance Corporal X, from Ontario, occurred under less honourable circumstances. The casualty report states he died at An Hoa near Da Nang as a result of:

> multiple fragmentation wounds of both legs, scrotum and penis with traumatic amputation of a right hand sustained as the result of the accidental detonation of a grenade.... L. Cpl. [X] at the time of his death had involuntarily absented himself from his appointed place of duty. He had in his possession a grenade and pistol. While under the influence of alcoholic beverages, he threatened several South Vietnamese civilians. When a fellow marine tried to calm him down, a scuffle between the two ensued, during which the grenade held by [X] detonated. The marines were aware that no liberty was permitted at An Hoa, the area in which the incident occurred.

While the media emphasized the atrocity side of American actions, little if anything was written of military personnel who killed their comrades who were threatening or attacking Vietnamese civilians.

While the case of William Calley involving the massacre at My Lai was the most publicized atrocity, there were also cases of torture and execution of Viet Cong prisoners. Such things happened, and more often than in previous American conflicts because of the nature of the war and the enemy. This was a guerrilla war without a front fought in a foreign land where tired and frustrated American troops were often unable to differentiate Vietnamese civilians from the Viet Cong. The brutality of the Vietnam War witnessed on television helped convince many that the United States should pull out of this conflict.

The Canadian government was fortunate during the Vietnam War in that no Canadian citizen serving in the U.S. armed forces was ever taken prisoner. Had any been captured and had their citizenship been disclosed, some explaining would have been necessary. Canada's membership on the International Commission for Supervision and Control for Vietnam would likely have been questioned, as well as its diplomatic efforts for peace between Washington and Hanoi.

Missing in Action

Prior to the American Civil War, those killed in battle were not always given proper burial. Men of noble status were often shown preference. During the Civil War, the Union forces set portions of former battlefields aside for burial purposes and erected markers at the graves that showed, where possible, the names of the men buried there. The French and Germans followed suit in the Franco-Prussian War, and thus began the tradition of accounting for and commemorating those killed in action. Canadians killed overseas in wartime were buried near where they fell. Whether Americans killed in the First or Second World War were permanently buried overseas or brought home depended on the preference of their next of kin. All Americans killed in Korea were repatriated.

In every war those whose bodies have never been recovered are listed as missing in action. In the First World War, the nature of trench warfare and the destructive aspect of explosives resulted in many such casualties. The problem of accounting for those missing in action also manifested itself during the Second World War and the Korean conflict.

The U.S. Department of Defense has used three categories for missing personnel: missing in action (MIA); prisoners of war (POW);

and killed in action, body recovered or body not recovered (KIA/BR, KIA/BNR). An initial determination of which category to apply is made by the field commander. After 12 months there is a review of the evidence on a case-by-case basis for those in the missing status to determine if a serviceman should continue to be classified as captured or missing, or be reclassified as deceased.

Status reviews for personnel missing in Southeast Asia were withheld until known American POWs were returned and debriefed. Regarding the determination on Vietnam missing, the status of all but one of the missing servicemen had been changed through this review process to a finding of KIA/BNR. In the case of Colonel Charles E. Shelton (USAF), the sole individual whose status remains unchanged, the secretary of the air force decided to leave him in POW status as a symbolic gesture for all missing personnel.

Private POW lobby groups categorized those missing in action and prisoners of war according to varying degrees of information about them: (1) confirmed, (2) suspect, (3) doubtful, (4) unknown and (5) unrelated. One of the Canadian citizens listed as missing in action was Warrant Officer Ian McIntosh of the army. He was in a helicopter struck by ground fire on 24 November 1970 that crashed in Quang Tri Province, South Vietnam, about 20 miles southeast of Khe Sanh, not far from the border with Laos. Another Canadian, Lance Corporal John Howard Reeves of Winnipeg, a marine whose body was considered non-recoverable, was reported missing on 23 December 1966. His demise was due to drowning about 15 miles southwest of Hoi An in Quang Nam Province. He was swept away by a strong current while crossing a stream during a patrol. There are also several other Canadians listed as missing in action.

The Vietnamese maintain that there are no live Americans in their custody. Yet Americans who were seen parachuting close to Indochinese Communist forces did not return and have yet to be accounted for. Such persons were probably killed or have since died in captivity.

Various theories have been expounded concerning the first-hand sightings that have been reported in Indochina of those alleged to be Americans, both in and out of captivity. One theory is that these may be American defectors. Another suggested explanation is that they are not Americans but Soviets or Eastern Europeans. The POW question and that concerning the return of the remains of those missing in action are issues deserving of resolution on strictly humanitarian grounds.

National League of POW/MIA Families

The National League of POW/MIA Families is a non-profit organization consisting solely of relatives of American prisoners of war, missing in action, killed in action (body not recovered) and returned Vietnam POWs. The league's position is that some Americans are alive in Indochina. It believes that divisiveness of effort and theatrics, such as offering public rewards and performing stunts to advertise them, only serve to weaken the efforts of the American government and discredit the seriousness of the issue. The third Friday of every September marks National POW/MIA Recognition Day in the United States.

Canada's Department of External Affairs is responsible for any Canadian citizens being held prisoner in Southeast Asia. Thus far, no firm evidence has been received that any such cases exist.

Many of the reasons for fighting the war given by the American government at the time, such as the domino theory of the spread of communism, proved fallacious. The Vietnam experience left many veterans extremely distrustful of government and bureaucrats. The prisoner-of-war issue is a legacy of that mistrust.[10]

Those who have never served in the military may find it difficult to understand the furore over possible POWs and MIAs. During the fighting in Vietnam, men who were wounded on the battlefield or shot down felt sure that their buddies would be coming to rescue them. It was an unwritten rule that often cost the Americans much higher casualties than would have been the case had they just abandoned them. Vietnam veterans especially cannot tolerate the possibility that any of their comrades may be held against their will, particularly in view of the inhumane treatment accorded American pilots shot down over North Vietnam. Many Vietnam veterans and the families of those missing have vowed never to cease lobbying, demonstrating or complaining until the situation is resolved to their satisfaction.

AGENT ORANGE

Some Canadian Vietnam veterans were exposed to a defoliant used in Vietnam to kill unwanted vegetation that otherwise would have provided cover for the enemy. The herbicide was called "Agent Orange" because it was shipped to Vietnam in orange-striped barrels. Spraying was stopped by order of the deputy secretary of defenCe in 1971.

By 1978, a concern was expressed by American Vietnam veterans that those exposed to Agent Orange might be subject to delayed health effects. These fears were based on the fact that it contained minute traces of the chemical dioxin. Dioxin is of concern because animal studies have shown it to be toxic. There was some testing of the herbicide on Canadian vegetation at Camp Gagetown, New Brunswick, in 1966. Some of the defoliant was produced at Elmira, Ontario.[11]

Members of the U.S. Air Force who handled and sprayed Agent Orange were most heavily exposed. Some in the army, navy and marines also received substantial doses. Studies are continuing to determine the relationship between military service in Vietnam, exposure to Agent Orange, cancer and birth defects. Those exposed directly to Agent Orange reported immediate symptoms, most of which related to a skin problem resembling acne. Many later complaints were of a psychological nature, such as headache, loss of drive, irritability and change of personality.[12] Whether such problems were caused by Agent Orange or the war itself remains debatable.

Initially, the lawyers on both sides of the issue, those representing some 10,000 to 15,000 Vietnam veterans suffering from exposure to Agent Orange and those representing the seven chemical companies that manufactured the defoliant, arrived at an out-of-court settlement for $180 million as compensation. This averted a trial. Some 300 Vietnam veterans then individually took the chemical companies to court seeking higher individual damages, and this resulted in the temporary setting aside of the $180 million.

With the dismissal by the U.S. Supreme Court of the lawsuits mounted by the veterans who challenged the class-action settlement, the way was cleared in 1988 for disbursement of the Agent Orange fund, which had grown to $240 million. To qualify, veterans had to be totally disabled and prove that they had served in Vietnam in an area where the herbicide was used. Survivors of deceased veterans received lump-sum payments. Some money was also set aside to fund social service projects that benefit Vietnam veterans and their families.

During the summer of 1988 a U.S. federal judge handed over $5 million to Australian and New Zealand officials for distribution to their soldiers exposed to Agent Orange while fighting in Vietnam. The payment represents the two countries' share of the Agent Orange settlement fund.[13] For compensation purposes, Canadians have been lumped together with the Americans.

The U.S. Veterans Administration at first refused to give Vietnam veterans the benefit of the doubt, demanding proof of a causal relationship between Agent Orange and a medical disorder. Only those with the skin ailment chloracne were eligible. A lawsuit brought by the Vietnam Veterans of America organization resulted in this strict interpretation being overruled by a California judge in May 1989. The Veterans Administration did not appeal this ruling, thus making it possible for Vietnam veterans to receive compensation for other health problems relating to exposure to Agent Orange.

The Americans used Agent Orange and other chemicals in Vietnam without knowing their long-term effects. The eventual health and genetic consequences for the children of Canada's Vietnam veterans are not fully known. For many former servicemen and their families, this is possibly the worst part of the Agent Orange nightmare.[14]

During the war, over 100 million pounds of herbicides were sprayed over millions of acres of South Vietnam, destroying forests, vegetation and crops. The residue of the herbicides will continue to negatively affect the Vietnamese people and all forms of life in that country for many years to come.

VIETNAM VETERANS' GROUPS

Together Then! Together Again!

Voluntary contributions to patriotic funds provide an indication of the measure of public support for a war and its veterans. For volunteers fighting in the South African War, money was raised to help their families. These funds later supplemented the British pensions given to widows, orphans and disabled veterans. The Canadian Patriotic Fund of the First World War also helped the families of Canadian soldiers. The response this time was even more enthusiastic. However, the massive casualties suffered in the fighting necessitated government assistance to help veterans and their families. Unlike Canada's Vietnam volunteers, who had no organized support, the Canadians who fought in the Spanish Civil War had the moral and financial help of the Friends of the Mackenzie-Papineau Battalion prior to and following their return. Ineligible to join the Royal Canadian Legion as full members, Canadian Vietnam veterans have had to create their own organization.

In the last several years, autonomous Vietnam veterans' groups have been springing up in the major cities across this country. Groups in Halifax, Montreal, Ottawa, Toronto, Winnipeg, Calgary, Edmonton and Vancouver together form the Canadian Vietnam Veterans Coalition. Consequently, Canadian Vietnam veterans living in or close to the major cities have access to groups of their peers. But for those Vietnam veterans living in isolated smaller towns or in northern communities, there is no meeting place or group. They are on their own.

The veterans' groups and their meetings provide an opportunity to make or renew bonds of friendship among men who have experienced many trying, stressful and dangerous times. Together again, the veterans, as well as having fun and sharing happy occasions, support each other through difficult times. It helps to have fellow Vietnam veterans nearby in times of unemployment, marriage breakdown and death.

All veterans are products of their generation and the war in which they fought. The nature of the war and how they served is reflected by the veterans and their groups. Those who attend reunions of veterans' groups will be struck by the differences in outlook and taste between Second World War/Korea and Vietnam War veterans.

Group Meetings

A common phenomenon at some Canadian Vietnam veterans' meetings is to have a complete stranger appear who has only recently learned about the existence of the group. A typical first reaction, often tearful, is "All these years ... I thought I was the only one" (i.e., the only Vietnam veteran in this area).

Some Canadian Vietnam veterans attend one meeting and never return, often because many unhappy memories are rekindled. At times tears are shed for those who did not come home or have since died. Those who served with the same American unit, perhaps in the same area of South Vietnam or even at the same time, feel a deep bond of friendship with one another. Canada's Vietnam veterans remain the only group from the post-Second World War baby boom that has seen war, albeit a limited war, first-hand. We can learn from them the consequences of war.

At gatherings among Canada's Vietnam veterans there is a wide variety of opinion expressed about the war. Some regret having volunteered. One native Canadian who saw heavy combat in Vietnam remarked: "If they ever want me to go again, they will have to come and get me with guns and I will be waiting for them with a loaded M-16." Many others would go again.

At meetings, routine business is discussed, such as unit reunions in the United States, finances, the sale of memorabilia (including badges, pins, shirts, caps, etc.), social activities, and other efforts to help raise money for the group. Following the formal part of the meeting, there is a chance to relax, sometimes over beer, and chat.

The sad and traumatic aspects of the war are usually not discussed. In fact, the men enjoy telling stories about the non-violent side of the war. For example, they will talk about when they lost their virginity. (It was usually in a South Vietnamese brothel.) Sex overseas in general is a popular topic at get-togethers among vets — when wives or girlfriends are absent.

Sex Overseas

Canadians who took part in previous conflicts could not be described as being totally chaste during their wartime service overseas. Victorian inhibitions declined even during the First World War. During the Second World War sex was more readily available both on a romantic basis, especially in Britain and the Netherlands, and by purchase. British servicemen fighting in various parts of the world complained that Canadian servicemen based in Britain for the invasion of the Continent were taking away their women. There was similar resentment by South Vietnamese soldiers against Americans.

With the availability of large amounts of American money and the flood of rural people seeking safety and sustenance in the urban areas of South Vietnam, prostitution was bound to flourish. Vietnamese women became available to fill the American demand. They could be found in bars in downtown Saigon or in areas adjacent to military camps, even out in the country.

Canadians, like Americans, were entitled to a total of 30 days' leave prior to and following one-year tours in Vietnam. There was also about one week of rest and relaxation (R&R) and one week of leave during the one-year tours. In addition, one-, two- or three-day furloughs were sometimes available. It was possible to take leave both in and outside of Vietnam. R&R sites in South Vietnam existed at Vung Tau in the south and China Beach near Da Nang in the north. R&R away from Vietnam was permitted in Australia, Bangkok, Hawaii, Hong Kong, Kuala Lumpur, Manila, Penang, Singapore, Taipei and Tokyo. Where an individual chose to spend his R&R was usually an indication of his personality. For example, Bangkok was for those with a penchant for a wild time, while Taipei was better suited for those with a more subdued disposition. In 1970 the amount of leave was increased to two weeks to enable some soldiers to travel back to the United States.

In Vietnam there was an abundance of sex, which was generally a physical means of releasing tension, not a means of communicating affection and love. Sex was a commodity readily available for sale either in South Vietnam or out of the country. There were many bar girls, each with a slightly different story of how she came to be in that profession. When the North Vietnamese took over the South, one of the problems they faced was how to find alternative employment for the large number of prostitutes.

Canadian Vietnam vets now married or with girlfriends have generally been unwilling to go public with their sexual exploits. An exception is Marc Danis of Montreal, now living in Oregon:

> I was in Vietnam from December 1968 to August 1969 with Company B, 9th Supply and Transport Battalion, 9th Infantry Division. I was stationed at Dong Tam located approximately 40 miles southwest of Saigon.
>
> During one of many times spent on guard duty overlooking the My Tho River among the deltas, I noticed a sampan heading towards a friendly village. Standing in the sampan was a Cambodian woman with a broad and wholesome smile. As I waved back at her, she asked me in the customary colloquial jargon if I wanted to "boom-boom." I replied in the affirmative and told her to send a boy-san to pick me up at 4 p.m. Disregarding off-limits orders, I found myself guided by a group of boy-sans warning me where the booby traps lay and to stay away from impending danger. Shortly thereafter I reintroduced myself to the Cambodian woman. We decided we would go for a swim, and into the waters of the Mekong Delta we went. (I thought for sure I would contract some disease from those muddy waters, but I didn't.) Around dinner time we ate and she rolled me a few joints of pot which I smoked. As the candlelight burned gently in a little corner of the thatched hut, we gradually found ourselves naked in each other's arms. Surprisingly, we hit it off sexually. After consummation, she adamantly said to me that I was not to pay anymore for sex with her, since I was "GI No. 1," which is considered a compliment. Unfortunately, I never saw her again.
>
> I was able to find some sleep that night even though the Tet offensive was in full bloom and I was armed to the teeth. The next morning I made it back just in time for formation and no one was the worse for it.
>
> I was never granted any real R&R. I was later fined and demoted two ranks for smoking marijuana, possession of a flare tube converted into a water pipe and illegal possession of an M-1 carbine with two banana clips. So much for my R&R.[15]

Private Marc Danis at Dong Tam, Vietnam, 1969. (Courtesy M. Danis.)

Guy Mathieu also recalled his only contact with Vietnamese women:

When I was in Qui Nhon I think the entire village was involved in prostitution. Everytime we walked into a bar we were propositioned. I remember their price was $1.69 in American money and their ages ranged from about 13 to the early 20s. Every bar also had a mama-san, usually an older woman, who carried a large pocketbook and collected the money.

You could also get a Vietnamese girl to live with you for $20 a month. I think that was a form of prostitution. I went to the "boom-boom" room quite a few times. Thank God I never got VD. In Saigon they also had the French quarter. It was the place to go.[16]

The widespread prevalence of prostitution throughout South Vietnam was only one indication of the disruption of that society caused by the war and American spending. Much of that money did not go to its intended uses but to high officials of the South Vietnamese government. There was involvement, direct and indirect, of high-ranking members of the Saigon government and military in prostitution, drugs and graft.

Outward Appearance of the Canadian Vietnam Vets

How does one distinguish Canadian Vietnam veterans from the rest of the population? There is no easy way. They are usually males, 38 to 48 years old, who function in all parts of our society. The large majority are hard-working, politically conservative, industrious and well adjusted. Most speak favourably about Americans and the United States. Some wear a single metal bracelet bearing the rank, name, branch of service and date of loss of one of their comrades originally listed as missing in action. The bracelet is both a symbol of the lost comrade and a reminder that if he remains a prisoner of war, he has not been forgotten.

While there is an evident bond among veterans of any war, particularly between those who served alongside each other, there is an especially strong closeness among Vietnam veterans. Their war experiences have deeply affected them. As a result of not being welcomed home as heroes but instead ignored or shunned, the initial closeness that was born in combat has grown.

The emphasis in North American society has been and continues to be on the need to win and succeed. Thus, the fact that these men returned as "losers" was particularly difficult for them to accept. Initially, Canadian Vietnam veterans withdrew to their own communities, merged among the general populace, and refused to be recognized or come forward. With the passage of time, however, Vietnam veterans have begun to see what happened in greater perspective. They feel a strong need to justify what they did and defend the righteousness of their cause.

Among Canadian Vietnam veterans, a very small proportion have withdrawn to a simpler way of life. They live in isolation in remote areas. Some have found their way to forest areas in the American Pacific Northwest and Vancouver Island. They feel more comfortable living in the rain forest area than in cities.

For those Canadians who fought in Vietnam, the war did not end when peace was made or they returned home. The war will be over for them when not only the physical but also the psychological wounds have healed and they are fully accepted within society.

Organizational Heroes

The real heroes at this stage in the post-Vietnam War era in Canada, in addition to the wives and girlfriends, are the members of the executive, particularly the presidents, of the Canadian Vietnam veterans' groups. These presidents have voluntarily spent long hours, often to the detriment of their own personal lives and jobs, helping many individuals. There is still a significant number of Vietnam veterans scattered across the country in need of counselling or self-help support groups. Their problems will continue to affect our society in one form or another for years to come.

Conclusion

Canadian Vietnam veterans include a wide range of individuals with many different interests, philosophies and ideas. While there is no guarantee that every veteran who becomes a member of a group in Canada will feel comfortable in such a group, it is likely that those who enjoy interesting company will find personal rewards from belonging, supporting or being associated with Canada's Vietnam vets. Unable to qualify for direct government funding, Canada's Vietnam veterans have had to finance their own groups and are consequently more self-reliant than many other publicly funded organizations.

The establishment of Vietnam veterans' groups in Canada has given Vietnam veterans a chance to socialize freely with others who have lived through a similar experience. It is beneficial just to see that one is not the only Canadian who served in Vietnam. The emotional support of fellow Vietnam veterans is important, as is the sharing of information about veterans' benefits, health problems and news about other groups and fellow members. For some, communicating with other Canadian Vietnam veterans helps them to relate better to other people in general.

IMPOSTERS

While the overwhelming majority of Vietnam veterans are honest, as among any group of veterans from any war, some stories of theirs become exaggerated in the retelling. There are a few "vets" whose claims to have seen action in Vietnam cannot be verified. Places, dates and units do not fit with established facts. Such individuals are unwilling or unable to produce their record of military service for verification when asked to do so. After repeating their stories countless times, the imposters become "legends in their own minds." One Maritimer spoke clandestinely to me over the telephone of serving in Korea and being sent on secret assignments to Vietnam, Cambodia and Laos. He was unwilling, however, to discuss specifics. One Westerner wrote that he was held prisoner by the Viet Cong but escaped. He would not provide specifics. Another Canadian Vietnam veteran — let us call him Fred — claimed he served three tours with the U.S. Special Forces or Green Berets. Although in possession of what appeared from a distance to be a DD-214 form (his record of American military service), Fred was unwilling to allow the interviewer to make a copy or look it over. Fred would not discuss any particulars of his Vietnam service because, he said, of being sworn to secrecy. Are Fred and the others telling the truth? I invite the reader to consider the probabilities.

A Dutchman living in Canada applied to become a member of a Vietnam veterans' group in British Columbia. He claimed to have seen some action in South Vietnam with his country's special forces in 1973-74 while observing the American withdrawal. Checking revealed that the individual in question was a retired officer of the Royal Netherlands Air Force, but the Dutch never sent military observers to Vietnam.

There is a well-known female imposter from Toronto known as "Andy." She claimed to have served as a nurse in Vietnam. Andy was prominently in attendance at events for Canadian Vietnam veterans. It turned out that her DD-214 was forged. In both Canada and the United States it is a criminal offence to wear a uniform or medal to which one is not entitled. It is also illegal to falsify or forge a military discharge paper or a record of military service. Andy was questioned in the United States by the FBI and henceforth no longer posed as a Vietnam veteran. Her motivations remain unclear.

According to Section 419 of Canada's Criminal Code:

> Every one who without lawful authority, the proof of which lies on him, (a) wears a uniform of ... any other navy, army or air force or a uniform that is so similar to the uniform of any of those forces that it is likely to be mistaken therefor, (b) wears a distinctive mark relating to wounds received or service performed in war, or a military medal, ribbon, badge, chevron or any decoration or order that is awarded for war services, (c) has in his possession a certificate of discharge, certificate of release, statement of service or identity card that has not been issued to and does not belong to him, or (d) has in his possession a certificate of release, statement of service ... that contains any alteration that is not verified ... is guilty of an offence punishable on summary conviction....
>
> Every one who is convicted of an offence punishable on summary conviction is liable to a fine of not more that two thousand dollars or to imprisonment for six months or to both.

Another woman, "Brandy," stated she served as a nurse with the Canadian Women's Army Corps in 1965 in Phnom Penh. However, nurses belonged to the Royal Canadian Army Medical Corps. As a result of heavy fighting in Phnom Penh, she claims to suffer from severe PTSD. A bit of checking showed that Brandy was never in the Canadian Army or with the International Control Commission in Cambodia. As well, there was no heavy fighting in the Cambodian capital during the year she claimed to be there. Furthermore, Canadian servicewomen were never sent to Cambodia.

A self-styled Vietnam veteran of Moncton, New Brunswick,

claimed to have served in Vietnam in 1969 as a member of the 101st Airborne Division and to have been awarded the Silver Star Medal, two Bronze Star Medals and two Purple Hearts. The National Personnel Records Center at St. Louis, Missouri, can find no record of his serving in Vietnam or of his receiving these awards. (Replicas of such medals may be obtained through mail-order houses.) Genuine Vietnam veterans are embarrassed by imposters, who usually have an oft-repeated tale for those who might be interested.

One heart-rending story came from a woman whose "dear friend" was a Canadian Vietnam veteran living in the United States. He was a former member of the U.S. Army and a paraplegic. It turned out that he had never been to Vietnam but had broken his neck in an accident a few years after leaving the service. As he was lonely, the young man wanted to be comforted.

It is relatively rare in Canada for someone to falsely claim to be a veteran of the First or the Second World War or Korea. With a revival of interest in the Vietnam War has come a growing tendency by some to masquerade as Vietnam veterans. They have read a few books on the subject, seen some movies or television programs and picked up a bit of jargon. Some have even purchased medals, clothing and equipment from dealers in militaria.

Even some Canadian Vietnam veterans claim to have been awarded decorations to which they are not entitled. Genuine recipients of awards for bravery should be able to produce actual citations or proof on their DD-214 form. There are also some non-combatants who are evasive about the details of their service. They claim to have seen action as marines or paratroopers yet are unwilling to give their specific units. Mike said he was a combat infantryman, but he was really a clerk back at headquarters. There is nothing dishonourable in serving as a clerk — there is in being dishonest to everyone.

One individual who claimed to have been a combat marine in Vietnam presented himself for an interview wearing a few medals. He was of small stature, bearded, tattooed and unwashed, and he sought financial help. When questioned about his unit or its location, he pleaded an inability to remember because of severe PTSD. His service record was with a family member who was very ill and could not be contacted. As with some other imposters, a main motivation seemed to be to convey to the listener a "macho" image.

As the Canadian Vietnam veteran gains greater acceptance or publicity, the number of imposters will likely increase. The media can assist in keeping their numbers down by checking out their authenticity prior to giving them the publicity and attention which some of them crave.

PROBLEMS WITH THE
ROYAL CANADIAN LEGION

In Vietnam, most Canadians served honourably and performed well either in combat or in the rear echelon. They did their tour of duty. They won their share of medals for bravery. Then they faced isolation at home. Similarly, Canadians who lost relatives and loved ones in Vietnam remain isolated and ignored. They have not had the sympathy, for example, of those who had family members killed in the First and Second World War.

It might be expected that, while faced with a generally uncaring Canadian public, Canada's Vietnam veterans would be regarded with sympathy and understanding by the Royal Canadian Legion. Such is not the case. The Dominion Command of the Royal Canadian Legion opposes full membership for Canada's Vietnam veterans and cenotaph plaques honouring Canadians killed in Vietnam. The position was taken in January 1988[17] as a result of a storm of controversy that arose six months earlier.

At the 33rd Biennial Convention of delegates to the Manitoba and Northwestern Ontario District of the Legion in June 1987, a resolution was passed opposing the placement on cenotaphs of plaques commemorating Canadian service with the United States forces in Vietnam. This resolution was a response to a proposal to install such a plaque on the Winnipeg cenotaph.

"We want no plaques in memory of mercenaries," said legion delegate Harold Bastable. "We'd have to do the same for Canadians who fought in the Falklands War or the '67 War in the Middle East, or for any Canadian mercenaries that go all over the world shooting people."[18]

Said Fred Smith, the second vice-president of the branch: "They are U.S. veterans, not Canadian ones. There are a lot of other people who want to lay wreaths such as anti-nuclear groups."[19] Another legion spokesman stated: "If the government recognizes them, then we'll recognize them." In turn, a spokesman for Veterans Affairs said the federal government did not recognize the group as Canadian veterans because they did not fight in a war in which Canada was "officially involved."[20]

In a retort to the Royal Canadian Legion, Jack Rabb in his column in the *Record News* from Smith Falls, Ontario, wrote:

> Now we quite realize that Canada was not officially en-
> gaged in the Vietnam conflict, but I wonder how many
> people recognize the fact that some 30,000 Canadians
> chose to join their U.S. counterparts to attempt to contain
> communism on foreign soil.... The fact that American
> people got carried away by the Jane Fonda peacenik
> groups and practically reviled their servicemen upon their
> return from that God-forsaken land should have no bearing
> on the Canadian Legion turning its back on them. The
> veterans of Vietnam don't deserve to be ostracized in this
> manner, they've already served their time in Hell.[21]

The Manitoba and Northwestern Ontario Branch dismissed Canadians in U.S. and other forces as mercenaries, saying they should not be accorded exactly the same status as Canadian Korean War veterans. The legion maintains that those Canadians who enlisted to fight in Canada's armed forces during a war declared or officially supported by the Canadian government (the South African War, the two world wars, the Korean War) ought to be considered distinct from those who enlisted to fight in wars not declared or officially supported by Canada (Spain, Vietman).

A main purpose of the Canadian Legion is to help Canadian veterans across Canada, and Canada's Vietnam and other veterans are in need of that support. As full membership is only open to veterans of wars in which Canada was officially involved, to former and current members of the Canadian Forces, and to members of the reserves and of the Royal Canadian Mounted Police, Vietnam vets are only eligible as individual associate members.

During Remembrance Day services, the position of Dominion Command of the Canadian Legion is:

that it conducts ceremonies at war memorials across Canada to honour those who paid the supreme sacrifice in any conflict in which Canada was officially engaged. Anyone wishing to honour these veterans may do so by simply attending the ceremony or by placing a wreath with the appropriate groups. Where the Legion controls the parades associated with Remembrance Day ceremonies, it is generally not considered appropriate for non-Canadian organizations to march as a group. Traditionally, Canadian veterans' groups that participate in these ceremonies do so because of their association with those who served with and within Canada's forces ... and under no circumstances should these occasions be used by any organization seeking publicity, platform for protest or recognition of other groups.[22]

Robert Purvis at the Vietnam Veterans Memorial, Washington, D.C., September 1986. (Courtesy of Leatherneck.*)*

Denied participation at the Remembrance Day ceremony in Winnipeg on 11 November 1987, Canadian Vietnam veterans there held their own ceremony to honour those Manitobans killed or missing in the Vietnam War. Early that day fresh red paint was found dumped at the base of the cenotaph. The city fire department managed to remove the paint just prior to the commencement of the Canadian Vietnam veterans' service. At the ceremony, a Canadian and an American flag, and also a black and white banner representing prisoners of war and those still missing, were lowered in remembrance. Veterans sang "The Star Spangled Banner" followed by "O Canada" and laid wreaths. Robert Purvis, the Winnipeg Vietnam veterans' spokesman said: "We're here to send a message to our younger generation that war is not glamorous as depicted in the Hollywood movies. War is hell."[23]

Purvis's father, who served in the Lord Strathcona's Horse, quit the legion as a result of the dispute.

Some in the Royal Canadian Legion have put down Canada's Vietnam veterans as "mercenaries." They are not being quite fair, as the motives of most Canadians who joined to fight in Vietnam were not monetary. "The basic pay of a private in the U.S. Army [in May 1968] was $97.50 per month. That isn't a lot of money to put your life on the line," says Robert Purvis. In spite of the death of one of his friends, 21-year old Larry Collins, and a tour as a U.S. Army Ranger, Purvis's support for the war never wavered. "The majority of us fought for the same principles of freedom and democracy as our fathers did before us." Patrick Tower from Dauphin, Manitoba, who became a sergeant in a U.S. Marine artillery battery, remembers driving around South Vietnam with a huge Canadian flag on the side of his truck. He still thinks the fight was a just cause. "We [Canadians] should have been there."[24]

R.B. Warke of Port Coquitlam, British Columbia, president of the Veterans of the Indo-China Expeditionary Wars, in an open letter to *Legion* magazine and to Canada's Vietnam Veterans stated:

As a 4th generation Canadian military man I am appalled and disgusted that Legion members such as Fred Smith and Harold Bastable should be given media exposure for their exceedingly narrow-minded, pompous and hypocritical views on Canadian Vietnam veterans.

It is bad enough that our smug and complacent society ignores, trivializes and/or denigrates the sacrifices made by better men than those which now seem to make up the balance of today's populace, but the sorry spectacle of one generation of veterans slandering another generation of veterans is deplorable in the extreme.

Wars today are no longer (and indeed have not been for years) contests of clearly defined borders, distinctly uniformed armies, or governed by any pretense of rules or fair play. They have become struggles of ideologies that begin obscurely, endure for decades, and never really come to any final or defined conclusions. No amount of denial, no amount of ignoring reality, and no amount of wishing to the contrary will obviate the fact that, like it or not, we are locked into a grim and relentless struggle to the death with a monstrous and remorseless enemy.

I have always had a deep and abiding respect for my forefathers and their comrades who served this country in the World Wars and Korean War. But times and events have changed, and it is no longer a question of going forth to do battle every 15 or 20 years with some would-be world-beater or other. We are now, whether one realizes it or not, at war with communism and it is a global war.[25]

James Cook of Bancroft, Ontario, after a great deal of soul-searching on the subject of Canadian Vietnam veterans, wrote a letter to the *Legion* which was published in May 1988:

... At age 18, I enlisted and served in north-west Europe for nearly five years. My father had served in WW I and the Boer War. My grandfather, who lived in England, served five years in the American Civil War, then returned to England. What is a veteran? All were in hell and anyone who goes to war becomes a veteran. What we are discussing are the untold thousands who went to defend those freedoms and beliefs we are raised and educated to cherish. Please do not segregate me from those of different generations who were doing the same as I at my time in history.

We all served for the betterment of mankind according to our conscience. There have been unpopular wars since time began, but the soldiers are still veterans.

The Canadian Legion's executive is faced with a complex situation with reference to Canadian Vietnam veterans. On the one hand, there is substantial good will within some of the local branches towards these veterans. On the other hand, many members are unwilling to accept them. With the passage of time and the dying off of legion veterans who saw action in wartime, the only surviving Canadian combat veterans — unless Canada again becomes involved in hostilities — will be this country's Vietnam veterans.

All Canadian veterans of the First and Second World War, the Korean conflict and peacekeeping operations are proud of their contribution to this country. Many of them regard the Vietnam War as a foreign conflict. The wish of most — that Remembrance Day services in Canada should honour only those killed in the service of this country — is deserving of respect.

In contrast to the situation vis-à-vis the Royal Canadian Legion, Canadian Vietnam veterans or Americans who served in Vietnam are free to join as full members the Army, Navy and Air Force Veterans Association in Canada. While that organization's purpose in Remembrance Day ceremonies is the same as the legion's, Vietnam veterans are free to march and take part in its ceremonies.

THE WALL AND THE DEAD

The Vietnam Veterans Memorial

The establishment of a memorial in Washington has provided a focus where Canadians, both veterans and relatives, may go to grieve and remember. A good number of Canadian Vietnam veterans seem to require some sort of catharsis as a result of the hostility or indifference they encountered in Canada upon their return. For some it may be marching in a parade. Others find a visit to the Vietnam Memorial in Washington an opportunity to vent suppressed feelings.

In front of the black granite wall of the Vietnam War Memorial in Washington on 20 September 1986, nearly 100 men and women were present as a small Canadian maple leaf flag and a rose were placed under 56 names. Some members of the group choked with grief, others wept openly. They were there to honour their fellow Canadians killed fighting with the American forces in Vietnam.

After what some members of this group describe as two decades of disgrace, they have come forward. As Ronald Mella from Vancouver said: "For so many years, I wouldn't even tell people I was a Vietnam vet. To get together with these guys after 20 years, when six months ago I thought I was all by myself in this — it's a relief, a big relief."[26]

For some, a psychological wall was broken down as a result of this visit. Gary Craig, originally from Calgary and a former member of the 173rd Airborne Brigade, remarked: "Until coming here, I'd mentally blocked it all out. I never told anyone I was in Vietnam. I never tried to contact another vet. But when I looked at the Wall, it all started coming back." Memories returned; Craig recalled having to identify 80 of his slain comrades whose faces had been mutilated by the North Vietnamese. "For the first time, I could remember their faces as they were when they were alive," he said, the tears streaming from behind his sunglasses.[27]

"I was 19 when I enlisted in the marines," recalled Alexander Mills from the Toronto area. "The reason I went was pure adventure." His world had a John Wayne tilt to it. He wanted to fight not only for the cause but for the glory. However, when he, his cousin Kenneth Craig and friend Allen Mack jumped out of the doors of a helicopter on 6 April 1968, near Camp Carroll not far from the Demilitarized Zone (DMZ), to retrieve the body of a dead reconnaissance officer, the enemy was lying in wait. Mortar fire blew Mack's head to bits and Mills was wounded by shrapnel in the face, right arm and thigh. At the Wall of the Vietnam Memorial, Mills remembered his friend who was 19 when killed. "I left part of my soul in 'Nam,' but I got part of it back here. The real heroes are the ones that gave their lives in the name of freedom ... and our wives and girlfriends who have put up with our nightmares."[28]

Alexander Mills came out of Vietnam in January 1969 after being wounded two weeks before his tour of duty ended. Walking through a swamp, Mills was using his M-79 grenade launcher to probe the murky water when something tripped the safety and then snagged the trigger. A grenade went off, ripping his hand apart. "In Vietnam, there was boredom, bitterness, exhaustion and fear. You didn't know who the hell to trust," he admitted. "I was in a convoy when a 10-year-old threw a grenade into a pack of guys. Somebody had to shoot that kid. I couldn't do it, but somebody did. The experiences were brutal enough in the combat zones, but seemed worse once we got home."[29] For some, the trip in 1986 to the Wall was a form of pilgrimage. But for others, the "coming home" process will not be complete until they are fully accepted by their communities.

For many Canadians, that pilgrimage to the Vietnam Memorial was a time and place to remember those killed, a time and place to share memories and problems and, for some, an occasion to exorcise the demons still haunting them. One Canadian remarked, "I can stop living in the past now."

Canadian Vietnam veterans more often go to the Vietnam Memorial as individuals or with their families rather than in a group.

Some have visited the Wall more than once; others are not yet ready to make that journey. Those who have been there find it a very emotional experience.

Like many Canadian Vietnam veterans, the next of kin of those killed in Vietnam are also generally unwilling to speak openly about their loss to a stranger. Some feel guilt or shame; others are hostile and very defensive of that war and America's part in it. For most, however, there remains a deep wound that they bear every day and that they are unwilling to have probed.

On the Vietnam Memorial in Washington are the names of 58,000 American service personnel. To many visitors the names convey absolutely nothing; to others they mean brothers, fathers, husbands, sons or friends. It is difficult for those with no connection whatsoever with any of the names to realize that behind every inscription is someone who was loved.

Those Lost

For most, service in the American military had a maturing effect. They acquired new skills and became more responsible individuals. In other cases, however, service in Vietnam had negative physical and mental consequences. And then there were those who didn't return. For the victims and their loved ones, the Vietnam War represents a deep personal sacrifice. As well as those killed in Vietnam, there are others who have since died — some of wounds or by suicide or from drugs. The Vietnam experience has had effects from which many others will never fully recover.

FRANCIS DELMARK

Service: Marines   Date of Death: 18 August 1965

Francis Delmark of Lethbridge, Alberta, had attended the University of Alberta (Edmonton) for a year. He went to Alaska in order to earn enough money to return to university, and while up north decided to join the U.S. Marines. He was sent to Vietnam in May 1965, a member of Company I, 3rd Battalion, 3rd Regiment, 3rd Marine Division. He was killed a few months later. The following is the last letter he wrote:

Private Francis Delmark in San Diego, California, 1965. He was killed 18 August 1965. (Courtesy Elizabeth Delmark.)

1 July 1965

Dear Mom:

Have a few minutes so I am going to try to scratch out a word or two and thank you for all the things you've done this last while and let you know I received your letter. Back at the outpost again so you can get more writing — we're finally getting some slack after a month of hard patrolling night and day. September and the monsoons are drawing near and the emphasis is shifting from all-out offensive action to defensive, as in the heavy rains and dense cloud cover our jets can't operate effectively and the Viet Cong can move virtually at will, so sandbagged bunkers are drawing the sweat that muddy rice paddies or the rocky brush-covered hills or the burning sand dunes did a short week ago. There's been a lot of changes this last while since my last letter — the company has finally dug in and sent down some roots — which is a welcome change from a solid two months of hitting and moving which although is interesting always adds to the confusion, so will be good to take a breather and gather ourselves for the coming months.

They're starting to send guys out on rest and recuperation — R&R — senior corporals (one per platoon, one platoon at a time in a cycle) were to get 10 days at Hong Kong, while just lately senior lance corporals were to go to Bangkok in Thailand for a 5-day break, two per platoon simultaneously, so I guess the Marine Corps feels it's got its pound of flesh (or sweat at any rate) from us this past two months. They've also got a people-to-people program going to try and help the Vietnamese who were victims of air strikes and our sweeps which in some instances practically levelled entire villages.

Feel quite fortunate in how well my carcass has been holding up, and knowing full well it's bad luck to talk about something when it's going decent but will take a chance and probably get myself shot tomorrow. Haven't been bothered yet by heat exhaustion as some of the guys have; some guys are getting malaria and so far while the mosquitoes are practically in clouds at night, in the morning no itches, no pains; haven't even caught the small infections that seem to form in every cut no matter how large or small. Am in Nam free and fortunate and healthy and as a matter of fact, enjoying this outdoor stuff like nobody's business. One complaint is the 120 degrees and plus weather. Then I am like a big lizard in the afternoon as all I can find ambition to do when we're not on operation is to find myself a spot in the shade. That's about it for the Vietnam scene for now....

So long for now and say hi to everyone and say a prayer for me now and then.

Loads of love from your son[30]

EDWARD GERALD SHARPE

Service: Marine Corps   Date of Death: 25 April 1967

One day Gerald Sharpe saw a newspaper ad for a papermaker in Calhoun, Tennessee. He wrote to the Bowater Paper Company there and was hired. Both he and his wife, Leah, had been born and raised in Pine Falls, Manitoba. They decided to move to a warmer climate and to see a bit more of the

Private Edward Sharpe (middle row, 2nd from right) in front of his bunker, Chu Lai, March 1967. (Courtesy Mrs. G.S. Sharpe.)

world. They took their two young sons with them, and two other sons were born in the States. Eddie was the oldest (born 30 April 1948). He volunteered for the Marine Corps and was killed while on a patrol in northern Quang Nam Province. Eddie's younger brother also joined the marines but protests from family and friends along with his mother's mental state following Eddie's death stopped him from being sent to Vietnam. As a result of Eddie's death, the Sharpes moved away from Calhoun to a nearby town. They both remain Canadian citizens, residing in the United States with permanent visas.

The following are a selection of letters Eddie sent from Vietnam:

3 February 1967

Dear Mom, Dad and brothers,

Well, guess what? I finally found my address and I expect letters to come in by the plane load. I am stationed just south of Chu Lai. I stayed in Da Nang for two days waiting for a plane to this place. Finally got transportation and hooked up with my actual unit today. As much as you hear about Da Nang, it's a fairly secure place. I hoped to be stationed there but no such luck. However, the area I'm in now is a little more hairy. No sweat though. They issued me my M-14 rifle and I even sleep with the thing.

10 March 1967

Dear Family,

Well, it has been at least a week since I last wrote. Just came off an operation which lasted four days. We really messed up the gooks right and left. We lost eight men in the platoon from booby traps — two from my squad. I saw seven of them get it. War is most definitely hell!

15 March 1967

Dear Family,

How is everyone? I just came off a two-day operation you all probably know about. A navy destroyer blew a Viet Cong supply ship right out of the water. My company was heli-lifted to the area to pick up the pieces — close to 2,000 Chinese and Russian rifles, machine guns, ammo, also medical supplies and food. It all was scattered over a radius of two square miles. It seemed like every high-ranking official in Vietnam came to see the mess. Reporters and photographers galore! To beat it all, we had to walk back — 15,000 metres. I thought I'd drop. Finally made it though.

Received my first "care" package from the mission study class. The fudge brownies were delicious. My whole squad and I enjoyed them tremendously. Will write them thank you today. As far as other mail, it is coming in regularly now. Just about six days to get here. No, I am not supposed to have U.S. currency. I traded the $2 for Vietnamese money. Also, let me add it is impossible for me to call you. I'm on the front lines so to speak and there are no conveniences whatsoever. I am truly the American/Canadian fighting man. Our humour and our mail are the only things that keep our morale high. I am just fine — the Lord is taking good care of me. Don't worry. Say hello to everyone.

Love
Your son and brother
Eddie

7 April 1967

Dear Family,

Well, I just came off Operation "Boone." I wondered if I was going to make it through this one! I can truthfully say I am now a combat veteran. One man in our platoon was killed. I cried in my foxhole when I found out he had died on the chopper en route to the hospital. I just can't take it, I guess. Got the word from a buddy that my platoon sergeant said I was a damn good marine.

Got my two packages today. Boy, was I happy! Thank you again and again; this appears to be my month! Will be going on R&R soon. Could make it as far as Hawaii if I knew my family would be there. Obviously I'm hoping for Tokyo, the largest city in the world.

I have so much to be thankful for — there is one thing that is bothering me as far as my spiritual life is concerned. Countless times I have broken God's commandment "Honour thy Father and Mother." I feel before I can receive the Lord's forgiveness I must first receive that of my parents. Forgive me. How many times I have been so wrong. I can only hope to honour you both in the future. Believe me, I will do my utmost. I miss you all very much.

> Your son and brother,
>
> Eddie

P.S. Will write again, I hope. Thanks again for the packages. My thoughts are very scrambled in this letter as I'm exhausted. Decided to mail it anyway and let you know I'm fine. Good-night.[31]

VERNON THORSTEINSON

Service: Marine Corps   Date of Death: 12 August 1967

Vernon was born in Winnipeg, Manitoba, 7 February 1945, but grew up in Atikokan, Ontario. He was an army cadet in high school. At the University of Toronto, he dropped out and joined the U.S. Marines. While a scout with Company I, 3rd Battalion, 9th Regiment, 3rd Marine Division, he was killed as a result of mistaken identity during a night ambush west of Cam Lo. His mother could barely bring herself to go through Vernon's letters and other items from Vietnam. Several letters are reproduced:

> 11 April 1967

Dear Mom,

I got your parcel yesterday and it was very welcome. I am not sure what I said in my last letter but concerning these packages, don't send them air mail because it will be much too expensive for you.

We were supposed to make two patrols, the first to a quiet area, and the second, to the north, to a hot area. As it turned out, both

Private Vernon Thorsteinson, summer, 1966. (Courtesy Mrs. S. Thorsteinson.)

were hot areas. I, with one other scout, made the first patrol with a squad from Charlie Company. There were to have been 10 men altogether but one guy had to stay behind. We went in by helicopter to a landing zone south of Mutter's Ridge which itself is a few miles south of the Demilitarized Zone. We were supposed to cross over the ridge to find a downed helicopter on the other side.

On the first day we made it about a third of the way up the ridge. One guy got heat exhaustion, and we had to wait about four hours for him to recover. Next morning we continued up the ridge. At 8:15 we had just reached the crest when we ran into a North Vietnamese

Army ambush. Only the first five guys in the patrol got into the firefight. I was the rear point and was still 20 metres down the ridge when the firing broke out. The four of us in the rear ran almost 100 metres back down the hill and set up a covering force. The rest broke off, came down running, and we all took off. The North Vietnamese did not follow, probably because they had one killed, three more wounded and probably killed, and didn't want any more. We had casualties, but of a different type. Two guys got nicked in the face by grenade fragments, receiving slight cuts, and two more guys sprained their ankles while they were running down the hill. At one o'clock in the afternoon, we were lifted out by chopper. Two days later I returned to Camp Carroll.

The weather here is still cool, at times very hot, but generally quite comfortable. I wonder how long it will last.

Vernon

30 April 1967

Dear Aunty Anne,

I have received all three parcels that you sent and thank you very much for them. It rained for about 10 days straight (not continuously) during the last two weeks. Lately it has been sunny and windy. The wind is nice because it keeps the temperature down to a comfortable level.

Tomorrow is May Day, the revered day of all Communists, and, I suspect, all sorts of things will break out here. One of the guys got a record from home — "Aftermath" by the Rolling Stones. This must be the most popular record album over here. There is something about that record album, particularly the song "Paint It Black," that just gets you. Believe it or not that song has a soothing effect.

There is a big battle going on southwest of here at Khe Sanh which has been going on for several days now. Company B, 1st Battalion, 9th Marines, assaulted Hill 881 and ran into a lot of trouble. They took heavy casualties.

There is some talk that we may be able to get R&R. I hope to go to Sydney, Kuala Lumpur or Singapore. On this R&R few people get any rest and less relaxation. They have to return to Vietnam to recuperate.

Vernon

20 June 1967

Dear Mom, Larry and Jack,

I apologize for not having written for so long but I have been out on operations for a month and a half. A fellow showed me a picture from *Time* magazine showing us when we took Hill 881 South. On 15 May the whole battalion was one of many involved in Operation "Hickory." Two battalions went into the Demilitarized Zone and the rest of us were just to the south.

On 5 June we returned to Camp Carroll. On the 7th, the whole battalion moved to Dong Ha. On the 13th, the battalion went on a search-and-destroy mission north of Con Thien. We just returned today.

It gets very hot during the days now, at least 100 Fahrenheit. As hot as it is we still move around in it. On the last operation, we destroyed over 500 bunkers and all kinds of guns. I have heard that our battalion may get a unit citation for taking Hill 881 South.

One thing we found in an abandoned village near the Demilitarized Zone were wild chickens. When the people left, they abandoned the chickens. We also found all kinds of wild pineapples which are hell to eat if they are not ripe. They are quite a bit different from the ones we buy. We also found bananas which never seem to get yellow. I think it is a little too early yet to find them ripe on the stalk.

The time goes by very quickly over here, especially when you are on an operation. Our days run from about six in the morning to eight at night in the field. By nine we go to sleep. I became the radioman for my squad which means I carry a 30-pound radio on my back in addition to everything else. I usually carry anywhere from 40 to 60 pounds or more of gear on operation. What surprises me most is that I can carry it. I will admit that it does get heavy, that my shoulders hurt after a while, that I do get quite tired.

Vernon

After looking at some of Vernon's letters mentioning his accomplishments as a youth, including academic achievements, his mother further remarked, "What a waste!"

PETER KMETYK

Service: Marines   Date of Death: 14 November 1967

Lance Corporal Peter Kmetyk on patrol in Vietnam, 1967. He was killed in action on 14 November of that year. (Courtesy V. Baranoski.)

In 1966 at the age of 18, Jonathan Peter Kmetyk, a Canadian from St. Catharines, Ontario, a former cadet working as a machinist, decided with three friends to join the U.S. Navy. They had been told education was free and that there were many other great benefits, but they were rejected. Peter alone decided to join the U.S. Marine Corps in July 1966. He had a Grade 10 education and had heard there would also be educational benefits with the marines. Peter found he loved the U.S. Marine Corps and was anxious to go

*to Vietnam. He landed in Vietnam 9 March 1967. Originally stationed with
his platoon at Da Nang, he was moved further north.*

*Excerpts from an account by Corporal Robert Versey give some idea of
what it was like to be on Kmetyk's seven-man reconnaissance patrol:*

It is only a 30-minute ride in the CH-46 Sea Knight helicopter to the
drop point in enemy territory. The men aren't talking much and
they'll talk even less during the next four days. The chopper drops
down into a bamboo patch 10 feet tall. In less than 20 seconds, the
marines scoot into the underbrush while another Sea Knight, two
Huey gunships and two marine jet fighters-bombers circle overhead.
Suddenly, they're all gone and the patrol is alone. After the noise of
the choppers the silence is gripping in the hot and humid jungle....
We must try to be quiet. Noise is an enemy just as dangerous as
Charlie (Viet Cong). We don't talk, we try not to break off bamboo
shoots, we step over dry twigs wherever possible. We must not let
our weapons or gear bang against the rocks and trees. Nobody wears
a steel helmet.

Around our waists and in our packs, everything is padded from
our canteens to the cans of C-rations wrapped in old socks. Our
grenades are secure with the pins taped down.

Private 1st Class Kmetyk is the point man. He stops every 50
metres and "listens up." Everyone stops, listens and studies the
surrounding jungle. Then we move ahead.

Kmetyk takes no shortcuts, never the easy way. He heads for the
thickest brush and much of the time we are crawling on our knees
through tunnels of thorned plants. Our flesh is torn and our knees
are raw. At last we reach the "harbor site," a place to spend the night
in the thickest undergrowth we can find. A rough perimeter is
formed and we sit down, rifles ready to start the long vigil....

We don't eat and we don't talk at the harbor site. We can smoke
while it is still light but only when a wind is blowing.

After the exhausting hours, sleep should be easy, but it doesn't
come. The rocks and roots make a rough bed, and the bugs and
mosquitoes are eating me alive. I know that spiders are crawling all
over me, but I can't move.

Suddenly, I'm awakened by a branch tapping me on the shoul-
der and I realize that I finally had dozed off after all.... I just know I'll
awaken another man the same way after my watch.

My partner is awake, but I can't see or hear him either. I can only
stare into the jungle blackness and listen for noises that might signal
approaching danger. It is so dark I'm not sure if my eyes are still
open or not. My back aches from the rough ground and the bugs

never let up. I was sweating all afternoon and now it's freezing cold. I can't help but shake, shake and even that makes noise.

A slow drizzle starts and soon we're soaked. We can't use our ponchos now — too much noise. I'm thirsty so I start to take a drink of water. Sounds simple, but it isn't. Carefully, I unsnap the canteen cover. Slipping it out takes even longer. I take a full minute to unscrew the top. The water is cool and refreshing but it must be conserved and every swallow sounds as if it could be heard 50 yards away. Then comes the delicate act of returning the canteen to its place. Then comes trouble. One of the men has started talking in his sleep. The noise is terrible before a man can reach him to wake him up. Men subject to nightmares are assigned to jobs.

Next comes a frightening noise from the brush, a crashing sound not made by some small rodent. I become tense, weapon ready, terribly scared. A whisper in my ear: "Don't worry, it's just an ape"....

Morning comes and I'm grateful for the first hint of light. I'm still dead tired and sore all over.... We move for hours. Finally, we eat! Eating is as complex as everything else while on patrol. Removing cans from the pack may take five minutes of noiseless movement and opening a can requires three or four minutes of silent twisting. Then the empties must be buried still without noise.

Why do men go out day after day on their patrols that are probably the most dangerous job in Vietnam? They are sent out each day because despite the talk about sophisticated new detection devices, the only way to find out what the enemy is doing is to go out into the brush where he is.

There are two force reconnaissance companies in Vietnam — the 3rd Force Reconnaissance Company attached to the 3rd Marine Division and the 1st Force Reconnaissance Company assigned to the 1st Marine Division. Their mission is to spy out targets of men and equipment, make raids, gather intelligence and call in artillery fire and air attacks....

It was on the final day that it happened. The patrol was working its way through the brush when the point man's fist suddenly shot upwards. Like a chain reaction the signal flew down the line until each man was a frozen statue. The steps of the enemy were close — very close. Seconds passed like minutes and minutes like hours. Nobody moved! Even a deep breath might make enough noise to turn the silent jungle into a holocaust of blazing gunfire and death.

This time the luck held. The steps of the 32 enemy faded away and the tensions eased, ever so slowly. Ten minutes later we had moved to better ground and had an artillery fire mission crashing down into the enemy's ranks, and then it's quiet again. We move out of the area.

....It's a welcome sight to see the sun of the fifth-day morning. But it's also time for another tense moment. This is the extraction or pickup when the marines can no longer hide.

Suddenly we see something that makes our blood run cold. It is a large pit some six feet deep with stakes covered with brush. A man who stumbled into it at night or any other time would die a horrible death.

Kmetyk leads the way down from the hills to search for a suitable landing zone. We sit and wait to see who reaches us first, the choppers or the enemy. After agonizing minutes of waiting, jet fighter-bombers streak in above us and begin to circle, four specks appear in the sky and grow hazy. Two are Huey gunships who will protect the CH-46 when it comes in to get us. And two are the CH-46 Yellow Knights. A yellow smoke grenade marks the spot and we mash the bamboo flat. The big chopper lumbers down and everyone is aboard in seconds — 30 minutes away are the hot showers and cold beer at Da Nang.

For the men of patrol "Killer Kane" it was just another mission. Within a very few days they would be back for more of the same.

The footsteps that had frozen the men in the jungle had been replaced by the reassuring "flop-flop" of the chopper blades. At last noise was no longer a problem. The faces around me are still black and greasy but it's not difficult to spot the faint smiles.[32]

In late November of 1967, Kmetyk's family of five brothers and two sisters received the heart-breaking news of his death. Another letter arrived not long after to his mother who had remarried:

Headquarters
1st Reconnaissance Battalion
1st Marine Division
San Francisco, California

1 December 1967

Dear Mrs. Baranowski:

The untimely death of your son, Lance Corporal Jonathan Peter KMETYK, U.S. Marine Corps, on 14 November 1967, in the Republic of Vietnam is a source of great sorrow to me and to all the officers and men of the 1st Reconnaissance Battalion. Please accept our deepest sympathy in your bereavement.

Your son, Jonathan, was participating in a long-range reconnaissance patrol 25 miles southeast of Da Nang, Republic of Vietnam.

The patrol was operating in very rugged terrain characterized by a thick growth of 30 foot high trees and six to seven foot underbrush. The patrol was 10 miles from the nearest friendly force, and the only way to get into, or out from the area is by helicopter. At approximately 10:30 a.m. on November 14, 1967, the patrol was taken under fire by a Viet Cong force. Jonathan was shot by enemy small arms fire and death was instantaneous. Attempts were made to get a helicopter to evacuate your son's body, however, monsoon season weather was such that the helicopter could not make the evacuation. The patrol members carried Jonathan, for over a mile through the jungle to a preplanned helicopter landing zone. At approximately 11:30 a.m. on November 15, 1967, while the patrol was still proceeding to the landing zone, the rear of the patrol was hit by automatic weapons fire, and the marines carrying your son had to place him down and seek cover. Repeated attempts were made to get your son's body back, but each time the effort was repulsed. One member of the patrol was wounded in the last attempt. An additional search was made from 20 November 1967 to 24 November 1967 with negative results. However, when the tactical situation permits a further search will be conducted for Jonathan's remains....

Following notification of Peter's death, his mother cried for many nights and was unable to sleep. For years she was haunted by an image of him lying alone in a field. The loss of Peter is more deeply felt at family reunions at Christmas than at other times of the year.

One of Peter's American friends from Iowa who was on that ill-fated patrol has continued to correspond with Peter's family. He was there when a sniper shot Peter, the point man, in the head. He made a pilgrimage to Washington and sent a rubbing from the Wall of Peter's name. His mother recently wrote: "All these years I couldn't have Peter's picture out where I could look at him — it hurt too much — but after talking to some Canadian Vietnam vets, it did something to me and now I have Peter's picture out with all our others. It still pains me to look at it."[33] She has decided to go to Washington to actually see his name on the Wall.

RANDOLPH HATTON

Service: Army   Date of Death: 14 November 1968

Randolph E. Hatton was born in Toronto in 1939. He served in the Royal Canadian Navy and then worked for Toronto's public transit system. In search of better wages he became a bus driver for Grey-

Private Randolph Hatton, 1967. He was killed in Vietnam 14 November 1968. (Courtesy Linda James.)

hound. While working out of New York City he registered for the draft. He returned to Toronto and was employed at a service station when he received his draft notice. He could have ignored it, but he voluntarily enlisted in the U.S. Army at Buffalo, giving a false birth date to enhance his chances of being sent to Vietnam. He declared he was a U.S. citizen born in 1946 in San Diego, California. As for his parents, he falsely described them as being born in the States and his mother deceased (which was untrue). He also lied when he stated he was a high school graduate, a Roman Catholic and unemployed. Pressure to fill quotas resulted in recruiters not properly checking out information.

Hatton's military training was at Fort Dix, New Jersey, and Fort Benning, Georgia. He commenced his tour in Vietnam on 20 January

1968 with Company E, 2nd Battalion, 8th Cavalry Regiment, 1st Cavalry Division (Airmobile). He was wounded in battle and evacuated to Japan, but was later returned to his unit in the northern part of the country. His letters home became increasingly pessimistic. He wondered if he would ever make it back alive. He felt "an ugly bad feeling in the air. Things were not just right." On 14 November Randy wrote his mother and father:

> We have dead gooks all over the place outside the wire and mass graves for the ones that were inside or close at hand. They don't stink too much anymore but they are still there. Company A found 1,000 rounds of 82-mm mortar ammunition the other day. I hope they can't replace it in a hurry. Well, time to go. I'll finish this letter tomorrow.

He never did finish the letter. He was killed by a mortar round that day at an air strip.

PFC Hatton's body was brought back to Toronto in a grey coffin on an American Airlines plane. At the funeral was a 10-man U.S. military honour guard. At the gravesite at Pine Hills cemetery, soldiers aimed their rifles into the air and fired three times. The Stars and Stripes was removed from the coffin and folded. The officer in charge took the flag, walked up to Randy's mother, and placed it in her hands. "From the president of the United States," he said. Her husband Harold, then led her away. Mr. Hatton remarked to reporters: "I've only developed feelings about this war since I lost my boy. I think it's the ugliest, the craziest thing there ever was."[34]

ADOLF KROISENBACHER

Service: Marines   Date of Death: 7 March 1969

Adolf Joseph Kroisenbacher was born in Austria in 1938. He immigrated to Canada in 1960. After a stay in Montreal, he moved west in 1961 to Montmartre, Saskatchewan, where he worked for a baker. He quickly learned English on his own and was able to speak it without a trace of an accent. Adolf lived in a boarding house near the Laturnis family and became friends with their two sons. He soon became a part of the family.

In 1968 Adolf decided to join the U.S. Marines for three years. In search of a better life, he hoped to do his tour in Vietnam and eventually become an American citizen. He enlisted in Spokane and took basic training at San Diego from 8 April to 4 June 1968.

Lance Corporal Kroisenbacher was a member of the 3rd Marine Division in Vietnam from early September 1968 until his death on 7 March

*Private Adolf Kroisenbacher, 1968. He was killed 7 March 1969.
(Courtesy K. Laturnis.)*

*1969 from "a hostile explosive device while on a patrol." His remains were
sent to Austria for burial. So mutilated was the body that his elderly parents
were unable to identify their son. They could not believe the body was that
of Adolf and speculated that he might still be alive somewhere. Adolf's best
friend, Ken Laturnis, now a member of the RCMP, remembers the good
times they spent together. Married with two daughters, Ken thinks of what
Adolf might have done with his life had he survived Vietnam.*

*The following is a letter sent by Adolf on 1 August 1968 to Mr. and
Mrs. Laturnis from Vietnam:*

Dear Family!

Writing this letter in the light of a small candle and can't see too good. But what's the difference. My writing is bad anyway. We go by helicopter in the mountains and stay there for about 7 to 20 days. It all depends what we find out there. We run patrols every day and ambushes at night. If we make contact with the Viet Cong we have to chase them out. In other words, we have to kill them and blow up their bunkers. Those guys are clever. We found some hospitals underground and well equipped. At night we sleep on the ground and sometimes we go without chow for two days. The choppers can't come in while it is raining or fog. This country could be beautiful if it were not at war all the time. Well, I see my candle is going down so I had better close this letter. Bye for now.

Adolf

P.S. I'd like to know how football is going.[35]

ROBERT HOLDITCH

Service: Army   Date of Death: 2 July 1969

Robert Holditch was born in Port Robinson, Ontario. He enlisted in the U.S. Army to "get away from a woman" and was assigned to the 82nd Airborne Division. He joined the Special Forces and served as advisor for two tours in Vietnam, 1962-63 and 1964.

Bob served his first six-month tour in Vietnam between November 1962 and May 1963 with a detachment consisting of 12 men of the Special Forces (Green Berets). In South Vietnam, he was based near Cung Son in Phu Yen Province in the central highlands. His rank was staff sergeant.

The covert mission of the Green Berets at this time was to recruit and train South Vietnamese to defend their hamlets against Communist guerrillas. Initially, the Special Forces performed more medical than combat work. Malnutrition and parasitic diseases were more of a problem than the enemy.

Holditch, with the rest of his unit, arrived on a C-123 aircraft at Tuy Hoa. They had U.S. passports and international drivers' licences. The team had obsolete weapons rather than standard U.S. Army equipment. Such weapons were also given to the Vietnamese trainees. The maps issued had been prepared in 1927 by the French with no contour lines; hence, users could easily get lost. For food, they carried a stocking full of rice and supplemented that diet by living off the land. They used local currency to purchase blankets, pots and occasionally South Vietnamese livestock for meat.

Staff Sergeant Robert Holditch (right), holding a python, Cung Son, South Vietnam, January 1963. (Courtesy B. Holditch.)

After two six-month tours in Vietnam, Bob managed to enter flight school, where he qualified as a helicopter pilot. His third tour, in 1968-69, was with the 2nd Squadron, 17th Cavalry Regiment, 101st Airborne Division, as a warrant officer. He was killed when his helicopter crashed into the sea. Bob is survived by his wife, Barbara, of Fayetteville, North Carolina, and two sons. Both his parents are now deceased. His friend, Marvin Wells, a master sergeant with the Special Forces during his first tour, sheds some light on this Canadian and his experience in Vietnam:

Exodus

I met Bob in October 1962 while forming a special team to go to South Vietnam. There were few Americans in the country then. The team had a clandestine mission to recruit and lead indigenous personnel in defence of their hamlets against Communist guerrillas. The Vietnamese government called this the defended hamlet program. After being met at Tuy Hoa by the province chief, the team was transported to the village of Cung Son. With local labour, we began to build a small military camp and to recruit the locals.

Bob was the engineer sergeant. After completing his work of supervising the building of the camp and its defences, he began to participate in the combat missions of the team. Initial operations consisted mainly of reconnaissance to determine what the enemy situation was and what could be done about it. Winning over the local population was a high priority, so convincing them that we were friends was very important.

Our intelligence sergeant had received word from one of his agents that a small village, high in the rugged forested mountainous area not far away, was being used by the Viet Cong to hold local civilians prisoner to produce foodstuffs and do other work for them. These civilians had been captured by the Viet Cong at different times and carried away.

We decided to mount an operation and rescue these people. Since the program was very new, only a small number would be available for the rescue. The Americans who would participate would be myself, Bob and the medical sergeant. The strike force would consist of three 5-man squads, each under command of one of the American sergeants.

To ensure secrecy, only we three Americans had been informed what the mission was. We could not be certain that some of our recruits were not enemy agents. A route was planned that would appear to be for a normal reconnaissance patrol. It would start out in the opposite direction from the hidden village. After two days, it was altered to move higher into the mountains and to come around behind the village.

When the unit was within striking distance of the village, a final reconnaissance was made and a plan of action developed. One squad was to seal the most obvious escape route and the other two were to move in from two different directions attempting to take out the guards and not to hurt the civilians. Luckily for us there were only seven guards and they were caught unaware. Initially, the civilians were frightened but were assured by our men that they were now safe and would be returning.

Three of the guards managed to escape. We knew they would soon inform their leaders of what had transpired. Those held consisted of about 250 people ranging from babies to old men and women. One old man was unable to walk and had to be carried in a makeshift litter. Some of the people had been held captive several years, while others had been there for only a short time.

We knew that we were going to have a hard time getting back without being ambushed but decided to take a route through the thick underbrush. This way the enemy would not be able to set up an ambush because we would be changing our direction frequently. One squad would lead the way and do the scouting and trail clearing, a second squad would assist the people and perform flank security, and a third squad would conduct rearguard action. Though the enemy might not know where we were going they could easily follow us. We had with us small voice radios but were out of range of our camp so we could not call for any kind of assistance.

The villagers insisted on taking their personal belongings, which included household goods and even livestock. They did not believe we would resupply them. So off we went herding people, dogs, ducks, chickens, pigs and cows. It took us five days to move a total distance of about 25 miles to a place where we intersected a gravelled highway which also put us in a favourable position to transmit a message on our radio. While discussing our problems someone remarked that he now knew what Moses felt like leading the children of Israel out of bondage with the Egyptians in pursuit. We were able to establish radio contact with our camp and transportation was sent by the South Vietnamese army to take these civilians back to our camp. With these people we built a small village nearby which we named Phouc Thuan. One happy incident was that one of the women that we brought back was the wife of one of our Vietnamese recruits. She had been carried off two years before. More amazing to us was the fact that the prison village was only 35 miles from Cung Son and that nothing had been done to free and return the captive people.[36]

GUY BLANCHETTE

Service: Army   Date of Death: 26 August 1969

Guy Blanchette was born and raised in St. Gerard, Quebec. For a better economic future, his family moved to the United States. The family settled in Manchester, New Hampshire, where Guy married Lise, a French Canadian girl. He joined the New Hampshire National Guard in order to fulfil his military service. In 1968 Guy's unit, the 3rd Battalion, 197th Field Artillery, was activated into federal service for a one-year tour in Vietnam beginning in September. The 3rd Battalion suffered six combat deaths. Two Canadians, including Guy, were among five killed when their military vehicle detonated a mine. As Guy had applied to become an American citizen prior to his death, President Nixon granted him American citizenship posthumously.

The following surviving letters from Guy to his parents offer some insight into the man:

Corporal Guy Blanchette, with a prisoner at Fire Support Base Thunder, South Vietnam, 1969. (Courtesy Gerard Blanchette.)

Phu Loi
1 October 1968

Dear Mom and Dad,

To begin with, I would like to wish Dad a happy birthday. I hope next year to be there. I am no longer manning the guns. Instead I drive the captain and am kept busy taking care of the jeep's radios which are worth about $2,000.

Saturday we are going out into the field some 45 miles from here. We will have a company of the 1st Infantry Division with us. They are one of the best units out here.

I bought a camera for $51. Back home it would cost more than double. Is everything alright back home? The leaves must have begun to fall. Here the good weather ought to begin soon.

Lise probably told you I went to Saigon to try and find our trucks. I don't think there is any city in the United States as dirty as Saigon. Really, it is something to see; I had never imagined that there were people so filthy.

> Good-bye for now,
>
> Guy

> Fire Base Thunder III
> 2 January 1969

Dear Mom and Dad,

How are all of you this evening? As for me things are not so good. It is extremely hot with no rain and lots of dust on the roads. But it remains rather tranquil here, apart from yesterday night when six Viet Cong were killed on a fire mission. It was no laughing matter recently when a helicopter suddenly flew in front of us when we were firing our guns. I think the pilot must have gotten the scare of a lifetime!

I received a tape-recording from Lise saying you took her out to a restaurant and that she spent Christmas eve and slept over. She said everybody was delighted with their presents. Did Dad like his camera? He might have some trouble initially but after a while he will be able to take pictures that are just out of this world. Lise was quite pleased with the coat you gave her. Let us all look forward to next year when I am sure the holidays will be much happier.

You probably have lots of snow this time of year. When I return, I am going to buy a ski-doo and have some fun.

Good-bye from your son who often thinks of you.

> Guy

> Fire Base Thunder III
> 21 August 1969

Dear Mom and Dad,

I am not doing much these days as my tour of duty will soon be coming to an end (I'm short). On the 26th we are supposed to go down by truck to Long Binh and stay there until 3 September — our unit's date of departure. After 27 hours by airplane, we are supposed to arrive back in New Hampshire.

Today was a rather quiet day. We were hit by some mortar rounds and captured two of the enemy just outside the perimeter wire. It appears that the enemy are about to begin something, but there is no way that they can win.

Could you please do me a favour? Please buy a dozen roses and have them delivered to Lise for 2 September, the day before I arrive. I will pay you back on my return.

Only 12 more days and a wake-up to go.

Love,

Guy[37]

JOHN RODEN

Service: Army   Date of Death: 11 October 1969

On 16 October 1969, an American army officer came to the house of Mr. and Mrs. Bernard Roden of Halifax. He brought bad news — their son Sergeant John Joseph Roden, a Canadian citizen and member of the 5th Special Forces Group (Airborne), had been killed in Vietnam. The only information available concerning the circumstances of his death was that John had drowned while on a special mission. His body was returned on a commercial airline accompanied by a Green Beret sergeant.

Following a memorial service at St. Catherine's church on 23 October 1969, the body of John Roden was lowered into the snow-swept ground as eight fellow Green Beret sergeants in olive-coloured uniforms fired a three-gun salute and a lone bugler played "The Last Post." The American flag and John's green beret were presented to Mr. Roden, a civilian employee of the Halifax dockyard. The trail that ended in tragedy for the 26-year-old Haligonian had begun in 1965 when John joined the U.S. Army. He had liked it so much that after his first hitch he re-enlisted for six more years.

On leave at home from the war in August 1969, John described his job with the Green Berets as mainly teaching South Vietnamese how to fight. Their training included weaponry, guerrilla warfare and patrolling. John would go out on a reconnaissance patrol with them for a week at a time. Each patrol consisted of two U.S. soldiers and 20 Vietnamese. If the enemy were spotted in significant numbers, the patrol would radio headquarters for support. While in the field, John ate the same food as the Vietnamese, such as dehydrated fish and rice and whatever they came across, rather than regular U.S. Army rations.

Sergeant John Roden has just been presented the U.S. Army's Commendation Medal, September 1969. He was lost on a patrol shortly after. (Courtesy M. Roden.)

While home on leave, John displayed the Bronze Star and Army Commendation Medal he had been awarded for bravery in September and November 1968. The Bronze Star Medal for valour was awarded to SP-4 Roden, Company C, 5th Special Forces Group (Airborne):

> Specialist Roden distinguished himself by exceptionally valorous actions on 27 and 28 September 1968 while serving as a Special Forces advisor to Camp Thuong Duc. He constantly exposed himself to withering automatic weapons, mortar, and rocket fire from the enemy as he manned a 106 recoilless rifle bringing effective fire on entrenched enemy positions. Specialist Roden's accurate fire on the enemy relieved pressure on other defense positions within the camp. His accurate fire and his fearlessness in the face of such intensive enemy fire was an inspiration to the men manning the positions near him. When ammunition was getting low in the positions, he left what little cover he had and moved under intensive enemy fire to the ammo bunker to secure ammunition and then moved from position to

position distributing it. His timely distribution of ammunition and his complete disregard for his own safety under
intense enemy fire gave great encouragement to his comrades. Specialist Roden's personal bravery and devotion
to duty were in keeping with the highest traditions of the
military service and reflect great credit upon himself, the
Special Forces, and the United States Army.

Prior to John's return to Vietnam, his father was questioned by a
newspaper reporter about the possibility of his son getting killed. He
replied: "My wife and I worry, it is a nagging type of worry but
John's well trained and knew the consequences when he joined the
army."[38] Interviewed after his son's death, Mr. Roden said, "I am not
bitter. John wasn't drafted or forced to serve. He chose that life and
loved it. His death — that's just the way things worked out."[39]

BRIAN JOHN DEVANEY

Service: Army   Date of Death: 30 May 1970

*Brian John Devaney was born in Toronto on 14 June 1946. He moved to the
United States at an early age but retained his Canadian citizenship. As a
helicopter gunship pilot, Brian served a year in Vietnam and was then
granted a six-month extension. Most of his time in Vietnam was spent at
Pleiku, and the end of his tour at Kontum. Although he usually flew gunships, Brian was killed while flying a rescue helicopter to extract Special
Forces troops under heavy fire outside the borders of South Vietnam. He was
shot and killed as he was about to land. His helicopter crashed and a relatively recent arrival, Lieutenant Robert Talmadge, a co-pilot on the rescue
helicopter, tried to save him.*

Talmadge sent in his recollections:

I never really knew very much about B.J.'s life. He kept pretty much
to himself. He certainly wasn't anti-social but he had come to the
point of not getting too close to anyone by the time I arrived and took
over the first lift platoon of the 170th Assault Helicopter Company at
Kontum. When I arrived in Vietnam, B.J. had already completed one
complete tour in gunships and was most of the way through his six-
month extension. He had been an aircraft commander and fire team
lead in the gunship section of the 170th. At the time the 170th's experienced aircraft commanders had all been killed, wounded or returned home.

Chief Warrant Officer 2 Brian Devaney with the unit mascot, Slick,
flying over Kontum, South Vietnam, 1970. (Courtesy Bill Watson.)

B.J. volunteered to stay on in order to train the fresh replacements like myself. The 170th was the primary support company for C Team of the 5th Special Forces Group detachment stationed in Kontum. The 170th's mission was dangerous — so dangerous in fact that it was rotated every so often among the companies of the 52nd Battalion of the 1st Aviation Brigade. The mission consisted of armed reconnaissance of territories outside of South Vietnam in order to obtain data in preparation for the invasion of Cambodia.

The 170th supplied the transport helicopters. The main gunship support came from another company. The U.S. Air Force provided forward air controllers and fighters for additional firepower. The flight lead of our helicopters functioned as the air mission com- mander of these operations. The skill required to utilize the various elements was only obtained through combat experience. B.J. was, quite literally, the only aircraft commander in our company with that experience at that time.

B.J.'s bravery was legendary. For inexperienced pilots such as myself, his flying skills and knowledge of the area of operations and enemy tactics were a constant source of amazement. B.J. had been shot down on two different occasions that I know of. One instance was so traumatic that the co-pilot was never quite able to shake the memory, and was later sent home because of alcohol dependency. B.J., however, would shrug off danger as if it didn't exist. He seemed to be able to detach himself mentally from the heat of the moment and the gripping fear that accompanies combat at close range. I never saw a cooler, more capable flight lead than B.J.

I flew with B.J. on many missions and felt the sting of his caustic instruction until I sometimes wondered if I was just that bad a pilot or if he, like many of the other warrant officers in my charge, just didn't like commissioned officers. It wasn't until I was thrust into the po- sition of flight lead of the missions on FOB (forward operating base) that I began to understand the reason for the exacting standards and his near fanatical bent toward protecting the lives in his charge both on the ground and in the air. He taught me the meaning of leadership and command responsibility.

B.J. was bigger than life. He was our company's good luck charm. He seemed invincible.

I remember the day he was killed just as I remember the day when President Kennedy was assassinated. B.J. wasn't assigned to fly on the 30th because he had completed his extension and was due to go home. However, the night before, he had gone down into the operations bunker and put himself on the mission board for one last mission as lead. He was assigned to fly with Chief Warrant Officer Mike Taylor of Louisville, Kentucky.

As normally was the practice, the team (called the FOB mob) would go to Dak To and wait for instructions or calls for moving the Special Forces teams if they got in contact with the enemy and needed to be pulled out of the area. The call came just before noon on the 30th of May.

I was flying as co-pilot for Chief Warrant Officer 2 Rich Glover. We were the reserve ship of the four-ship team. (Two ships would insert/extract the reconnaissance teams, and two ships were held in reserve in case of maintenance problems or combat losses to the insert ships.) I recall sitting in the heat under a tarpaulin listening to the radios that carried our aircrafts' radio traffic. I can only remember two words. They were — "Lead's down." No one could believe it. We all knew it was B.J. We scrambled to launch and headed for the area where B.J. and Mike had been recovering a team in contact. It was a place we called the bra because of the shape of where two streams came together near the tri-border area of Laos, Cambodia and South Vietnam.

We couldn't get in immediately. The team on the ground was receiving heavy machine-gun fire and they didn't want anyone to come in until they could move to a safer location for the helicopters to pick them up.

We learned about two minutes after we arrived on station that the crew had been hit pretty badly and could see them pinned down in a bomb crater surrounded by jagged tree stumps. Without waiting for confirmation that the landing zone had been secured, Rich Glover put the helicopter into a high overhead approach that ended about five yards from the crater. We took small-arms fire the entire time we were waiting for the crew and some injured members of the reconnaissance team to get on. I remember seeing Mike Taylor trying to lift B.J. up to the helicopter. We couldn't land on the ground because of the debris and trees and elephant grass. As soon as B.J.'s crew and the injured members of the reconnaissance team were on the helicopter's skids, Rich started backing away from the crater. As we did so, we inadvertently hit a tree stump with the tail rotor blade, causing tremendous noise and vibration that could be felt throughout the ship.

Rich managed to maintain control of the ship and we headed to Ben Het at maximum speed. As soon as we got out of the hole I looked back at B.J. and Mike. Mike looked at me and shook his head very slowly from side to side. He was holding B.J.'s head in his lap. He had B.J.'s sunglasses in his other hand. I got out of my crew seat and went off to assist the wounded.

I saw immediately that two reconnaissance team members had bullet and shrapnel wounds to their arms and legs. They were applying bandages from the ship's first-aid kits that we had thrown to them. I moved B.J. to the middle of the helicopter to get him away from the slipstream of the aircraft (the doors were open) so that shock would not set in so rapidly. I removed his chicken plate (chest protector) and began administering mouth-to-mouth resuscitation. I saw a massive wound in his right side and applied pressure with a knapsack and the first-aid pouch. I yelled at Glover that we had to try to make Pleiku where the evacuation hospital was located. Glover shouted that he didn't know if the ship would hold together that long. I worked on B.J. At one time I thought I felt a pulse. I managed to oxygenate his blood somewhat because the cyanosis left his face just as we reached the evac hospital at Pleiku. As soon as Rich got the ship on the deck, the evac people were up in the helicopter and carrying B.J. into the hospital.

Rich had brought the loaded ship back with almost three inches missing from the tips of both tail rotor blades. One blade still had a four-inch piece of wood stuck in it.

In about 10 minutes a young, frail-looking blond nurse came out to the helipad. She told us B.J. "didn't make it." Her name was Lieutenant Taylor. She asked us if anyone else was hurt. We said no. She took a towelette out of her fatigues and wiped my face. Then she started crying and hurried back inside the evac hospital.

The doctor later explained to us that B.J. had been dead when we picked him up. I didn't want to believe him but he said that B.J.'s heart had been hit by the remnants of a large-calibre projectile. Apparently when his ship was hit, the rounds entered from below and behind. Several of them had gone through the floor of the aircraft and hit the back of B.J.'s armoured seat. One of the rounds went through the small crack between the back panel and the side panel of the seat. From there it ricocheted through B.J.'s side to his chicken plate, where it bounced back into his body and entered his heart.

It is ironic that B.J. would lay down his life for the United States. This sacrifice from a Canadian citizen is especially significant in contrast to the number of American citizens who fled to Canada.[40]

Effects on Families

Canadians who have lost loved ones in Vietnam have had a difficult time. Some parents have even been told, "He got what he deserved," "It's his own fault," or "It serves him right." Some families bear the death as a mark of shame. They lie about the circumstances. Some will tell strangers that their son was killed in an auto accident or as a result of some other cause, such as drowning.

The grief of those Canadians who lost a loved one in Vietnam has been expressed in various ways. Most next of kin have kept silent. In some cases, rooms of sons have not been disturbed since the time of death. One mother could not bear to go through her late son's letters from Vietnam. Brothers and sisters still imagine what it would be like if their sibling had not been killed. Children miss the father they hardly knew.

These brief biographies of some of those Canadians killed in

Vietnam will bring home to the reader that these were real people. Because they died in a futile war, their loss has been all the more difficult to take. Every time there is talk of new American military involvements, the spectre is raised of another war like that in Vietnam. The longer that war continues to haunt American governments, the greater the possibility that a similar mistake will not occur again.

CONCLUSION

The United States—a country able to put a man on the moon—failed to achieve victory in Vietnam. A technologically superior superpower was beaten by an enemy prepared to make tremendous sacrifices of human lives. The North Vietnamese and Viet Cong were able to convince the American people that the war was not worth the losses.

This was a war of ideas as much as a war of guns and helicopters. The South Vietnamese government and its allies were never able to convince the Vietnamese peasants that the government was deserving of their active support. Vietnam's war for national reunification and self-government, albeit Communist, was successful in spite of the Americans' efforts to shape the country in their own image. How long the Communist government of Vietnam will hold on to power remains to be seen.

Who was to blame for the American failure in Vietnam? The responsibility lies with America's highest political, civilian and military leaders of the time. If America had a bit less confidence, had listened more carefully to its friends, and had better understood its own limitations in fighting a prolonged limited war, perhaps the Vietnam imbroglio could have been avoided. But it did happen and there is no turning back of the calendar. It was a very painful lesson, but such lessons sometimes turn out to be the most beneficial in the long term.

One result of the Vietnam War was the passage of the War Powers Resolution of 1973 over the veto of President Nixon. The act requires the president to consult with Congress before intervening with U.S. forces in an armed conflict. The involvement may not continue beyond 90 days without further authorization by Congress.

The year 1990, 15 years after the fall of Saigon, will mark the 25th anniversary of the arrival of American combat troops in Vietnam.

Time is supposed to be the great healer. However, more time will be needed before the wounds from this war will be fully healed.

The Vietnam War created a temporary economic boom in certain Canadian sectors that sought to help meet the needs of U.S. war industries. A more lasting impact on Canada was caused by the influx of Americans who left the United States and the refugees from Indochina who have made this country their home. As for Canada's Vietnam veterans, they remain an isolated fragment left in the wake of that war.

A significant proportion of Canada's Vietnam War veterans remain troubled, confused and isolated. They need sympathy, not scorn. It is on the level of individual to individual that the healing process, exemplified by the Wall, can progress.

Canadian citizens continue to enlist in the armed services of the United States, though in relatively small numbers. Many of these individuals cannot seem to find a niche in the armed forces of their own country. American culture remains an important influence in Canada. As there is relatively little exposure to Canadian military history through the media or in the schools, it is likely that the American forces will continue to exert an appeal to our country's youth, particularly if the U.S. is at war and Canada is not.

Many of the Canadians who fought in Vietnam feel they wasted the best years of their lives. They returned not as heroes but as pariahs; like ex-convicts, they concealed where they had been and what they had done. The building of the Vietnam Veterans Memorial represented an important first step in giving them some measure of acceptance, but much more remains to be done — particularly for those living in this country. The Canadians who served in Vietnam were courageous. Not all had to go there, but whatever their motivation, they went. The vast majority served honourably. The courage they drew upon in time of battle continues to sustain them in coping with the psychological and physical effects of that war.

The American effort in Vietnam can be likened to an animal stuck in a swamp. The more the Americans struggled, the more deeply they sank. When they finally left, they were not covered in glory but with the stigma of a lost cause. The Canadian Vietnam veterans who returned home reeked of that stigma, causing many in this country to shun them. A good number of years have now since passed, and the time has come to make these veterans feel welcome.

The Canadians who went to fight in Vietnam left quietly and returned the same way. These Canadians made a contribution not yet recognized in Canada or the United States. Let us hope that this book will help make some of their experiences better known to future generations.

APPENDIX A

Canadian Casualties of the Vietnam War

VIETNAM VETERANS MEMORIAL						
Name	Rank	Service	Panel	Line	Date of Birth	Date of Death
ANDERSON, John Austin	SP-4	Army	59E	16	10 Feb 47	13 May 68
BEAUDOIN, Gaetan	Sgt.	Army	19W	116	05 Sep 48	26 Aug 69
BENCHER, Alvin Kenneth	Sgt.	Army	54W	36	03 Apr 40	02 Jul 68
BERNARD, Vincent	L. Cpl.	USMC	43W	51	07 Sep 45	21 Sep 68
BLANCHETTE, Guy André	Sgt.	Army	19W	117	30 Nov 46	26 Aug 69
BOLDUC, Daniel Alphonse	Cpl.	Army	20W	13	03 Feb 46	29 Jul 69
BOMBERRY, Gregory Lee	Sgt.	Army	45W	48	04 Apr 47	06 Sep 68
BROEFFLE, Ivan Clifford	Cpl.	Army	57E	15	20 Mar 46	09 May 68
BROWN, Thomas Edward	S. Sgt.	Army	15W	13	21 Mar 46	02 Dec 69
BRUYERE, Peter Norbert	SP-4	Army	10W	94	15 May 51	25 May 70
BUTT, Gary	S. Sgt.	Army	4W	103	09 May 51	03 Apr 71
CAMPBELL, Michael Frances	PFC	Army	52E	15	08 Apr 42	26 Apr 68
CAMPBELL, Randall Kenneth	L. Cpl.	USMC	1E	109	18 Sep 44	25 Apr 65

VIETNAM VETERANS MEMORIAL						
Name	Rank	Service	Panel	Line	Date of Birth	Date of Death
CARON, Bernard John	S. Sgt.	Army	36E	48	10 Oct 36	09 Feb 68
COLLINS, Larry Richard	SP-4	Army	26W	90	15 Jul 46	01 May 69
COLLINS, Mark Paine	SP-4	Army	64E	12	01 Oct 46	21 May 68
CONRAD, Andrew Charles, Jr	SP-5	Army	24E	94	07 Nov 31	09 Aug 67
CORBIERE, Austin Morris	L. Cpl.	USMC	7E	42	19 Feb 43	09 May 66
CORBIN, Normand Alfred	L. Cpl.	USMC	20W	100	16 Jun 48	06 Aug 69
CRABBE, Frank Edward	PFC	USMC	5E	40	20 Jun 46	16 Feb 66
DAVIES, Donald Paul	SP-5	Army	21W	32	05 Oct 48	29 Jun 69
DEARBORN, Patrick John	L. Cpl.	USMC	29E	9	17 Nov 48	02 Nov 67
DELMARK, Francis John	L. Cpl.	USMC	2E	55	05 Nov 42	18 Aug 65
DEVANEY, Brian John	CWO	Army	10W	120	14 Jun 46	30 May 70
DEVOE, Douglas Wayne	PFC	USMC	41W	15	02 Nov 48	05 Oct 68
DEXTRAZE, Richard Paul	L. Cpl.	USMC	26W	31	09 May 47	23 Apr 69
DICKIE, Guy Douglas	Pvt.	USMC	38E	25	04 Mar 48	08 Feb 68
EADIE, Gordon Patterson	L. Cpl.	USMC	24E	113	11 Apr 47	15 Aug 67

Name	Rank	Service	Panel	Line	Date of Birth	Date of Death
FRANCIS, John Fredric	Lt.	Navy	11E	109	12 Apr 33	26 Oct 66
FRIGAULT, Joseph O.	S. Sgt.	Army	20E	15	12 Oct 26	17 May 67
GAUTHIER, Gérard Louis	AlC	USAF	25E	99	24 Mar 46	04 Sep 67
GENERAL, Leslie Neil	Cpl.	USMC	3E	31	26 Jun 46	01 May 68
GRAHAM, Gilbert James	SN	Navy	27E	24	24 Feb 46	28 Sep 67
GREEN, Larry	PFC	USMC	35W	60	15 Jun 45	09 Jan 69
HATTON, Randolph Edward	PFC	Army	39W	16	15 Dec 39	14 Nov 68
HAWES, Wayne Lindsay	SP-4	Army	35W	16	03 Sep 34	01 Jan 69
HOLDITCH, Robert Wilson	CWO	Army	21W	45	04 Feb 33	02 Jul 69
HOUSE, Willis Francis	M. Sgt.	Army	29W	30	30 May 24	13 Mar 69
JMAEFF, George Victor	Cpl.	USMC	30W	4	14 Aug 45	01 Mar 69
JOBEY, Andrew John	PFC	Army	52E	2	15 May 49	29 Apr 68
KELLAR, Harry David	PFC	USMC	31W	51	05 May 49	25 Feb 69
KELLY, John William	Cpl.	Army	13W	15	19 May 45	15 Feb 70
KENNEDY, Bruce Thomas	PFC	USMC	46W	31	08 Jan 49	26 Aug 68

VIETNAM VETERANS MEMORIAL

Name	Rank	Service	Panel	Line	Date of Birth	Date of Death
VIETNAM VETERANS MEMORIAL						
KENNY, Robert W.	Sgt.	Army	14E	74	19 Mar 42	24 Jan 67
KMETYK, Jonathan Peter	L. Cpl.	USMC	29E	96	17 Aug 47	14 Nov 67
KROISENBACHER, Adolf J.	L. Cpl.	USMC	30W	66	26 Nov 38	07 Mar 69
LAWSON, Darryl Dean	Cpl.	USMC	26E	79	26 Dec 42	16 Sep 67
LOW, Kevin Douglas	Sgt.	Army	21W	29	24 Apr 49	28 Jun 69
LUKEY, Geoffrey John	L. Cpl.	USMC	17W	46	26 Aug 49	06 Oct 69
MacGLASHAN, John Williams	T. Sgt.	USAF	74E	73	27 Jun 29	03 Aug 67
McINTOSH, Ian	WO	Army	6W	79	21 Sep 45	24 Nov 70
MANNING, David Karl	L. Cpl.	USMC	35W	66	17 Jun 48	10 Jan 69
MARIER, Maurice John	SP-4	Army	15W	48	09 May 48	16 Feb 67
McSORLEY, Rob George	SP-4	Army	12W	107	26 Mar 51	08 Apr 70
MARTIN, Alan, Jr.	Sgt.	USAF	29W	15	21 Jul 46	08 Mar 69
MONETTE, R. Albert	SP-4	Army	28W	113	28 Feb 50	06 Mar 72
MORIN, Donald William	L. Cpl.	USMC	13W	20	26 Feb 49	16 Feb 70
NESBITT, Calvin Ian	PFC	USMC	52E	22	07 Jan 49	26 Apr 68

VIETNAM VETERANS MEMORIAL						
Name	Rank	Service	Panel	Line	Date of Birth	Date of Death
PISACRETA, Roger Melvin	CWO	Army	4W	45	06 Jun 40	10 Mar 71
REEVES, John Howard	L. Cpl.	USMC	37E	76	28 Oct 43	23 Dec 66
ROBSON, William Reid	Lt.	Navy	37E	67	22 Nov 28	06 Feb 68
RODEN, John Joseph	Sgt.	Army	17W	69	02 Mar 43	11 Oct 69
SANTORO, Robert John	SP-4	Army	48W	15	19 May 46	14 Aug 68
SAULER, Charlie F	SP-4	Army	27E	50	22 Sep 39	04 Oct 67
SAUVE, Daniel Louis	PFC	USMC	6E	127	15 Oct 47	21 Apr 66
SEMENIUK, Larry Stephen	Cpl.	Army	34E	64	14 May 49	17 Jan 68
SHARPE, Edward Gerald	PFC	USMC	18E	88	30 Apr 48	25 Apr 67
SHERIN, John C., III	WO	Army	42W	64	09 Jun 41	02 Oct 68
SOMERS, Frank J.	S. Sgt.	Army	14E	77	24 Jun 36	25 Jan 67
SOSNIAK, Tadeusz	M. Sgt.	Army	45W	10	09 Jan 41	30 Aug 68
STALINSKI, Stefan Z.	PFC	USMC	2E	32	29 May 45	08 Jul 65
STEEL, Robert James	PFC	Army	11E	47	28 Mar 47	04 Oct 68
STURDY, Alan MacDonald	Sgt.	Army	22E	116	21 Jan 45	02 Jul 67

VIETNAM VETERANS MEMORIAL						
Name	Rank	Service	Panel	Line	Date of Birth	Date of Death
SUTHONS, Melvin Harold	PFC	USMC	2E	13	03 Feb 44	18 Jun 65
THORSTEINSON, Vernon J.	Cpl.	USMC	24E	104	07 Feb 45	12 Aug 67
WARREN, Baxter	Sgt.	Army	12W	50	02 Apr 48	27 Mar 70
WELSH, Rutherford J.	WO	Army	4E	82	09 Jun 42	27 Jul 66
WHITE, Gordon Glenn	L. Cpl.	USMC	29W	26	25 Sep 45	12 Mar 69
WILLIAMS, Thomas Murray	Sgt.	Army	9E	35	27 Apr 28	18 Jul 66

APPENDIX B

Ranks

ARMY	NAVY	MARINE CORPS	AIR FORCE
General	Admiral	General	General
Lieutenant General	Vice Admiral	Lieutenant General	Lieutenant General
Major General	Rear Admiral	Major General	Major General
Brigadier General	Commodore	Brigadier General	Brigadier General
Colonel	Captain	Colonel	Colonel
Lieutenant Colonel	Commander	Lieutenant Colonel	Lieutenant Colonel
Major	Lieutenant Commander	Major	Major
Captain	Lieutenant	Captain	Captain
1st Lieutenant	Lieutenant Junior Grade	1st Lieutenant	1st Lieutenant
2nd Lieutenant	Ensign	2nd Lieutenant	2nd Lieutenant
W-4 Chief Warrant Officer	W-4 Chief Warrant Officer	W-4 Chief Warrant Officer	W-4 Chief Warrant Officer
W-3 Chief Warrant Officer	W-3 Chief Warrant Officer	W-3 Chief Warrant Officer	W-3 Chief Warrant Officer
W-2 Chief Warrant Officer	W-2 Chief Warrant Officer	W-2 Chief Warrant Officer	W-2 Chief Warrant Officer
W-1 Warrant Officer	W-1 Warrant Officer	W-1 Warrant Officer	W-1 Warrant Officer

Ranks

Pay Grade	ARMY		NAVY	MARINE CORPS	AIR FORCE
E-9	Specialist Sergeant Major	SP-9	Master Chief Petty Officer	Sergeant Major or Master Gunnery Sergeant	Chief Master Sergeant
E-8	1st Sergeant or Master Sergeant	SP-8	Senior Chief Petty Officer	1st Sergeant or Master Sergeant	Senior Master Sergeant
E-7	Sergeant, 1st Class	SP-7	Chief Petty Officer	Gunnery Sergeant	Master Sergeant
E-6	Staff Sergeant	SP-6	Petty Officer 1st Class	Staff Sergeant	Technical Sergeant
E-5	Sergeant	SP-5	Petty Officer 2nd Class	Sergeant	Staff Sergeant
E-4	Corporal	SP-4	Petty Officer 3rd Class	Corporal	Sergeant
E-3	Private 1st Class		Seaman	Lance Corporal	Airman 1st Class
E-2	Private		Seaman Apprentice	Private 1st Class	Airman
E-1	Private		Seaman Recruit	Private	Basic Airman

APPENDIX C

Chronology

1954
July

Geneva agreement on the cessation of hostilities. Canada, India and Poland appointed to the ICSC (International Commissions for Supervision and Control) to oversee the agreement.

1955

Canada submits minority statement to ICSC (Vietnam) supporting President Diem of South Vietnam.

1959

President Eisenhower makes commitment to preserve South Vietnam as a separate national state. Hanoi decides to unify Vietnam by force.

1960
December

Approximately 900 U.S. military "advisors" in South Vietnam.

1961

President Kennedy renews U.S. commitment to South Vietnam.

1962

MACV (U.S. Military Assistance Command Vietnam) formed with headquarters in Saigon.

1963

U.S. aid to South Vietnam totals $400 million. Kennedy assassinated; Johnson becomes president.

1964

23,300 U.S. military advisors in Vietnam. Johnson elected president in landslide victory.

1965
February-March

The bombing of North Vietnam begins. Canada defends bombing in minority statement of ICSC.

March

3rd Marine Regiment, 3rd Marine Division, sent to Vietnam from Okinawa and also 1st Marine Aircraft Wing.

May

173rd Airborne Brigade to Vietnam from Okinawa.

July	1st Brigade, 101st Airborne Division, to Vietnam from Fort Campbell, Kentucky.
August	7th Marine Regiment, 1st Marine Division, to Vietnam from Camp Pendleton. F. Blair Seaborn, Canada's representative on the ICSC, serves as an intermediary for messages between the United States and North Vietnam. Canada begins its aid program to South Vietnam under the Colombo Plan.
September	1st Cavalry Division (Airmobile) in Vietnam from Fort Benning, Georgia.
November	The North Vietnamese attempt to cut South Vietnam in two is prevented by the 1st Cavalry Division.

1966

March	Chester Ronning begins special mission to Hanoi in an attempt to mediate. Large American military sweeps around Saigon.

1967	The build-up of American and Communist forces continues. Canada builds anti-tuberculosis hospital in Quang Ngai Province.

1968

January	The North Vietnamese siege of Khe Sanh commences.
January 31	The beginning of Communist Tet offensive.
March	LBJ announces he will not run for re-election.
May	Peace talks begin in Paris.
September	537,800 U.S. military personnel in Vietnam.
October	All bombing of North Vietnam halted.
November	Nixon elected president.

1969	The fighting continues.
July	Army begins to withdraw major units.
October 15	Massive anti-war demonstrations throughout the United States.
November 15	Large anti-war demonstration held in Washington.

344   Unknown Warriors

1970	The reduction of U.S. forces continues.
April 29	U.S. forces invade Cambodia.
May 4	Anti-war protests. Four students killed at Kent State University.

1971	
February 8	South Vietnamese invasion of Laos a disaster. Large numbers of American troops withdrawn from South Vietnam. Nine Canadian medical centres to be built in An Giang Province, South Vietnam.
December 26-30	Heavy bombing of North Vietnam.

1972	
March	Troop withdrawals continue. North Vietnamese launch a major offensive but are unsuccessful.
May	Mining of North Vietnamese waters.
November	Nixon re-elected president.
December 18-29	Bombing of Hanoi and Haiphong.

1973	
January 27	Peace pact signed in Paris. U.S. government ends the draft.

1974	The fighting continues.

1975	
April 30	Vietnam civil war ends with Communist victory.

NOTES

Retrospect

1. The Foreign Enlistment Act was first enacted in Canada in 1937. Maximum penalty was a fine not exceeding $2,000 dollars or imprisonment for up to two years or both. The basic act, with subsequent revisions in 1952 and 1985, continues to be in force. (See *Statutes of Canada, 1937*, c. 32; R.S.C. 1952, c. 124; and R.S.C. 1985, c. F-28.)

2. Victor Hoar, *The Mackenzie-Papineau Battalion* (Ottawa, 1986), p. 235.

3. The Queen's Regulations and Orders for the Canadian Forces, Art. 601.

4. See National Archives, RG 330, Records of the Office of the Secretary of Defense and U.S. Navy, State Summary of War Casualties, Territories and Possessions of the United States and Foreign Countries (Washington, D.C.: U.S. Government Printing Office, 1946), pp. 12-15. See Appendix B.

5. *Globe and Mail* (Toronto), 9 March 1965.

Part I: **Historical Introduction**

1. Paul Starr, *The Discarded Army: Veterans after Vietnam* (New York, 1973), pp. 54-55; see also William Jayne, "Immigrants from the Combat Zone," in A.D. Horne, ed., *The Wounded Generation: America after Vietnam* (Englewood Cliffs, N.J., 1981).

2. The Foreign Enlistment Act, 10 April 1937, *S.C., 1937*, c. 32, s. 3. "Any person, being a Canadian National, within or without Canada, who voluntarily accepts or agrees to accept any commission or engagement in the armed forces of any foreign state at war with any friendly foreign state ... such person shall be guilty of an offence under this Act."

3. Clare Culhane, *Why Is Canada in Vietnam?* (Toronto, 1972), pp. 102-104.

4. This information was obtained in the summer of 1986 from federal Cabinet minutes obtained under the Access to Information Act. See *Vancouver Sun*, 2 July 1986.

5. House of Commons Debates, 24 February 1966, pp. 1706-7, and 9 March 1966, p. 2438. External Affairs, Consular Affairs, Military Service for Canadian Nationals Abroad, 1 Dec. 1963- , vol. 1, file no. 80-15-1-1; External Affairs, Foreign Enlistment Act, 7 June 1963-18 May 1967, file no. 27-10-3-2.

6. Letter from B.V. Shanks to Fred Gaffen, 16 June 1988. Most Canadians who enlisted in the American forces specifically to fight in Vietnam did so mainly between 1965 and 1970. Based on information supplied by the Statistical Analysis Branch of the Immigration and Naturalization Service

of the U.S. Department of Justice, the following list indicates the number of Canadians who became American citizens as a result of previous military service in the U.S. forces. Many of these were Canadian Vietnam veterans who, after several years of military service, decided to remain in the United States. These figures provide a more accurate idea of numbers involved:

Year	No. of Canadians in U.S. Forces Who Became Naturalized Americans
1967	245
1968	258
1969	330
1970	585
1971	543
1972	415
1973	377
1974	257
1975	234
	3,244

7. Letter to author from Veterans Administration, Office of Public Affairs, 10 February 1988.
8. *Sunday Star (Toronto)*, 6 July 1986.
9. *Press Republican* (Plattsburgh), 6 December 1987.
10. Ibid.
11. *Ottawa Citizen*, 18 June 1983, p. 51.
12. *Toronto Star*, "Saturday Magazine," 20 April 1985.
13. *Sault Star*, 10 November 1987.

Part II: War Experiences of Canadians

1. Letter from Reid Feltmate, 25 August 1989.
2. Letter from C.J. Phelps, 11 August 1988.
3. Letter from Thomas Tompkins, 5 February 1989.
4. Letter from Arne Sund, 27 October 1989.
5. Letter from Nicholas Caruso, 25 January 1989.
6. Letter from David S. Mitchell, 1 August 1989.
7. Letter from Gerald Giroldi, 11 February 1989.
8. Letter from David Dear, 10 December 1989.
9. Letter from Lorne Sims, 18 May 1988.

10. Letter from Guy Mathieu, 14 August 1989.

11. Letter from Michel Brodeur, 1 September 1989.

12. Letter from William Bricker, 15 July 1988.

13. Letter from William Bricker, 27 September 1989.

14. Letter from Graeme Webster, 28 July 1989.

15. Letter from Dominic Bilotta, 12 June 1989.

16. Letter from Dominic Bilotta, 4 July 1989.

17. Tape recording from Philip Hocking, 17 February 1990.

18. Letter from Michael Male, 1 July 1989.

19. Letter from William Yoachim, 15 September 1989.

20. Letter from Norman Malayney, 14 November 1988.

21. Letter from James M, 8 July 1988.

22. Letter from Thomas Hill, 30 June 1989.

23. Letter from Howard Walker, 8 March 1989.

24. Letter from Timothy LaBute, 15 September 1989.

25. Letter from Jack Savage, 5 October 1989.

26. Letter from Walter Mullaney, 14 August 1989.

27. Letter from Robert Crepeau, 6 June 1989.

28. Letter from T.D. Hornell, 31 May 1989.

29. Letter from John Ridout, 23 October 1989.

30. Letter from Malcolm Symons, 11 January 1990.

31. Letters from Edward Bowes, 14 December 1988.

32. Letter from John Laurin, 5 September 1989.

33. Letter from Bob Johnson, 15 June 1988.

34. Letter from Ernest Neville, 18 August 1989.

35. Letter from Edward Lamour, 30 August 1989.

36. Letter from Shane Pollock, 11 June 1988.

37. Letter from Dwight Anderson, 28 January 1989.

38. Letters sent by Dwight Anderson from Vietnam.

39. Interview with Eric Walsh, 11 May 1988.

40. Letter from David Ross, 31 December 1989.

41. Letter from George Tissington, 28 March 1989.

42. Letter from Reid Feltmate, 25 August 1989.

43. Letter from Intrepid Sea-Air-Space Museum, 4 May 1988.

44. Interview with Peter Lemon, 13 May 1988.

45. Letters from Joseph Edwards, 10 and 11 May 1989.

46. Letter from Marsha Jordan, 6 August 1988.

47. Letters from Daniel Cunningham, 7 and 8 April 1989.
48. Letter from Frank Kett, 27 June 1989.
49. Letter from Frank Kett, 27 July 1989.
50. Letter from Michael X, 11 May 1989.
51. Letter from Hugh and Sharon Hargrave, 30 October 1989.
52. Letter from Hugh and Sharon Hargrave, 4 December 1989.
53. Letters from Brian Lewis, 16 and 24 June 1989.
54. Letters from Vincent DeRossi, 16 August and 12 September 1989.
55. Letter from Kent Malcolm, 1 July 1989.
56. Letter from Brock McMahon, 21 June 1989.
57. *Toronto Sun*, 14 January 1987; *New York Times*, 27 March 1987.

Part III: **Coming Home**

1. E.G. Fortune, "The American Legion, Department of Canada: A Summary," unpublished manuscript.
2. In Canada, additional information may be obtained from National Victims Resource Centre, Ministry of the Solicitor General, 340 Laurier Avenue West, Ottawa, Ontario, K1A OP8.
3. Letter from George Crockett, 9 November 1988.
4. Letter from Renée Edwards, 14 May 1989.
5. Letter from David Dear, 15 February 1990.
6. Letter to author from John Evans, Combat Stress Unit, V.A. Hospital, Buffalo, 14 July 1988.
7. Interview with Frank Landry, 23 December 1988.
8. Letter from Robert White, 15 March 1989.
9. C.M. Johnson, *Action with the Seaforths* (New York, 1954), p.169; Cornelius Ryan, *The Longest Day* (New York, 1959), p. 246; Tony Foster, *Meeting of Generals* (Toronto, 1968), p. 323; interview with Fernand Larocque of the Régiment de la Chaudière.
10. "MIA, Are Any Still Alive? 25 Compelling Cases from Vietnam," *Life*, November 1987, p. 114.
11. *Montreal Gazette*, 24 January 1981; *Toronto Star*, 24 January 1981, 14 February 1990; *Globe and Mail*, 24 January 1981.
12. Veterans Administration, "Veterans Administration Steps Up Agent Orange Activities," *Agent Orange Review* 1, no. 1 (November 1982): 1-3.
13. *Ottawa Citizen*, 23 July 1988; *Toronto Star*, 25 July 1988.
14. *Agent Orange Review*, p. 4, *Globe and Mail*, 9 July 1984.
15. Letter from Marc Danis, 5 April 1988.

16. Letter from Guy Mathieu, 12 September 1989.

17. Circular No. 88/1/2 from Dominion Command to all branches, 15 January 1988 ("Membership Eligibility and Remembrance Day Ceremonies").

18. *Legion,* September 1987, p. 27.

19. *Ottawa Citizen,* 21 October 1987.

20. Ibid., 19 October 1987.

21. *Record News* (Smiths Falls), 4 November 1987, p. 14.

22. Circular No. 88/1/2 from Dominion Command to all branches, 15 January 1988 ("Membership Eligibility and Remembrance Day Ceremonies").

23. *Alberta Report,* 2 November 1987, p. 44.

24. *Winnipeg Free Press* and *Winnipeg Sun,* 12 November 1987; *Western Report,* 2 November 1987.

25. Unpublished letter, 11 November 1987.

26. *Ottawa Citizen,* 22 September 1986.

27. *Toronto Sunday Sun,* 22 September 1986.

28. Ibid.

29. *Sunday Star* (Toronto), 6 July 1986; *Leatherneck* 43 (December 1986): 2.

30. Letter from Mrs. Elizabeth Delmark, 25 January 1989.

31. Letter from Mrs. Gerald Sharpe, 15 November 1989.

32. *Buffalo Evening News Magazine,* 15 July 1967.

33. Letter to Lee Hitchins, 18 April 1988.

34. Letter from Mrs. Linda James, 24 January 1989.

35. Letter from Ken Laturnis, 6 February 1989.

36. Letter from Marvin Wells, 3 May 1990.

37. Letter from Gerald Blanchette, 10 November 1989.

38. *Mail-Star* (Halifax), 27 August 1969, pp. 3, 44.

39. Ibid., 24 October 1969, pp. 3, 35.

40. Letter from Bob Talmadge, 21 March 1990.

BIBLIOGRAPHY

Books

Alvarez, Everett, Jr., and A.S. Pitch. *Chained Eagle*. New York: D.I. Fine, 1989.

Anderson, William C. *BAT-21: Based on the True Story of Lieutenant Colonel Iceal E. Hambleton, USAF*. Englewood Cliffs, N.J.: Prentice Hall, 1980.

Arlen, Michael J. *Living-Room War*. New York: Viking Press, 1969.

Baritz, Loren. *Backfire: A History of How American Culture Led Us into Vietnam and Made Us Fight the Way We Did*. New York: William Morrow and Co., 1985.

Baskir, Lawrence M., and William A. Strauss. *Chance and Circumstance: The Draft, the War and the Vietnam Generation*. New York: A.A. Knopf, 1978.

Beeching, William C. *Canadian Volunteers: Spain, 1936-1939*. Regina: Canadian Plains Research Center, 1989.

Bender, David L., ed. *The Vietnam War: Opposing Viewpoints*. San Diego, Calif.: Greenhaven Press, 1984.

Berman, Larry. *Planning a Tragedy: The Americanization of the War in Vietnam*. New York: W.W. Norton, 1982.

——. *Lyndon Johnson's War: The Road to Stalemate in Vietnam*. New York: W.W. Norton, 1989.

Blakey, Scott. *Prisoner at War: The Survival of Commander Richard A. Stratton*. Garden City, N.Y.: Doubleday, Anchor Press, 1978.

Blank, Arthur. *The Stresses of War: The Example of Vietnam*. New York: Macmillan, Free Press, 1981.

Bleier, Rocky, and Terry O'Neil. *Fighting Back*. Briarcliff Manor, N.Y.: Stein and Day, 1975.

Boettcher, T.D. *Vietnam: The Valor and the Sorrow*. Boston: Little, Brown and Co., 1985.

Bonior, David, et al. *The Vietnam Veteran: A History of Neglect*. New York: Praeger, 1984.

Bourne, P.G. *Men, Stress and Vietnam*. Boston: Little, Brown and Co., 1970.

Boyle, Richard. *The Flower of the Dragon: The Breakdown of the U.S. Army in Vietnam*. San Francisco: Ramparts Press, 1972.

Brace, Ernest C. *A Code to Keep: The True Story of America's Longest-Held Civilian Prisoner of War in Vietnam*. New York: St. Martin's Press, 1988.

Brende, Joel Osler, and Erwin Randolph Parson. *Vietnam Veterans: The Road to Recovery*. New York: Plenum Press, 1985.

Buckingham, William A., Jr. *Operation Ranch Hand: The United States Air Force and Herbicides in Southeast Asia, 1961-1971*. Office of Air Force History. Washington, D.C.: U.S. Government Printing Office, 1982.

Burchett, Wilfred G. *Grasshoppers and Elephants: Why Vietnam Fell?* New York: Urizen Books, 1977.

——. *The China-Cambodia-Vietnam Triangle.* Chicago: Vanguard Books, 1981.

Buttinger, Joseph. *Vietnam: A Political History.* New York: Praeger, 1968.

——. *Vietnam: The Unforgettable Tragedy.* New York: Horizon Press, 1977.

Camp, Norman M., Robert H. Stretch, and William C. Marshall. *Stress, Strain and Vietnam: An Annotated Bibliography.* New York: Greenwood Press, 1988.

Cawthorne, Nigel. *Prisoners of War.* Eyewitness Nam No. 13. Aldbourne, Wiltshire: Orbis Publishing, 1988.

Cayer, Marc. *Marc Cayer: Prisonnier au Vietnam.* Montreal: Ferron, 1973.

Charlton, Michael, and Anthony Moncrieff. *Many Reasons Why: The American Involvement in Vietnam.* New York: Hill and Wang, 1978.

Chomsky, Noam. *American Power and the New Mandarins.* New York: Pantheon Books, 1969.

——. *At War with Asia.* New York: Random House, 1970.

Christy, Jim. *The New Refugees.* Toronto: Peter Martin Associates, 1972.

Cincinnatas. *Self-Destruction: The Disintegration and Decay of the United States Army During the Vietnam Era.* New York: W.W. Norton, 1981.

Clodfelter, Mark. *The Limits of Air Power: The American Bombing of North Vietnam.* New York: Macmillan, Free Press, 1989.

Coffee, Gerald L. *Beyond Survival: Building on the Hard Times — A POW's Inspiring Story.* New York: Putnam, 1990.

Colby, William, with James McCargar. *Lost Victory: A Firsthand Account of America's Sixteen Year Involvement in Vietnam.* Chicago: Contemporary Books, 1989.

Collins, Margaret Graham. *I'll Ride the Lightning When I Go: Destination Vietnam.* Victoria: Cappis Press, 1982.

Colvin, Rod. *First Heroes: The POWs Left Behind in Vietnam.* New York: Irvington Publishers, 1987.

Cooper, Chester L. *The Lost Crusade: America in Vietnam.* New York: Dodd, Mead and Co., 1970.

Culhane, Claire. *Why Is Canada in Vietnam?* Toronto: NC Press, 1973.

Currey, Cecil B. *Self-Destruction: The Disintegration and Decay of the United States Army in the Vietnam Era.* New York: W.W. Norton, 1981.

Curry, G. David. *Sunshine Patriots: Punishment and the Vietnam Offender.* Notre Dame, Ind.: University of Notre Dame Press, 1985.

Davis, Larry. *Wild Weasel: The SAM Suppression Story.* Carrollton, Tex.: Squadron/Signal Publications, 1986.

Dean, Chuck, with Bob Putman. *Nam Vet: Making Peace with Your Past.* Mountlake Terrace, Wash.: Point Man International, 1988.

Dengler, Dieter. *Escape from Laos*. Novato, Calif.: Presidio Press, 1979.

Denton, Jeremiah A. *When Hell Was in Session*. New York: Reader's Digest Press, 1976.

Désiré, Michel. *La Campagne d'Indochine (1945-1954): Bibliographie*. 3 vols. Vincennes: Service historique de l'Armée de terre, 1971, 1973, 1976.

Dickson, Paul. *The Electronic Battlefield*. London: Marion Boyars, 1977.

Dimas, David D. *Missing in Action — Prisoner of War: A Report to the American People*. La Mirada, Calif.: privately printed, 1986.

Duiker, William J. *The Communist Road to Power in Vietnam*. Boulder, Col.: Westview Press, 1981.

Dumbrell, John, ed. *Vietnam and the Antiwar Movement: An International Perspective*. Aldershot, Eng.: Avebury, 1989.

Dung, Van Thien. *Our Great Spring Victory*. London: Monthly Review Press, 1977.

Dziuban, Stanley W. *Military Relations between the United States and Canada, 1939-1945*. Washington, D.C.: Department of the Army, 1959.

Eayers, James. *In Defence of Canada, Indochina: Roots of Complicity*. Toronto: University of Toronto Press, 1983.

Egendorf, Arthur. *Healing from the War: Trauma and Transformation after Vietnam*. Boston: Houghton Mifflin, 1985.

Emerick, Kenneth. *War Resisters Canada*. Knox, Penn.: Pennsylvania Free Press, 1972.

Engelbrecht, Charles V. *The Guns Fell Silent and the War Began*. Laurel, Md.: Engelbrecht and Associates, 1987.

Fall, Bernard. *Street Without Joy*. 4th ed. Harrisburg, Penn.: Stackpole Co., 1967.

——. *The Two Vietnams: A Political and Military Analysis*. New York: Praeger, 1967.

——. *Hell in a Very Small Place: The Siege of Dien Bien Phu*. New York: Vintage Books, 1968.

Figley, Charles R., ed. *Stress Disorders among Vietnam Veterans: Theory, Research, and Treatment*. New York: Brunner/Mazel, 1978.

——. *Trauma and Its Wake: The Study and Treatment of Post-Traumatic Stress Disorder*. New York: Brunner/Mazel, 1985.

Figley, Charles R., and Seymour Leventman. *Strangers at Home: Vietnam Veterans Since the War*. New York: Praeger, 1980.

Fitzgerald, Frances. *Fire in the Lake: The Vietnamese and the Americans in Vietnam*. Boston: Atlantic Little, Brown and Co., 1972.

Fleming, Jim. *Vietnam: A Personal Impression*. Toronto: Rogers Broadcasting, 1968.

Gabriel, Richard A. *Military Incompetence: Why the American Military Doesn't Win*. New York: Hill and Wang, 1986.

Gabriel, Richard A., and Paul L. Savage. *Crisis in Command: Mismanagement in the United States Army*. New York: Farrar, Straus and Giroux, 1978.

Gaffen, Fred. *In the Eye of the Storm: A History of Canadian Peacekeeping Operations*. Toronto: Deneau and Wayne, 1987.

Gaither, Ralph. *With God in a P.O.W. Camp*. Nashville, Tenn.: Broadman Press, 1973.

Garrett, Richard. *P.O.W.* London: David and Charles, 1981.

Gelb, Leslie H., with Richard K. Betts. *The Irony of Vietnam: The System Worked*. Washington, D.C.: Brookings Institution, 1979.

Generous, Kevin M. *Vietnam: The Secret War*. New York: Gallery Books, 1985.

Giap, Vo Nguyen. *Unforgettable Days*. Hanoi: Foreign Language Publishing House, 1978.

Giap, Vo Nguyen, and Van Tien Dung. *How We Won the War*. Philadelphia: Recon Publications, 1976.

Gibson, James William. *The Perfect War: Technowar in Vietnam*. Boston: Atlantic Monthly Press, 1986.

Gitlin, Todd. *The Sixties: Years of Hope, Days of Rage*. New York: Bantam Books, 1987.

Gough, Michael. *Dioxin, Agent Orange: The Facts*. New York: Plenum Press, 1986.

Granatstein, J.L. *Canada, 1957-1967: The Years of Uncertainty*. Canadian Centenary Series. Toronto: McClelland and Stewart, 1986.

Grant, Zalin, ed. *Survivors: American POWs in Vietnam*. New York: W.W. Norton, 1975.

Grinter, Lawrence, and Peter Dunn, eds. *The American War in Vietnam: Lessons, Legacies, and Implications for Future Conflicts*. New York: Greenwood Press, 1987.

Groom, Winston, and Duncan Spencer. Conversations with the Enemy: *The Story of P.F.C. Robert Garwood*. New York: Putman, 1983.

Halberstam, David. *The Best and the Brightest*. New York: Random House, 1972.

Hallin, Daniel C. *The Uncensored War: The Media and Vietnam*. New York: Oxford University Press, 1986.

Hammer, Richard. *The Court-Martial of Lt. Calley*. New York: Coward, McCann and Geoghegan, 1971.

Hannah, Norman B. *The Key to Failure: Laos and the Vietnam War*. Lanham, Md.: Madison Books, 1987.

Hardy, René. *Les Zouaves Pontificaux Canadiens*. History Division Paper No. 19. Ottawa: National Museums of Canada, 1976.

Harnly, Caroline D., ed. *Agent Orange and Vietnam: An Annotated Bibliography*. Metuchen, N.J.: Scarecrow Press, 1988.

Harrison, James P. *The Endless War: Vietnam's Struggle for Independence*. New York: McGraw-Hill, 1982.

Hayslip, Le Ly, with Jay Wurts. *When Heaven and Earth Changed Places: A Vietnamese Woman's Journey from War to Peace*. New York: Doubleday, 1989.

Helle, Roger. *My War Beyond Vietnam*. Ventura, Calif.: Regal Books, 1985.

Helmer, John. *Bringing the War Home: The American Soldier in Vietnam and After*. New York: Macmillan, 1974.

Hendin, Herbert, and Ann P. Haas. *Wounds of War: The Psychological Aftermath of Combat in Vietnam*. New York: Basic Books, 1984.

Herring, George. *America's Longest War*. 2nd ed. New York: A.A. Knopf, 1986.

Hoar, Victor, and Mac Reynolds. *The Mackenzie-Papineau Battalion: The Canadian Contingent in the Spanish Civil War*. Ottawa: Carleton University Press, 1986.

Horne, A.D., ed. *The Wounded Generation: America after Vietnam*. Englewood Cliffs, N.J.: Prentice Hall, 1981.

Hubbell, John G. *POW: A Definitive History of the American Prisoner-of-War Experience in Vietnam, 1964-1973*. New York: Reader's Digest Press, 1976.

Isaacs, Arnold R. *Without Honor: Defeat in Vietnam and Cambodia*. Baltimore: Johns Hopkins University Press, 1983.

Jensen-Stevenson, Monika, and William Stevenson. *Kiss the Boys Goodbye: How the United States Betrayed Its Own POWs in Vietnam*. Toronto: McClelland and Stewart, 1990.

Just, Ward S. *To What End: Report from Vietnam*. Boston: Houghton Mifflin, 1968.

——. *Military Men*. New York: A.A. Knopf, 1970.

Karnow, Stanley. *Vietnam: A History*. New York: Viking Press, 1983.

Kasinsky, Renée. *Refugees from Militarism: Draft Age Americans in Canada*. New Brunswick, N.J.: Transaction Books, 1976.

Kelly, William E., ed. *Post-Traumatic Stress Disorder and the War Veteran Patient*. New York: Brunner/Mazel, 1985.

King, Edward L. *The Death of the Army: A Pre-Mortem*. New York: Saturday Review Press, 1972.

Kinnard, Douglas. *The War Managers*. Hanover, N.H.: University Press of New England, 1977.

Kolko, Gabriel. *Anatomy of a War: Vietnam, the United States, and the Modern Historical Experience*. New York: Pantheon Books, 1985.

Kovic, Ron. *Born on the Fourth of July*. New York: McGraw-Hill, 1976.

Krepinevich, Andrew F. *The Army and Vietnam*. Baltimore: Johns Hopkins University Press, 1986.

Kubey, Craig, et al. *The Viet Vet Survival Guide*. New York: Ballantine Books, 1985.

Kulka, Richard A. *Trauma and the Vietnam War Generation: Report of the Findings from the National Vietnam Veterans Readjustment Study*. New York: Brunner/Mazel, 1990.

Lepore, Randall F. *Post-Traumatic Stress Disorder — V.A. Disability Claims and Military Review*. Boston: Dominus Vobiscum Publishing, 1988.

Levant, Victor. *Quiet Complicity: Canadian Involvement in the Vietnam War*. Toronto: Between the Lines, 1986.

Levitt, Cyril. *Children of Privilege: Student Revolt in the Sixties*. Toronto: University of Toronto Press, 1984.

Lewy, Guenter. *America in Vietnam*. New York: Oxford University Press, 1978.

Lomperis, Timothy J. *The War Everyone Lost — and Won: America's Intervention in Vietnam's Twin Struggles*. Baton Rouge, La.: Louisiana State University Press, 1984.

Lonn, Ella. *Foreigners in the Union Army and Navy*. Baton Rouge, La.: Louisiana State University Press, 1951.

Maclear, Michael. *The Ten Thousand Day War, Vietnam: 1945-1975*. New York: Methuen, 1981.

MacPherson, Myra. *Long Time Passing: Vietnam and the Haunted Generation*. New York: Doubleday, 1984.

Marolda, Edward J., and G. Wesley Price, III. *A Select Bibliography of the United States Navy and the Southeast Asian Conflict, 1950-1975*. Washington, D.C.: Naval Historical Center, 1983.

——. *A Short History of the United States Navy and the Southeast Asian Conflict, 1950-1975*. Washington, D.C.: Naval Historical Center, 1984.

Marshall, Kathryn. *In the Combat Zone: An Oral History of American Women in Vietnam, 1966-1975*. Boston: Little, Brown and Co., 1987.

Mason, Patience, H.C. *Recovering from the War: A Woman's Guide to Helping Your Vietnam Vet, Your Family, and Yourself*. New York: Viking Press, 1990.

Matsakis, Aphrodite. *Vietnam Wives: Women and Children Surviving Life with Veterans Suffering Post Traumatic Stress Disorder*. Kensington, Md.: Woodbine House, 1988.

McCloud, Bill, ed. *What Should We Tell Our Children about Vietnam*. Norman, Okla.: University of Oklahoma Press, 1989.

McConnell, Malcolm. *Into the Mouth of the Cat: The Story of Lance Sijan, Hero of Vietnam*. New York: W.W. Norton, 1985.

McCoy, Alfred W. *The Politics of Heroin in Southeast Asia*. New York: Harper and Row, 1972.

McDaniel, Eugene B. *Scars and Stripes: The True Story of One Man's Courage in Facing Death as a Vietnam POW*. Irvine, Calif.: Harvest House, 1975.

McGrath, John M. *Prisoner of War: Six Years in Hanoi*. Annapolis, Md.: Naval Institute Press, 1975.

Merritt, William E. *Where the Rivers Ran Backward*. Athens, Ga.: University of Georgia Press, 1989.

Mersky, Peter, and Norman Polmar. *The Naval Air War in Vietnam 1965-1975.* Annapolis, Md.: Nautical and Aviation Publishing Co. of America, 1981.

Millet, Allen Reed, ed. *A Short History of the Vietnam War*. Bloomfield, Ind.: Indiana University Press, 1979.

Moffatt, Gary. *History of the Canadian Peace Movement Until 1969*. St. Catharines, Ont.: Grapevine Press, 1969.

Mrozek, Donald J. *Air Power and the Ground War in Vietnam: Ideas and Actions*. Maxwell Air Force Base, Ala.: Air University Press, 1988.

Murphy, Edward F. *Vietnam Medal of Honor Heroes*. New York: Ballantine Books, 1987.

Nasmyth, Virginia, and Spike Nasmyth. *Hanoi, Release John Nasmyth: A Family Love Story*. Santa Paula, Calif.: V. Parr, 1984.

Neilands, J.B. *Harvest of Death: Chemical Warfare in Vietnam and Cambodia*. New York: Macmillan, Free Press, 1972.

Nguyen, Van Cahn. *Vietnam under Communism, 1975-1982*. Stanford, Calif.: Stanford University Press, 1983.

Nixon, Richard. *The Real War*. New York: Warner Books, 1981.

——. *No More Vietnams*. New York: Arbor House, 1985.

Oberdorfer, Don. *Tet! The Turning Point in the Vietnam War*. New York: Da Capo, 1983.

O'Brien, Tim. *If I Die in a Combat Zone: Box Me Up and Ship Me Home*. New York: Delacorte Press, 1973.

O'Daniel, Larry J. *Missing in Action: Trail of Deceit*. New Rochelle, N.Y.: Arlington House, 1979.

O'Neill, Robert J. *General Giap: Politician and Strategist*. Sydney: Cassell Australia, 1969.

Papp, Daniel S. *Vietnam: The View from Moscow, Peking, Washington*. Jefferson, N.C.: McFarland and Co., 1981.

Parker, F. Charles, IV. *Vietnam: Strategy for a Stalemate*. New York: Paragon House, 1989.

Patterson, Charles L., and G. Lee Tippin. *The Heroes Who Fell from Grace: The True Story of Operation Lazarus, the Attempt to Free American POWs from Laos in 1982*. Canton, Ohio: Daring Books, 1985.

Peake, Louis A. *The United States in the Vietnam War, 1954-1975: A Selected Annotated Bibliography*. New York: Garland, 1986.

Peck, M.B. *Red Moon over Spain: Canadian Media Reaction to the Spanish Civil War, 1936-1939*. Ottawa: Steel Rail, 1988.

Peers, W.R. *The My Lai Inquiry*. New York: W.W. Norton, 1979.

Pike, Douglas. *Viet Cong: The Organization and Techniques of the National Liberation Front of South Vietnam*. Cambridge, Mass.: MIT Press, 1966.

———. *History of the Vietnamese Communist Party*. Palo Alto, Calif.: Hoover Institution, 1978.

———. *PAVN: People's Army of Vietnam*. Novato, Calif.: Presidio Press, 1986.

Podhoretz, Norman. *Why We Were in Vietnam*. New York: Simon and Schuster, 1982.

Polner, Murray. *No Victory Parades: The Return of the Vietnam Veteran*. New York: Holt, Rinehart and Winston, 1971.

Powers, Thomas. *Vietnam: The War at Home*. Boston: G.K. Hall, 1984.

Risner, Robinson. *Passing of the Night: My Seven Years as a Prisoner of the North Vietnamese*. New York: Random House, 1973.

Ross, A. Douglas. *In the Interests of Peace: Canada and Vietnam, 1954-1973*. Toronto: University of Toronto Press, 1984.

Rowan, Stephen A. *They Wouldn't Let Us Die: The Prisoners of War Tell Their Story*. Middle Village, N.Y.: J. David Publishers, 1973.

Rowe, James N. *Five Years to Freedom*. Boston: Little, Brown and Co., 1971.

Royal Canadian Legion. *The General Bylaws of the Royal Canadian Legion*. Ottawa: Dominion Command, 1986.

Salisbury, Harrison E., ed. *Vietnam Reconsidered: Lessons from a War*. New York: Harper and Row, 1984.

Saul, John, and Heron Craig, eds. *Imperialism, Nationalism and Canada*. Toronto: New Hogtown Press, 1977.

Schardt, Arlie, William Rusher, and Mark O. Hadfield. *Amnesty? The Unsettled Question of Vietnam*. Croton-on-Hudson, N.Y.: Sun River Press, 1973.

Schemmer, Benjamin F. *The Raid*. New York: Harper and Row, 1976.

Schlesinger, Arthur M., Jr. *The Bitter Heritage: Vietnam and American Democracy, 1941-1966*. Boston: Houghton Mifflin, 1987.

Schuck, Peter H. *Agent Orange on Trial: Mass Toxic Disasters in the Courts*. Cambridge, Mass: Harvard University Press, Belknap Press, 1986.

Schwinn, Monika, and Bernhard Diehl. *We Came to Help*. New York: Harcourt Brace Jovanovich, 1976.

Scruggs, Jan C., and Joel Swerdlow. *To Heal a Nation: The Vietnam Veterans Memorial*. New York: Harper and Row, 1985.

Severo, Richard, David Singer, and John Banks. *The Wages of War: When Americans Came Home — From Valley Forge to Vietnam*. New York: Simon and Schuster, 1989.

Sevy, Grace, ed. *The American Experience in Vietnam: A Reader*. Norman, Okla.: University of Oklahoma Press, 1989.

Shaplen, Robert. *The Road from War: Vietnam 1965-1970*. New York: Harper and Row, 1970.

Sharp, U.S. Grant. *Strategy for Defeat: Vietnam in Retrospect*. San Rafael, Calif.: Presidio Press, 1978.

Sheehan, Neil, et al. *The Pentagon Papers as Published by The New York Times*. New York: Bantam Books, 1971.

Simpson, Charles M., III. *Inside the Green Berets: The First Thirty Years*. Novato, Calif.: Presidio Press, 1985.

Smith, R.B. *An International History of the Vietnam War*. 2 vols. London: Macmillan, 1985.

Sonnenburg, Stephen M., Arthur Blank, and John Talbott, eds. *The Trauma of War: Stress and Recovery in Vietnam Veterans*. Washington, D.C.: American Psychiatric Press, 1985.

Stanton, Shelby L. *Vietnam: Order of Battle*. Washington, D.C.: U.S. News Books, 1981.

——. *The Rise and Fall of an American Army: U.S. Ground Forces in Vietnam, 1965-1973*. New York: Dell, 1985.

——. *Green Berets at War: U.S. Army Special Forces in Southeast Asia 1956-1975*. Novato, Calif.: Presidio Press, 1985.

——. *Anatomy of a Division: The 1st Cav in Vietnam*. Novato, Calif.: Presidio Press, 1987.

Starr, Paul, James F. Henry, and Raymond P. Bonner. *The Discarded Army: Veterans after Vietnam*. New York: Charterhouse, 1973.

Stockdale, Jim, and Sybil Stockdale. *In Love and War: The Story of a Family's Ordeal and Sacrifice During the Vietnam Years*. New York: Harper and Row, 1984.

Summers, Harry G., Jr. *On Strategy: A Critical Analysis of the Vietnam War*. Novato, Calif.: Presidio Press, 1982.

——. *Vietnam War Almanac*. New York: Facts on File Publications, 1985.

Taylor, Charles. *Snow Job: Canada, the United States and Vietnam, 1954 to 1973*. Toronto: Anansi, 1974.

Thayer, Thomas C. *War without Fronts: The American Experience in Vietnam*. Boulder, Col.: Westview Press, 1985.

Thompson, Leroy. *The U.S. Army in Vietnam*. Newton Abbot, Eng.: David and Charles, 1989.

Thompson, Robert. *Peace Is Not at Hand*. New York: McKay, 1974.

——. *Make for the Hills: Memories of Far Eastern Wars*. London: Leo Cooper, 1989.

Thompson, W. Scott, and Donaldson D. Frizzell, eds. *The Lessons of Vietnam*. New York: Crane and Russak, 1977.

Trooboff, Peter D., ed. *Law and Responsibility in Warfare: The Vietnam Experience*. Chapel Hill, N.C.: University of North Carolina Press, 1975.

Uhlig, Frank Jr., ed. *Vietnam: The Naval Story*. Annapolis, Md.: Naval Institute Press, 1986.

U.S. Department of Defense. *POW-MIA Fact Book*. Washington, D.C.: Department of Defense, July 1987.

Vennema, Alje. *The Viet Cong Massacre at Hue*. New York: Vantage Press, 1976.

Vietnam Veterans Memorial: Directory of Names. 6th ed. Washington, D.C.: Vietnam Veterans Memorial Fund, 1986.

Walt, Lewis. *Strange War, Strange Strategy*. New York: Funk and Wagnalls, 1970.

Walton, George. *The Tarnished Shield: A Report on Today's Army*. New York: Dodd, Mead and Co., 1973.

Walzer, Michael. *Just and Unjust Wars: A Moral Argument with Historical Illustrations*. New York: Basic Books, 1977.

Warner, Denis. *Certain Victory: How Hanoi Won the War*. Kansas City: Sheed, Andrews and McMeel, 1978.

Warnock, John W. *Partner to Behemoth: The Military Policy of a Satellite Canada*. Toronto: New Press, 1970.

Westmoreland, William. *A Soldier Reports*. New York: Dell, 1980.

Whittemore, Thomas. *The Vietnam War: A Text for Students*. Cambridge, Mass.: Cambridgeport Press, 1988.

Wilcox, Fred. *Waiting for an Army to Die: The Tragedy of Agent Orange*. New York: Random House, 1983.

Williams, Tom, ed. *Post-Traumatic Stress Disorders of the Vietnam Veteran: Observations and Recommendations for the Psychological Treatment of the Veteran and His Family*. Cincinnati, Ohio: Disabled American Veterans, 1980.

Wilson, John P. *Identity, Ideology, and Crisis: The Vietnam Veteran in Transition*. Cleveland: Cleveland State University, 1977.

Windchy, Eugene G. *Tonkin Gulf*. Garden City, N.Y.: Doubleday, 1971.

Zaffiri, Samuel. *Hamburger Hill, May 11-20, 1969*. Novato, Calif.: Presidio Press, 1988.

Zaroulis, Nancy, and Gerald Sullivan. *Who Spoke Up? American Protest against the War in Vietnam, 1963-1975*. Garden City, N.Y.: Doubleday, 1984.

Articles

Anonymous. "American Legion, Department of Canada: A Summary." Unpublished manuscript. American Legion Library, Indianapolis.

Atkinson, R.M., et al. "Assessment of Vietnam Veterans for Posttraumatic Stress Disorder in Veterans Administration Disability Claims." *American Journal of Psychiatry* 139 (1982): 1118-21.

Bartlett, Tony. "Canadians at the Wall." *Leatherneck* 43 (December 1986): 1-5.

Brooks, Tom. "British North Americans in the American Civil War." *The 1988 Journal of the Canadian Society of Medals and Insignia*, 1989, pp. 10-16.

Butterfield, Fox. "The New Vietnam Scholarship." *New York Times Magazine*, 13 February 1983, pp. 26-34, 45-61.

Clark, Doug. "Canada's Unknown Soldiers." *Maclean's*, 8 August 1983, pp. 12-13.

——. "The Loneliness and Pain of Canadian Veterans of the Vietnam War." *Globe and Mail*, 9 July 1984.

Ford, Catherine. "Mercenaries Deserve No Honor." *Calgary Herald*, 13 November 1986.

Frye, J.S., and R.A. Stockton. "Discriminant Analysis of Post Traumatic Stress Disorder among a Group of Vietnam Veterans." *American Journal of Psychiatry* 139 (1982): 52-56.

Gration, Peter. "On 1 ATF in Vietnam." *Journal of the Australian War Memorial*, no. 12 (April 1988): 45-46.

Harrison, Donald Fischer. "Computers, Electronic Data and the Vietnam War." *Archivaria*, no. 26 (Summer 1988): 18-32.

Holm, Tom. "Forgotten Warriors: American Indian Servicemen in Vietnam." *Vietnam Generation* 1, no. 2 (Spring 1989): 56-58.

Holt, C.A. "Nova Scotia's Brother Heroes." *Military Collectors' Club of Canada Journal*, January 1972, pp. 8-10.

Indra, Doreen. "Southeast Asians." In *The Canadian Encyclopedia*, 2nd ed., p. 2051. Edmonton: Hurtig Publishers, 1988.

Laughridge, Eugene N. "The Air Force in Books about Vietnam." *Aerospace Historian* 35, no. 4 (December 1968): 266-67.

Levant, Victor. "Vietnam War." In *The Canadian Encycloepedia*, 2nd ed., p. 2263. Edmonton: Hurtig Publishers, 1988.

Levine, Allan. "Soldiers of Fortune." In *The Canadian Encyclopedia*, 2nd ed., pp. 2043-44. Edmonton: Hurtig Publishers, 1988.

Life. "MIA. Are Any Still Alive? 25 Compelling Cases from Vietnam." *Life*, November 1987, pp. 111-24.

Lovett, Christopher. "We Held the Day in the Palm of Our Hand: A Review of Recent Sources on the War in Vietnam." *Military Affairs* 51, no. 2 (April 1987): 67-72.

Lyon, Peyton V. "Canada, the U.S. and Viet-Nam: A Comment." *Journal of Commonwealth Political Studies*, 6 July 1968.

MacGregor, Tom. "Combat Stress." *Legion*, October 1989, pp. 10-11.

Malott, R.K. "Canadian Medal of Honor Recipients." *Journal of the Military Collectors Club of Canada*, September 1970, pp. 14-16.

McIntosh, Dave. "War Veterans." In *The Canadian Encyclopedia*, 2nd ed., pp. 2276-77. Edmonton: Hurtig Publishers, 1988.

Monroe, Steve. "Wings of the Apocalype: A Canadian Helicopter Pilot Recalls the Hell That Was Vietnam." *Saturday Night* 100, no. 12 (December 1985): 56-61.

Ross, David. "The Canadian Pontifical Zouaves, 1868-70." *OMMC Bulletin* 2 (1973): 1-6.

Spetz, Steven. "Vietnam War: Exploding the Myths." *The Whig Standard Magazine*, 19 March 1988, pp. 5-9.

Stanley, G.F.G. "Dien Bien Phu in Retrospect." *International Journal* 10, no. 1 (Winter 1954-55): 38-50.

Strange, R.E., and D.E. Brown. "Home from the War: A Study of Psychiatric Problems in Vietnam Returnees." *American Journal of Psychiatry* 127 (1970): 488-92.

Stretch, R., J. Vail, and J. Maloney. "Post Traumatic Stress Disorder among Army Nurse Corps Vietnam Veterans." *Journal of Consulting and Clinical Psychology* 53, no. 5 (1972): 704-8.

INDEX

"Agent Orange", 282-283
Aircraft
  A-1 (Douglas Skyraider), 55
  A-7 (Vought Corsair II), 89, 255
  B-52 (Boeing Stratofortress), 24, 83,
    118, 254, 256, 273
  C-7 (de Havilland Caribou), 119,
    137
  C-47 (Douglas), 91, 109, 251
  C-123 (Fairchild Provider), 112,
    119, 233, 319
  C-130 (Lockheed Hercules), 53, 73,
    90, 108-109, 118-119, 169, 174,
    202, 232, 255
  C-141 (Lockheed StarLifter), 219
  EB-66 (Douglas Destroyer), 254
  EC-121 (Lockheed Constellation),
    255
  F-4 (McDonnell Douglas Phantom),
    76, 91-92, 115-116, 119, 147, 167,
    181, 201, 209, 249-50, 254
  F-105 (Fairchild Republic
    Thunderchief), 201, 254
  0-1 (Cessna Bird Dog), 44-45, 137
  P-3 (Lockheed Orion), 271
  KC-135 (Boeing Stratotanker), 256
Air Force, U.S.
  11 Squadron, 112
  12 Squadron, 112
  38 Squadron, 166
  56 Squadron, 219
  421 Squadron, 249
  432 Squadron, 249
American Legion, 9, 263
Anderson, Sgt. Dwight, 182-194
Army, Navy and Air Force Veterans in
  Canada, 298
Australia, 22, 26, 31, 107, 147, 283
Aviation (Helicopter) Companies,
  U.S. Army
  92nd, 42
  134th, 199-200
  155th, 106
  170th, 327-328

  195th, 137
  205th, 106, 196
  213th, 196
  478th, 162

Bases, Air Force
  Brooks, 219
  Cam Ranh Bay, 117-119, 145-147
  Clark, 90, 118, 219, 231, 234
  Da Nang, 73, 78, 97, 149, 151, 153,
    249-250
  Hill, 112
  Korat, 255
  Lackland, 90, 165
  McChord, 117
  McGuire, 196
  Phu Cat, 90-91
  Sampson 165
  Sheppard, 166, 219
  Stead, 166
  Takhli, 249
  Tan Son Nhut, 118, 122, 196
  Travis, 90, 117, 165, 231
  Tuy Hoa, 202
  Ubon, 166
  Udorn, 230, 232-233, 249-250
  Utapao, 179
  Yokota, 141, 219
Bases, Naval
  Cam Ranh Bay, 271, 274
  Newport, 123
  Norfolk, 123
  San Diego, 59, 123, 271
Bastable, Harold, 294, 297
Battalions, U.S. Army
  1st, 12th Cavalry, 70
  1st, 27th Artillery, 158
  2nd, 8th Cavalry, 316
  3rd, 197th Field Artillery, 322
  9th, Supply and Transport, 287
  11th Aviation, 196,
  16th Armor, 140
  39th Engineer, 111
  92nd Engineer, 126

326th Engineer, 246
504th M.P., 248
765th Transportation, 123
Bilotta, Sgt. Dominic, 101-105
Blanchette, Sgt. Guy, 321-324
Bowes, Sgt. Edward, 159-161
Bricker, Airman 1st Class William, 90-92
Brigades, U.S. Army
  1st Aviation, 137, 196, 328
  173rd Airborne, 48, 140-2, 257, 300
  196th Infantry, 110
  198th Infantry, 129
Brodeur, PO 1st Class Michel, 88-89

Cambodia, 23, 26, 66, 179-180, 182, 198, 275
Campaign Medals, U.S. see Honours and Awards)
Camps, South Vietnam
  Carroll, 101, 300, 308-309
  Eagle, 149, 151-153, 247
  Enari, 151
  Evans, 206
  Holloway, 87
  Reasoner, 73, 77
Camps, U.S.
  Lejeune, 84, 163, 219
  Pendleton, 78, 97, 163, 181, 219
Canadian Vietnam Veterans Coalition, 262, 284
Canadian Volunteers — Vietnam Battalion (CVVN), 35
Caruso, Sgt. N.P., 62-69
Chaplin, H.R., 263
Collard, Joseph, 39
Cook, James, 298
Craig, Gary, 299
Craig, Kenneth, 300
Crepeau, Sgt. Robert, 148-149
Crockett, L. Cpl. George, 266
Cunningham, Cpl. D.C., 219-229

Danis, Pvt. M.L., 287
Dear, Cpl. D.J., 78-84, 267-269
Delmark, Cpl. Francis, 301-3
Democratic Republic of Vietnam, 21
DeRossi, SP-4 Vincent, 248-249
Devaney, CWO 2 B.J., 326-330
Dextraze, Gen. J.A., 38-39
Dextraze, L. Cpl. Richard, 38

Diabo, Arthur, 38
Diefenbaker, J.G., 29, 35
Divisions, U.S. Army
  Americal (23rd Infantry), 129, 260
  1st Cavalry, 62-63, 69, 209, 316
  1st Infantry, 126, 148, 209, 270, 323
  4th Infantry, 106, 153, 162, 198, 249
  5th Infantry, 247
  9th Infantry, 287
  25th Infantry, 97, 126
  82nd Airborne, 64, 318
  101st Airborne, 110, 149-152, 198, 201, 204, 246-247, 274, 319
Draft. see Selective Service
Draft Evaders, 8
Dung, Gen Van Tien, 25

Edwards, L. Cpl. John, 267
Edwards, L. Cpl. Joseph, 211-217
Evans, S. Sgt. John, 269-270

Feltmate, WO Reid, 42-45, 207-209
Forts
  Belvoir, 111, 162
  Benjamin Harrison, 46, 168
  Benning, 46, 63, 125, 140, 159, 207, 316
  Bliss, 109
  Bragg, 64, 86, 154, 162
  Campbell, 64, 196
  Carson, 137, 249
  Dix, 126, 141, 162, 195, 316
  Eustis, 162, 195
  Hamilton, 168
  Hood, 125, 127, 199
  Jackson, 46
  Knox, 136-137, 209
  Leonard Wood, 112, 125
  Leavenworth, 177
  Lewis, 137, 162, 180, 207, 238
  McArthur, 168
  Meade, 109
  Ord, 105, 168-169, 180
  Polk, 197, 209
  Rucker, 105, 137, 197
  Sam Houston, 177, 238
  Sill, 158, 168, 196
  Wolters, 105, 158, 197

Giroldi, Cpl. G.M., 71-78
Green Berets, (see Special Forces)

Hargrave, Lt. Cmdr. Hugh, 241-246
Hargrave, Sharon, 241-246
Hatton, PFC Randolph, 315-316
Helicopters
    AH-1 (Cobra), 55, 108, 209
    CH-46 (Sea Knight), 311, 313
    CH-47 (Chinook), 99, 106, 108, 137,
        195-196
    CH-54 (Flying Crane), 162
    HH-43 (Huskie), 75, 166
    UH-1 (Huey), 42, 70, 106, 137-138,
        158, 196, 198, 207, 209, 313
    UH-34 (Choctaw)(Seahorse), 52,
        56, 75-76
Hill, SP-4 Thomas, 125-8
Hocking, WO Philip, 105-9
Ho Chi Minh, 21-22, 76, 98, 165, 192
Holditch, WO Robert, 318-321
Honours and Awards
    Bronze Star Medal, 50, 239, 274,
        325-326
    Medal of Honor, 50
    Silver Star Medal, 39, 50-51
Hornell, S. Sgt. David, 149-153

International Commission for Super-
    vision and Control for Vietnam
    (ICSC Vietnam), 21, 31, 279
International Commission of Control
    and Supervision (ICCS) for
    Vietnam (1973), 25, 196

Johnson, President L.B., 23-24, 34, 147
Johnson, Cpl. Robert, 163-165
Jordan, 1st Lt. Marsha, 218-219

Kennedy, President John F., 23, 328
Kett, S. Sgt. Frank, 229-237
Kmetyk, L. Cpl. J.P., 310-314
Korea, South, 22, 31, 119, 132, 176, 199
Korean War, 28, 30-31, 148-149, 213,
    265, 277, 279
Kroisenbacher, L. Cpl. Adolf, 316-318
Ky, Nguyen Cao, 22

LaBute, SP-5 Timothy, 137-140
Lamour, S. Sgt. Edward, 168-180
Landry, Sgt. Frank, 270
Laurin, S. Sgt. John, 162-163
Laos, 23, 26, 108, 115, 151, 185, 199,
    232-234, 247, 253, 275

Lemon, Sgt. Peter, 209-211
Lewis, SP-4, Brian, 246-247
Lodge, Henry Cabot, 17
Luongo, Patrick, 9

Mack, PFC Allen, 300
Malayney, S. Sgt. Norman, 117-123
Malcolm, S. Sgt. Kent, 249-253
Male, Sgt. Michael, 109-112
Marine Corps Stations, U.S.
    El Toro, Calif., 94, 97, 101, 183
    Quantico, Va., 219
Marine Corps Recruit Depots,
    U.S. Parris Island, S.C., 72, 84, 163,
        219
    San Diego, Calif., 180-181, 302, 317
Marine Corps, Units, U.S.
    Divisions
        1st, 84, 163, 181-182, 184, 190, 219,
            312-313
        3rd, 78, 85, 97, 101, 211, 213, 301,
            306, 312, 317
    Regiments
        1st, 84, 219, 224
        3rd, 72-3, 301
        4th, 101
        5th, 182, 184, 190
        7th, 163, 181, 184
        9th, 306, 308
        26th, 219
Martin, Paul, 35
Mathieu, PFC Guy, 86-88, 288-289
McIntosh, WO Ian, 280
McNamara, Robert, 23
McMahon, Sgt. Brock, 253-256
Mella, Cpl. Ronald, 299
Mills, Cpl. Alexander, 259, 300
Mitchell, S. Sgt. David S., 69-71
Mullaney, T. Sgt. Walter, 145-148
Murray, Charles, 260-261
My Lai, 278-279

National League of Families, 281
Neville, Maj. Ernest, 165-168
New Zealand, 22, 31, 283
Ngo Dinh Diem, 21-22
Nguyen Cao Ky. see Ky, Nguyen Cao
Nguyen Van Thieu. see Thieu,
    Nguyen Van
Nixon, President Richard M., 24, 322,
    332

Operations
  "Boone", 306
  "Apache Snow", 271
  "Double Eagle", 81, 84
  "Hastings", 99
  "Hickory", 103
  "Lam Son", 719, 247
  "Prairie", 99
  "Trailblazer", 74

Paris Accords (1973), 24, 30
Pearson, Prime Minister L.B., 29, 34-35
Phelps, Sgt. C.J., 46-48
Philippines, 22, 31, 78, 90, 118, 120,
  231
Pollock, PFC Shane, 180-182
Post-Traumatic Stress Disorder
  (PTSD), 264-276
Purvis, Robert, 296-297

Reeves, L. Cpl. J.H., 280
Regiments, U.S. Army
  4th Cavalry, 270
  8th Cavalry, 209, 316
  17th Cavalry, 319
  18th Infantry, 148
Republic of Vietnam, 21, 60, 155, 172
Ridout, S. Sgt. John, 154-157
Roden, Sgt. J.J., 324-6
Ross, CWO2 David, 197-202
Royal Canadian Legion, 14, 284, 294-8

Saigon, 20, 25, 90, 101, 108, 122, 126,
  139, 145, 151, 242, 286, 322
Savage, Cpl. David,140-145
Selective Service, 23, 35-36
Sharpe, PFC, E.G., 303-36
Sims, Cpl. L.T., 84-86
Skoumbros, Michael, 165
Socialist Republic of Vietnam, 25
Special Forces, 42, 71, 83, 103, 109, 140,
  155-156, 291, 318-321, 324-326,
  320
Stanfield, Robert, 29
Sund, PO 3rd Class Arne, 58-62
Symons, Malcolm, 157-159

Talmadge, Lt. Robert, 326-330
Tet Offensive, 22, 113, 119-120, 139,
  147, 151, 159, 184, 275
Thailand, 22, 31, 127, 166-168, 177-180,
  229-237, 253-256, 303
Thieu, Nguyen Van, 22, 25
Thorsteinson, Cpl. V.J., 306-309
Tissington, Sgt. George, 203-207
Tompkins, M. Sgt. T.B., 48-58
Tower, Sgt. Patrick, 296
Trudeau, Prime Minister Pierre, 29-30

Vessels
  Bennington, 271
  Braine, 60
  Catamount, 89
  Constellation, 88
  Coral Sea, 60
  Denver, 217
  Fresno, 267
  General W.H. Gordon, 97
  Kitty Hawk, 60
  New Jersey, 61
  Perkins, 59-61
  Philip, 60
  Upshur, 129

Veterans Administration, 262, 269-
  270, 283
Viet Cong, 22, 26, 61, 67, 73, 80, 97,
  111, 113, 122, 127, 132, 139, 155-
  156, 164, 181, 277-278, 320
Viet Minh, 228

Walker, Sgt. Howard, 129-137
Walsh, Sgt. Eric, 195-196
Warke, R.B., 297
War Powers Resolution, 332
Webster, Sgt. Graeme, 93-101
Wells, M. Sgt. Marvin, 319-321
Westmoreland, Gen. W.C., 19, 23, 100
White, PO3 R.N., 271-6
Wilby, Cpl. Edward, 257

Xuan Loc, 25

Yoachim, Capt. William, 112-116